Ōoku

☉ THE INNER CHAMBERS

by **Fumi Yoshinaga**

VOL. **7**

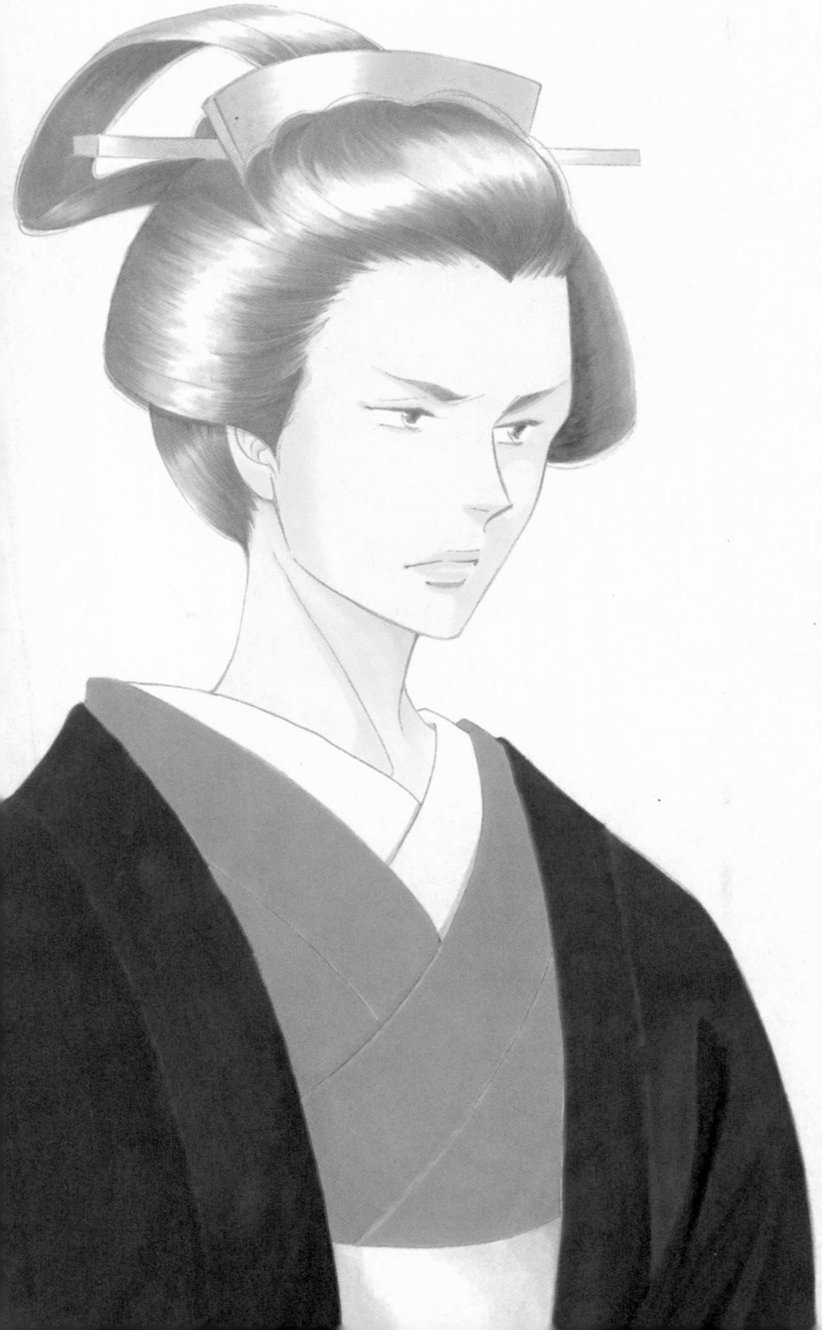

TABLE *of* CONTENTS

Ōoku

THE INNER CHAMBERS

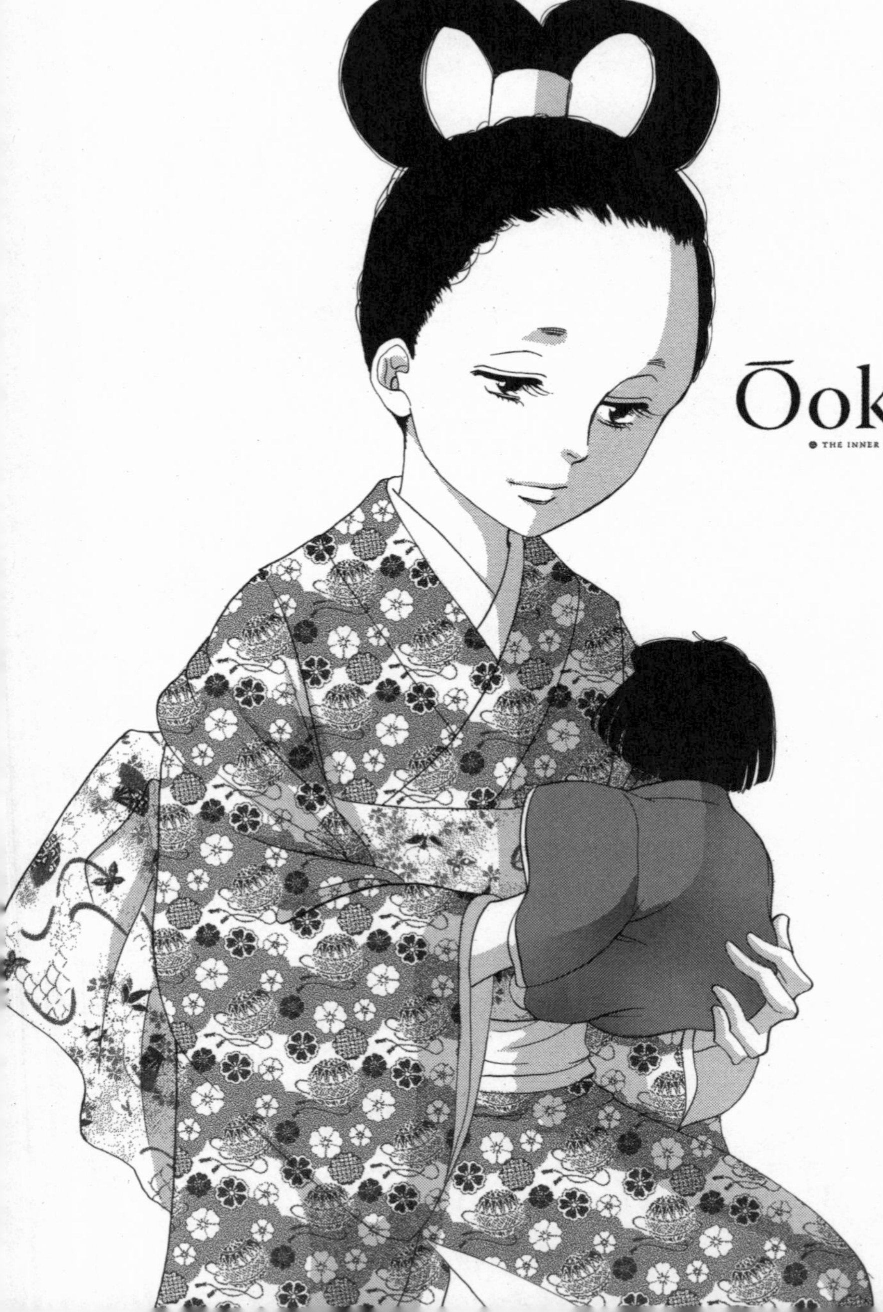

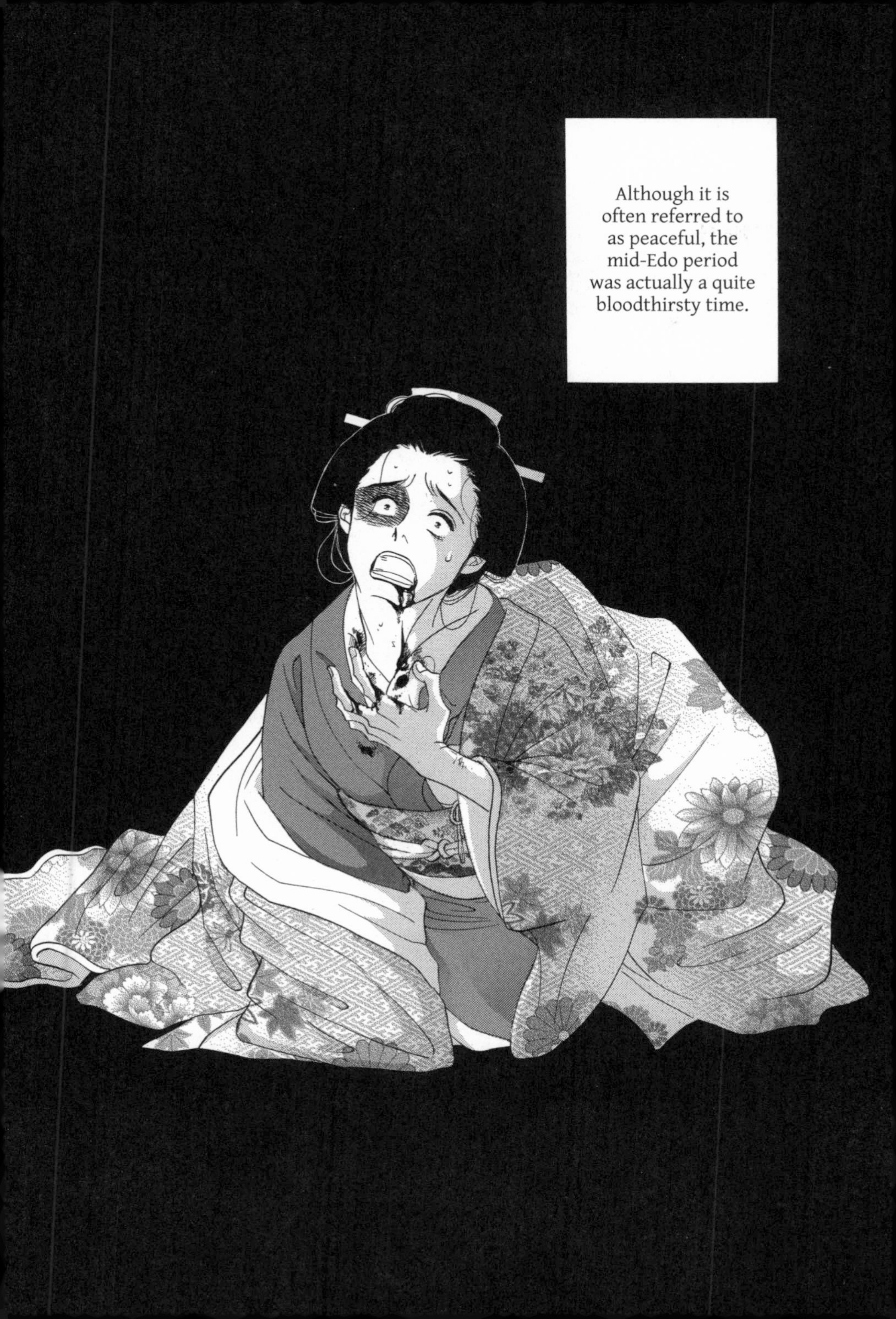
Although it is often referred to as peaceful, the mid-Edo period was actually a quite bloodthirsty time.

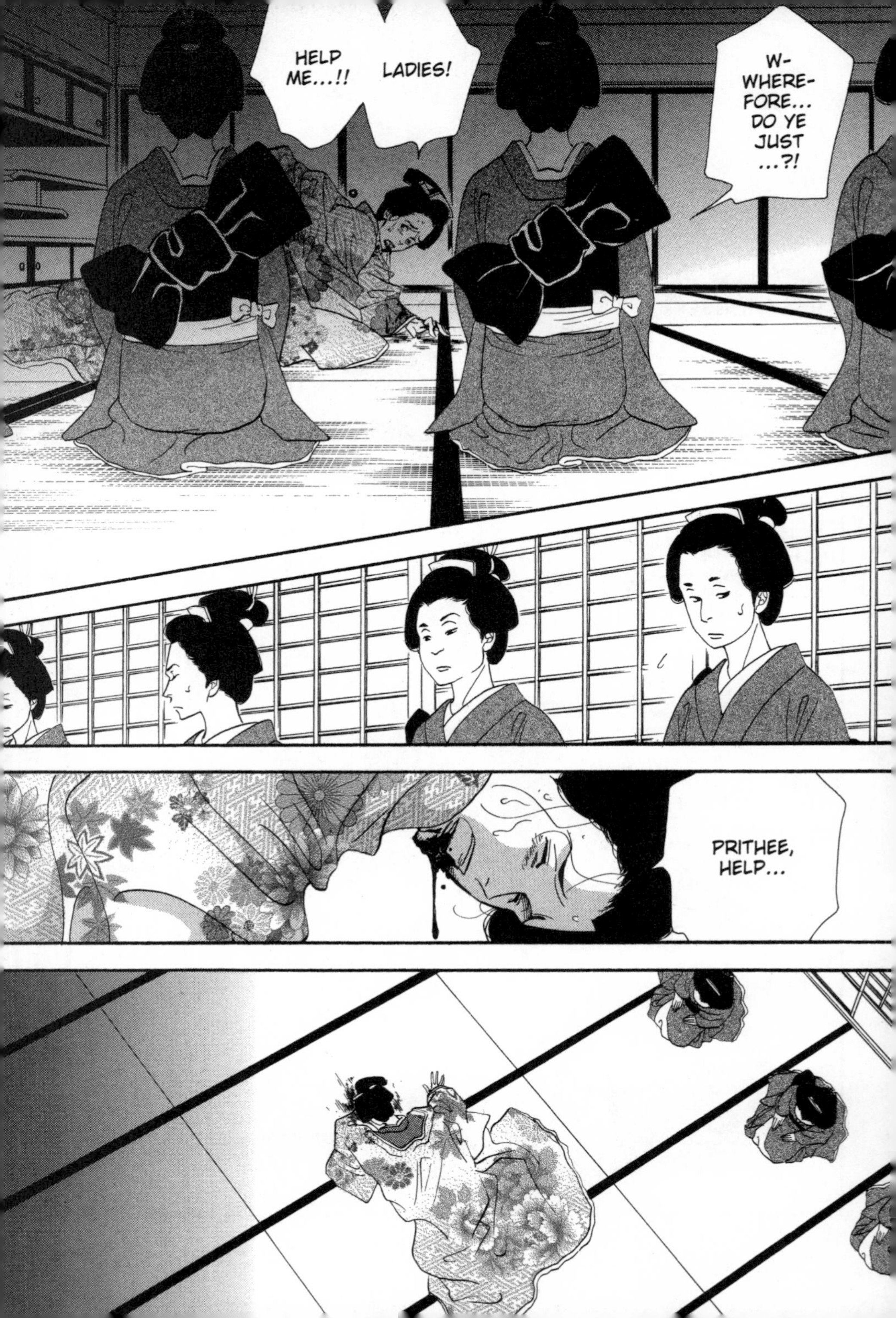
LADIES!
HELP ME...!!
W-WHEREFORE... DO YE JUST ...?!
PRITHEE, HELP...

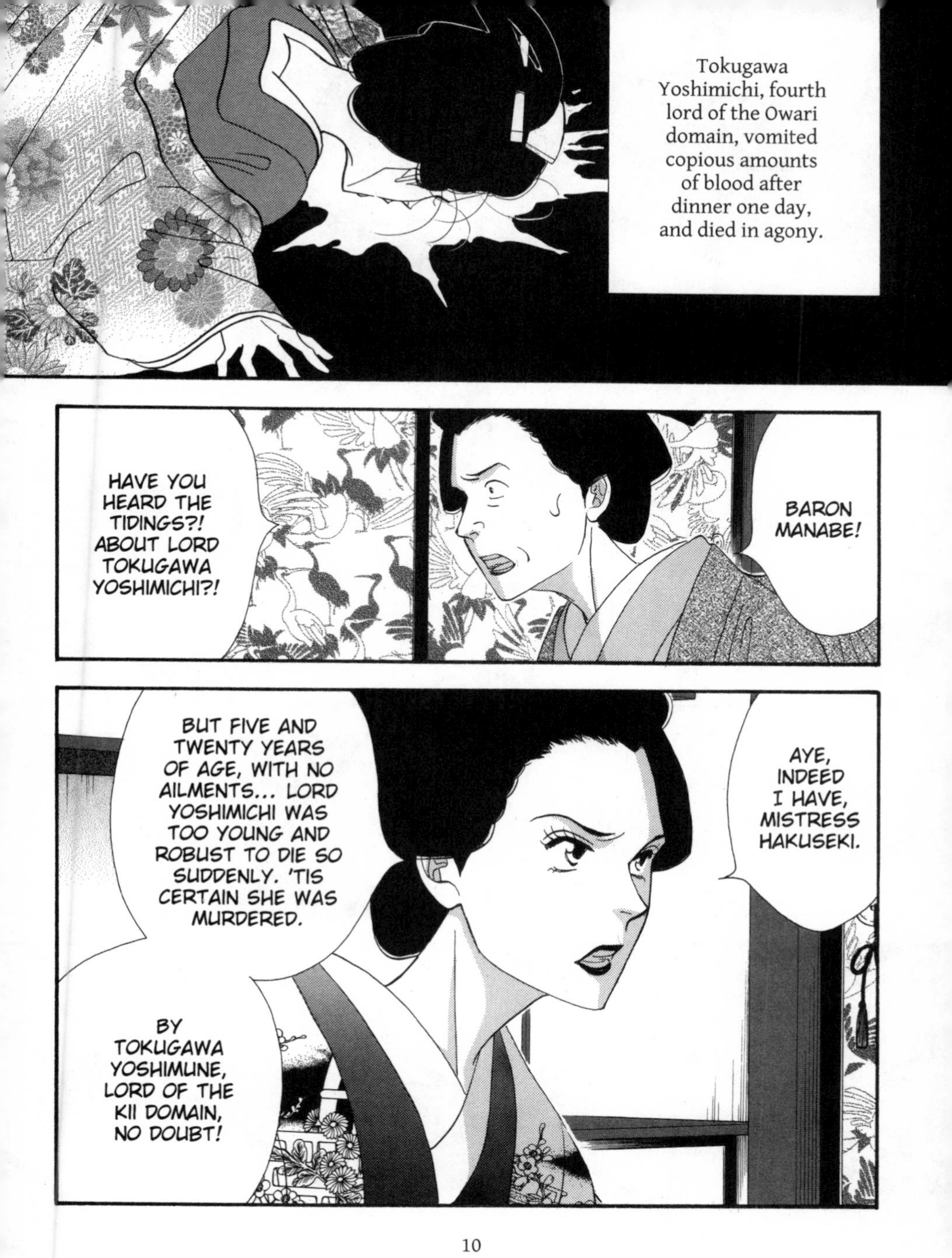
Tokugawa Yoshimichi, fourth lord of the Owari domain, vomited copious amounts of blood after dinner one day, and died in agony.
BARON MANABE!
HAVE YOU HEARD THE TIDINGS?! ABOUT LORD TOKUGAWA YOSHIMICHI?!
AYE, INDEED I HAVE, MISTRESS HAKUSEKI.
BUT FIVE AND TWENTY YEARS OF AGE, WITH NO AILMENTS... LORD YOSHIMICHI WAS TOO YOUNG AND ROBUST TO DIE SO SUDDENLY. 'TIS CERTAIN SHE WAS MURDERED.
BY TOKUGAWA YOSHIMUNE, LORD OF THE KII DOMAIN, NO DOUBT!

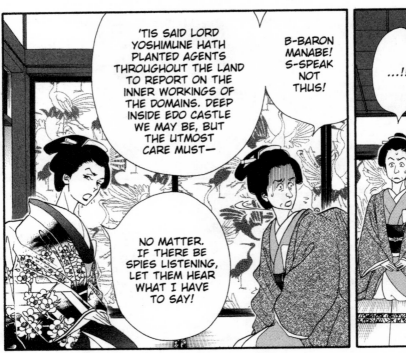

...!!
B-BARON MANABE! S-SPEAK NOT THUS!
'TIS SAID LORD YOSHIMUNE HATH PLANTED AGENTS THROUGHOUT THE LAND TO REPORT ON THE INNER WORKINGS OF THE DOMAINS. DEEP INSIDE EDO CASTLE WE MAY BE, BUT THE UTMOST CARE MUST—
NO MATTER. IF THERE BE SPIES LISTENING, LET THEM HEAR WHAT I HAVE TO SAY!
'TIS WHISPERED THAT WHEN LORD YOSHIMICHI OF OWARI DID COLLAPSE, NOT ONE OF THOSE PRESENT DID GO TO FETCH A PHYSICIAN, NOR E'EN RISE TO HELP OR COMFORT HER AS SHE DID WRITHE IN ANGUISH. THEIR OWN LORD, AND YET THEY SAT IN SILENCE AND WATCHED HER DIE...
WHO COULD SAY SUCH AN END IS NOT STRANGE?!
WE MAY WELL CONCLUDE THAT BY THE TIME OF LORD YOSHIMICHI'S DEMISE, MANY OF THOSE IN HER EDO MANSE WERE IN THE POCKET OF LORD YOSHIMUNE, THROUGH THE AGENCY OF HER INTELLIGENCERS WHO DID PENETRATE THEIR RANKS.

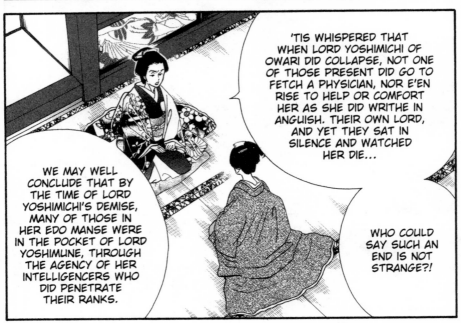

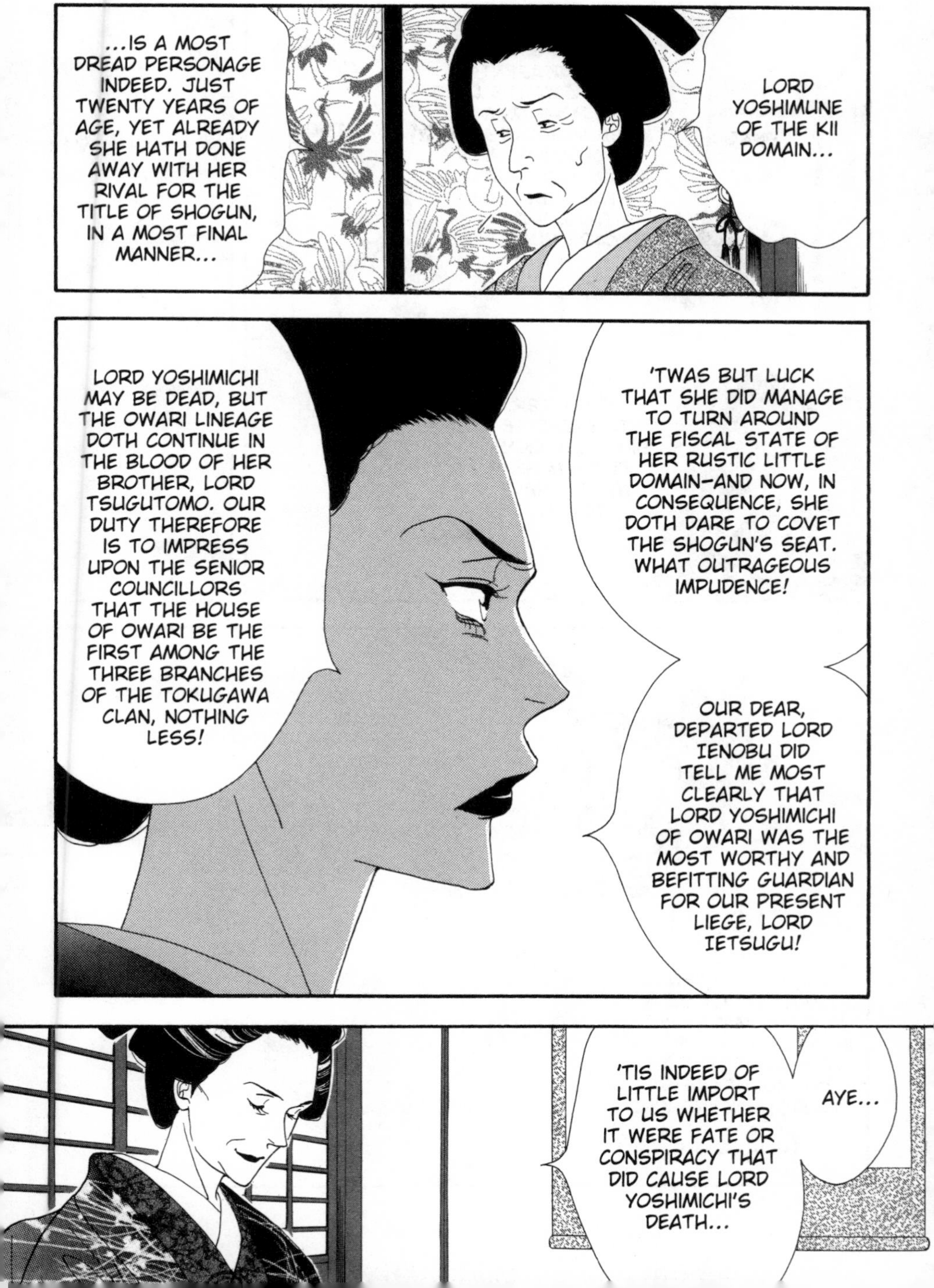
LORD YOSHIMUNE OF THE KII DOMAIN...
...IS A MOST DREAD PERSONAGE INDEED. JUST TWENTY YEARS OF AGE, YET ALREADY SHE HATH DONE AWAY WITH HER RIVAL FOR THE TITLE OF SHOGUN, IN A MOST FINAL MANNER...
'TWAS BUT LUCK THAT SHE DID MANAGE TO TURN AROUND THE FISCAL STATE OF HER RUSTIC LITTLE DOMAIN–AND NOW, IN CONSEQUENCE, SHE DOTH DARE TO COVET THE SHOGUN'S SEAT. WHAT OUTRAGEOUS IMPUDENCE!
OUR DEAR, DEPARTED LORD IENOBU DID TELL ME MOST CLEARLY THAT LORD YOSHIMICHI OF OWARI WAS THE MOST WORTHY AND BEFITTING GUARDIAN FOR OUR PRESENT LIEGE, LORD IETSUGU!
LORD YOSHIMICHI MAY BE DEAD, BUT THE OWARI LINEAGE DOTH CONTINUE IN THE BLOOD OF HER BROTHER, LORD TSUGUTOMO. OUR DUTY THEREFORE IS TO IMPRESS UPON THE SENIOR COUNCILLORS THAT THE HOUSE OF OWARI BE THE FIRST AMONG THE THREE BRANCHES OF THE TOKUGAWA CLAN, NOTHING LESS!
AYE...
'TIS INDEED OF LITTLE IMPORT TO US WHETHER IT WERE FATE OR CONSPIRACY THAT DID CAUSE LORD YOSHIMICHI'S DEATH...

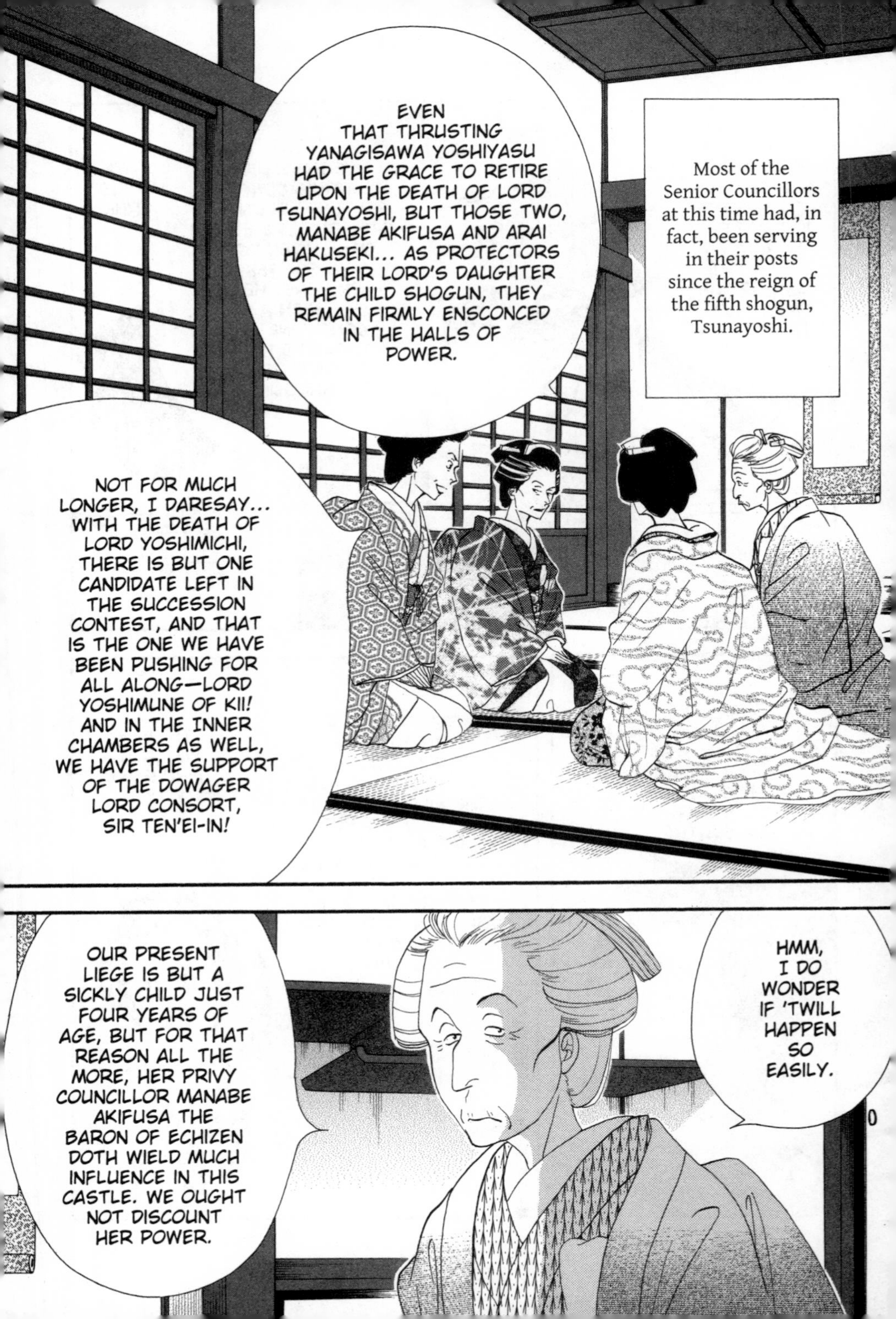
Most of the Senior Councillors at this time had, in fact, been serving in their posts since the reign of the fifth shogun, Tsunayoshi.
EVEN THAT THRUSTING YANAGISAWA YOSHIYASU HAD THE GRACE TO RETIRE UPON THE DEATH OF LORD TSUNAYOSHI, BUT THOSE TWO, MANABE AKIFUSA AND ARAI HAKUSEKI... AS PROTECTORS OF THEIR LORD'S DAUGHTER THE CHILD SHOGUN, THEY REMAIN FIRMLY ENSCONCED IN THE HALLS OF POWER.
NOT FOR MUCH LONGER, I DARESAY... WITH THE DEATH OF LORD YOSHIMICHI, THERE IS BUT ONE CANDIDATE LEFT IN THE SUCCESSION CONTEST, AND THAT IS THE ONE WE HAVE BEEN PUSHING FOR ALL ALONG—LORD YOSHIMUNE OF KII! AND IN THE INNER CHAMBERS AS WELL, WE HAVE THE SUPPORT OF THE DOWAGER LORD CONSORT, SIR TEN'EI-IN!
HMM, I DO WONDER IF 'TWILL HAPPEN SO EASILY.
OUR PRESENT LIEGE IS BUT A SICKLY CHILD JUST FOUR YEARS OF AGE, BUT FOR THAT REASON ALL THE MORE, HER PRIVY COUNCILLOR MANABE AKIFUSA THE BARON OF ECHIZEN DOTH WIELD MUCH INFLUENCE IN THIS CASTLE. WE OUGHT NOT DISCOUNT HER POWER.

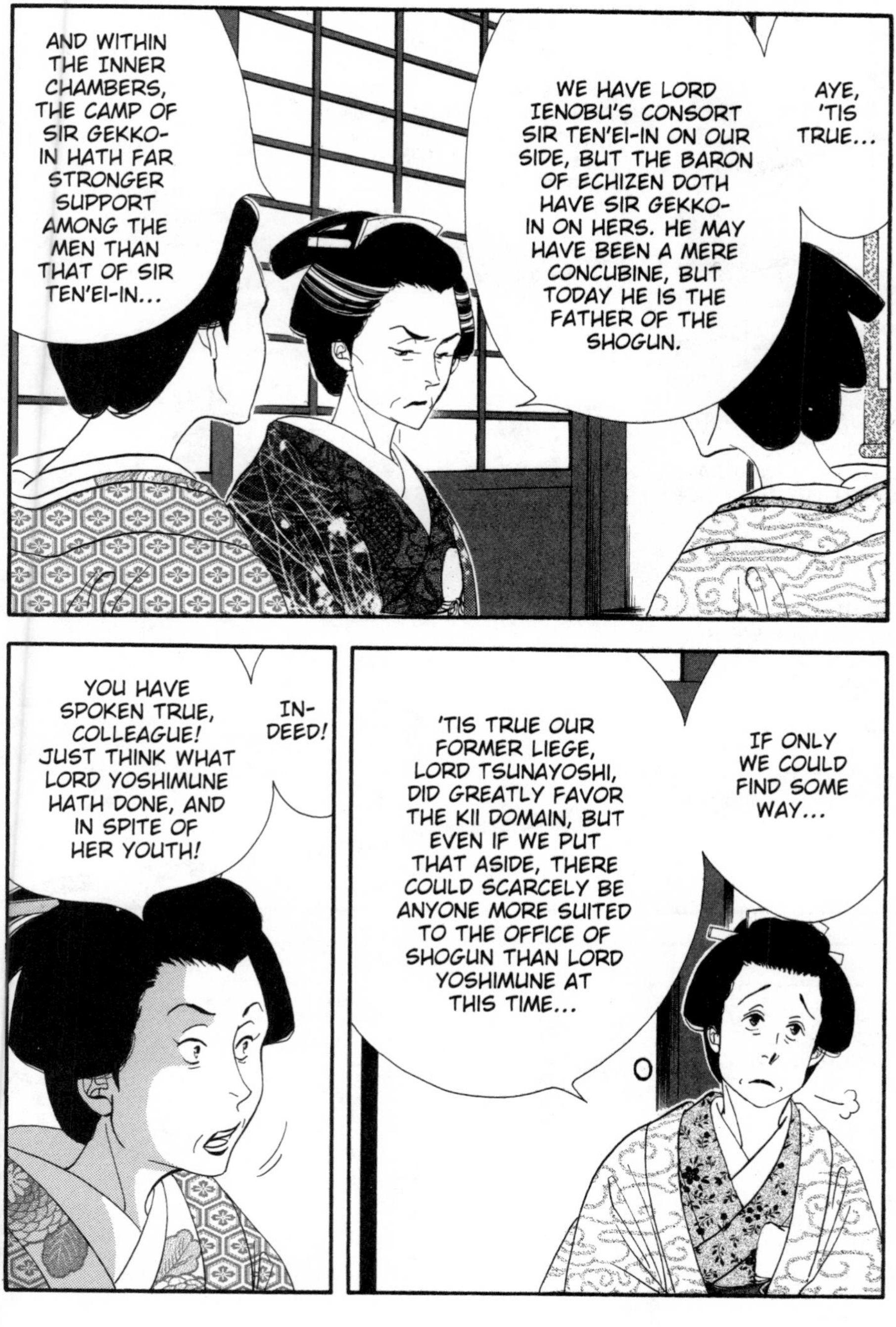
AYE, 'TIS TRUE...
WE HAVE LORD IENOBU'S CONSORT SIR TEN'EI-IN ON OUR SIDE, BUT THE BARON OF ECHIZEN DOTH HAVE SIR GEKKO-IN ON HERS. HE MAY HAVE BEEN A MERE CONCUBINE, BUT TODAY HE IS THE FATHER OF THE SHOGUN.
AND WITHIN THE INNER CHAMBERS, THE CAMP OF SIR GEKKO-IN HATH FAR STRONGER SUPPORT AMONG THE MEN THAN THAT OF SIR TEN'EI-IN...
IF ONLY WE COULD FIND SOME WAY...
'TIS TRUE OUR FORMER LIEGE, LORD TSUNAYOSHI, DID GREATLY FAVOR THE KII DOMAIN, BUT EVEN IF WE PUT THAT ASIDE, THERE COULD SCARCELY BE ANYONE MORE SUITED TO THE OFFICE OF SHOGUN THAN LORD YOSHIMUNE AT THIS TIME...
IN-DEED!
YOU HAVE SPOKEN TRUE, COLLEAGUE! JUST THINK WHAT LORD YOSHIMUNE HATH DONE, AND IN SPITE OF HER YOUTH!

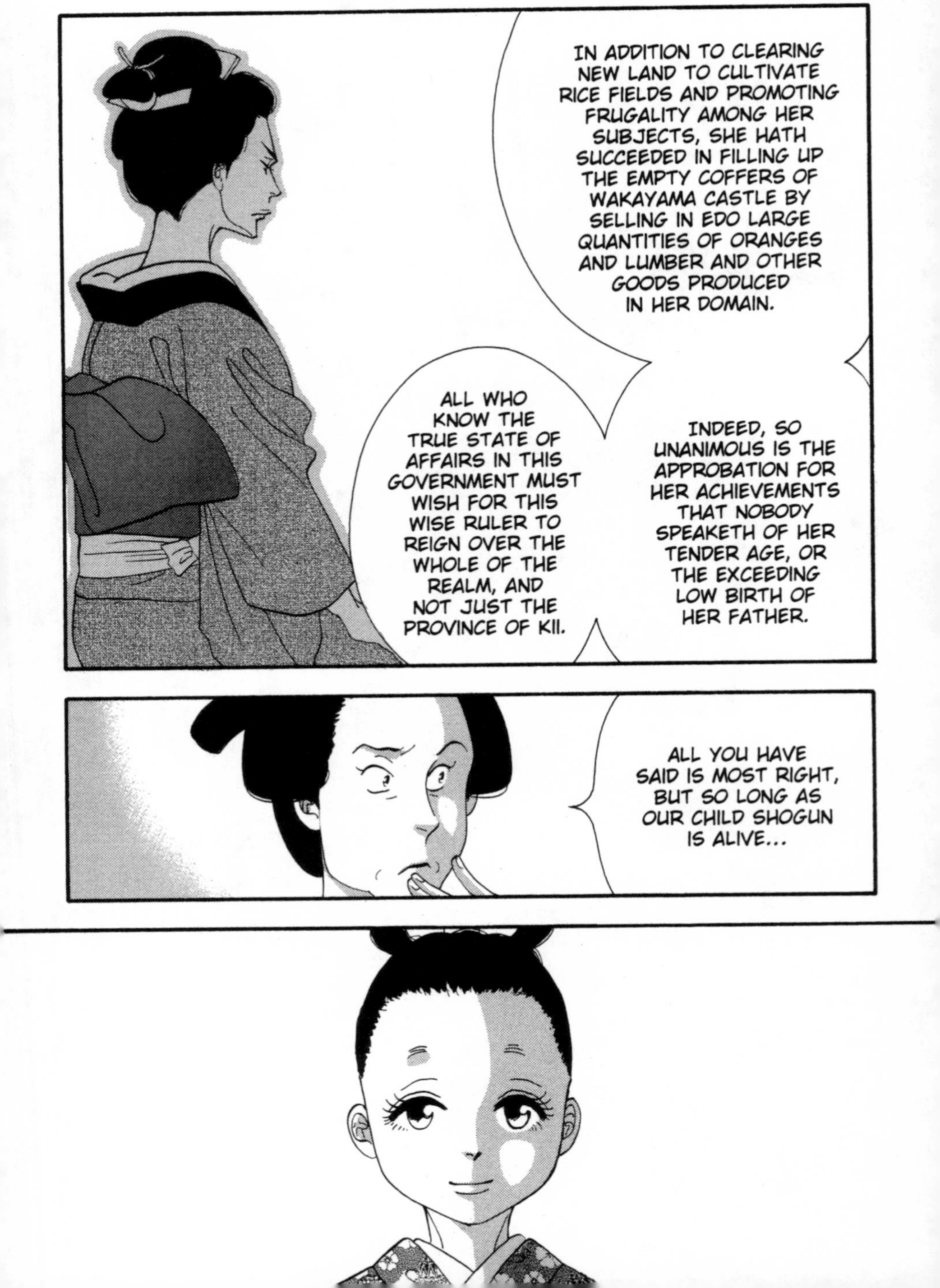
IN ADDITION TO CLEARING NEW LAND TO CULTIVATE RICE FIELDS AND PROMOTING FRUGALITY AMONG HER SUBJECTS, SHE HATH SUCCEEDED IN FILLING UP THE EMPTY COFFERS OF WAKAYAMA CASTLE BY SELLING IN EDO LARGE QUANTITIES OF ORANGES AND LUMBER AND OTHER GOODS PRODUCED IN HER DOMAIN.
INDEED, SO UNANIMOUS IS THE APPROBATION FOR HER ACHIEVEMENTS THAT NOBODY SPEAKETH OF HER TENDER AGE, OR THE EXCEEDING LOW BIRTH OF HER FATHER.
ALL WHO KNOW THE TRUE STATE OF AFFAIRS IN THIS GOVERNMENT MUST WISH FOR THIS WISE RULER TO REIGN OVER THE WHOLE OF THE REALM, AND NOT JUST THE PROVINCE OF KII.
ALL YOU HAVE SAID IS MOST RIGHT, BUT SO LONG AS OUR CHILD SHOGUN IS ALIVE...

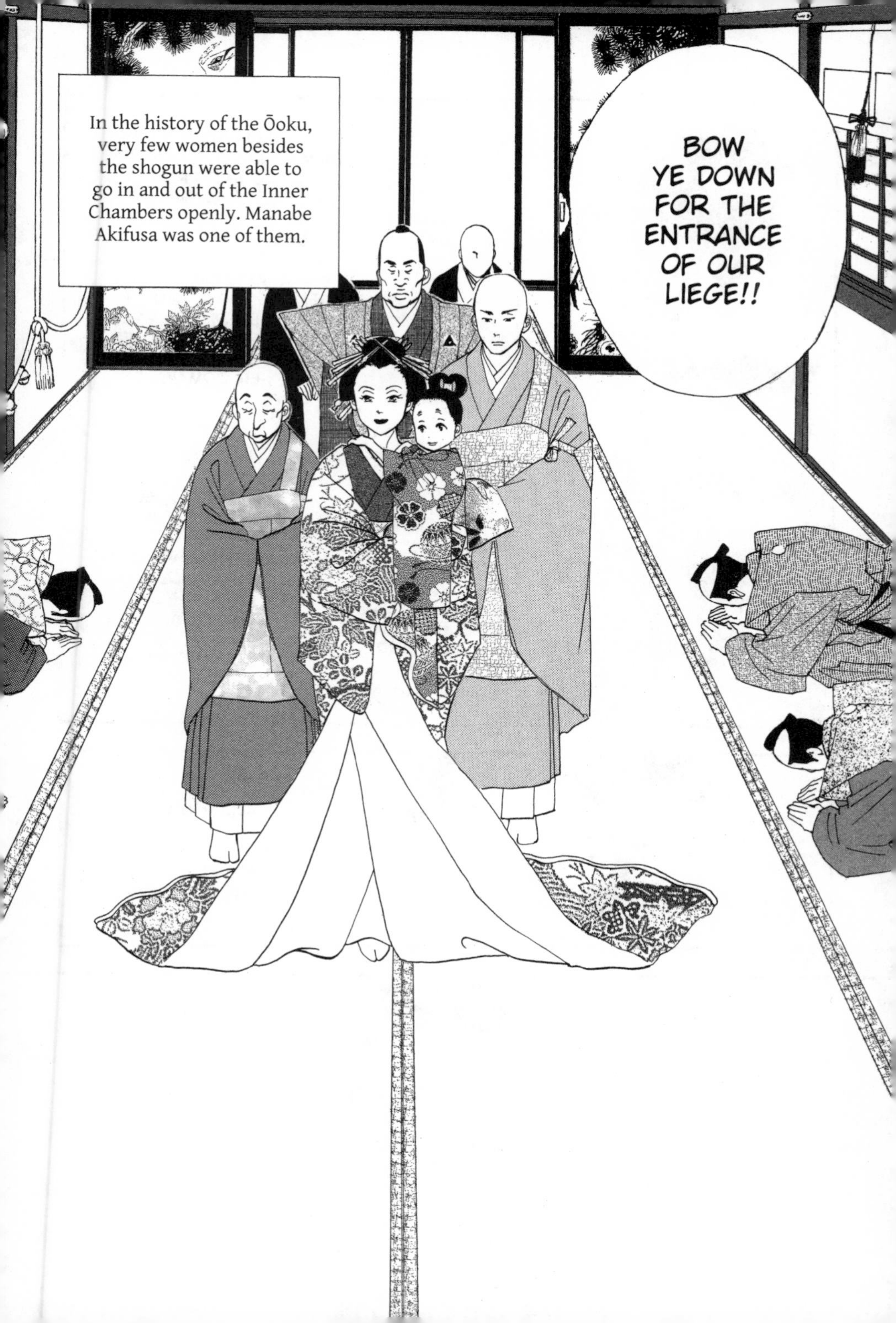
BOW YE DOWN FOR THE ENTRANCE OF OUR LIEGE!!
In the history of the Ōoku, very few women besides the shogun were able to go in and out of the Inner Chambers openly. Manabe Akifusa was one of them.

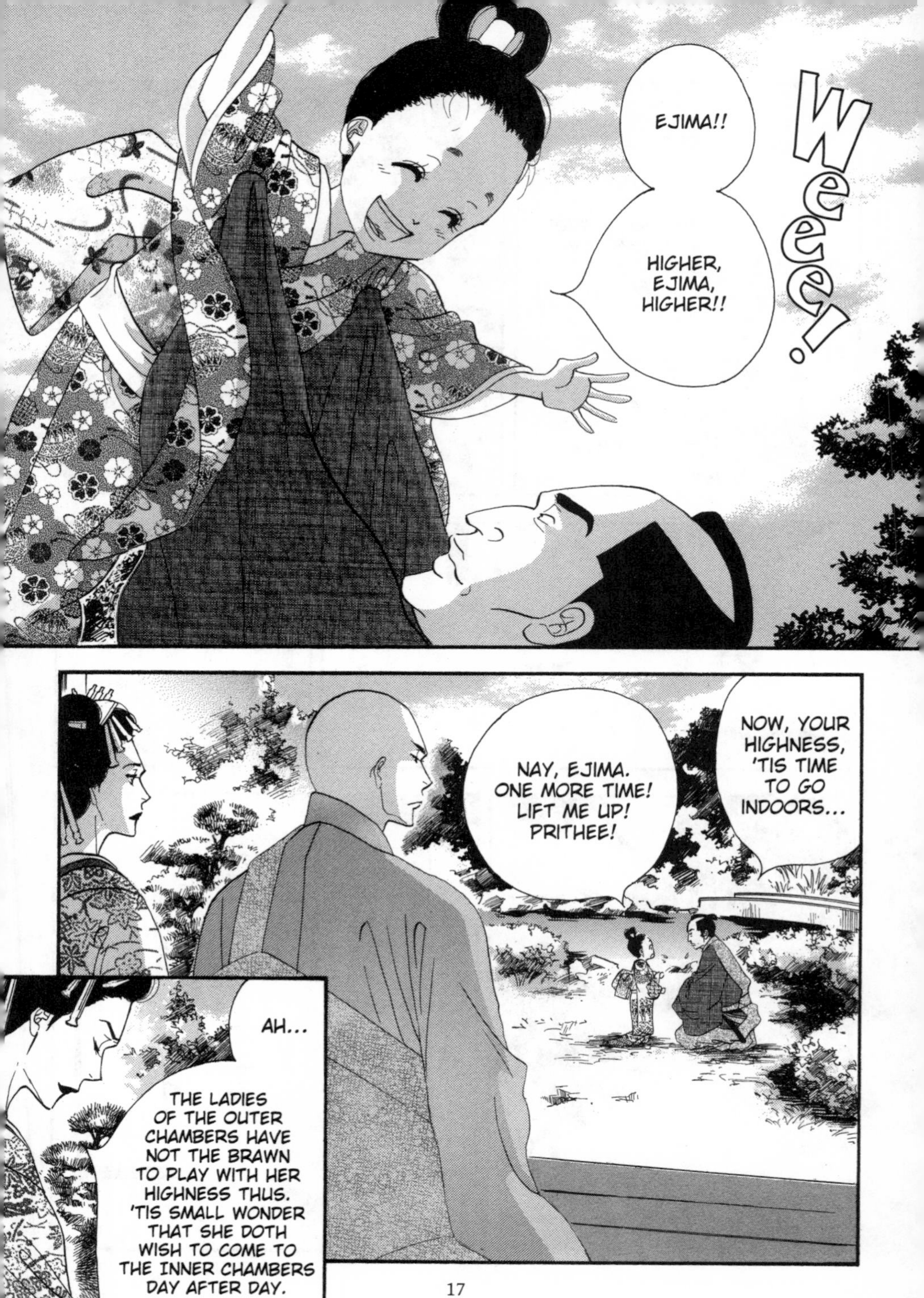
Weee!
EJIMA!!
HIGHER, EJIMA, HIGHER!!
NOW, YOUR HIGHNESS, 'TIS TIME TO GO INDOORS...
NAY, EJIMA. ONE MORE TIME! LIFT ME UP! PRITHEE!
AH...
THE LADIES OF THE OUTER CHAMBERS HAVE NOT THE BRAWN TO PLAY WITH HER HIGHNESS THUS. 'TIS SMALL WONDER THAT SHE DOTH WISH TO COME TO THE INNER CHAMBERS DAY AFTER DAY.

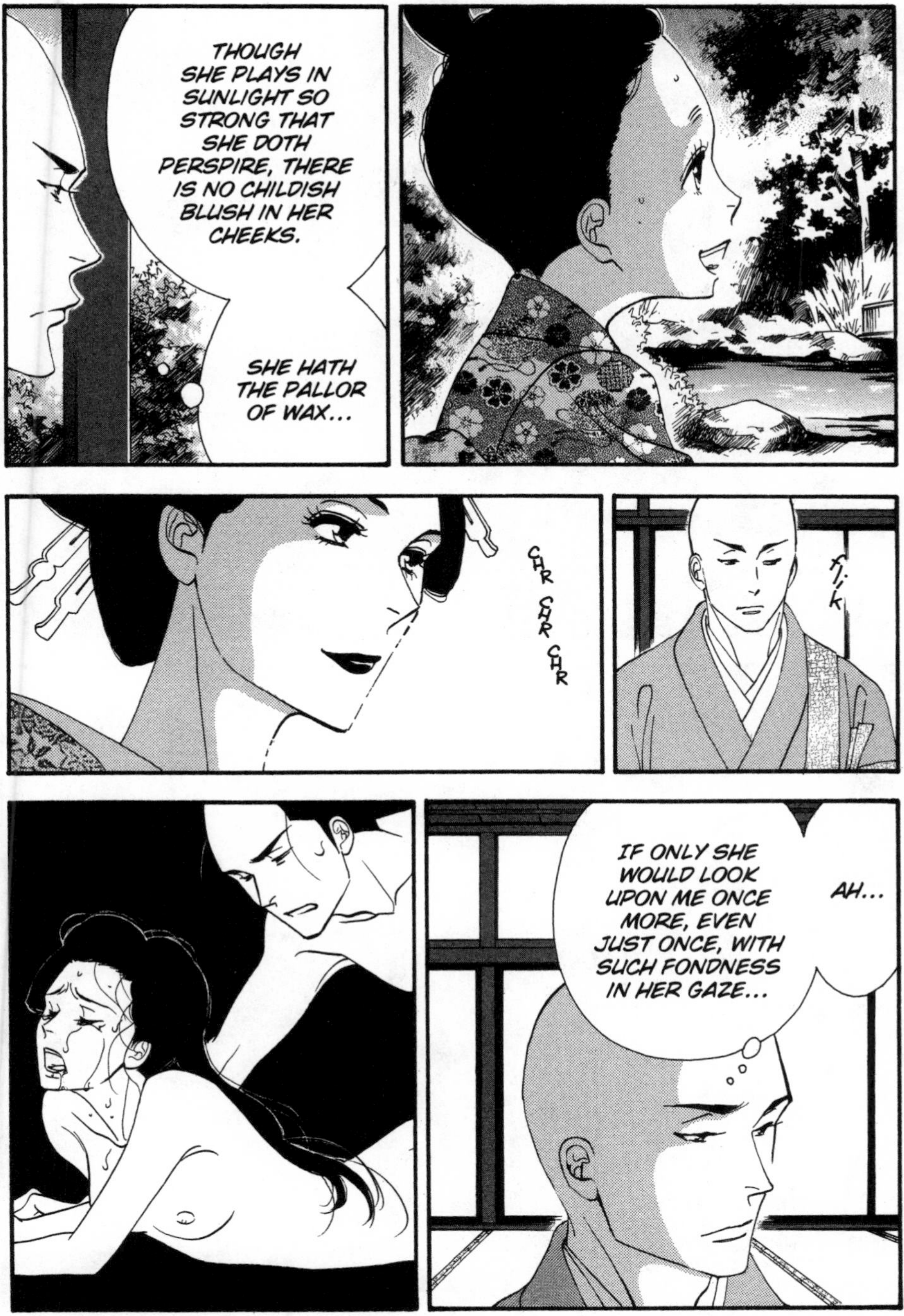
THOUGH SHE PLAYS IN SUNLIGHT SO STRONG THAT SHE DOTH PERSPIRE, THERE IS NO CHILDISH BLUSH IN HER CHEEKS.
SHE HATH THE PALLOR OF WAX...
FLIK
CHR CHR CHR CHR
AH...
IF ONLY SHE WOULD LOOK UPON ME ONCE MORE, EVEN JUST ONCE, WITH SUCH FONDNESS IN HER GAZE...

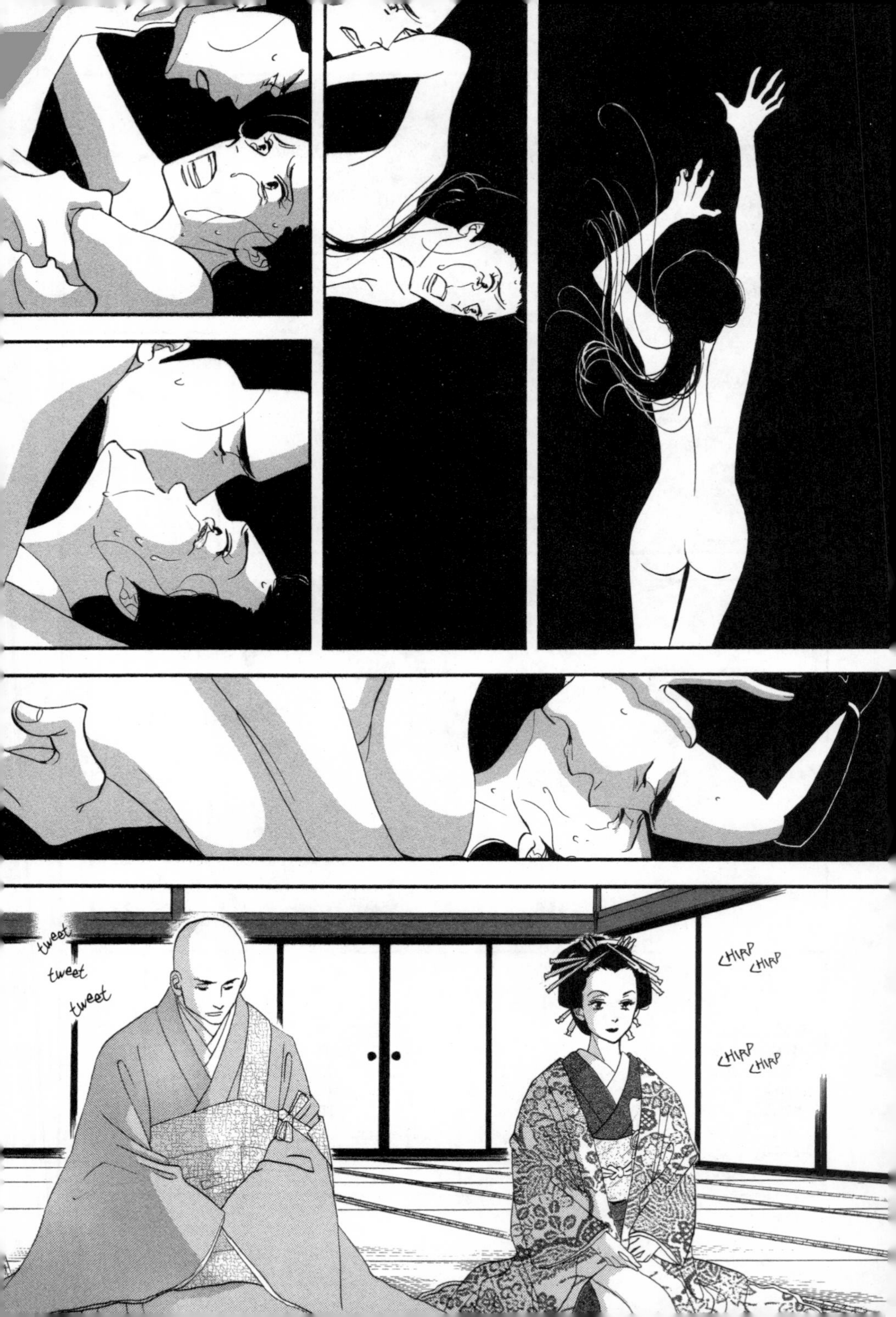
CHIRP CHIRP
CHIRP CHIRP
tweet
tweet
tweet

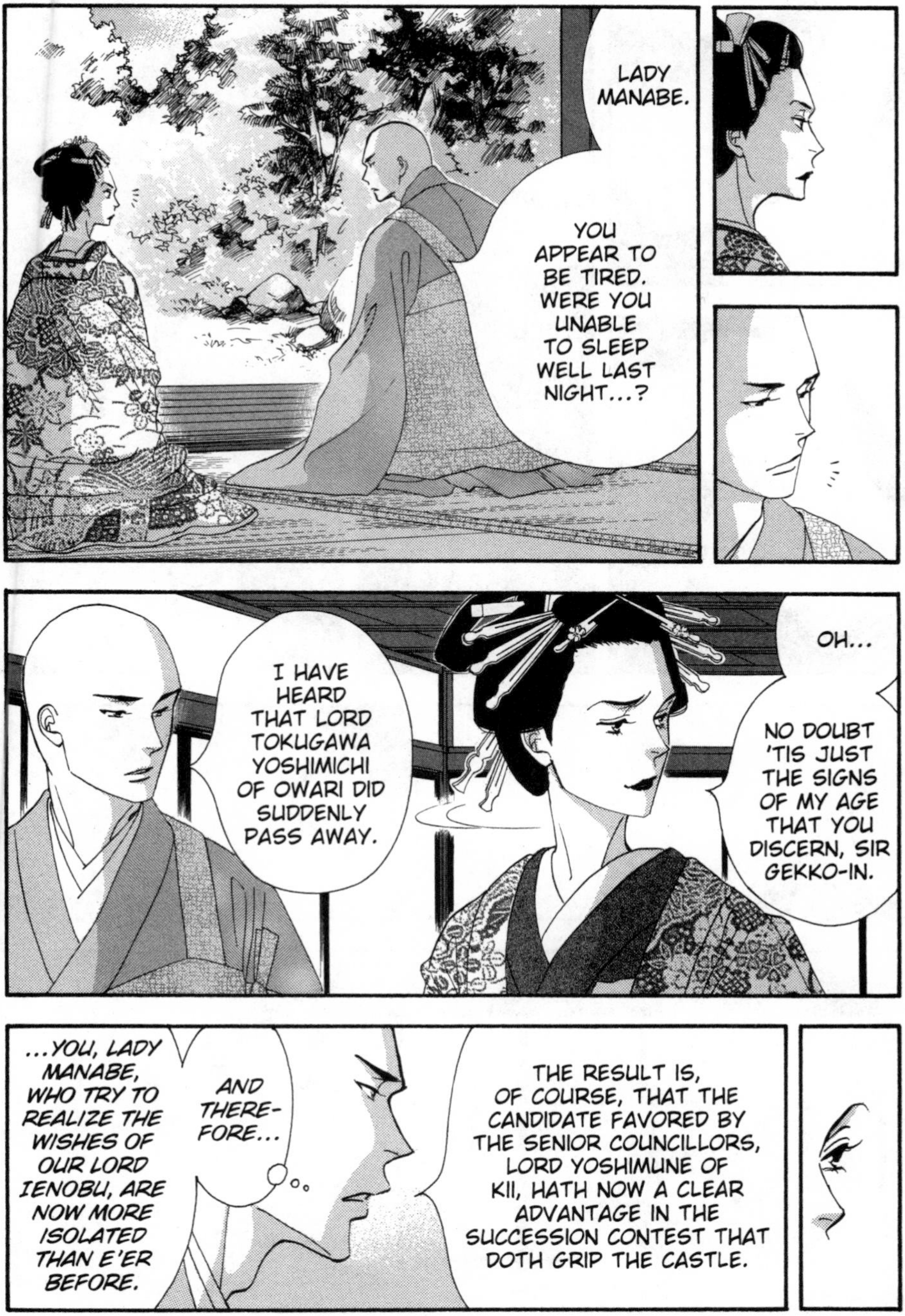
LADY MANABE.
YOU APPEAR TO BE TIRED. WERE YOU UNABLE TO SLEEP WELL LAST NIGHT...?
OH...
NO DOUBT 'TIS JUST THE SIGNS OF MY AGE THAT YOU DISCERN, SIR GEKKO-IN.
I HAVE HEARD THAT LORD TOKUGAWA YOSHIMICHI OF OWARI DID SUDDENLY PASS AWAY.
THE RESULT IS, OF COURSE, THAT THE CANDIDATE FAVORED BY THE SENIOR COUNCILLORS, LORD YOSHIMUNE OF KII, HATH NOW A CLEAR ADVANTAGE IN THE SUCCESSION CONTEST THAT DOTH GRIP THE CASTLE.
AND THEREFORE...
...YOU, LADY MANABE, WHO TRY TO REALIZE THE WISHES OF OUR LORD IENOBU, ARE NOW MORE ISOLATED THAN E'ER BEFORE.

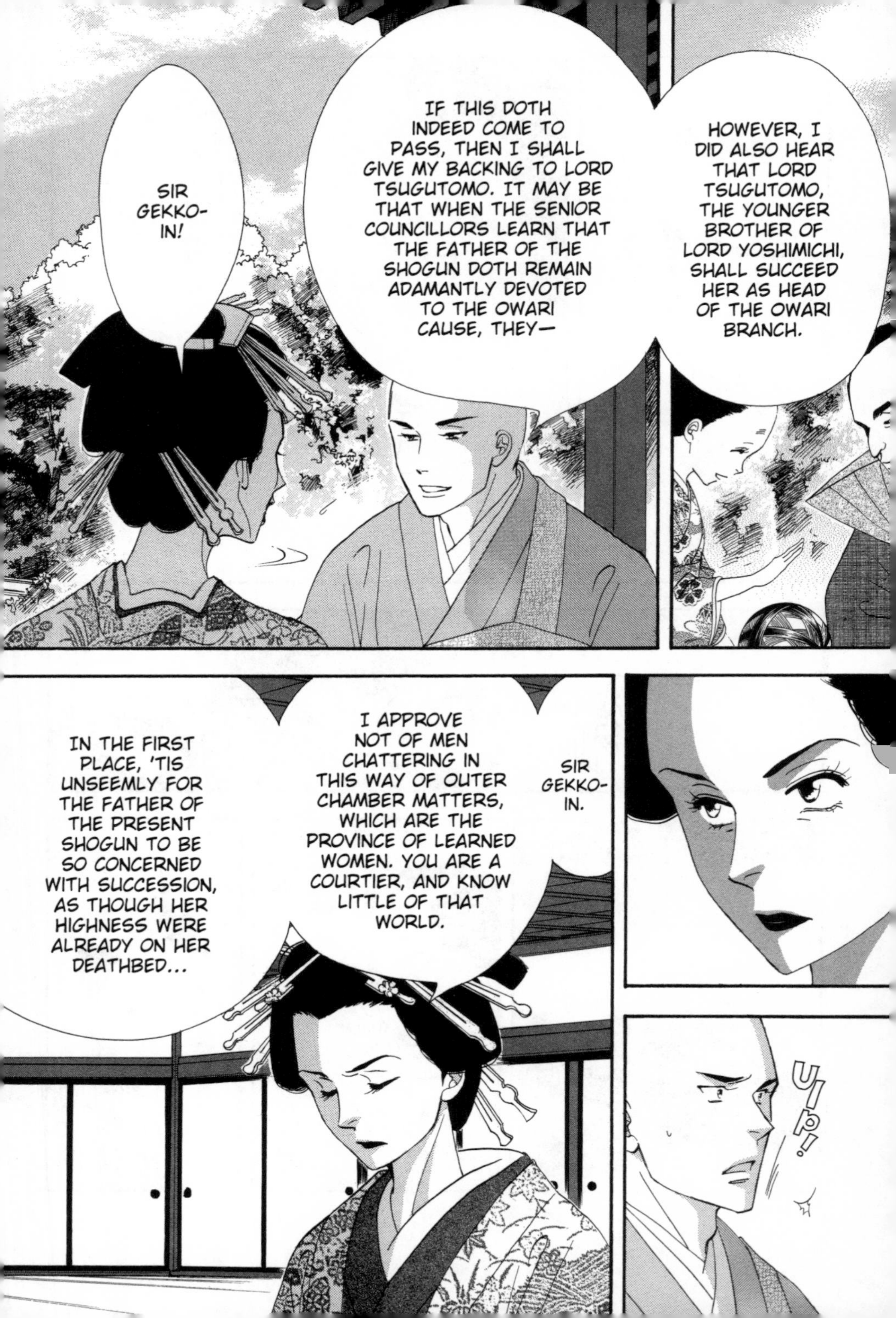
HOWEVER, I DID ALSO HEAR THAT LORD TSUGUTOMO, THE YOUNGER BROTHER OF LORD YOSHIMICHI, SHALL SUCCEED HER AS HEAD OF THE OWARI BRANCH.
IF THIS DOTH INDEED COME TO PASS, THEN I SHALL GIVE MY BACKING TO LORD TSUGUTOMO. IT MAY BE THAT WHEN THE SENIOR COUNCILLORS LEARN THAT THE FATHER OF THE SHOGUN DOTH REMAIN ADAMANTLY DEVOTED TO THE OWARI CAUSE, THEY—
SIR GEKKO-IN!
ULP!
SIR GEKKO-IN.
I APPROVE NOT OF MEN CHATTERING IN THIS WAY OF OUTER CHAMBER MATTERS, WHICH ARE THE PROVINCE OF LEARNED WOMEN. YOU ARE A COURTIER, AND KNOW LITTLE OF THAT WORLD.
IN THE FIRST PLACE, 'TIS UNSEEMLY FOR THE FATHER OF THE PRESENT SHOGUN TO BE SO CONCERNED WITH SUCCESSION, AS THOUGH HER HIGHNESS WERE ALREADY ON HER DEATHBED...

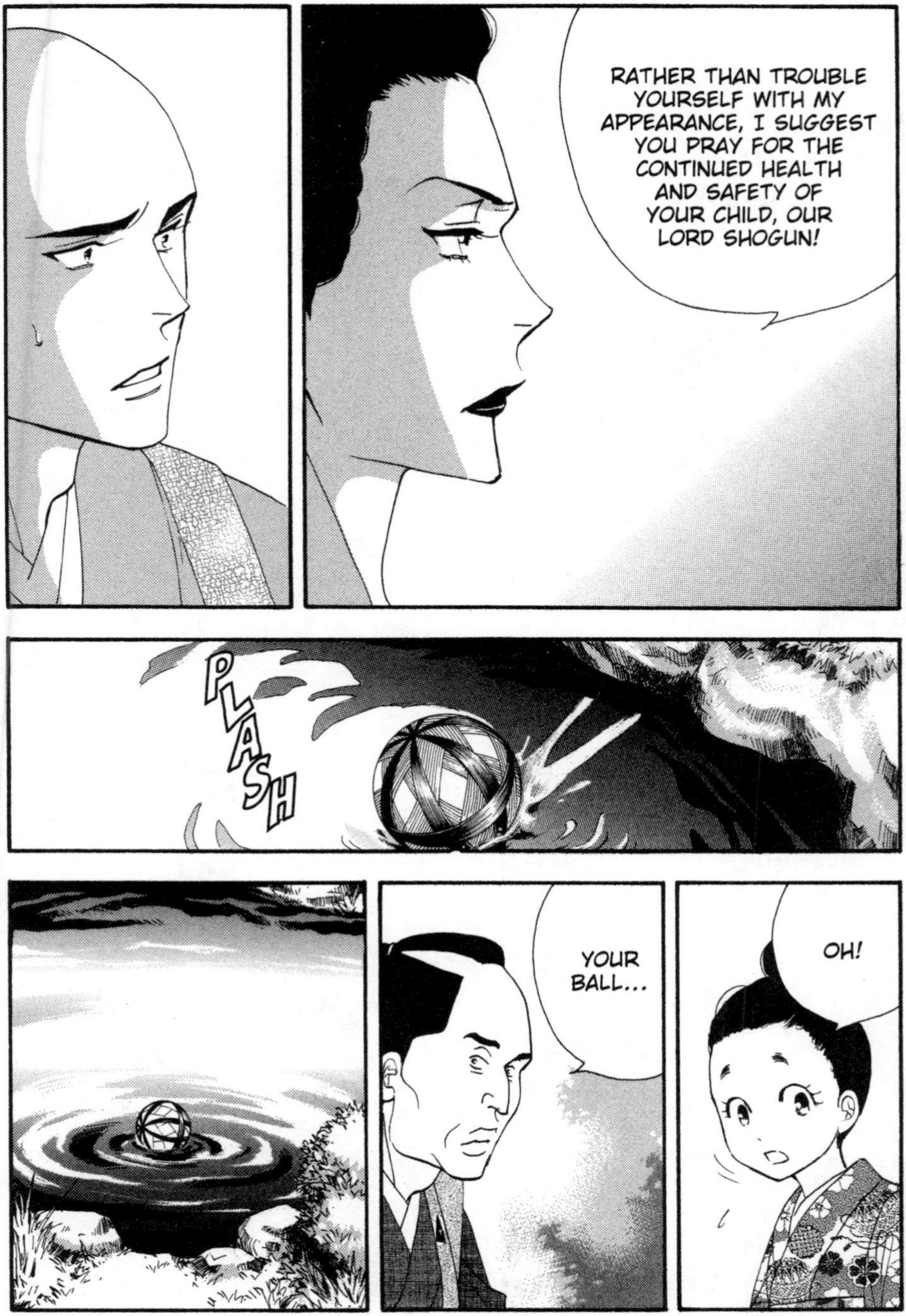
RATHER THAN TROUBLE YOURSELF WITH MY APPEARANCE, I SUGGEST YOU PRAY FOR THE CONTINUED HEALTH AND SAFETY OF YOUR CHILD, OUR LORD SHOGUN!
PLASH
OH!
YOUR BALL...

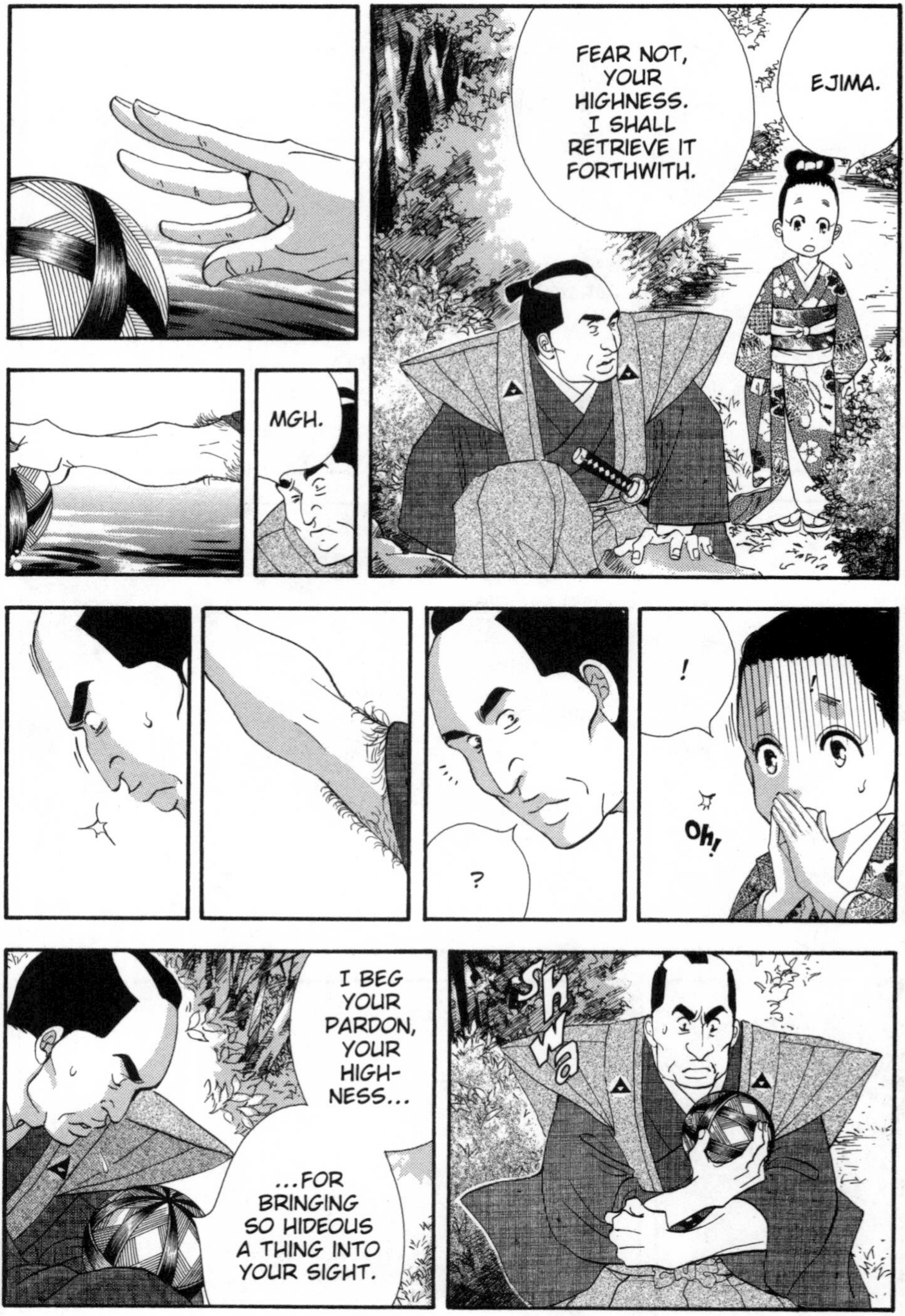
EJIMA.
FEAR NOT, YOUR HIGHNESS. I SHALL RETRIEVE IT FORTHWITH.
MGH.
!
!
Oh!
...
?
SHWA
I BEG YOUR PARDON, YOUR HIGH-NESS...
...FOR BRINGING SO HIDEOUS A THING INTO YOUR SIGHT.

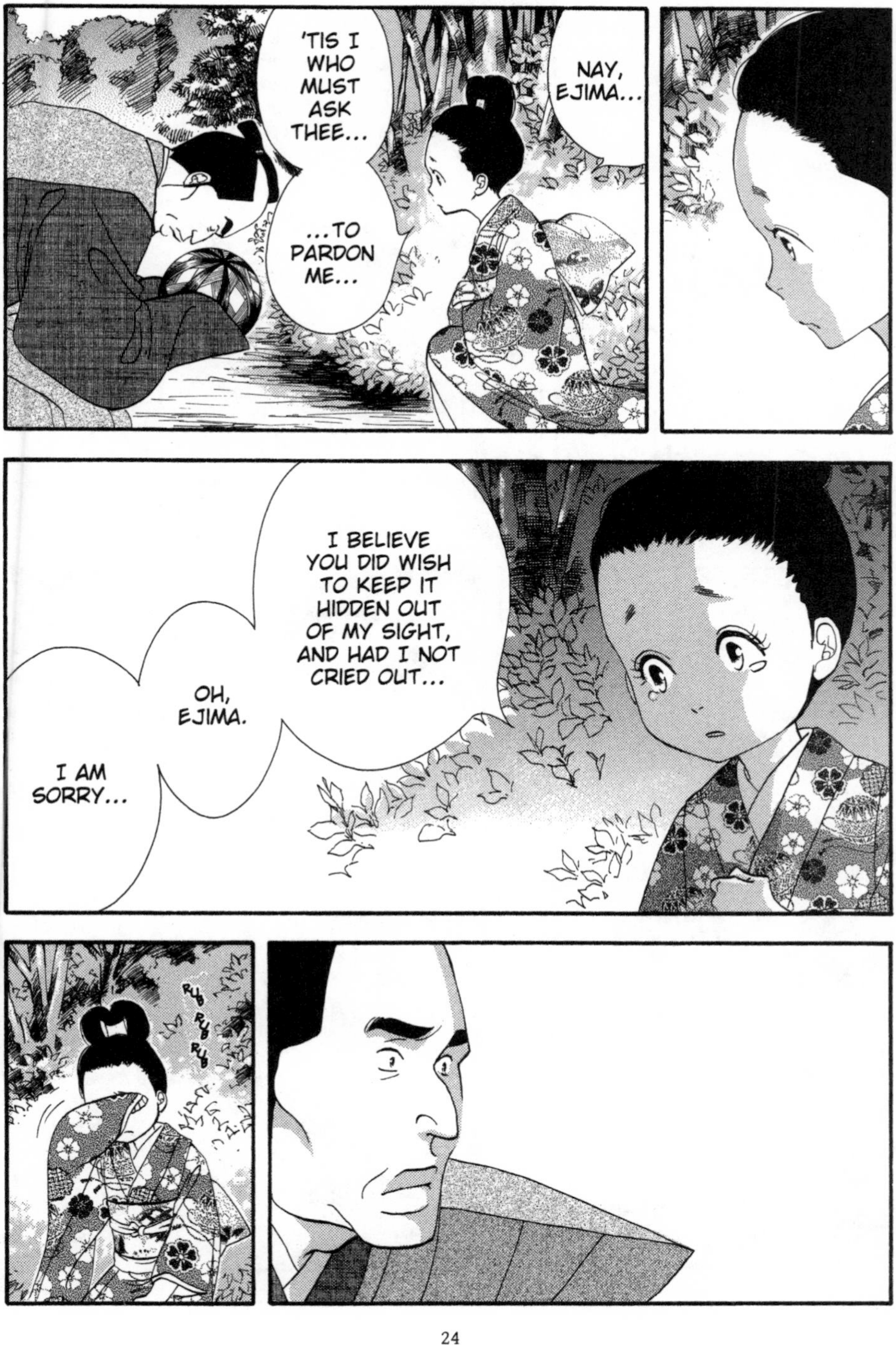
NAY, EJIMA...
'TIS I WHO MUST ASK THEE...
...TO PARDON ME...
I BELIEVE YOU DID WISH TO KEEP IT HIDDEN OUT OF MY SIGHT, AND HAD I NOT CRIED OUT...
OH, EJIMA.
I AM SORRY...
RUB RUB RUB

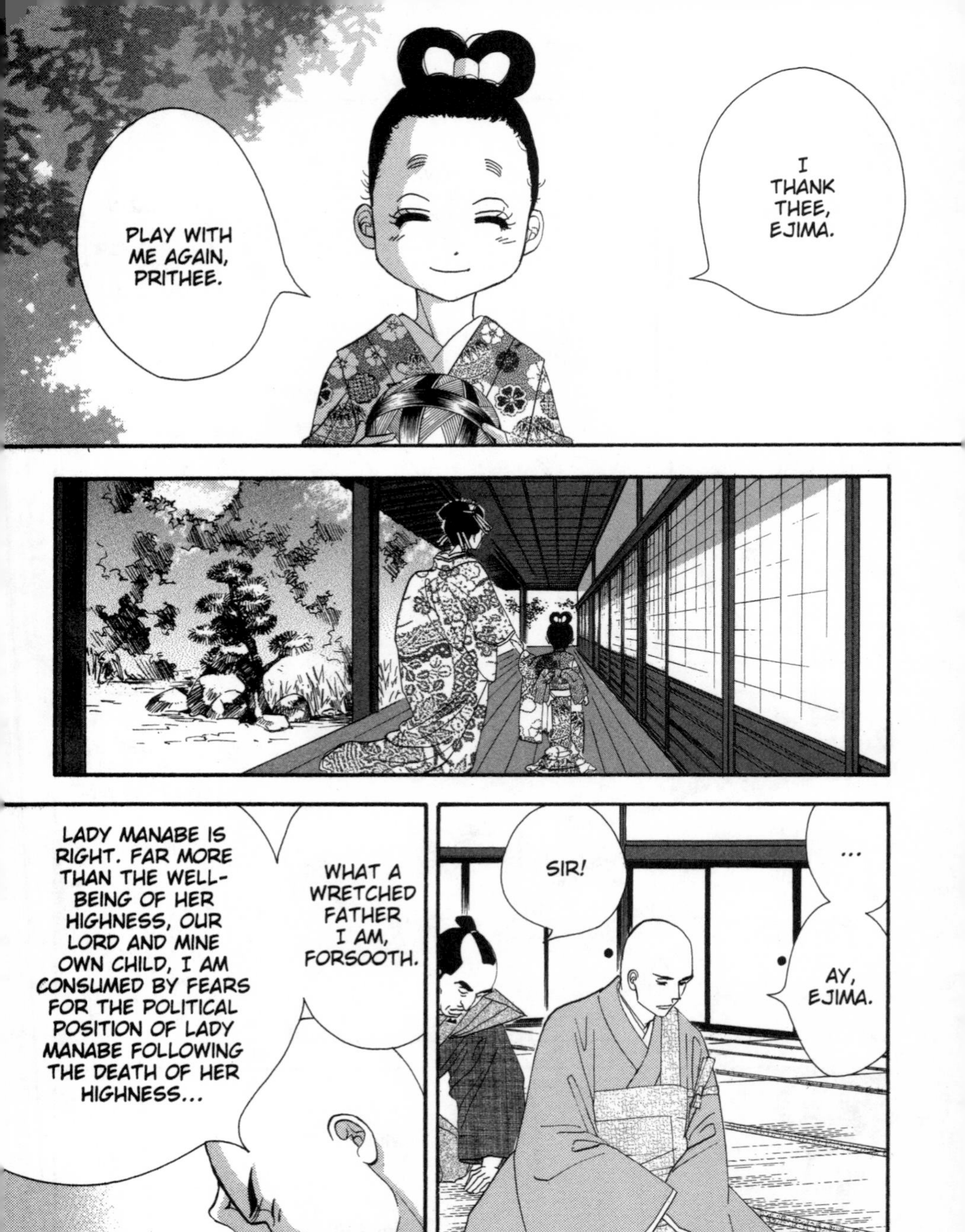
I THANK THEE, EJIMA.
PLAY WITH ME AGAIN, PRITHEE.
...
SIR!
AY, EJIMA.
WHAT A WRETCHED FATHER I AM, FORSOOTH.
LADY MANABE IS RIGHT. FAR MORE THAN THE WELL-BEING OF HER HIGHNESS, OUR LORD AND MINE OWN CHILD, I AM CONSUMED BY FEARS FOR THE POLITICAL POSITION OF LADY MANABE FOLLOWING THE DEATH OF HER HIGHNESS...

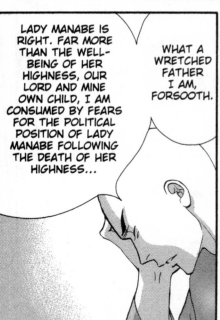

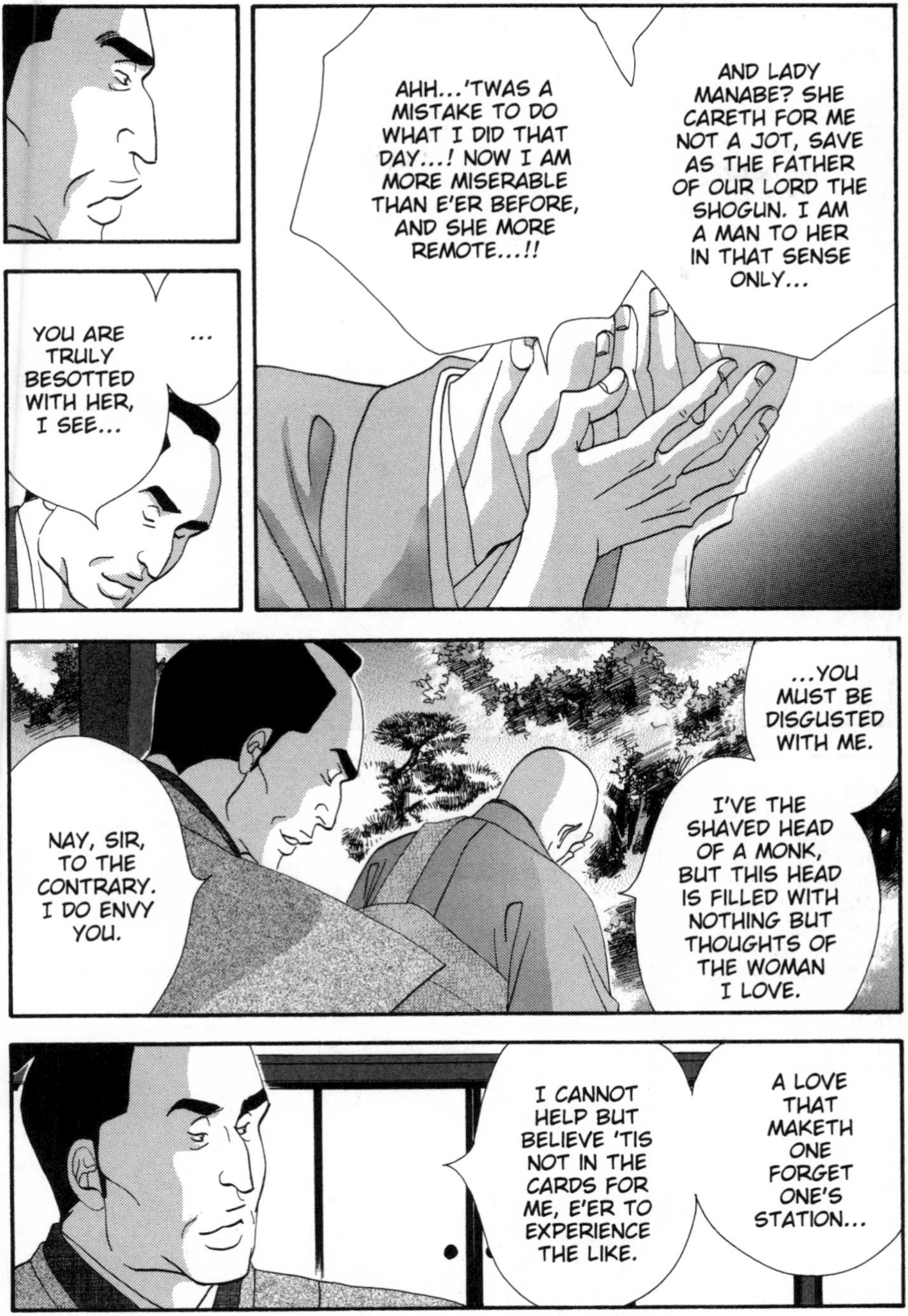
AND LADY MANABE? SHE CARETH FOR ME NOT A JOT, SAVE AS THE FATHER OF OUR LORD THE SHOGUN. I AM A MAN TO HER IN THAT SENSE ONLY...
AHH...'TWAS A MISTAKE TO DO WHAT I DID THAT DAY...! NOW I AM MORE MISERABLE THAN E'ER BEFORE, AND SHE MORE REMOTE...!!
...
YOU ARE TRULY BESOTTED WITH HER, I SEE...
...YOU MUST BE DISGUSTED WITH ME.
I'VE THE SHAVED HEAD OF A MONK, BUT THIS HEAD IS FILLED WITH NOTHING BUT THOUGHTS OF THE WOMAN I LOVE.
NAY, SIR, TO THE CONTRARY. I DO ENVY YOU.
A LOVE THAT MAKETH ONE FORGET ONE'S STATION...
I CANNOT HELP BUT BELIEVE 'TIS NOT IN THE CARDS FOR ME, E'ER TO EXPERIENCE THE LIKE.

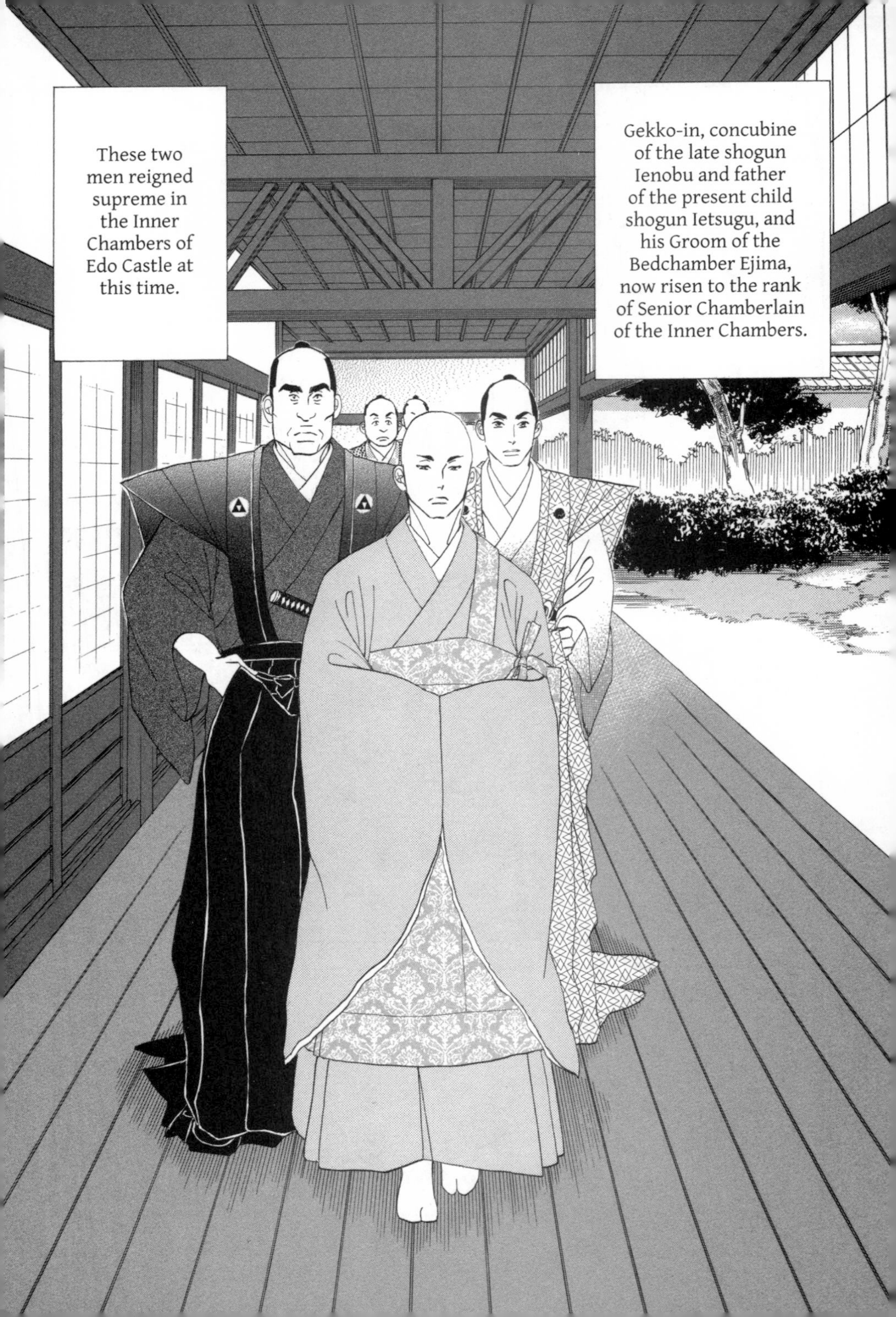
Gekko-in, concubine of the late shogun Ienobu and father of the present child shogun Ietsugu, and his Groom of the Bedchamber Ejima, now risen to the rank of Senior Chamberlain of the Inner Chambers.
These two men reigned supreme in the Inner Chambers of Edo Castle at this time.

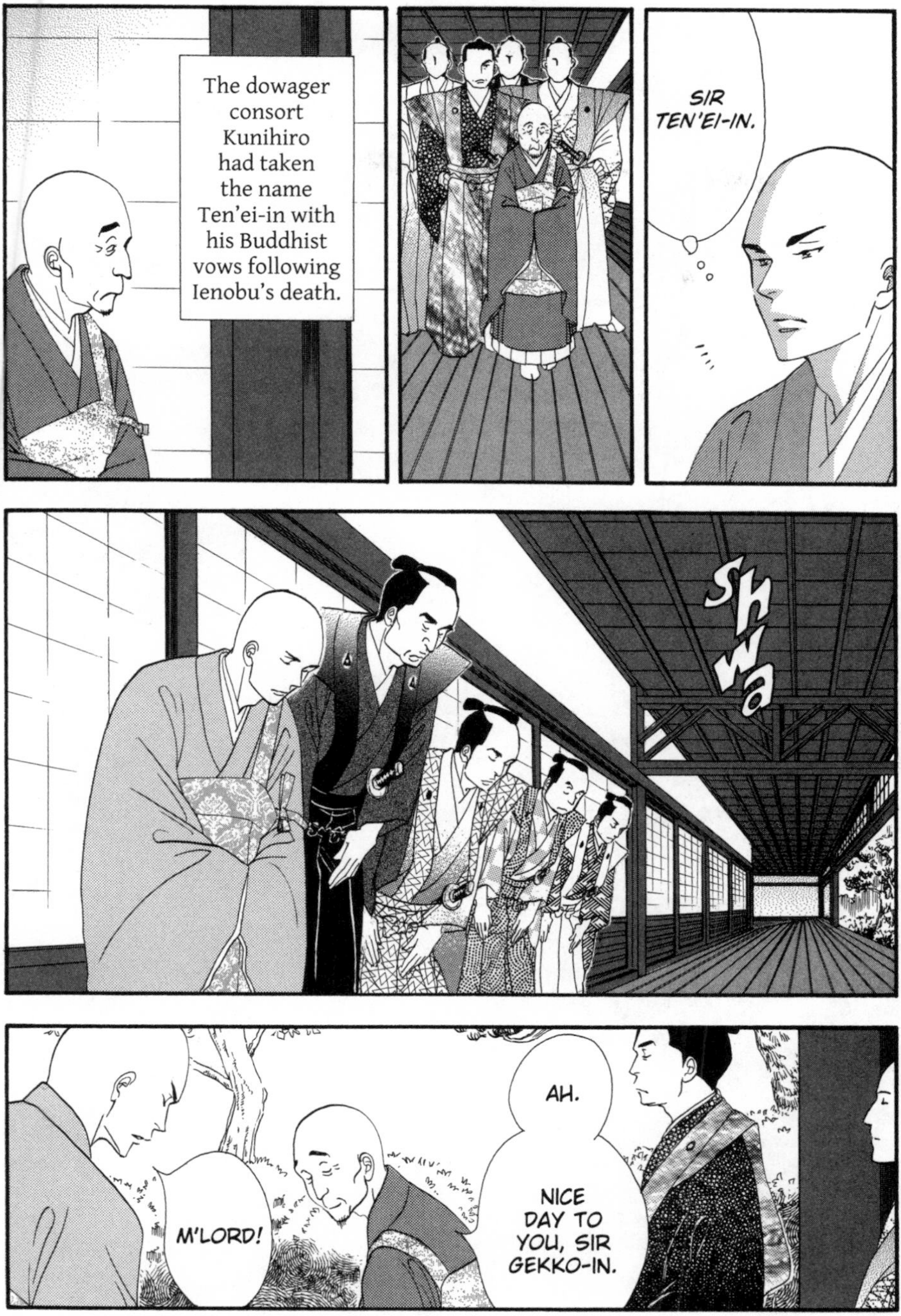
SIR TEN'EI-IN.
The dowager consort Kunihiro had taken the name Ten'ei-in with his Buddhist vows following Ienobu's death.
Shwa
AH.
NICE DAY TO YOU, SIR GEKKO-IN.
M'LORD!

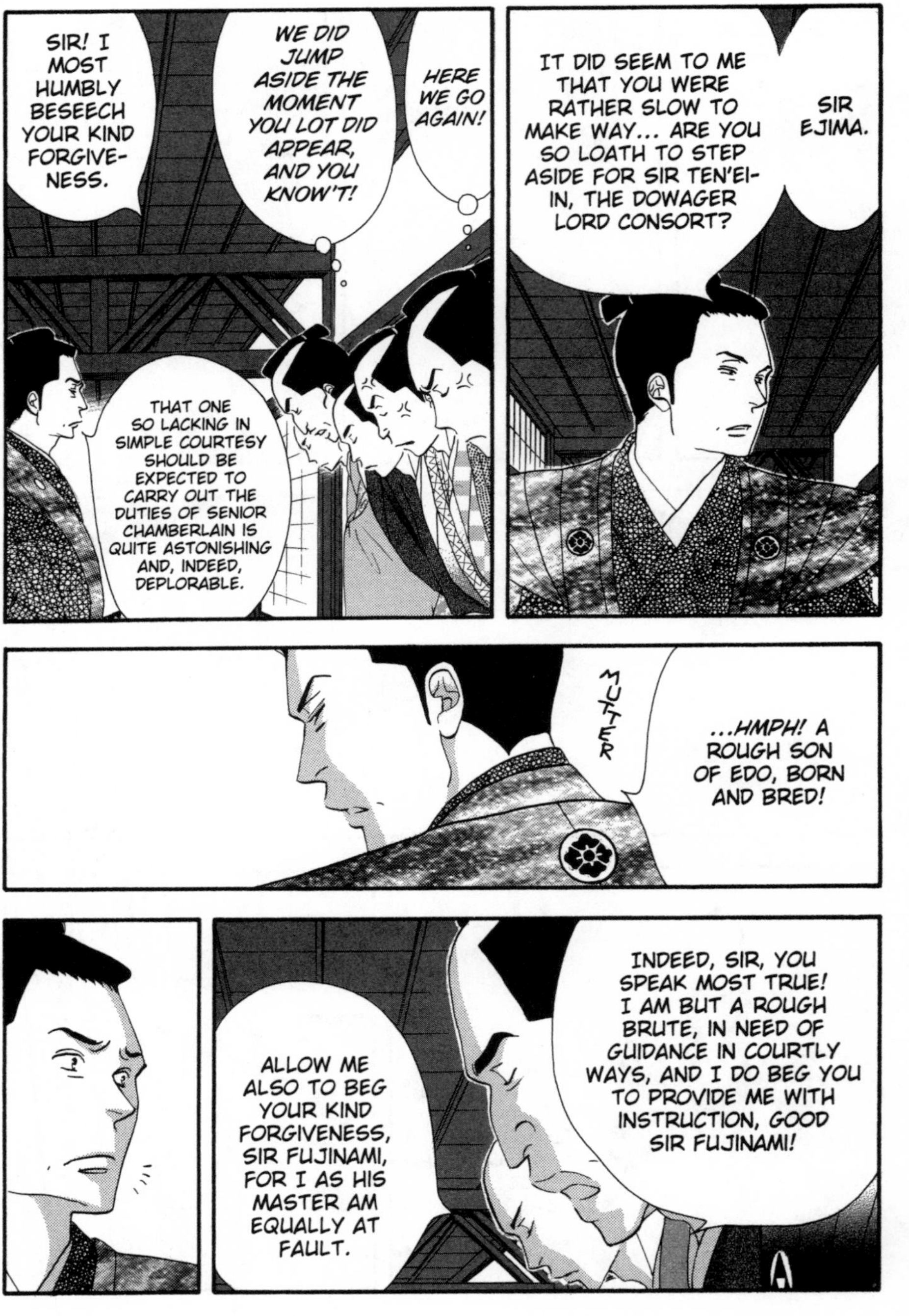
SIR EJIMA.
IT DID SEEM TO ME THAT YOU WERE RATHER SLOW TO MAKE WAY... ARE YOU SO LOATH TO STEP ASIDE FOR SIR TEN'EI-IN, THE DOWAGER LORD CONSORT?
HERE WE GO AGAIN!
WE DID JUMP ASIDE THE MOMENT YOU LOT DID APPEAR, AND YOU KNOW'T!
SIR! I MOST HUMBLY BESEECH YOUR KIND FORGIVENESS.
THAT ONE SO LACKING IN SIMPLE COURTESY SHOULD BE EXPECTED TO CARRY OUT THE DUTIES OF SENIOR CHAMBERLAIN IS QUITE ASTONISHING AND, INDEED, DEPLORABLE.
MUTTER
...HMPH! A ROUGH SON OF EDO, BORN AND BRED!
INDEED, SIR, YOU SPEAK MOST TRUE! I AM BUT A ROUGH BRUTE, IN NEED OF GUIDANCE IN COURTLY WAYS, AND I DO BEG YOU TO PROVIDE ME WITH INSTRUCTION, GOOD SIR FUJINAMI!
ALLOW ME ALSO TO BEG YOUR KIND FORGIVENESS, SIR FUJINAMI, FOR I AS HIS MASTER AM EQUALLY AT FAULT.

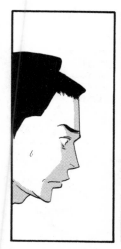

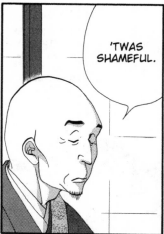

'TWAS SHAMEFUL.

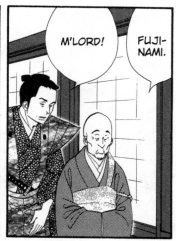

M'LORD!

FUJI-NAMI.

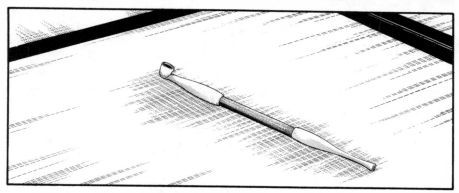

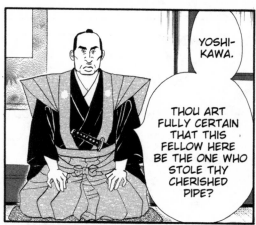

YOSHI-KAWA.

THOU ART FULLY CERTAIN THAT THIS FELLOW HERE BE THE ONE WHO STOLE THY CHERISHED PIPE?

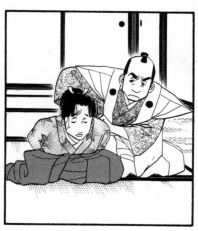

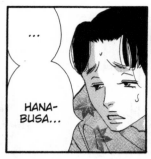

AYE, SIR EJIMA! THAT I AM!
THERE IS NO DOUBT WHATSOEVER OF'T, FOR I SAW HIM JUST A MOMENT AGO, PREENING HIMSELF WHILE SMOKING IN FRONT OF HIS FRIENDS THIS VERY PIPE OF MINE THAT WENT MISSING A FORTNIGHT AGO!
AND WHAT IS THY NAME, YOUNG FELLOW?
...
HANA-BUSA...
...THOU ART A CHAMBER BOY SERVING SIR FUJINAMI, ART THOU NOT?
SERVING SIR FUJINAMI?!
SIR EJIMA...! AT LAST WE CAN GIVE SIR FUJINAMI A DOSE OF HIS OWN BITTER MEDICINE!
MIYAJI!
M'LORD!
BRING ME MINE OWN PIPE TO THIS CHAMBER, FORTHWITH.

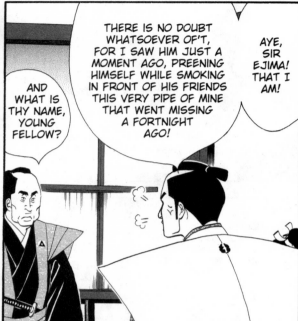

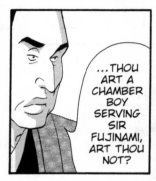

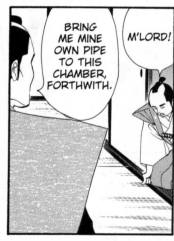

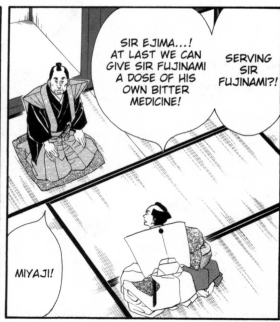

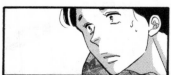

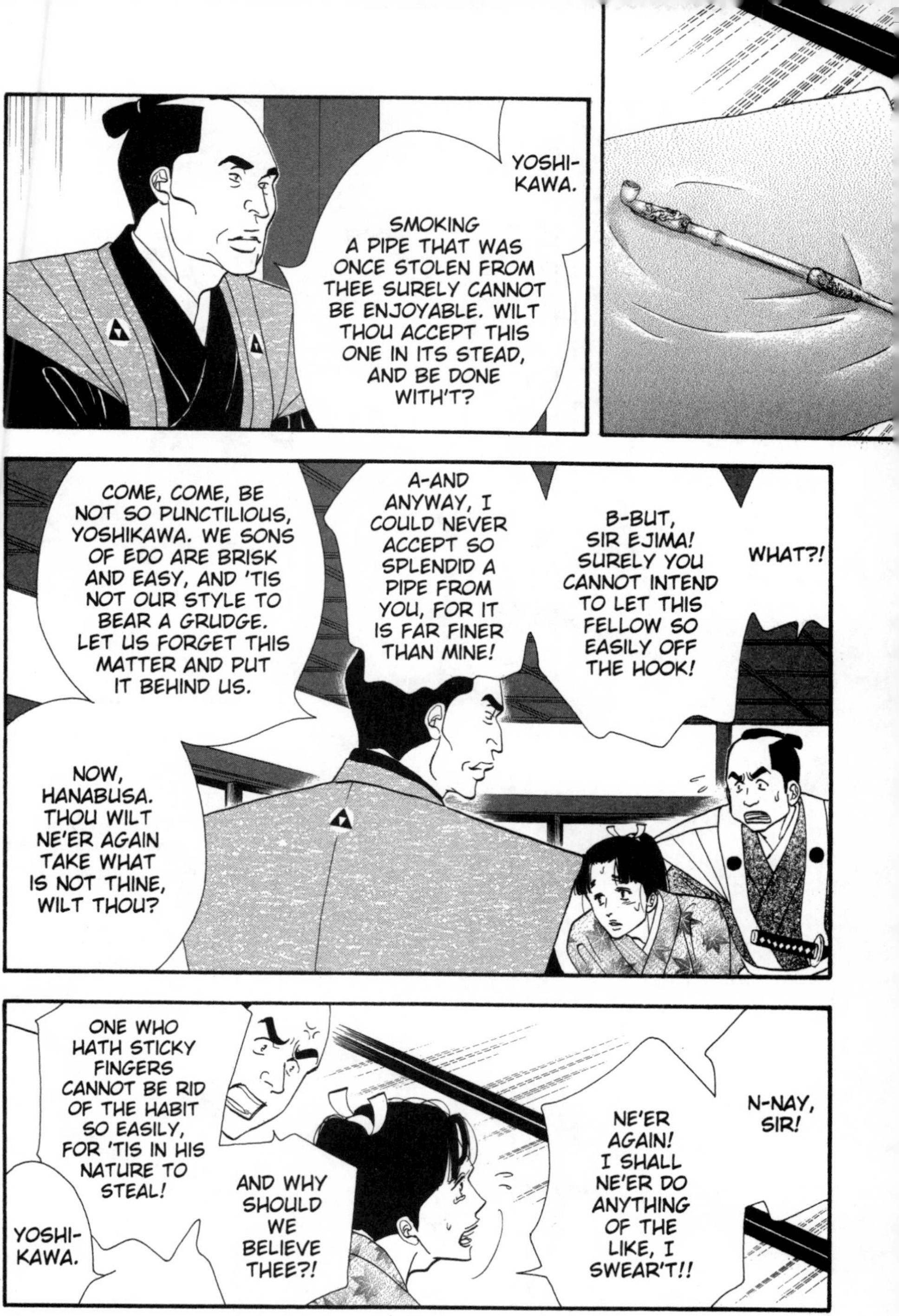
YOSHI-KAWA.
SMOKING A PIPE THAT WAS ONCE STOLEN FROM THEE SURELY CANNOT BE ENJOYABLE. WILT THOU ACCEPT THIS ONE IN ITS STEAD, AND BE DONE WITH'T?
WHAT?!
B-BUT, SIR EJIMA! SURELY YOU CANNOT INTEND TO LET THIS FELLOW SO EASILY OFF THE HOOK!
A-AND ANYWAY, I COULD NEVER ACCEPT SO SPLENDID A PIPE FROM YOU, FOR IT IS FAR FINER THAN MINE!
COME, COME, BE NOT SO PUNCTILIOUS, YOSHIKAWA. WE SONS OF EDO ARE BRISK AND EASY, AND 'TIS NOT OUR STYLE TO BEAR A GRUDGE. LET US FORGET THIS MATTER AND PUT IT BEHIND US.
NOW, HANABUSA. THOU WILT NE'ER AGAIN TAKE WHAT IS NOT THINE, WILT THOU?
N-NAY, SIR!
NE'ER AGAIN! I SHALL NE'ER DO ANYTHING OF THE LIKE, I SWEAR'T!!
ONE WHO HATH STICKY FINGERS CANNOT BE RID OF THE HABIT SO EASILY, FOR 'TIS IN HIS NATURE TO STEAL!
AND WHY SHOULD WE BELIEVE THEE?!
YOSHI-KAWA.

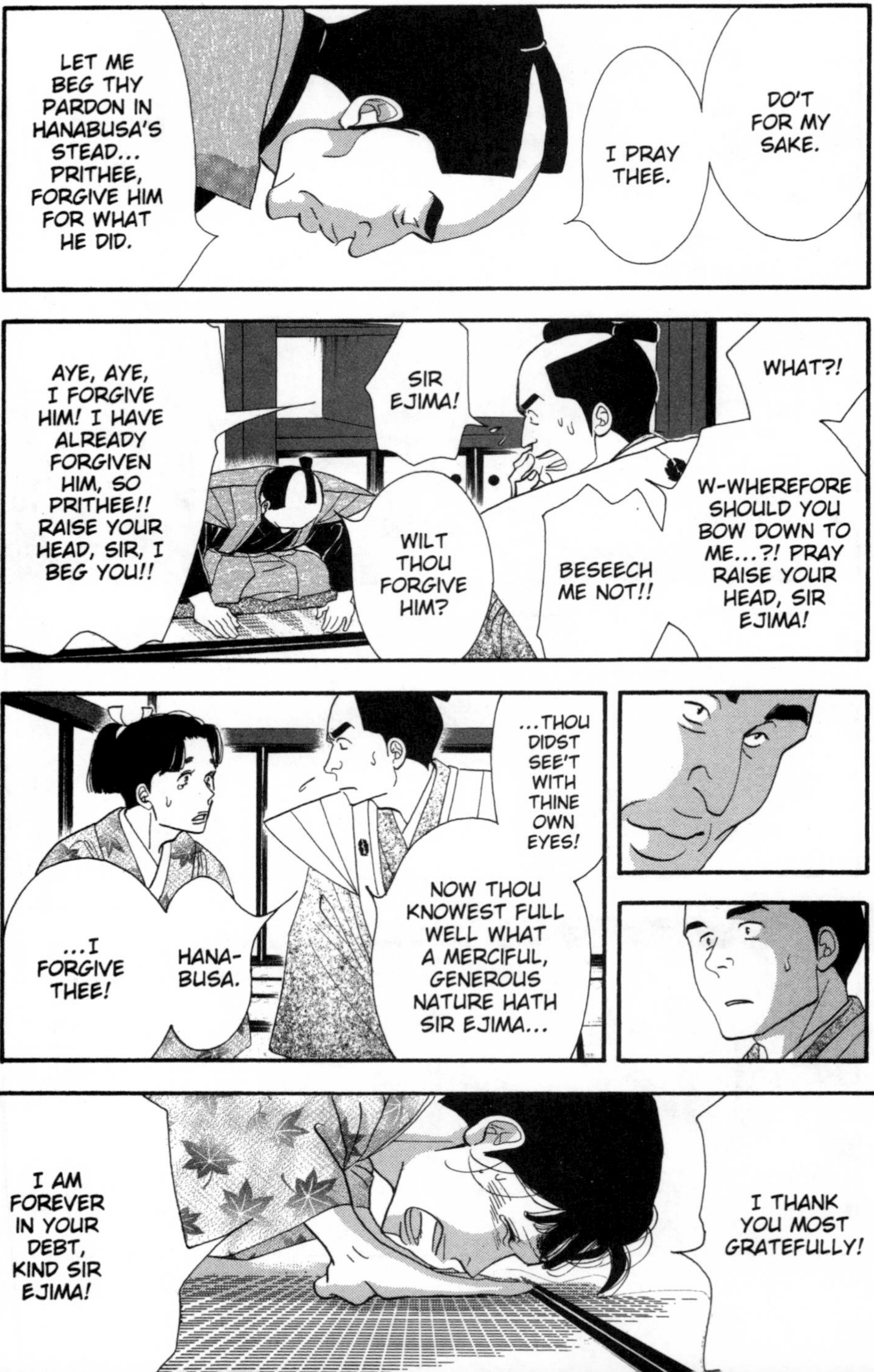
DO'T FOR MY SAKE.
I PRAY THEE.
LET ME BEG THY PARDON IN HANABUSA'S STEAD... PRITHEE, FORGIVE HIM FOR WHAT HE DID.
WHAT?!
W-WHEREFORE SHOULD YOU BOW DOWN TO ME...?! PRAY RAISE YOUR HEAD, SIR EJIMA!
BESEECH ME NOT!!
SIR EJIMA!
WILT THOU FORGIVE HIM?
AYE, AYE, I FORGIVE HIM! I HAVE ALREADY FORGIVEN HIM, SO PRITHEE!! RAISE YOUR HEAD, SIR, I BEG YOU!!
...THOU DIDST SEE'T WITH THINE OWN EYES!
NOW THOU KNOWEST FULL WELL WHAT A MERCIFUL, GENEROUS NATURE HATH SIR EJIMA...
HANA-BUSA.
...I FORGIVE THEE!
I THANK YOU MOST GRATEFULLY!
I AM FOREVER IN YOUR DEBT, KIND SIR EJIMA!

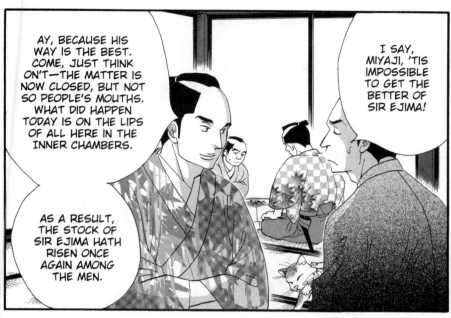

I SAY, MIYAJI, 'TIS IMPOSSIBLE TO GET THE BETTER OF SIR EJIMA!
AY, BECAUSE HIS WAY IS THE BEST. COME, JUST THINK ON'T—THE MATTER IS NOW CLOSED, BUT NOT SO PEOPLE'S MOUTHS. WHAT DID HAPPEN TODAY IS ON THE LIPS OF ALL HERE IN THE INNER CHAMBERS.
AS A RESULT, THE STOCK OF SIR EJIMA HATH RISEN ONCE AGAIN AMONG THE MEN.
GRRRR
I AM MOST MORTIFIED, SIR TEN'EI-IN!
AND WELL THOU SHOULDST BE.

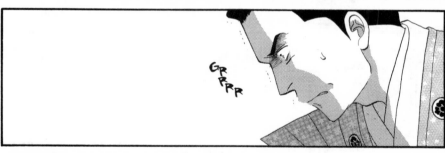

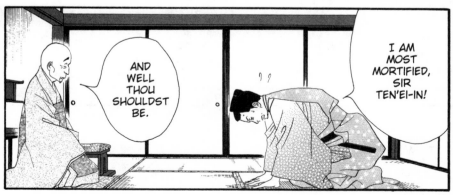

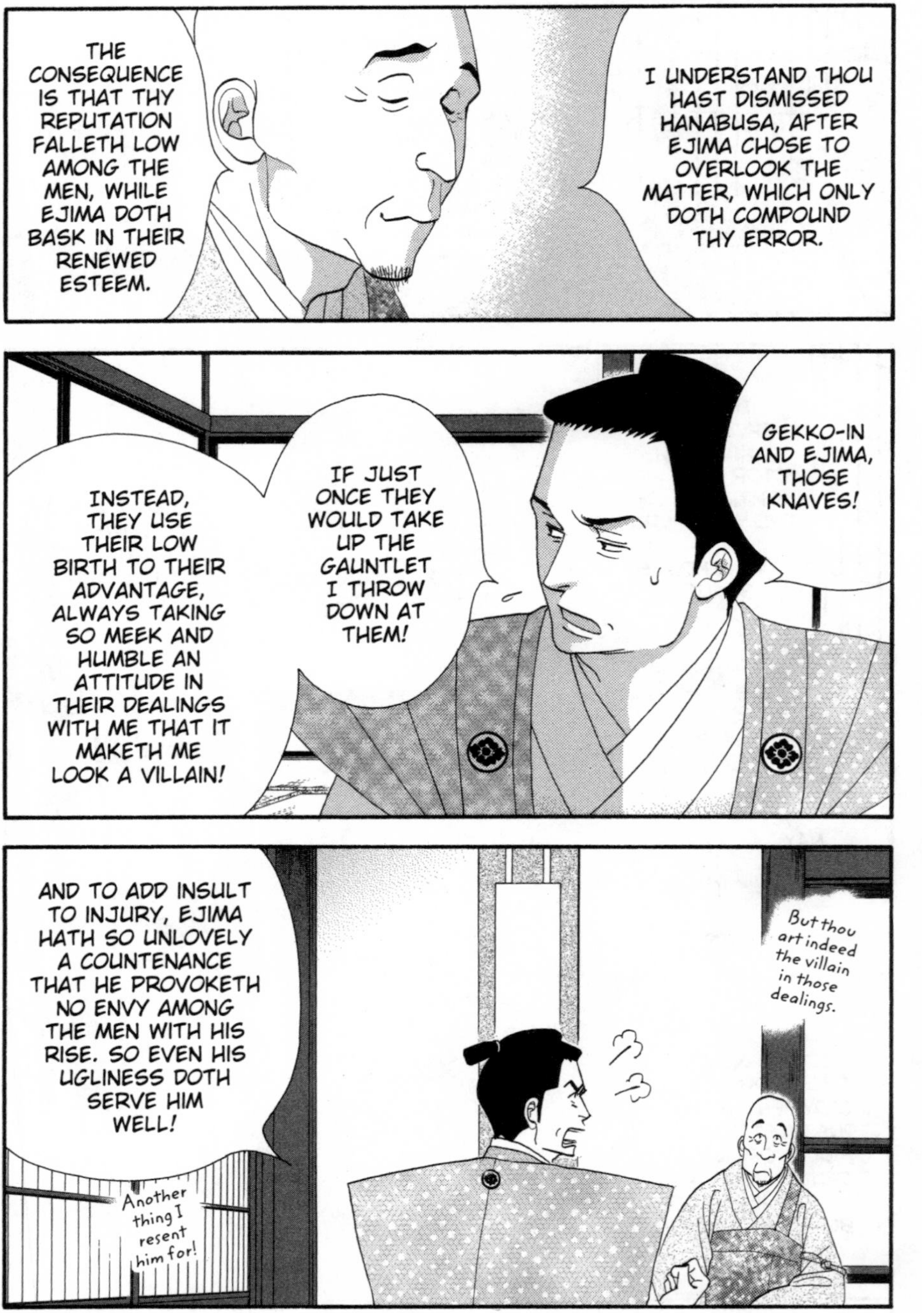
I UNDERSTAND THOU HAST DISMISSED HANABUSA, AFTER EJIMA CHOSE TO OVERLOOK THE MATTER, WHICH ONLY DOTH COMPOUND THY ERROR.
THE CONSEQUENCE IS THAT THY REPUTATION FALLETH LOW AMONG THE MEN, WHILE EJIMA DOTH BASK IN THEIR RENEWED ESTEEM.
GEKKO-IN AND EJIMA, THOSE KNAVES!
IF JUST ONCE THEY WOULD TAKE UP THE GAUNTLET I THROW DOWN AT THEM!
INSTEAD, THEY USE THEIR LOW BIRTH TO THEIR ADVANTAGE, ALWAYS TAKING SO MEEK AND HUMBLE AN ATTITUDE IN THEIR DEALINGS WITH ME THAT IT MAKETH ME LOOK A VILLAIN!
But thou art indeed the villain in those dealings.
AND TO ADD INSULT TO INJURY, EJIMA HATH SO UNLOVELY A COUNTENANCE THAT HE PROVOKETH NO ENVY AMONG THE MEN WITH HIS RISE. SO EVEN HIS UGLINESS DOTH SERVE HIM WELL!
Another thing I resent him for!

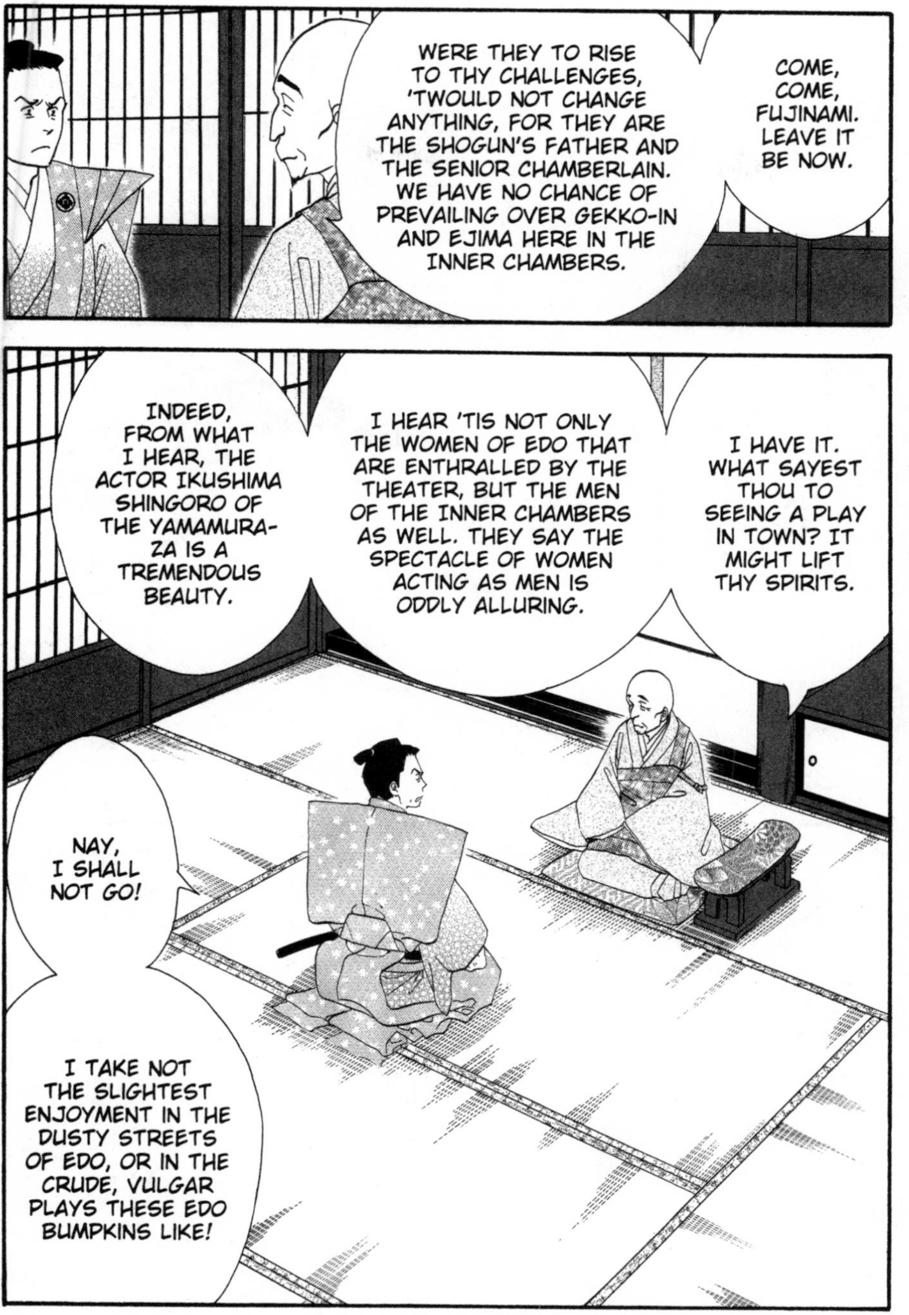
COME, COME, FUJINAMI. LEAVE IT BE NOW.
WERE THEY TO RISE TO THY CHALLENGES, 'TWOULD NOT CHANGE ANYTHING, FOR THEY ARE THE SHOGUN'S FATHER AND THE SENIOR CHAMBERLAIN. WE HAVE NO CHANCE OF PREVAILING OVER GEKKO-IN AND EJIMA HERE IN THE INNER CHAMBERS.
I HAVE IT. WHAT SAYEST THOU TO SEEING A PLAY IN TOWN? IT MIGHT LIFT THY SPIRITS.
I HEAR 'TIS NOT ONLY THE WOMEN OF EDO THAT ARE ENTHRALLED BY THE THEATER, BUT THE MEN OF THE INNER CHAMBERS AS WELL. THEY SAY THE SPECTACLE OF WOMEN ACTING AS MEN IS ODDLY ALLURING.
INDEED, FROM WHAT I HEAR, THE ACTOR IKUSHIMA SHINGORO OF THE YAMAMURA-ZA IS A TREMENDOUS BEAUTY.
NAY, I SHALL NOT GO!
I TAKE NOT THE SLIGHTEST ENJOYMENT IN THE DUSTY STREETS OF EDO, OR IN THE CRUDE, VULGAR PLAYS THESE EDO BUMPKINS LIKE!

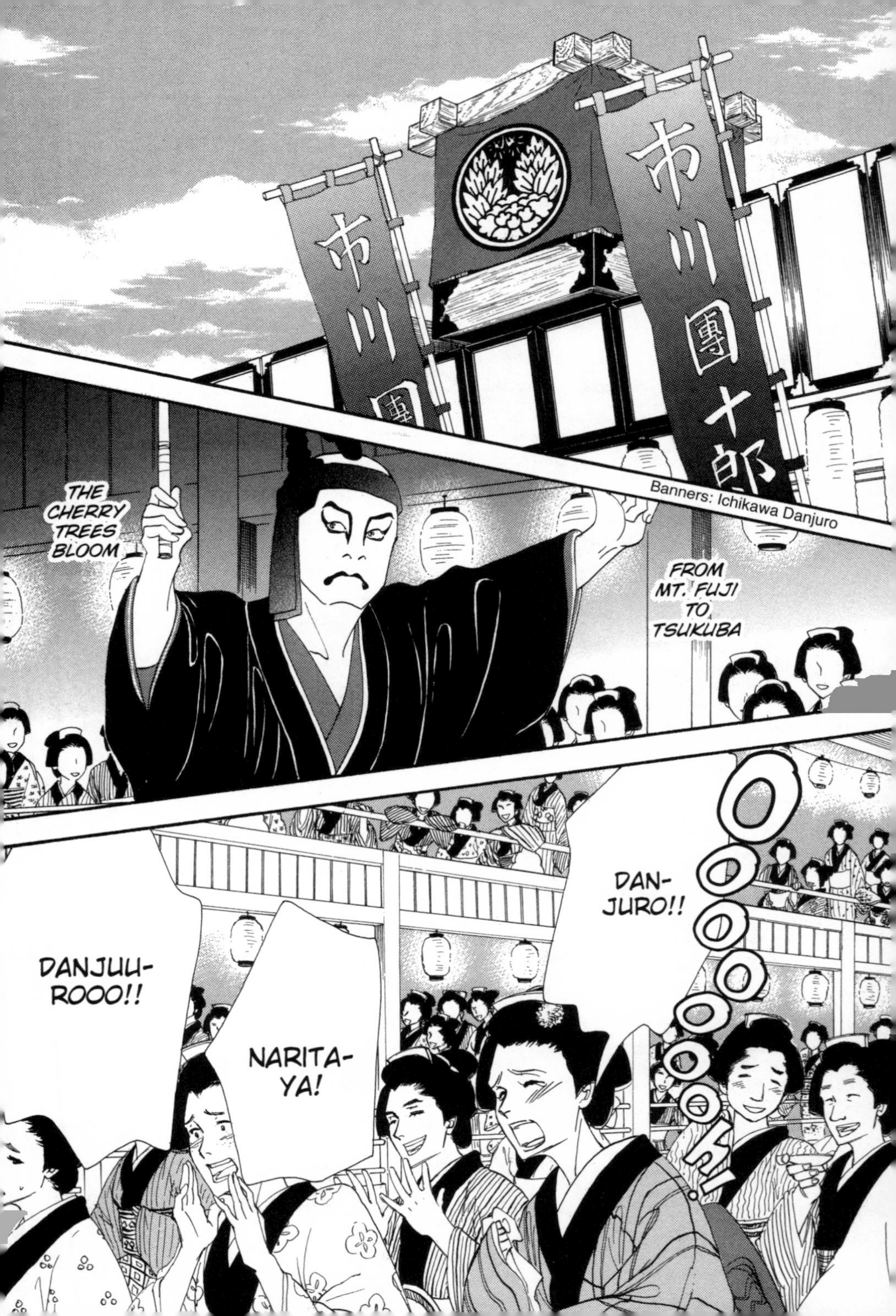
市川團十郎
Banners: Ichikawa Danjuro
FROM MT. FUJI TO TSUKUBA
THE CHERRY TREES BLOOM
OOOOOOOOOH!
DAN-JURO!!
NARITA-YA!
DANJUU-ROOO!!

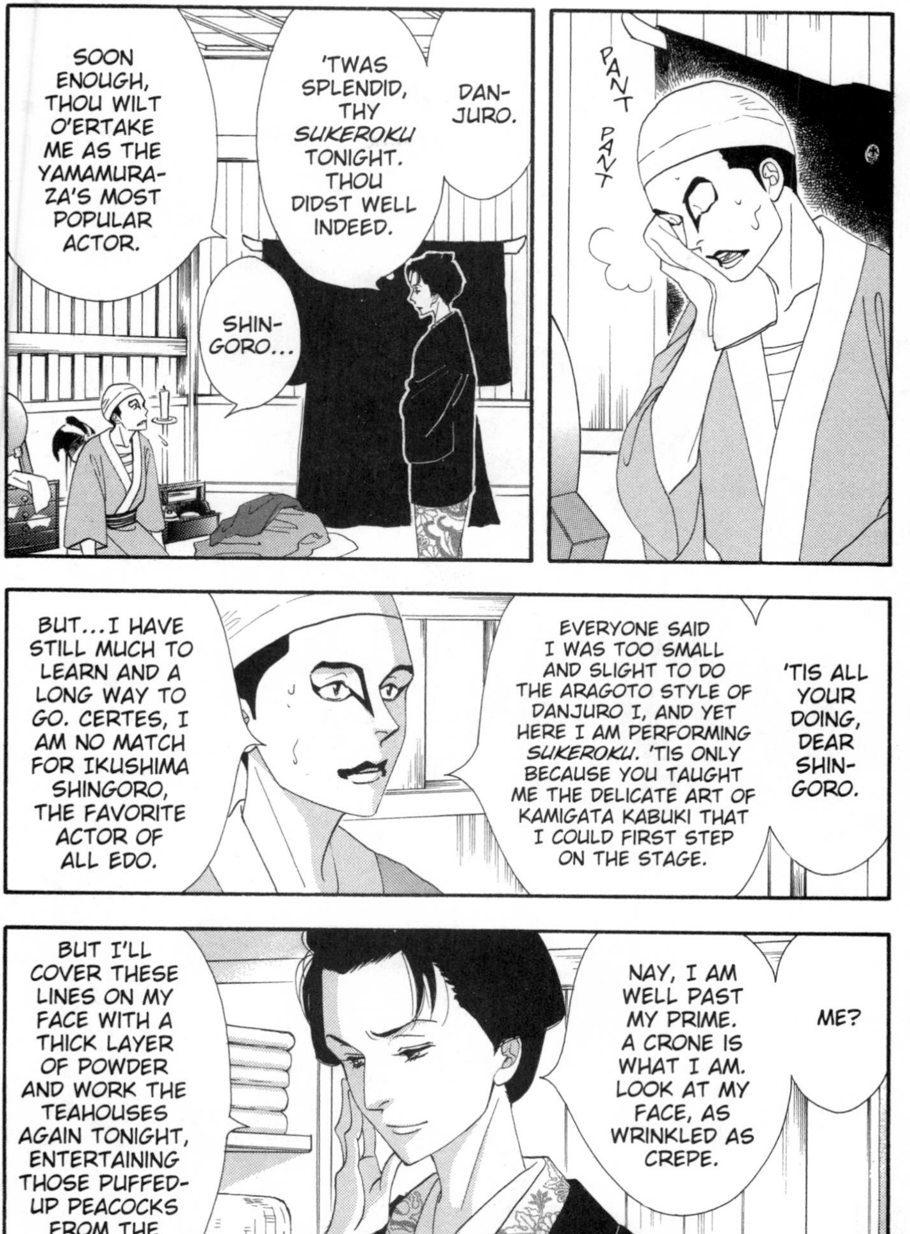
PANT PANT
DAN-JURO.
'TWAS SPLENDID, THY SUKEROKU TONIGHT. THOU DIDST WELL INDEED.
SOON ENOUGH, THOU WILT O'ERTAKE ME AS THE YAMAMURA-ZA'S MOST POPULAR ACTOR.
SHIN-GORO...
'TIS ALL YOUR DOING, DEAR SHIN-GORO.
EVERYONE SAID I WAS TOO SMALL AND SLIGHT TO DO THE ARAGOTO STYLE OF DANJURO I, AND YET HERE I AM PERFORMING SUKEROKU. 'TIS ONLY BECAUSE YOU TAUGHT ME THE DELICATE ART OF KAMIGATA KABUKI THAT I COULD FIRST STEP ON THE STAGE.
BUT...I HAVE STILL MUCH TO LEARN AND A LONG WAY TO GO. CERTES, I AM NO MATCH FOR IKUSHIMA SHINGORO, THE FAVORITE ACTOR OF ALL EDO.
ME?
NAY, I AM WELL PAST MY PRIME. A CRONE IS WHAT I AM. LOOK AT MY FACE, AS WRINKLED AS CREPE.
BUT I'LL COVER THESE LINES ON MY FACE WITH A THICK LAYER OF POWDER AND WORK THE TEAHOUSES AGAIN TONIGHT, ENTERTAINING THOSE PUFFED-UP PEACOCKS FROM THE LORDLY PALACES.

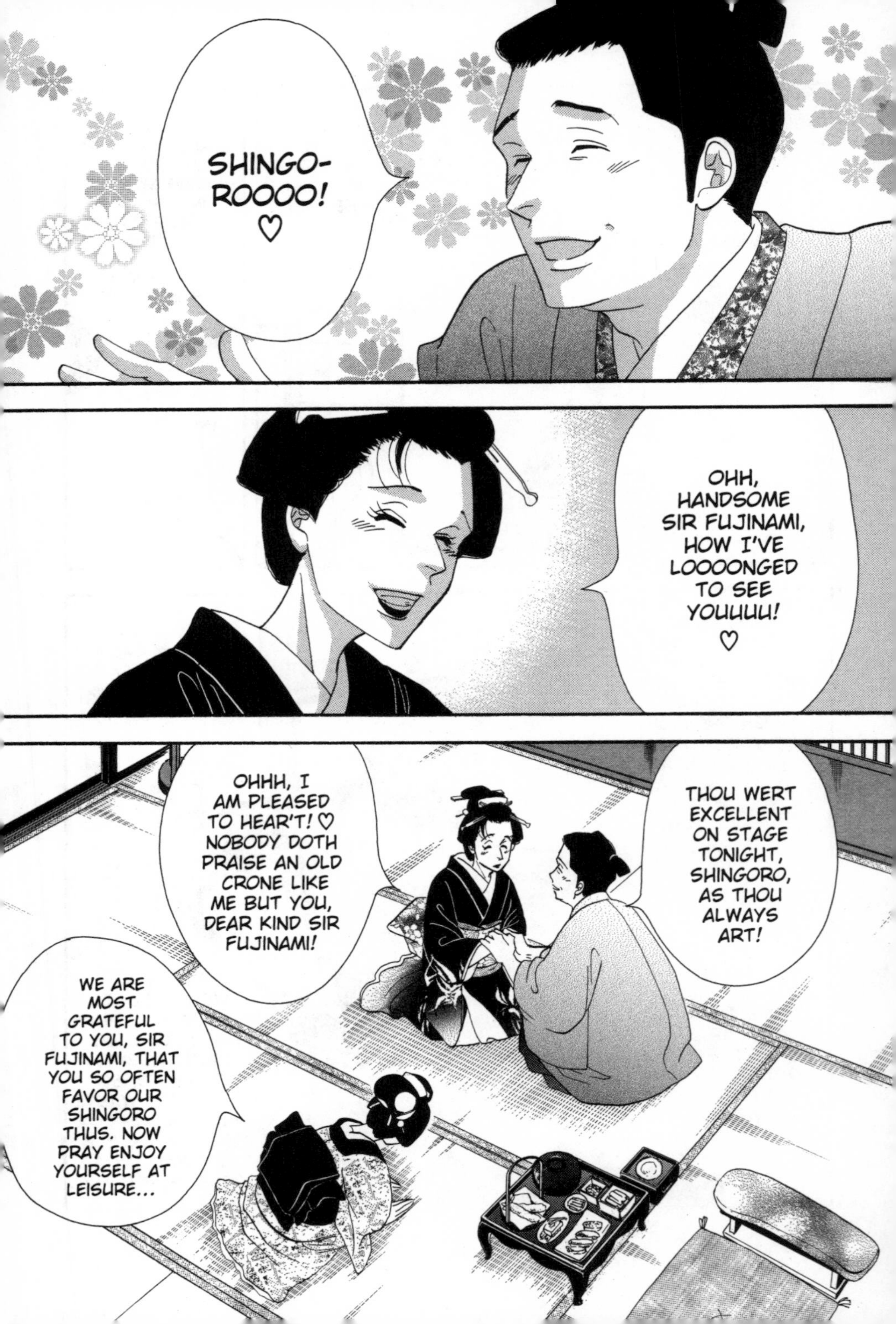
SHINGO-ROOOO! ♡
OHH, HANDSOME SIR FUJINAMI, HOW I'VE LOOOONGED TO SEE YOUUUU! ♡
THOU WERT EXCELLENT ON STAGE TONIGHT, SHINGORO, AS THOU ALWAYS ART!
OHHH, I AM PLEASED TO HEAR'T! ♡ NOBODY DOTH PRAISE AN OLD CRONE LIKE ME BUT YOU, DEAR KIND SIR FUJINAMI!
WE ARE MOST GRATEFUL TO YOU, SIR FUJINAMI, THAT YOU SO OFTEN FAVOR OUR SHINGORO THUS. NOW PRAY ENJOY YOURSELF AT LEISURE...

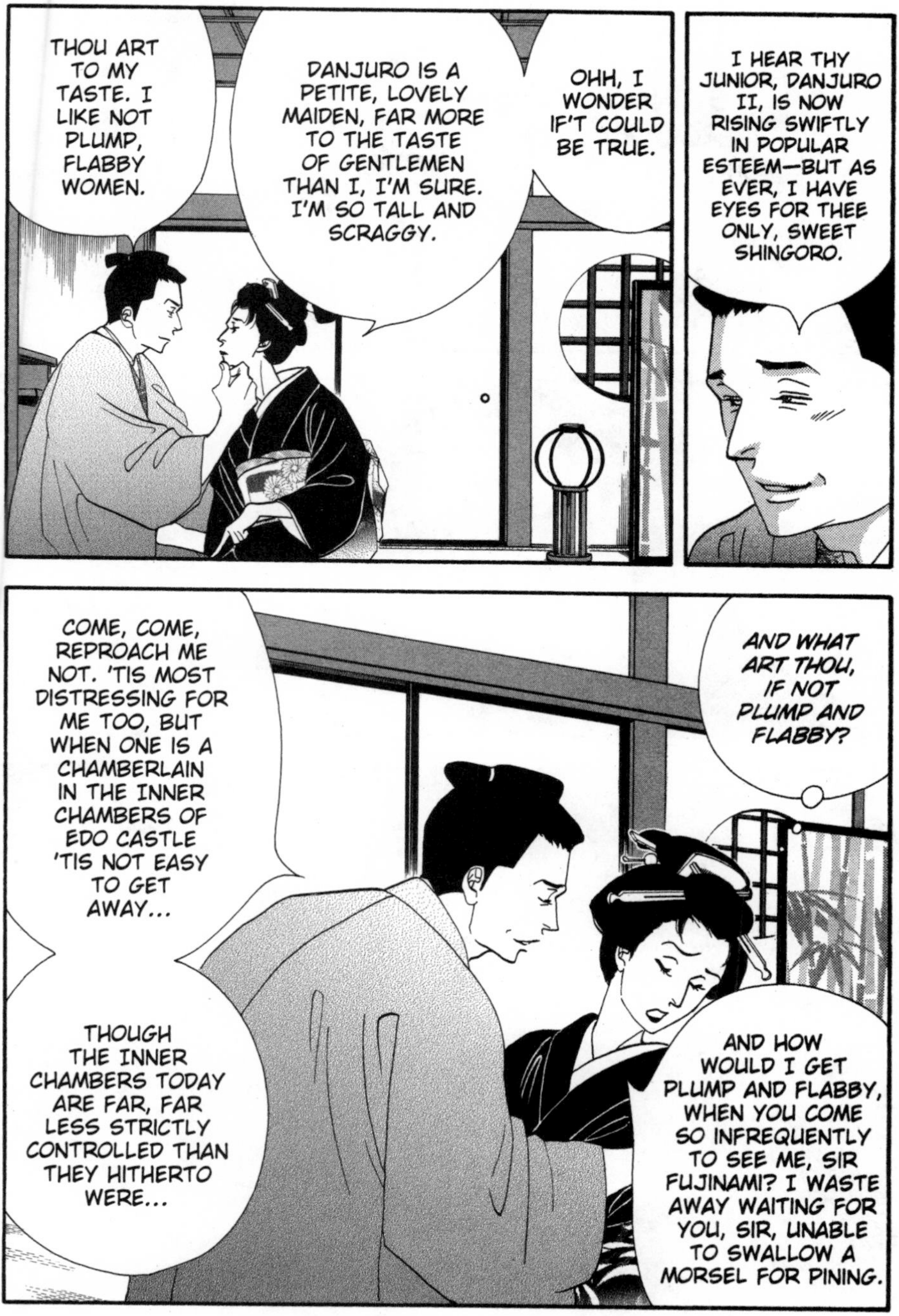
I HEAR THY JUNIOR, DANJURO II, IS NOW RISING SWIFTLY IN POPULAR ESTEEM—BUT AS EVER, I HAVE EYES FOR THEE ONLY, SWEET SHINGORO.
OHH, I WONDER IF'T COULD BE TRUE.
DANJURO IS A PETITE, LOVELY MAIDEN, FAR MORE TO THE TASTE OF GENTLEMEN THAN I, I'M SURE. I'M SO TALL AND SCRAGGY.
THOU ART TO MY TASTE. I LIKE NOT PLUMP, FLABBY WOMEN.
AND WHAT ART THOU, IF NOT PLUMP AND FLABBY?
AND HOW WOULD I GET PLUMP AND FLABBY, WHEN YOU COME SO INFREQUENTLY TO SEE ME, SIR FUJINAMI? I WASTE AWAY WAITING FOR YOU, SIR, UNABLE TO SWALLOW A MORSEL FOR PINING.
COME, COME, REPROACH ME NOT. 'TIS MOST DISTRESSING FOR ME TOO, BUT WHEN ONE IS A CHAMBERLAIN IN THE INNER CHAMBERS OF EDO CASTLE 'TIS NOT EASY TO GET AWAY...
THOUGH THE INNER CHAMBERS TODAY ARE FAR, FAR LESS STRICTLY CONTROLLED THAN THEY HITHERTO WERE...

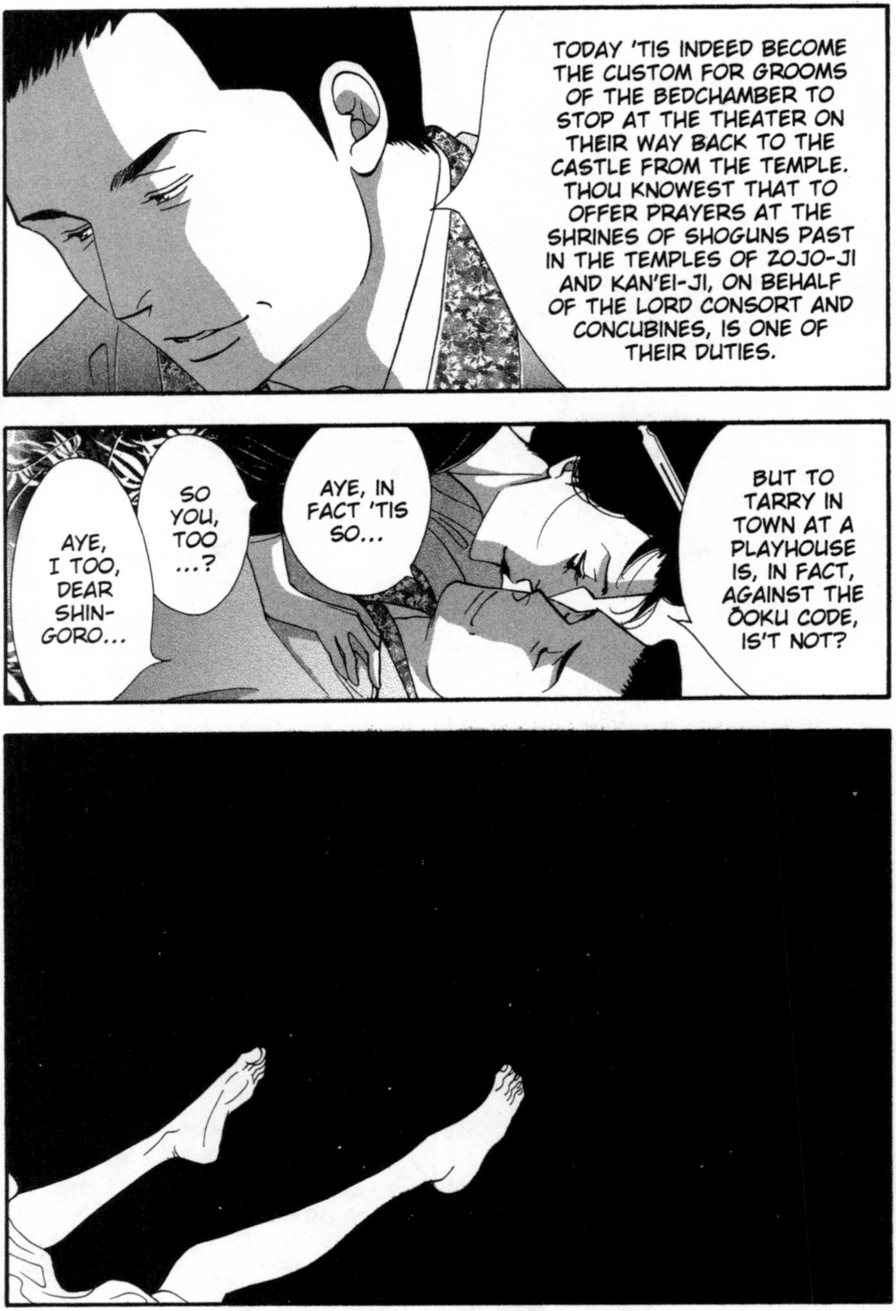
TODAY 'TIS INDEED BECOME THE CUSTOM FOR GROOMS OF THE BEDCHAMBER TO STOP AT THE THEATER ON THEIR WAY BACK TO THE CASTLE FROM THE TEMPLE. THOU KNOWEST THAT TO OFFER PRAYERS AT THE SHRINES OF SHOGUNS PAST IN THE TEMPLES OF ZOJO-JI AND KAN'EI-JI, ON BEHALF OF THE LORD CONSORT AND CONCUBINES, IS ONE OF THEIR DUTIES.
BUT TO TARRY IN TOWN AT A PLAYHOUSE IS, IN FACT, AGAINST THE ŌOKU CODE, IS'T NOT?
AYE, IN FACT 'TIS SO...
SO YOU, TOO...?
AYE, I TOO, DEAR SHIN-GORO...

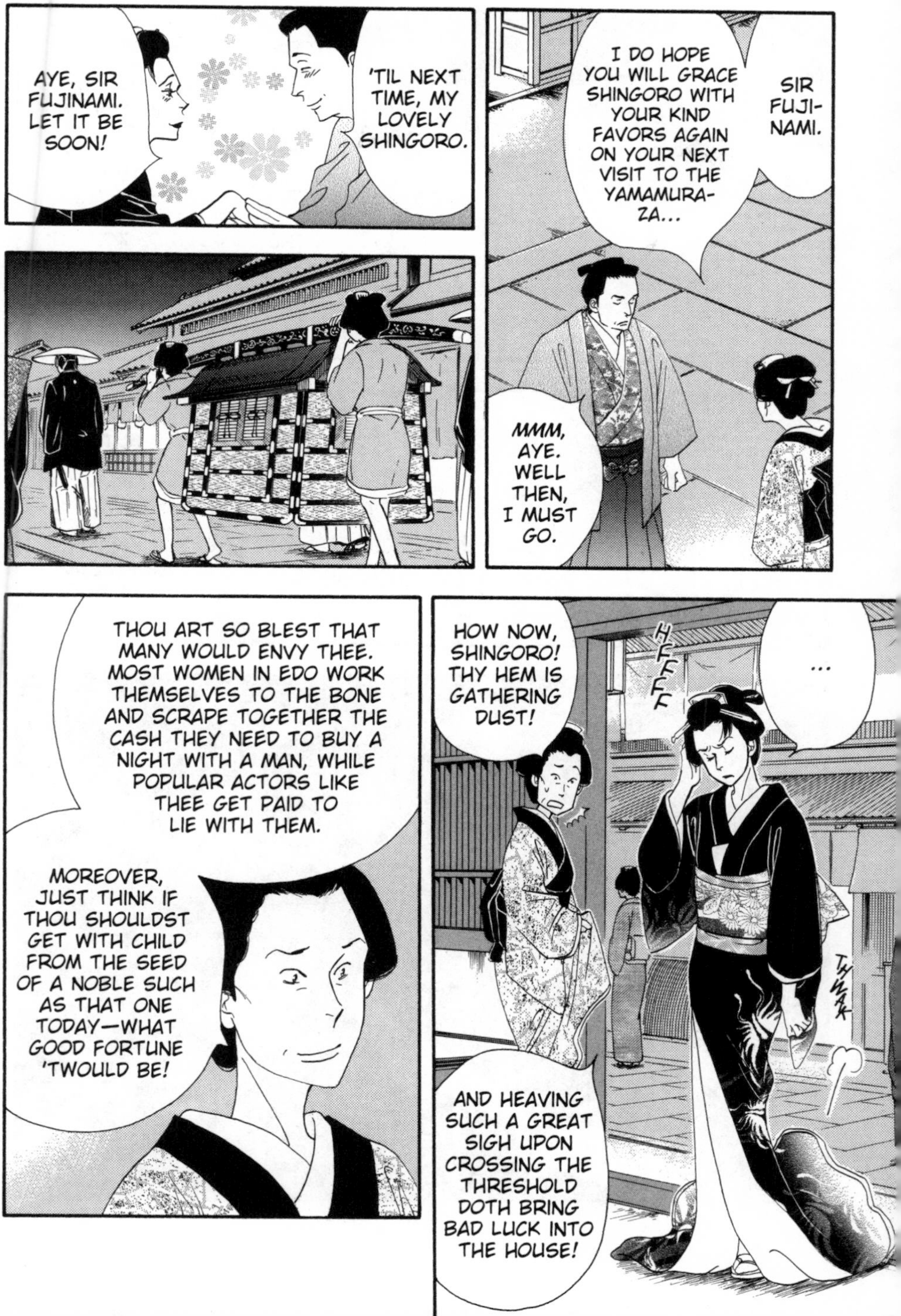
SIR FUJI-NAMI.
I DO HOPE YOU WILL GRACE SHINGORO WITH YOUR KIND FAVORS AGAIN ON YOUR NEXT VISIT TO THE YAMAMURA-ZA...
MMM, AYE. WELL THEN, I MUST GO.
'TIL NEXT TIME, MY LOVELY SHINGORO.
AYE, SIR FUJINAMI. LET IT BE SOON!
...
HFFFF
HOW NOW, SHINGORO! THY HEM IS GATHERING DUST!
THWAK
AND HEAVING SUCH A GREAT SIGH UPON CROSSING THE THRESHOLD DOTH BRING BAD LUCK INTO THE HOUSE!
THOU ART SO BLEST THAT MANY WOULD ENVY THEE. MOST WOMEN IN EDO WORK THEMSELVES TO THE BONE AND SCRAPE TOGETHER THE CASH THEY NEED TO BUY A NIGHT WITH A MAN, WHILE POPULAR ACTORS LIKE THEE GET PAID TO LIE WITH THEM.
MOREOVER, JUST THINK IF THOU SHOULDST GET WITH CHILD FROM THE SEED OF A NOBLE SUCH AS THAT ONE TODAY—WHAT GOOD FORTUNE 'TWOULD BE!

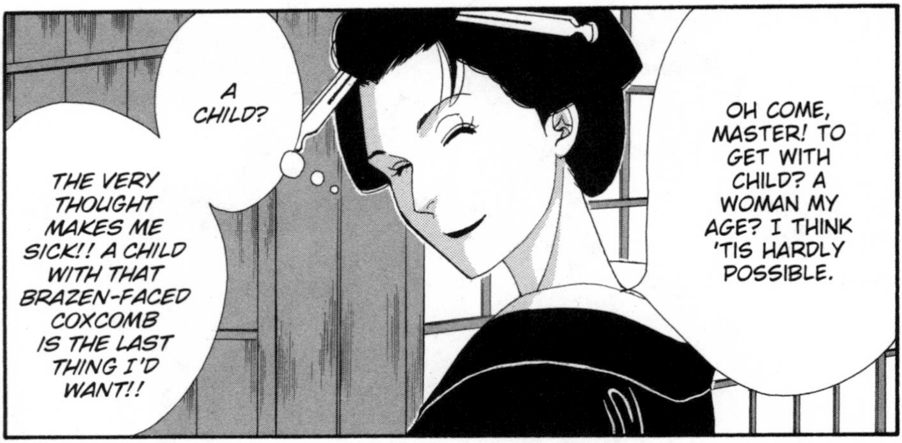
OH COME, MASTER! TO GET WITH CHILD? A WOMAN MY AGE? I THINK 'TIS HARDLY POSSIBLE.
A CHILD?
THE VERY THOUGHT MAKES ME SICK!! A CHILD WITH THAT BRAZEN-FACED COXCOMB IS THE LAST THING I'D WANT!!

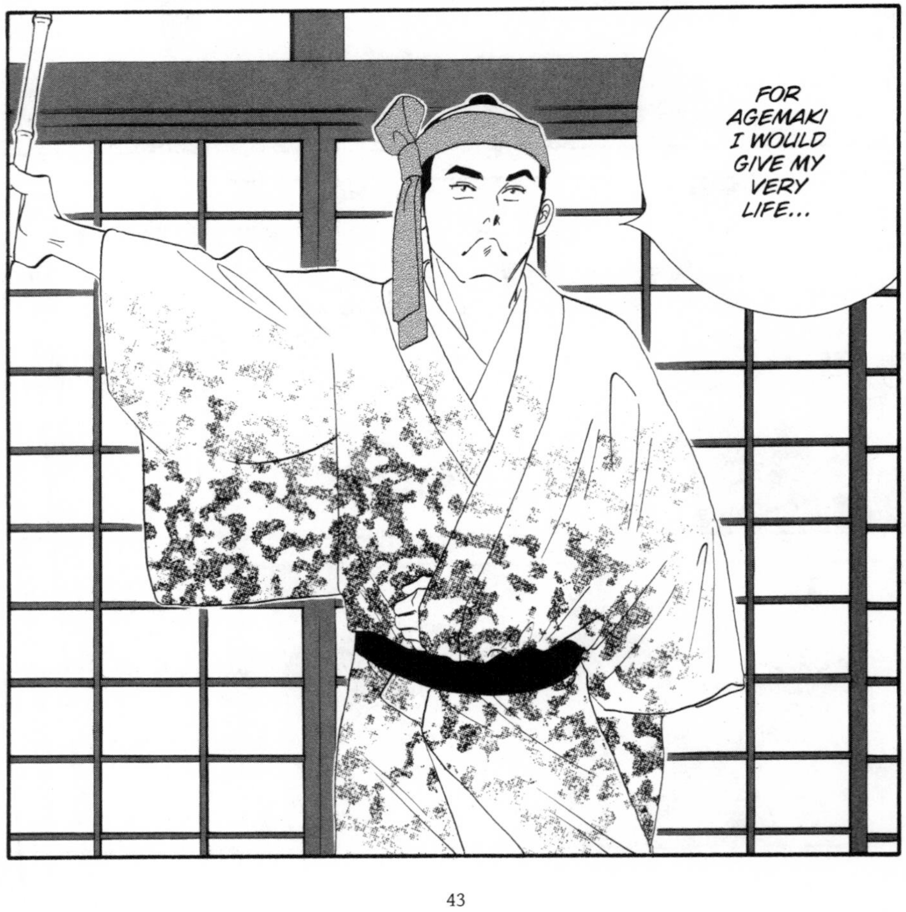
FOR AGEMAKI I WOULD GIVE MY VERY LIFE...

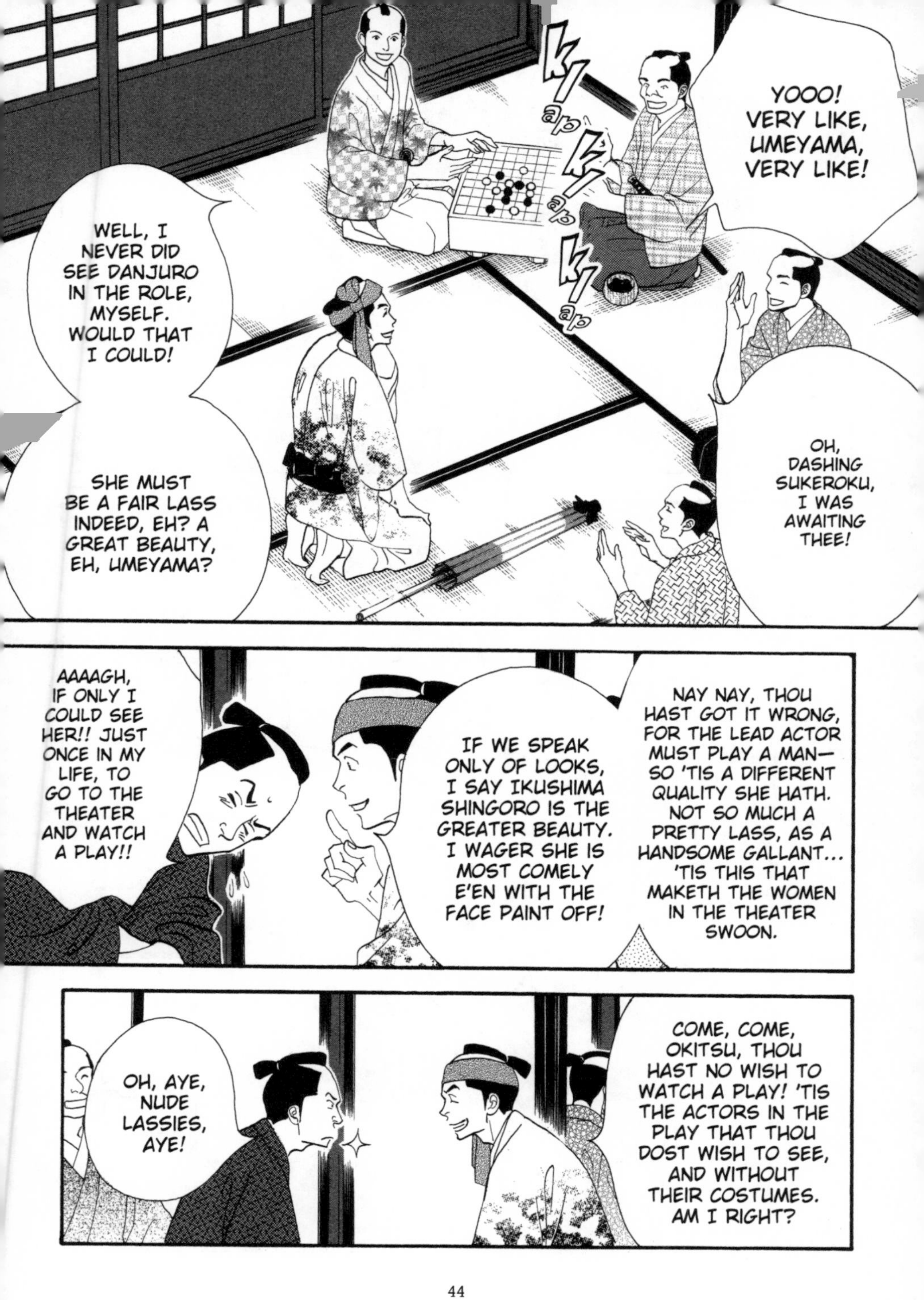
YOOO! VERY LIKE, UMEYAMA, VERY LIKE!
KLAP KLAP KLAP
WELL, I NEVER DID SEE DANJURO IN THE ROLE, MYSELF. WOULD THAT I COULD!
OH, DASHING SUKEROKU, I WAS AWAITING THEE!
SHE MUST BE A FAIR LASS INDEED, EH? A GREAT BEAUTY, EH, UMEYAMA?
NAY NAY, THOU HAST GOT IT WRONG, FOR THE LEAD ACTOR MUST PLAY A MAN— SO 'TIS A DIFFERENT QUALITY SHE HATH. NOT SO MUCH A PRETTY LASS, AS A HANDSOME GALLANT... 'TIS THIS THAT MAKETH THE WOMEN IN THE THEATER SWOON.
IF WE SPEAK ONLY OF LOOKS, I SAY IKUSHIMA SHINGORO IS THE GREATER BEAUTY. I WAGER SHE IS MOST COMELY E'EN WITH THE FACE PAINT OFF!
AAAAGH, IF ONLY I COULD SEE HER!! JUST ONCE IN MY LIFE, TO GO TO THE THEATER AND WATCH A PLAY!!
COME, COME, OKITSU, THOU HAST NO WISH TO WATCH A PLAY! 'TIS THE ACTORS IN THE PLAY THAT THOU DOST WISH TO SEE, AND WITHOUT THEIR COSTUMES. AM I RIGHT?
OH, AYE, NUDE LASSIES, AYE!

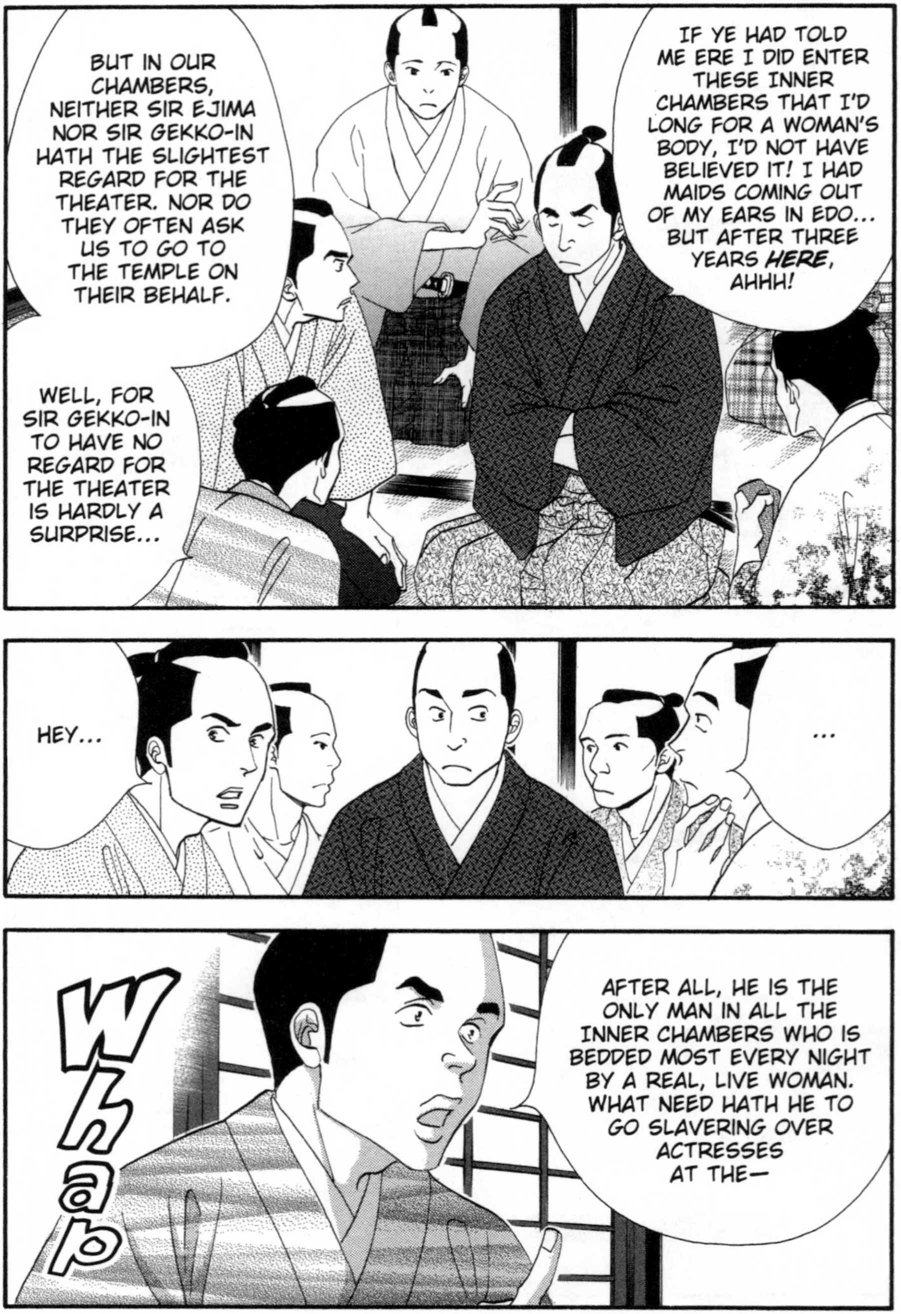
IF YE HAD TOLD ME ERE I DID ENTER THESE INNER CHAMBERS THAT I'D LONG FOR A WOMAN'S BODY, I'D NOT HAVE BELIEVED IT! I HAD MAIDS COMING OUT OF MY EARS IN EDO... BUT AFTER THREE YEARS *HERE*, AHHH!
BUT IN OUR CHAMBERS, NEITHER SIR EJIMA NOR SIR GEKKO-IN HATH THE SLIGHTEST REGARD FOR THE THEATER. NOR DO THEY OFTEN ASK US TO GO TO THE TEMPLE ON THEIR BEHALF.
WELL, FOR SIR GEKKO-IN TO HAVE NO REGARD FOR THE THEATER IS HARDLY A SURPRISE...
...
HEY...
AFTER ALL, HE IS THE ONLY MAN IN ALL THE INNER CHAMBERS WHO IS BEDDED MOST EVERY NIGHT BY A REAL, LIVE WOMAN. WHAT NEED HATH HE TO GO SLAVERING OVER ACTRESSES AT THE—
Whap

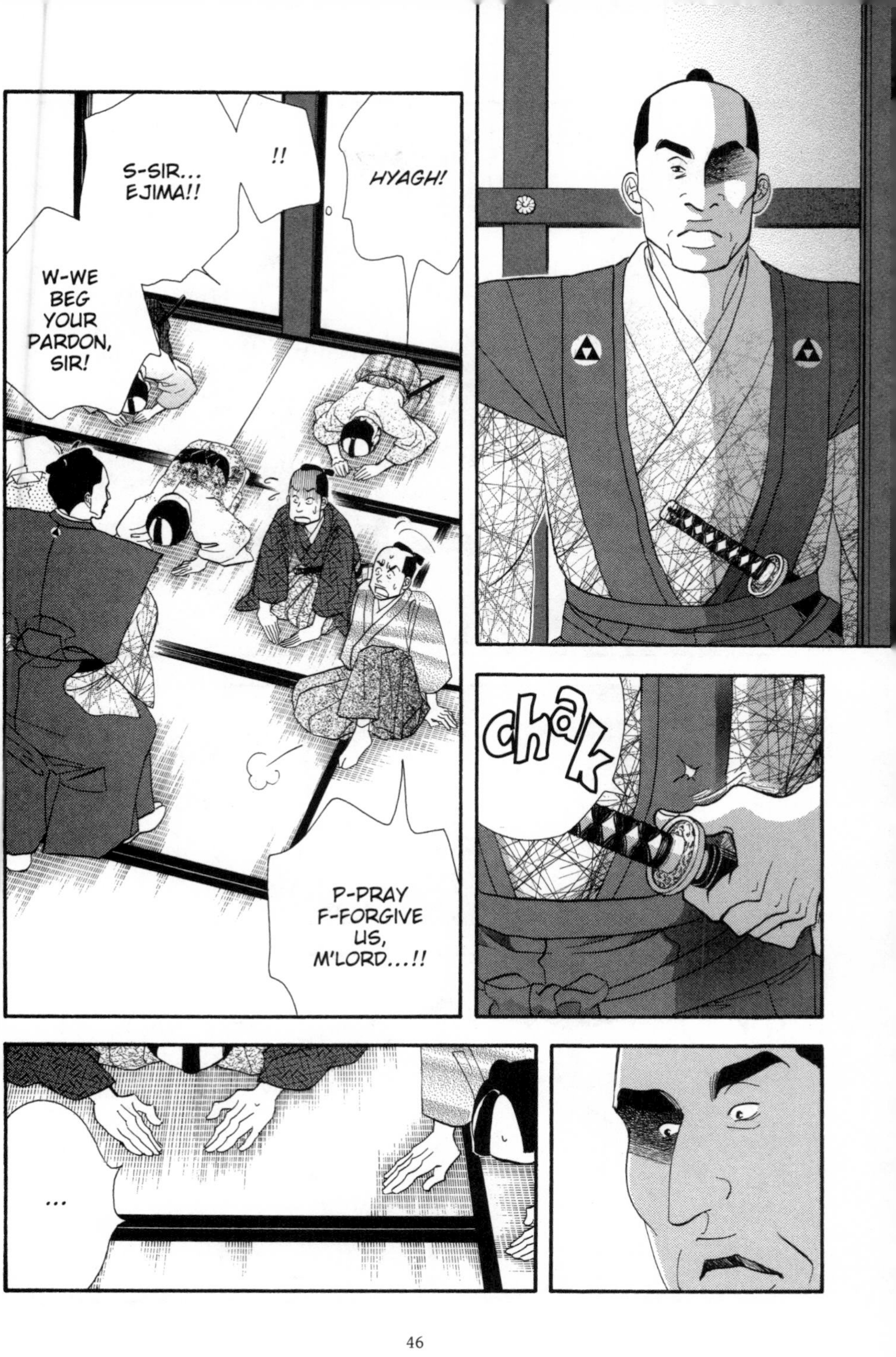
chak
HYAGH!
!!
S-SIR... EJIMA!!
W-WE BEG YOUR PARDON, SIR!
P-PRAY F-FORGIVE US, M'LORD...!!
...

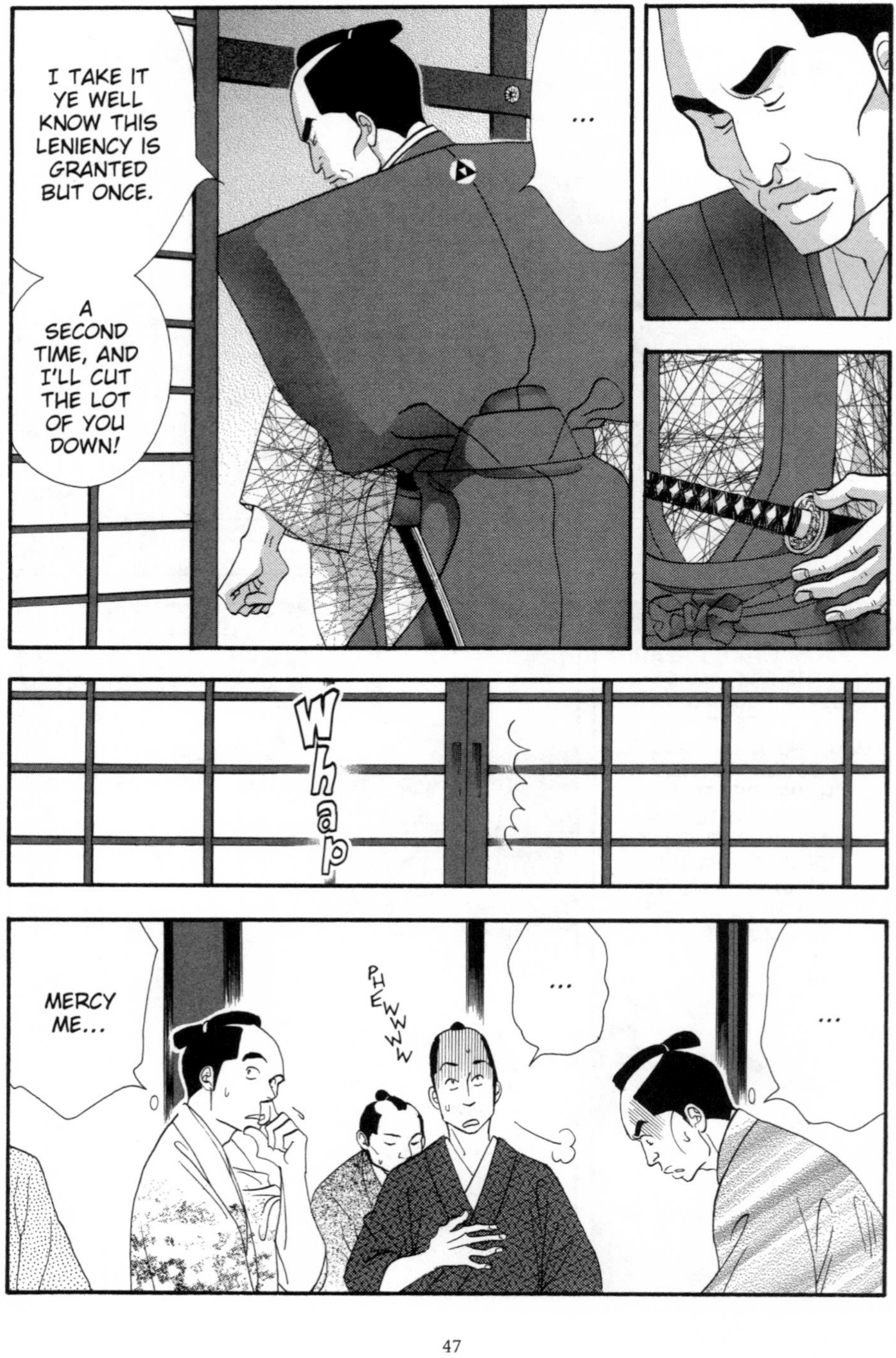
...
I TAKE IT YE WELL KNOW THIS LENIENCY IS GRANTED BUT ONCE.
A SECOND TIME, AND I'LL CUT THE LOT OF YOU DOWN!
Whap
...
...
PHEWWWW
MERCY ME...

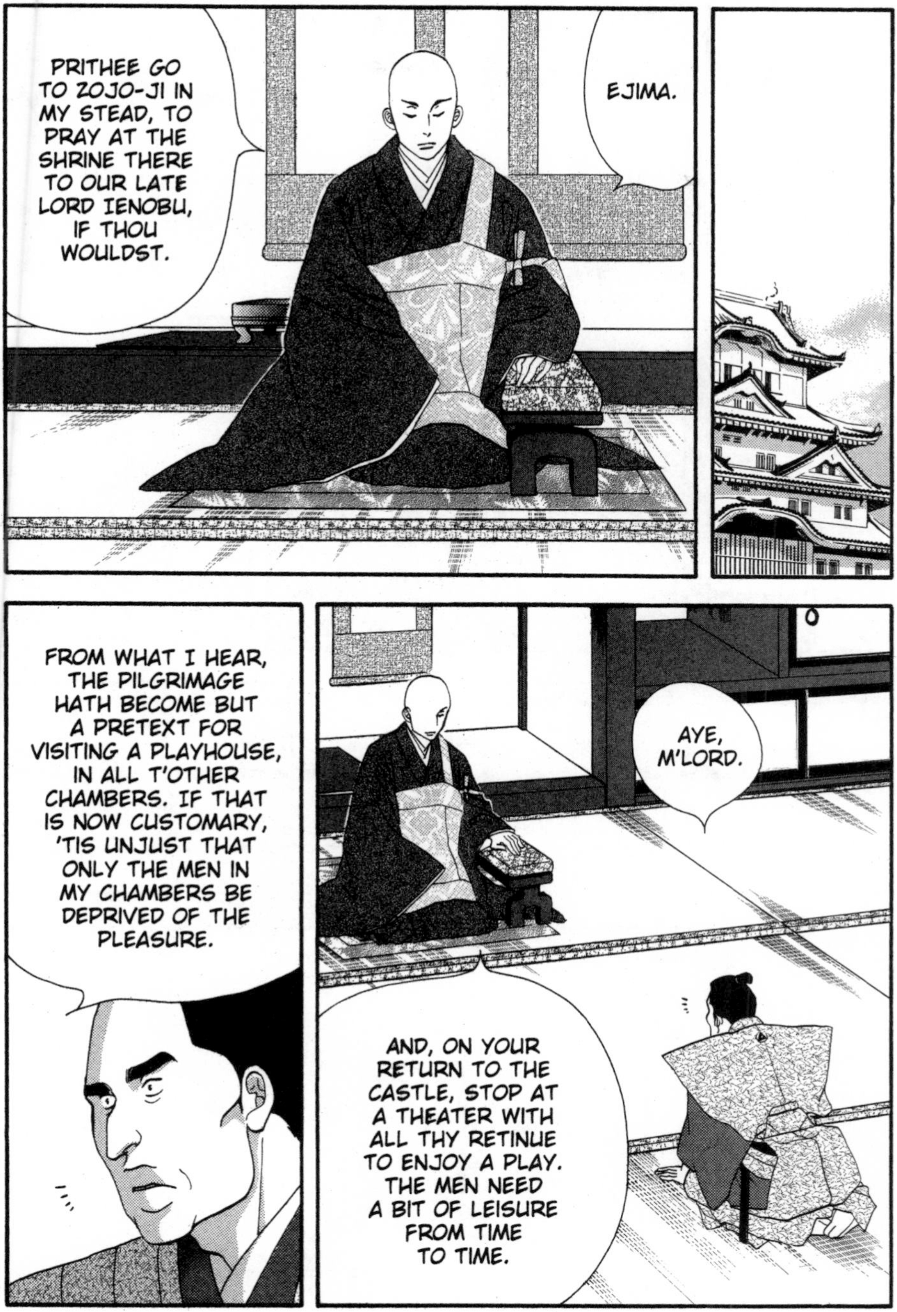
EJIMA.
PRITHEE GO TO ZOJO-JI IN MY STEAD, TO PRAY AT THE SHRINE THERE TO OUR LATE LORD IENOBU, IF THOU WOULDST.
AYE, M'LORD.
AND, ON YOUR RETURN TO THE CASTLE, STOP AT A THEATER WITH ALL THY RETINUE TO ENJOY A PLAY. THE MEN NEED A BIT OF LEISURE FROM TIME TO TIME.
FROM WHAT I HEAR, THE PILGRIMAGE HATH BECOME BUT A PRETEXT FOR VISITING A PLAYHOUSE, IN ALL T'OTHER CHAMBERS. IF THAT IS NOW CUSTOMARY, 'TIS UNJUST THAT ONLY THE MEN IN MY CHAMBERS BE DEPRIVED OF THE PLEASURE.

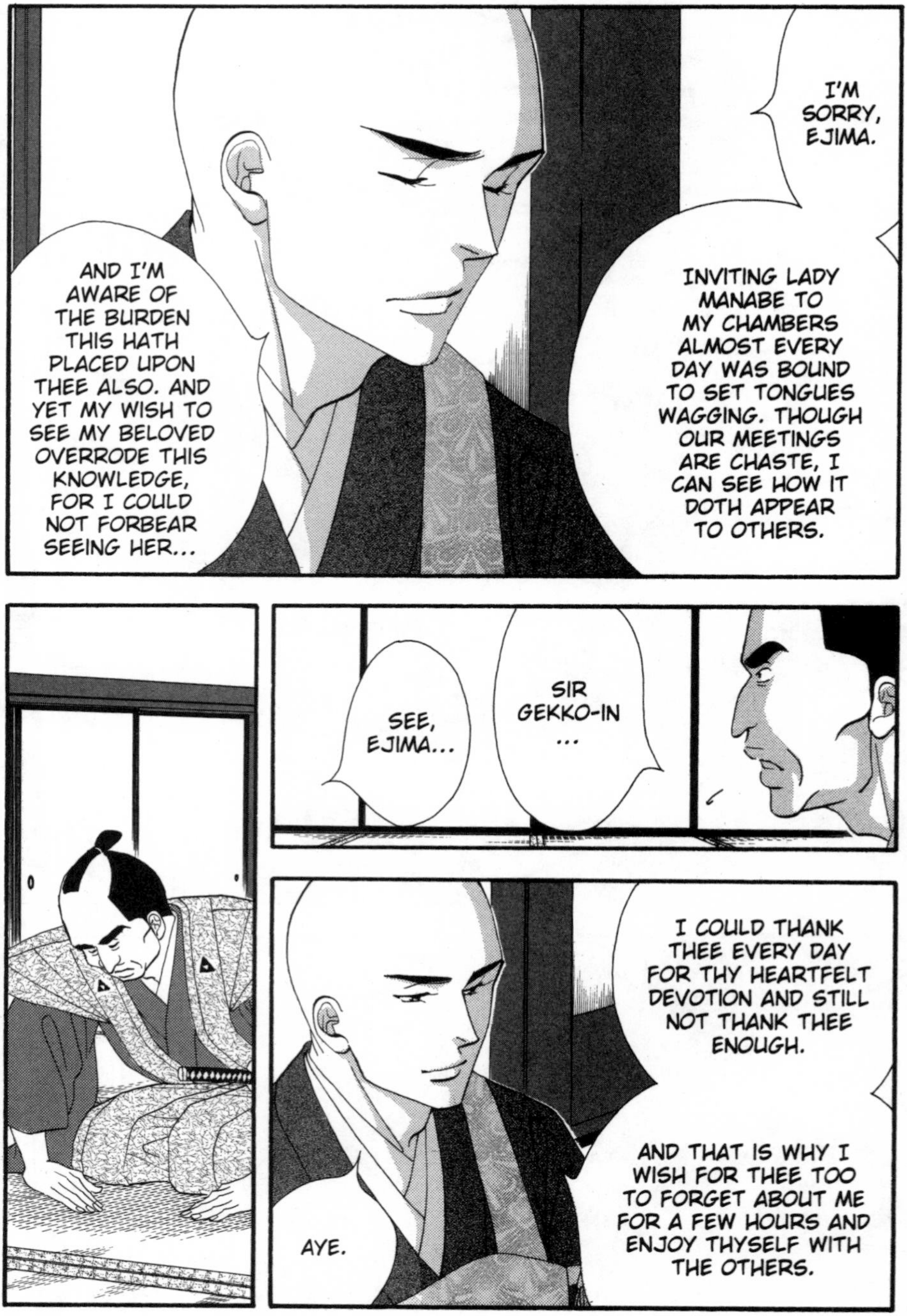
I'M SORRY, EJIMA.
INVITING LADY MANABE TO MY CHAMBERS ALMOST EVERY DAY WAS BOUND TO SET TONGUES WAGGING. THOUGH OUR MEETINGS ARE CHASTE, I CAN SEE HOW IT DOTH APPEAR TO OTHERS.
AND I'M AWARE OF THE BURDEN THIS HATH PLACED UPON THEE ALSO. AND YET MY WISH TO SEE MY BELOVED OVERRODE THIS KNOWLEDGE, FOR I COULD NOT FORBEAR SEEING HER...
SIR GEKKO-IN ...
SEE, EJIMA...
I COULD THANK THEE EVERY DAY FOR THY HEARTFELT DEVOTION AND STILL NOT THANK THEE ENOUGH.
AND THAT IS WHY I WISH FOR THEE TOO TO FORGET ABOUT ME FOR A FEW HOURS AND ENJOY THYSELF WITH THE OTHERS.
AYE.

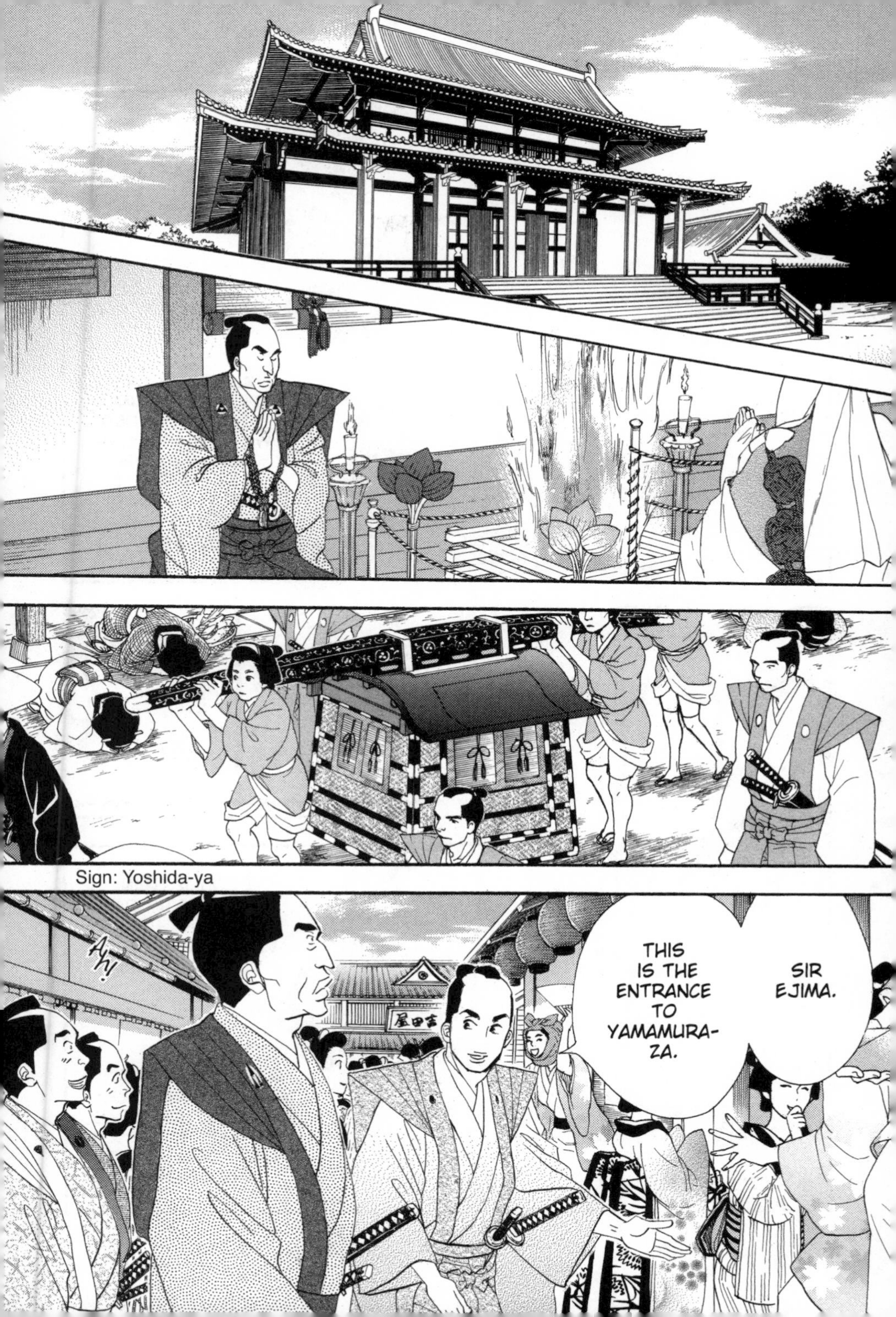
Sign: Yoshida-ya
SIR EJIMA.
THIS IS THE ENTRANCE TO YAMAMURA-ZA.
AH!

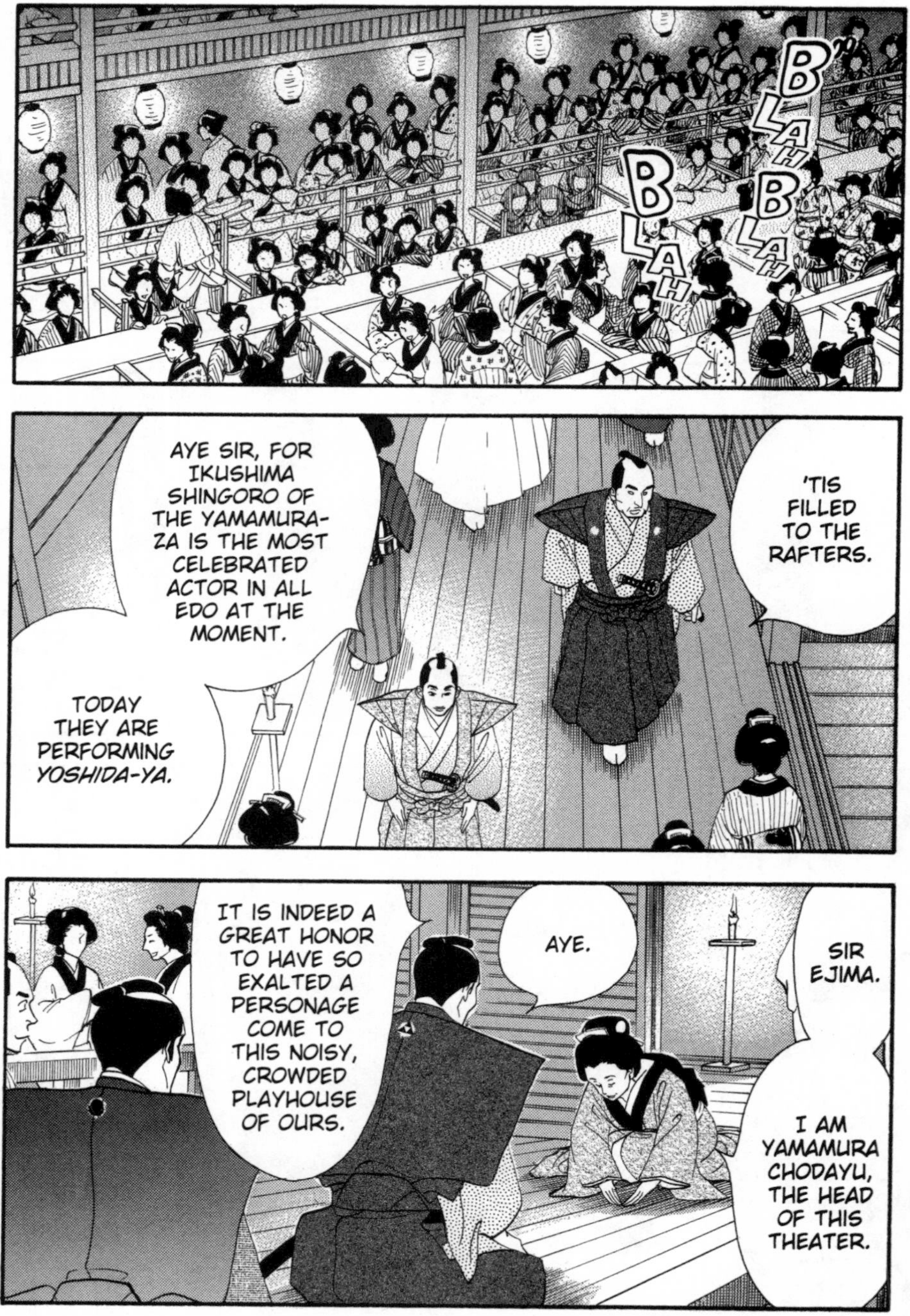
BLAH BLAH BLAH
'TIS FILLED TO THE RAFTERS.
AYE SIR, FOR IKUSHIMA SHINGORO OF THE YAMAMURA-ZA IS THE MOST CELEBRATED ACTOR IN ALL EDO AT THE MOMENT.
TODAY THEY ARE PERFORMING *YOSHIDA-YA.*
SIR EJIMA.
I AM YAMAMURA CHODAYU, THE HEAD OF THIS THEATER.
AYE.
IT IS INDEED A GREAT HONOR TO HAVE SO EXALTED A PERSONAGE COME TO THIS NOISY, CROWDED PLAYHOUSE OF OURS.

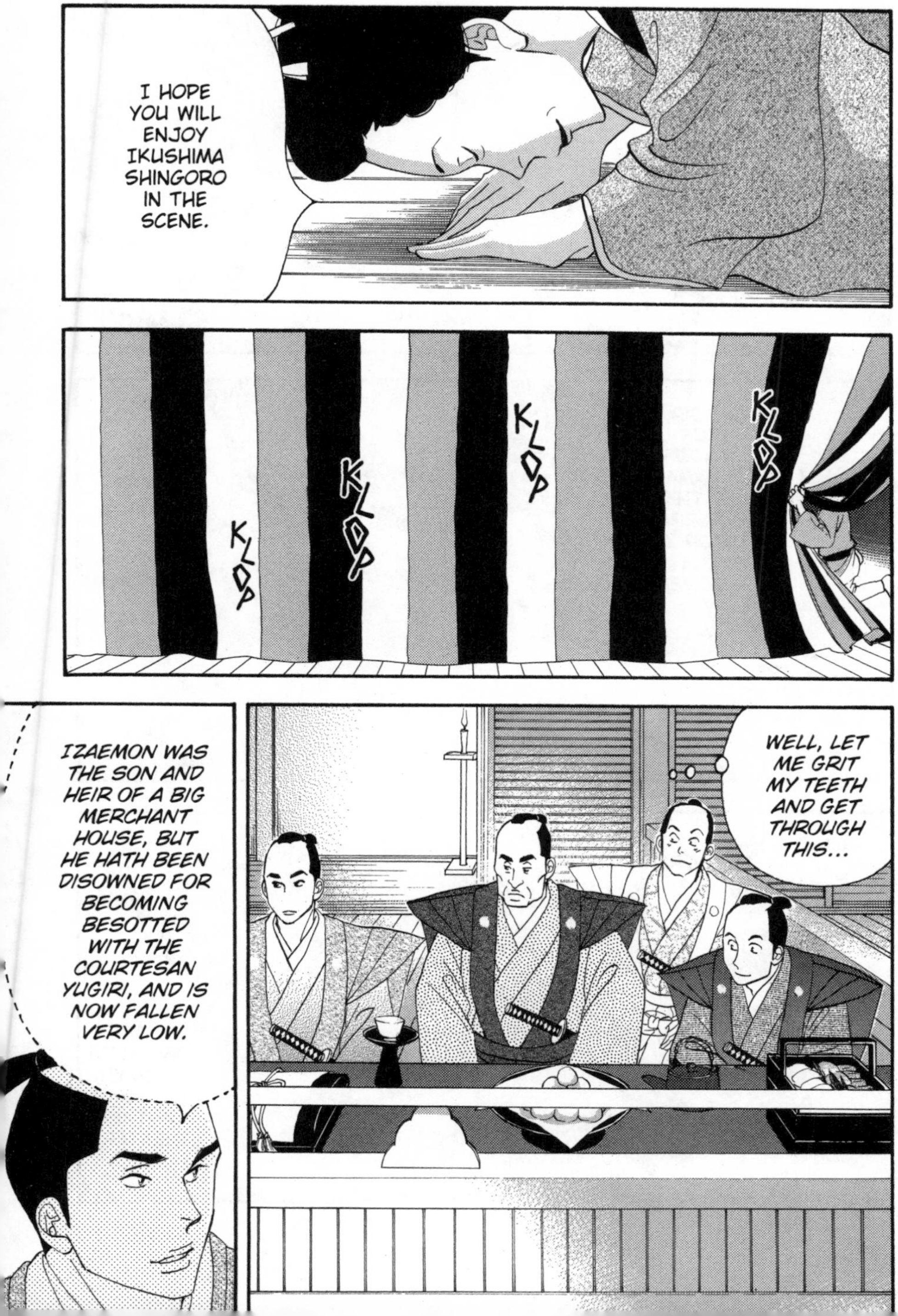
I HOPE YOU WILL ENJOY IKUSHIMA SHINGORO IN THE SCENE.
KLOP
KLOP
KLOP
KLOP
WELL, LET ME GRIT MY TEETH AND GET THROUGH THIS...
IZAEMON WAS THE SON AND HEIR OF A BIG MERCHANT HOUSE, BUT HE HATH BEEN DISOWNED FOR BECOMING BESOTTED WITH THE COURTESAN YUGIRI, AND IS NOW FALLEN VERY LOW.

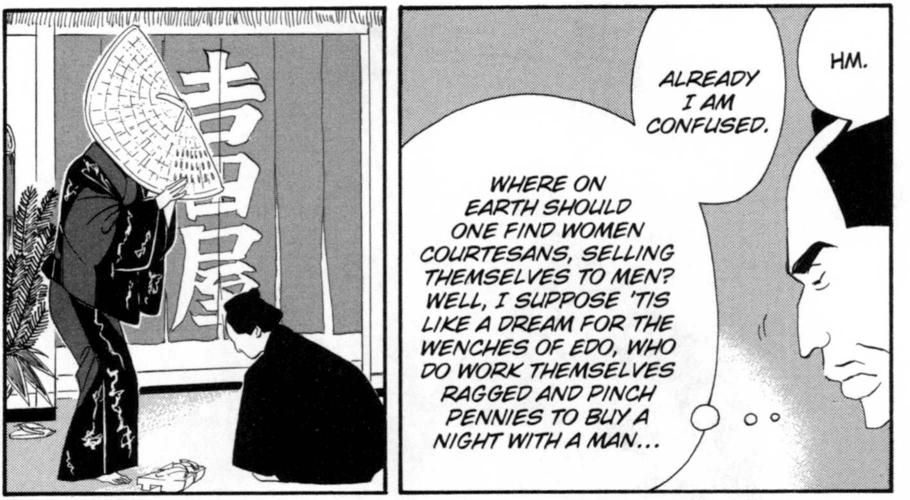
HM.
ALREADY I AM CONFUSED.
WHERE ON EARTH SHOULD ONE FIND WOMEN COURTESANS, SELLING THEMSELVES TO MEN? WELL, I SUPPOSE 'TIS LIKE A DREAM FOR THE WENCHES OF EDO, WHO DO WORK THEMSELVES RAGGED AND PINCH PENNIES TO BUY A NIGHT WITH A MAN...
Curtain: Yoshida-ya

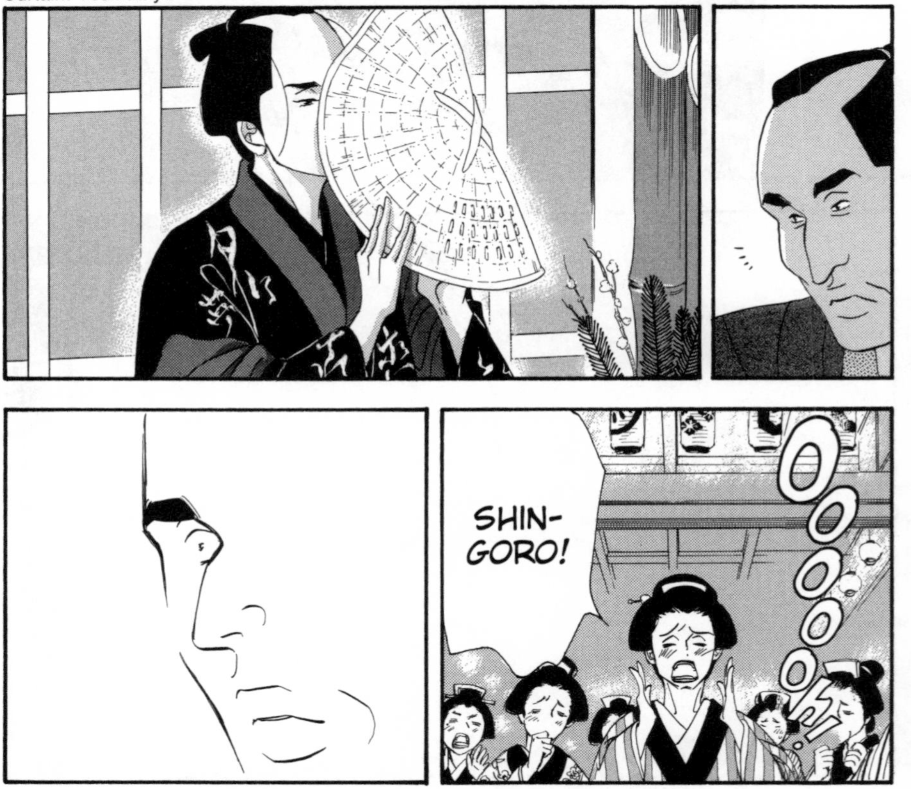
SHIN-GORO!
OOOOOOH!

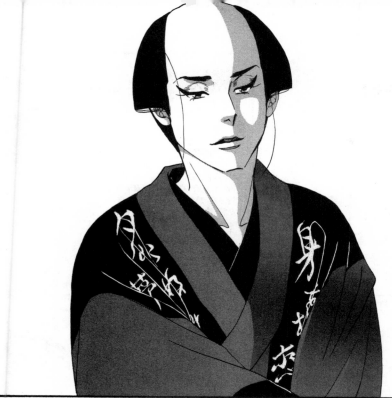

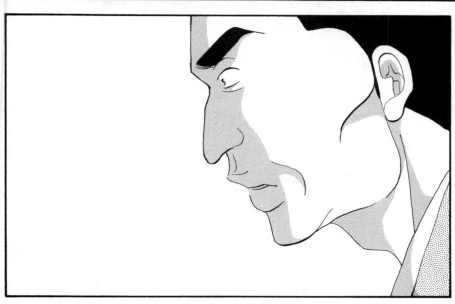

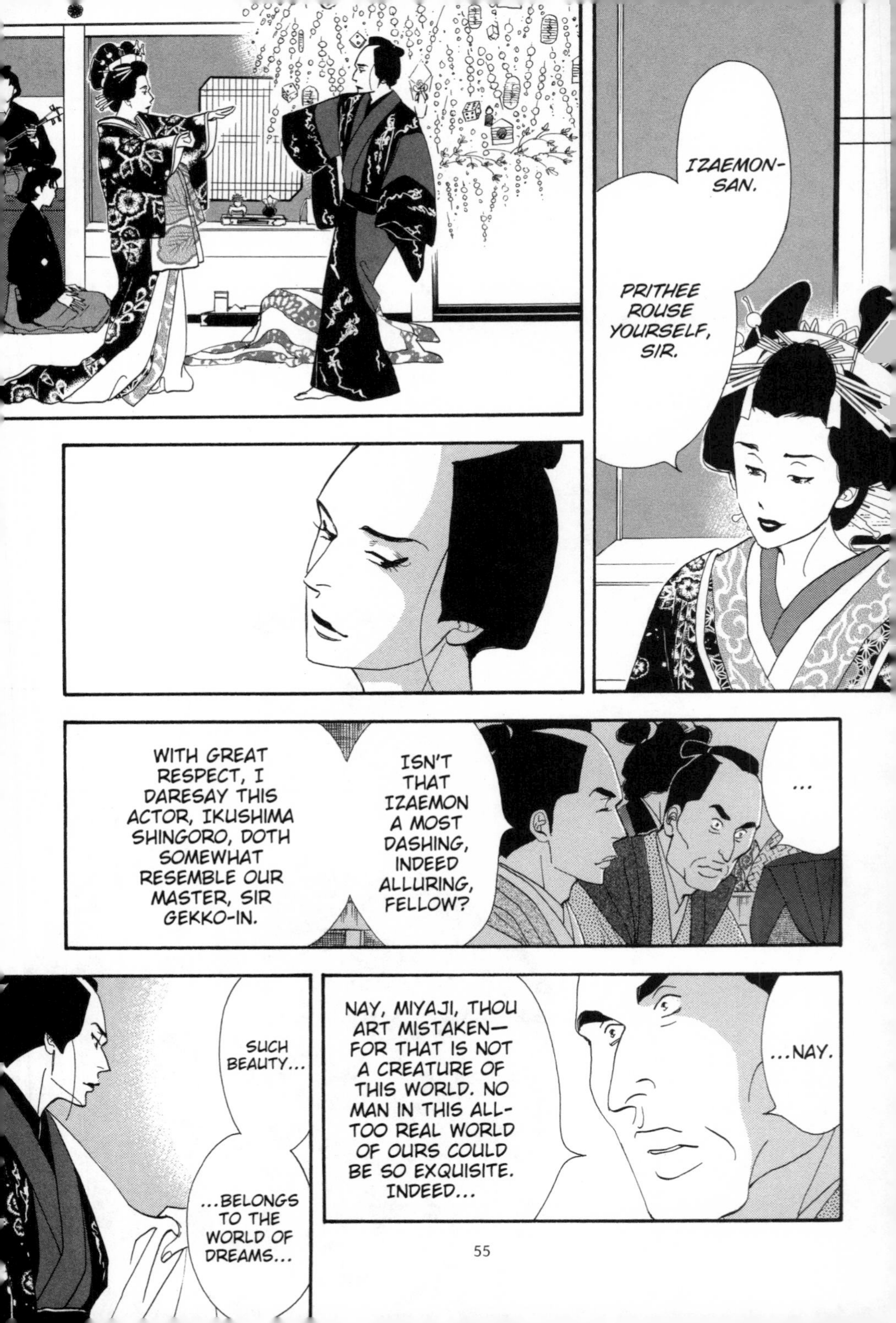
IZAEMON-SAN.
PRITHEE ROUSE YOURSELF, SIR.
...
ISN'T THAT IZAEMON A MOST DASHING, INDEED ALLURING, FELLOW?
WITH GREAT RESPECT, I DARESAY THIS ACTOR, IKUSHIMA SHINGORO, DOTH SOMEWHAT RESEMBLE OUR MASTER, SIR GEKKO-IN.
...NAY.
NAY, MIYAJI, THOU ART MISTAKEN—FOR THAT IS NOT A CREATURE OF THIS WORLD. NO MAN IN THIS ALL-TOO REAL WORLD OF OURS COULD BE SO EXQUISITE. INDEED...
SUCH BEAUTY...
...BELONGS TO THE WORLD OF DREAMS...

From that day
on, Ejima began
making frequent
visits to the
Yamamura-za
playhouse.

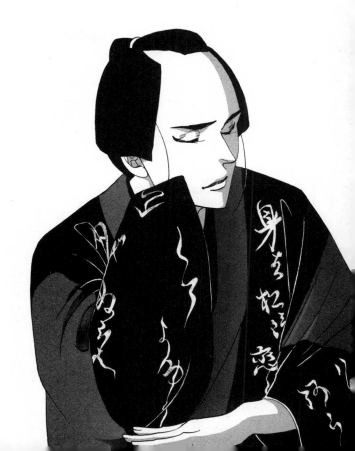

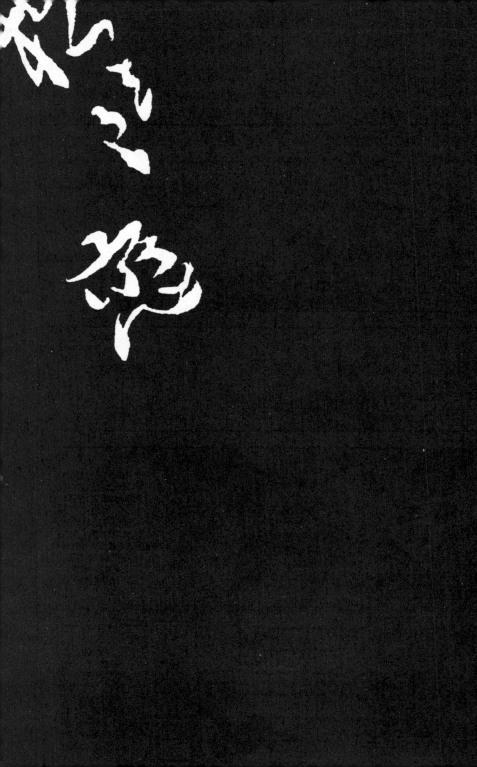

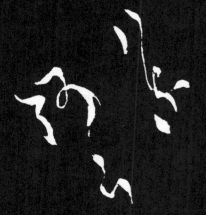

Ōoku
THE INNER CHAMBERS

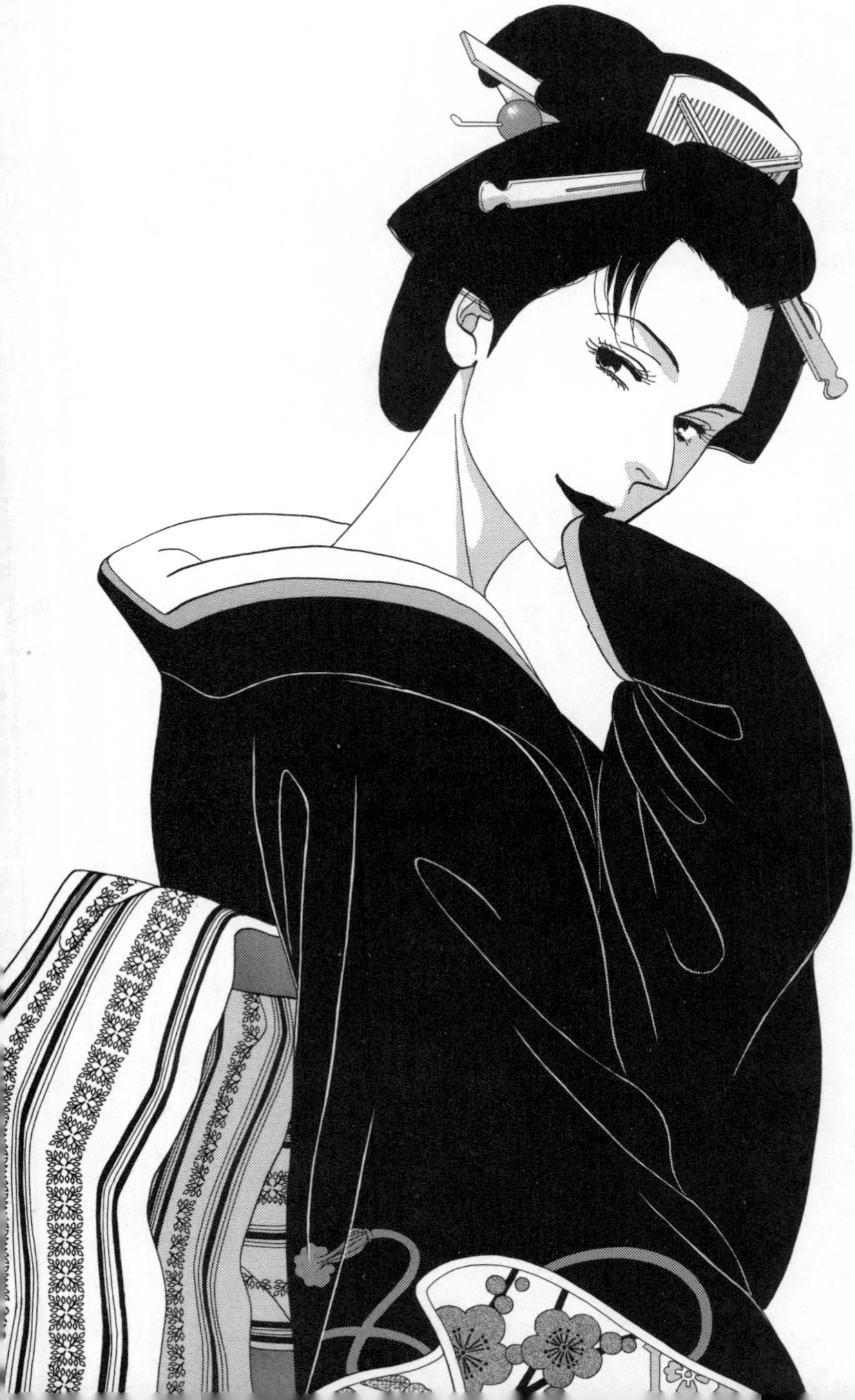

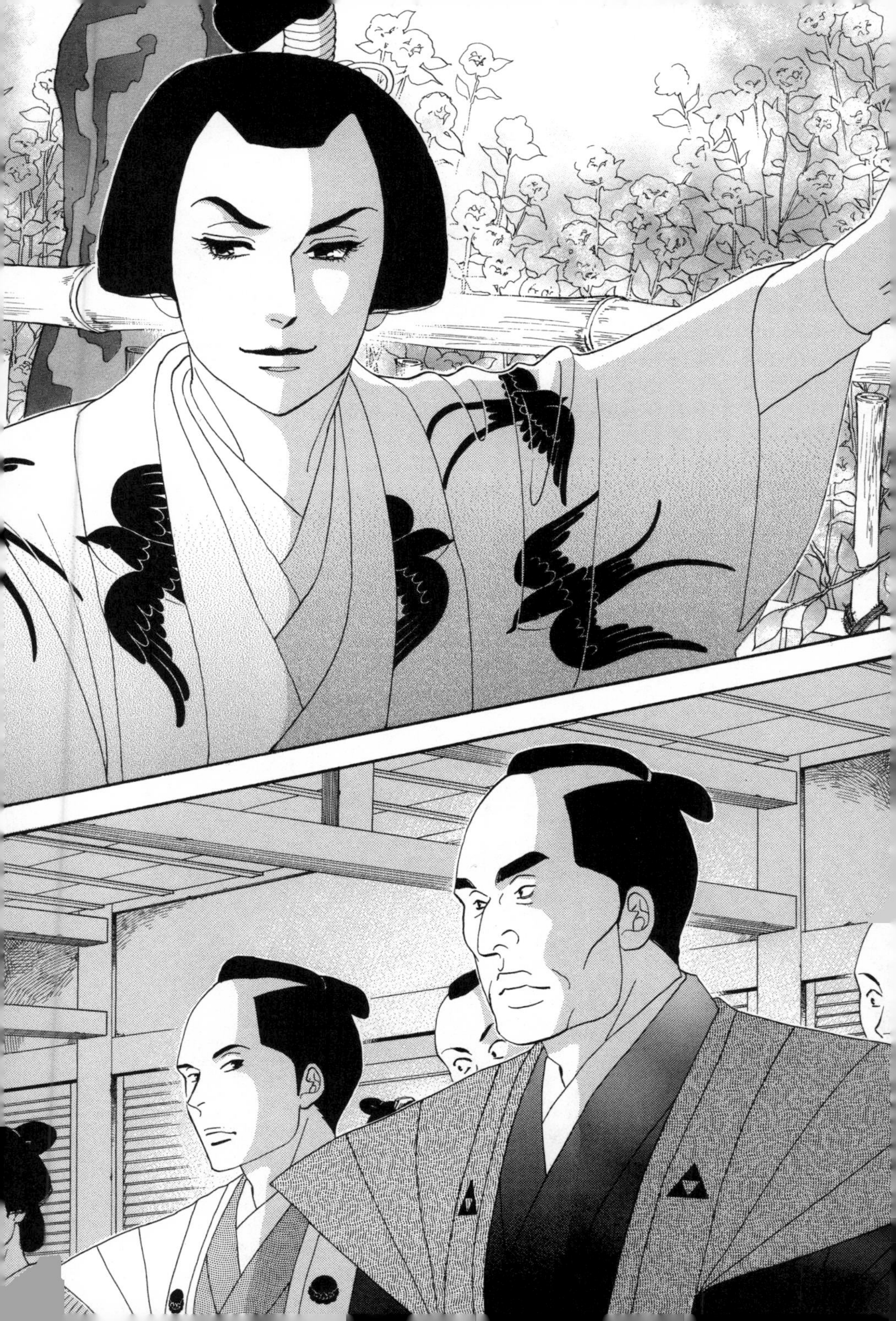

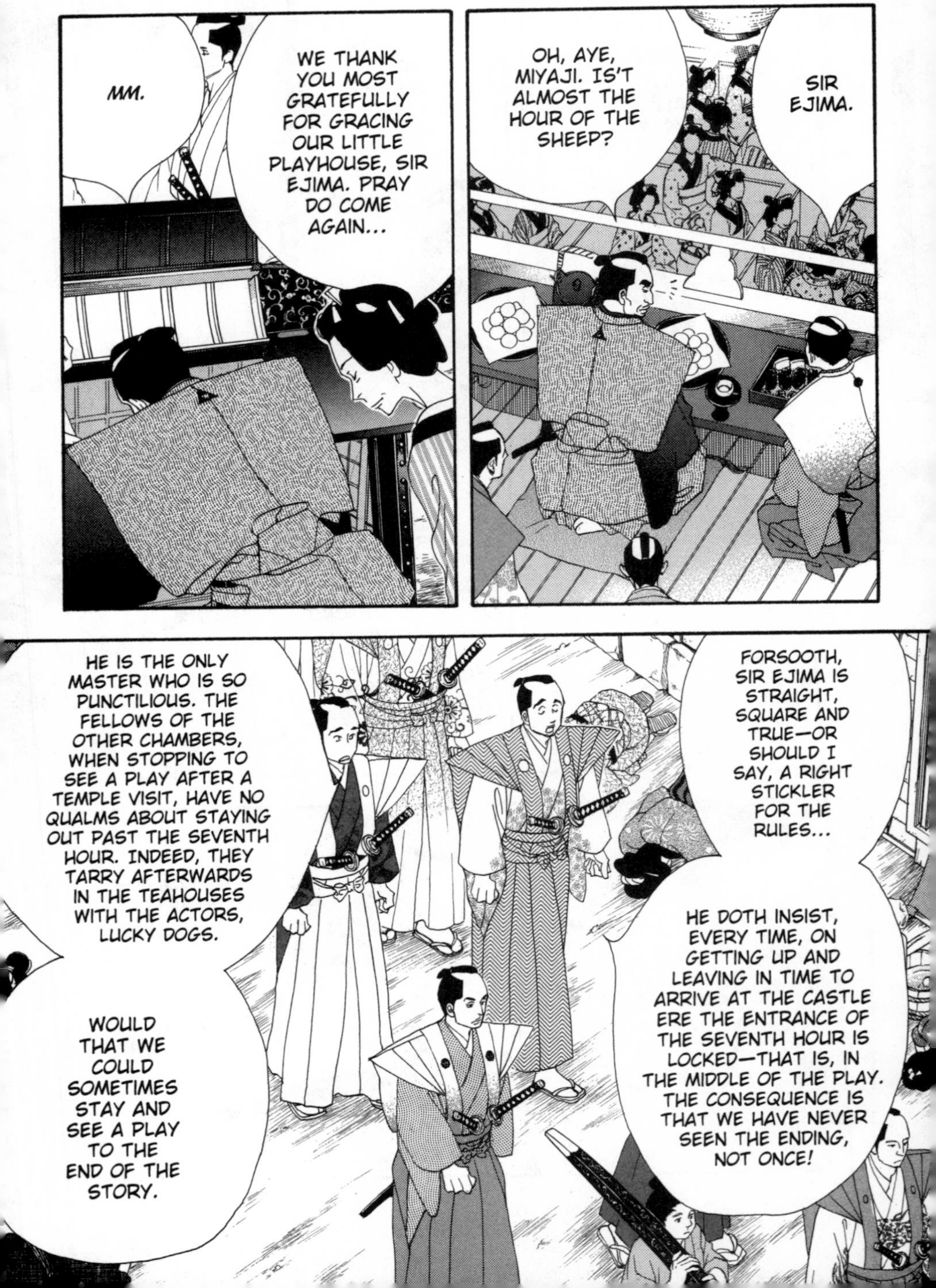
SIR EJIMA.
OH, AYE, MIYAJI. IS'T ALMOST THE HOUR OF THE SHEEP?
WE THANK YOU MOST GRATEFULLY FOR GRACING OUR LITTLE PLAYHOUSE, SIR EJIMA. PRAY DO COME AGAIN...
MM.
FORSOOTH, SIR EJIMA IS STRAIGHT, SQUARE AND TRUE—OR SHOULD I SAY, A RIGHT STICKLER FOR THE RULES...
HE IS THE ONLY MASTER WHO IS SO PUNCTILIOUS. THE FELLOWS OF THE OTHER CHAMBERS, WHEN STOPPING TO SEE A PLAY AFTER A TEMPLE VISIT, HAVE NO QUALMS ABOUT STAYING OUT PAST THE SEVENTH HOUR. INDEED, THEY TARRY AFTERWARDS IN THE TEAHOUSES WITH THE ACTORS, LUCKY DOGS.
HE DOTH INSIST, EVERY TIME, ON GETTING UP AND LEAVING IN TIME TO ARRIVE AT THE CASTLE ERE THE ENTRANCE OF THE SEVENTH HOUR IS LOCKED—THAT IS, IN THE MIDDLE OF THE PLAY. THE CONSEQUENCE IS THAT WE HAVE NEVER SEEN THE ENDING, NOT ONCE!
WOULD THAT WE COULD SOMETIMES STAY AND SEE A PLAY TO THE END OF THE STORY.

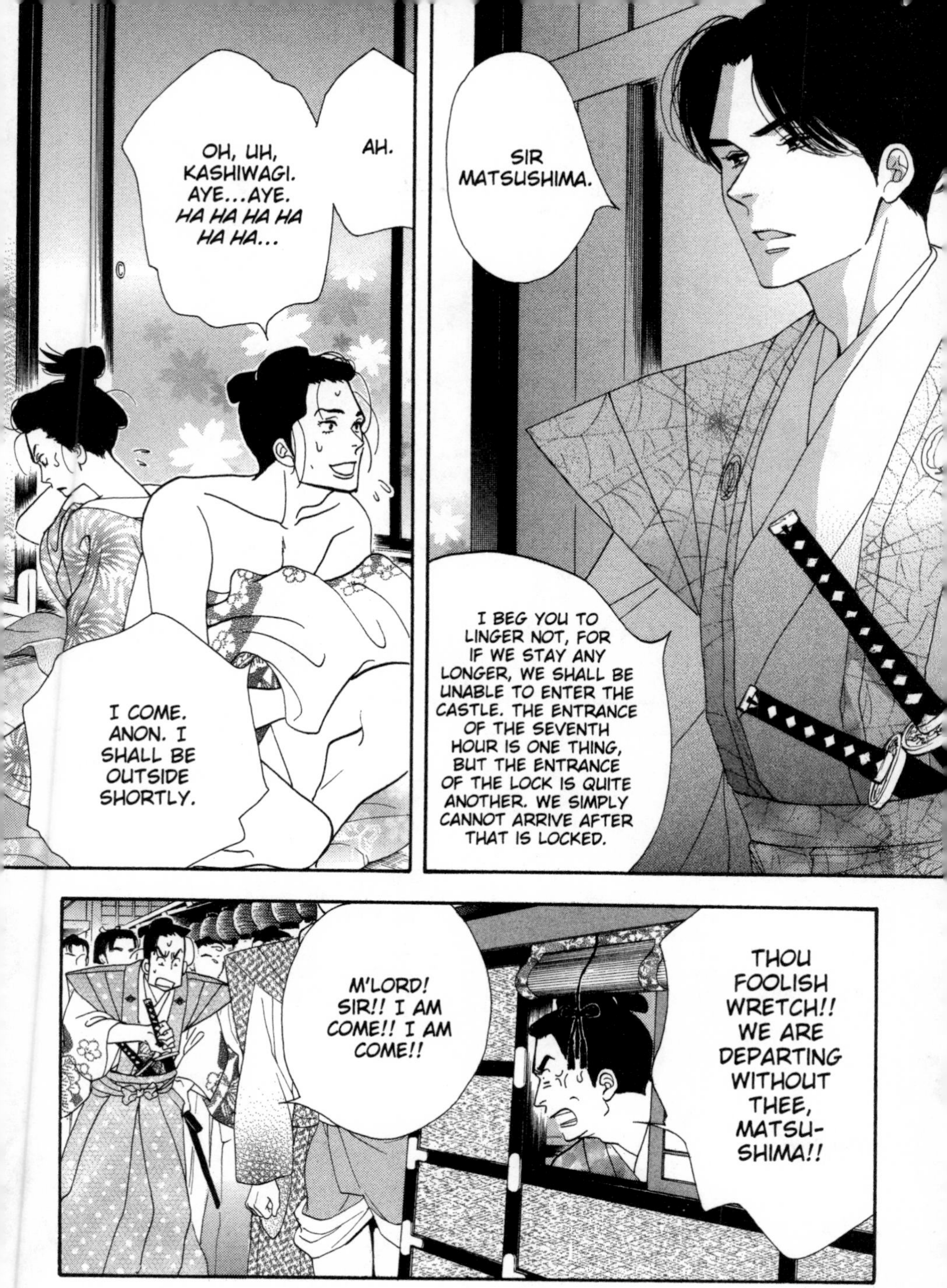
SIR MATSUSHIMA.
I BEG YOU TO LINGER NOT, FOR IF WE STAY ANY LONGER, WE SHALL BE UNABLE TO ENTER THE CASTLE. THE ENTRANCE OF THE SEVENTH HOUR IS ONE THING, BUT THE ENTRANCE OF THE LOCK IS QUITE ANOTHER. WE SIMPLY CANNOT ARRIVE AFTER THAT IS LOCKED.
AH.
OH, UH, KASHIWAGI. AYE...AYE. *HA HA HA HA HA HA...*
I COME. ANON. I SHALL BE OUTSIDE SHORTLY.
THOU FOOLISH WRETCH!! WE ARE DEPARTING WITHOUT THEE, MATSU-SHIMA!!
M'LORD! SIR!! I AM COME!! I AM COME!!

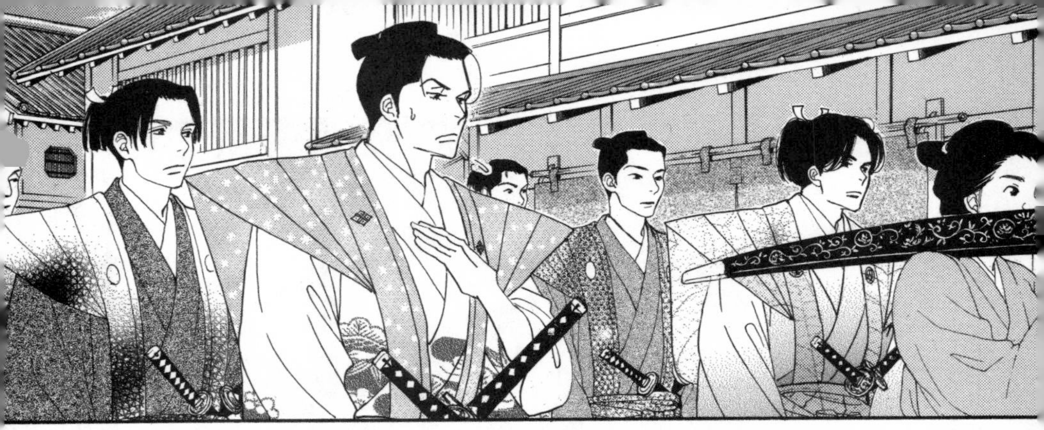

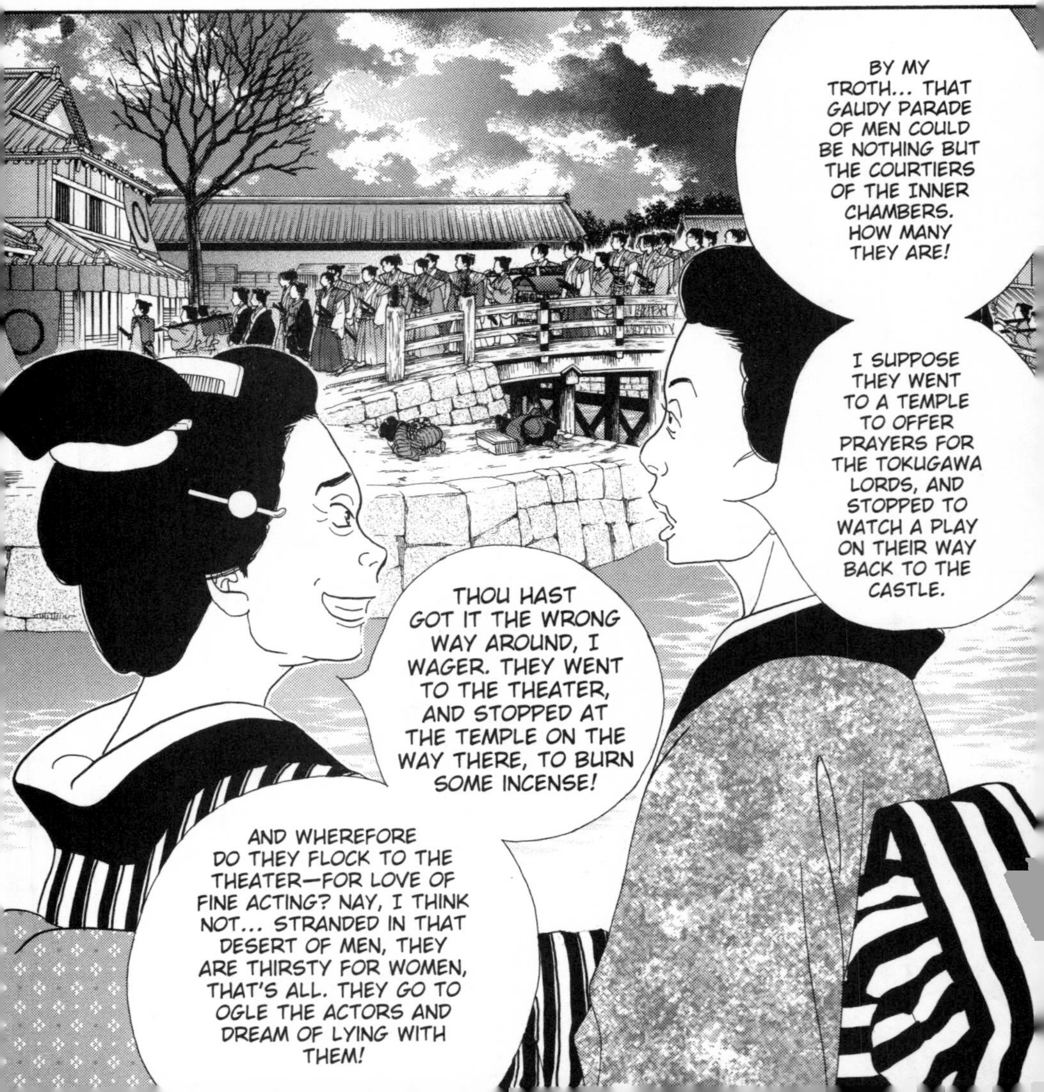
BY MY TROTH... THAT GAUDY PARADE OF MEN COULD BE NOTHING BUT THE COURTIERS OF THE INNER CHAMBERS. HOW MANY THEY ARE!
I SUPPOSE THEY WENT TO A TEMPLE TO OFFER PRAYERS FOR THE TOKUGAWA LORDS, AND STOPPED TO WATCH A PLAY ON THEIR WAY BACK TO THE CASTLE.
THOU HAST GOT IT THE WRONG WAY AROUND, I WAGER. THEY WENT TO THE THEATER, AND STOPPED AT THE TEMPLE ON THE WAY THERE, TO BURN SOME INCENSE!
AND WHEREFORE DO THEY FLOCK TO THE THEATER—FOR LOVE OF FINE ACTING? NAY, I THINK NOT... STRANDED IN THAT DESERT OF MEN, THEY ARE THIRSTY FOR WOMEN, THAT'S ALL. THEY GO TO OGLE THE ACTORS AND DREAM OF LYING WITH THEM!

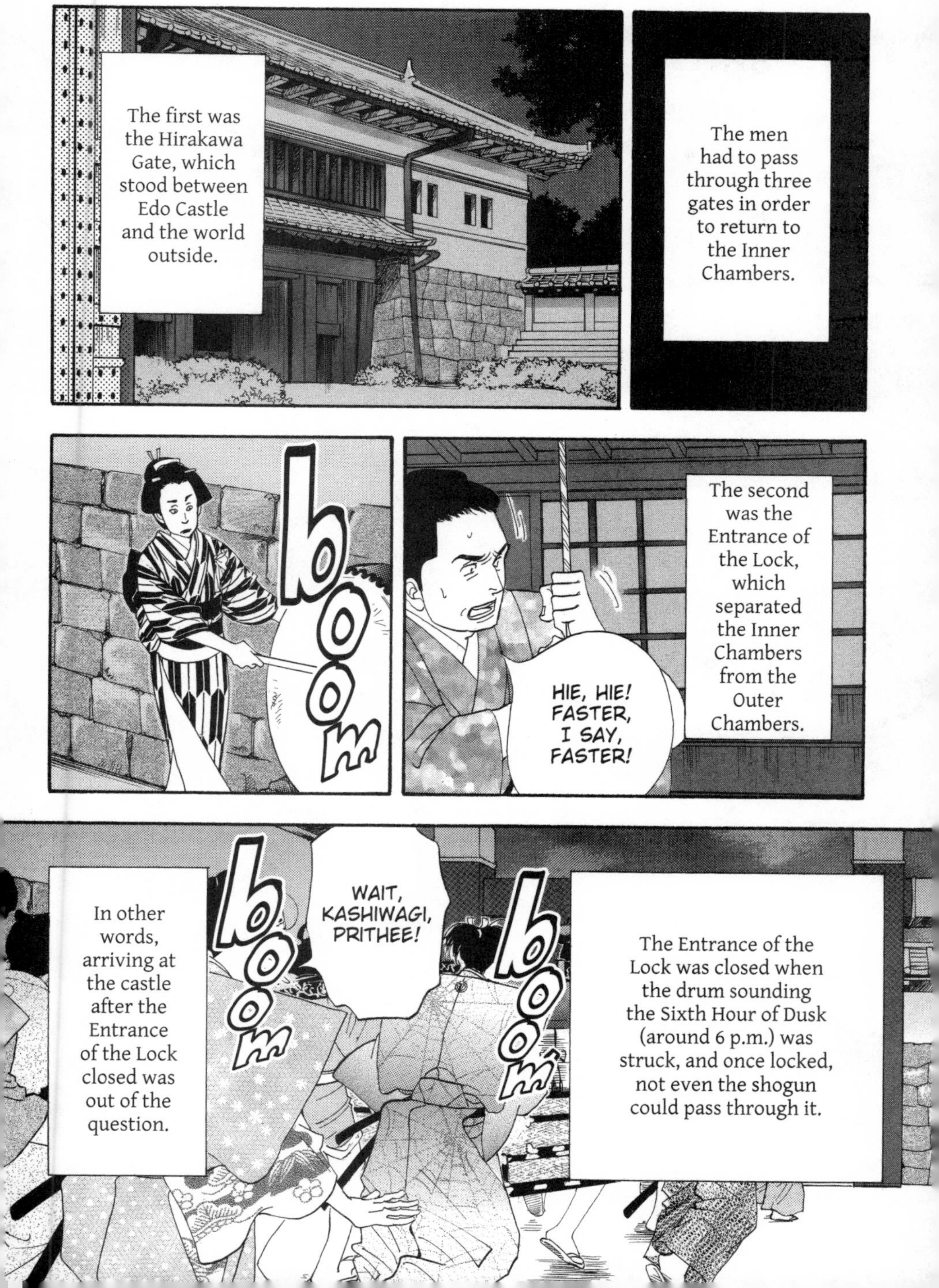
The men had to pass through three gates in order to return to the Inner Chambers.
The first was the Hirakawa Gate, which stood between Edo Castle and the world outside.
The second was the Entrance of the Lock, which separated the Inner Chambers from the Outer Chambers.
HIE, HIE! FASTER, I SAY, FASTER!
boom
The Entrance of the Lock was closed when the drum sounding the Sixth Hour of Dusk (around 6 p.m.) was struck, and once locked, not even the shogun could pass through it.
boom
WAIT, KASHIWAGI, PRITHEE!
boom
In other words, arriving at the castle after the Entrance of the Lock closed was out of the question.

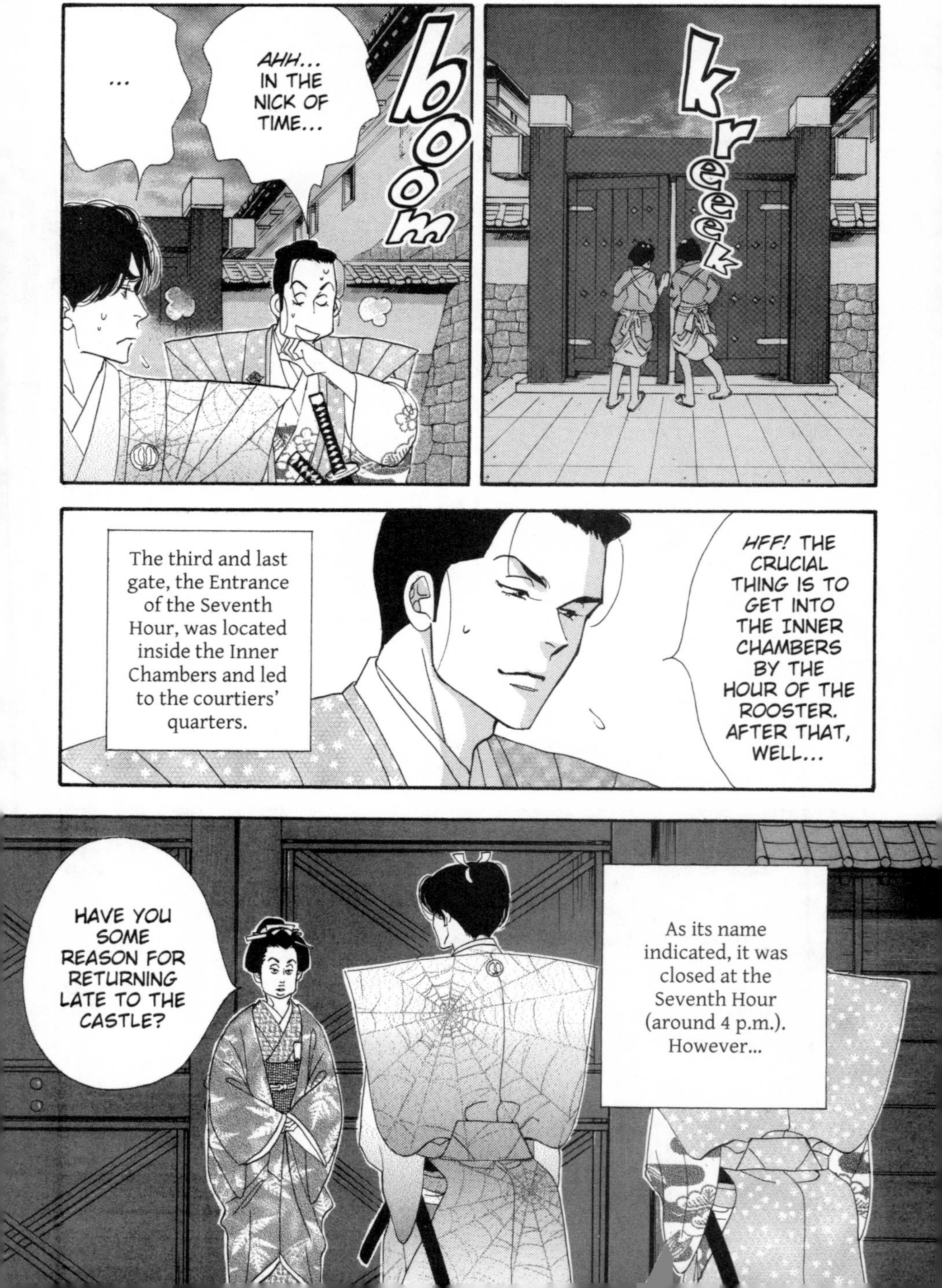
kreeek
boom
AHH... IN THE NICK OF TIME...
...
HFF! THE CRUCIAL THING IS TO GET INTO THE INNER CHAMBERS BY THE HOUR OF THE ROOSTER. AFTER THAT, WELL...
The third and last gate, the Entrance of the Seventh Hour, was located inside the Inner Chambers and led to the courtiers' quarters.
As its name indicated, it was closed at the Seventh Hour (around 4 p.m.). However...
HAVE YOU SOME REASON FOR RETURNING LATE TO THE CASTLE?

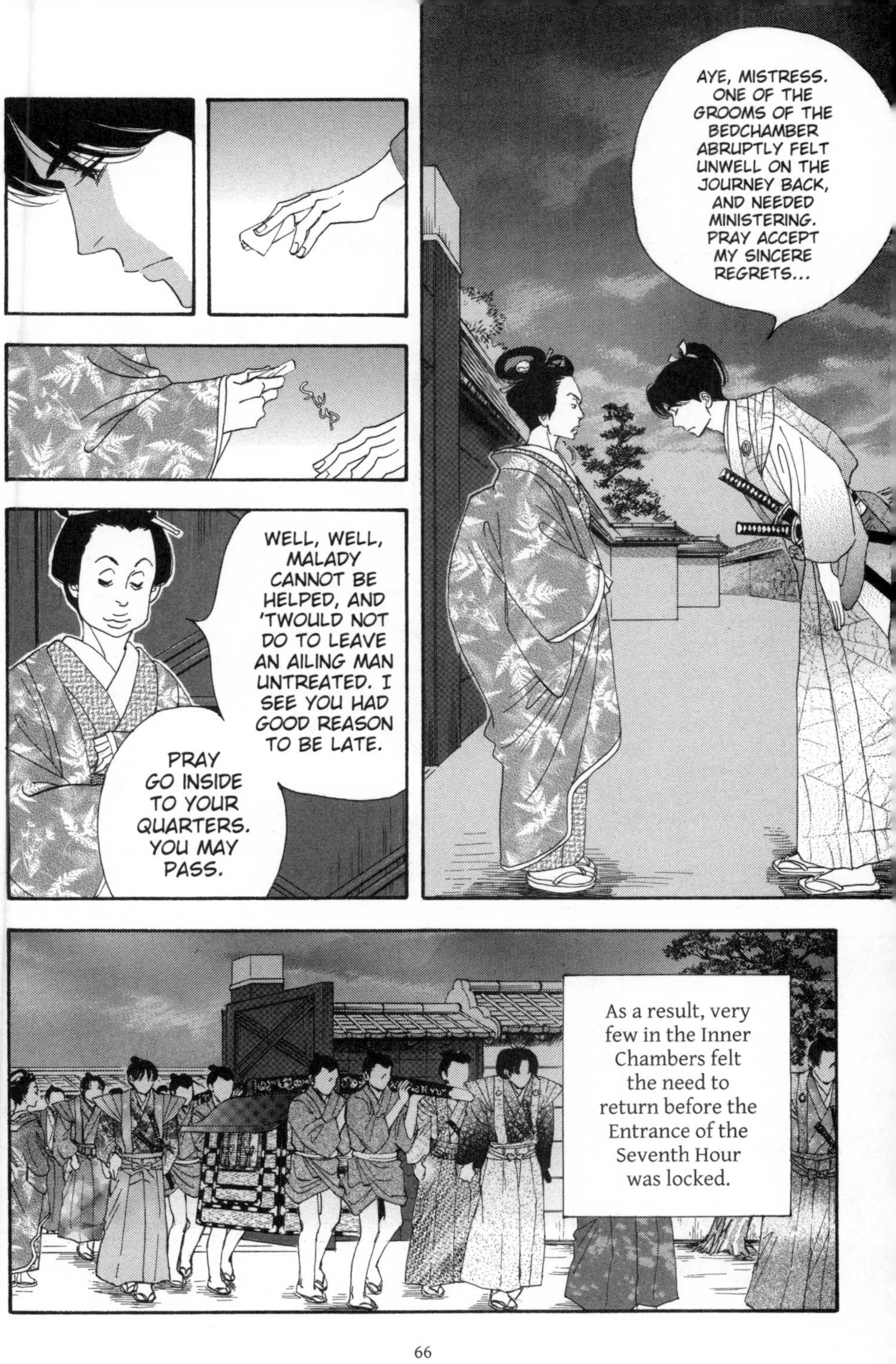
AYE, MISTRESS. ONE OF THE GROOMS OF THE BEDCHAMBER ABRUPTLY FELT UNWELL ON THE JOURNEY BACK, AND NEEDED MINISTERING. PRAY ACCEPT MY SINCERE REGRETS...
SWIP
WELL, WELL, MALADY CANNOT BE HELPED, AND 'TWOULD NOT DO TO LEAVE AN AILING MAN UNTREATED. I SEE YOU HAD GOOD REASON TO BE LATE.
PRAY GO INSIDE TO YOUR QUARTERS. YOU MAY PASS.
As a result, very few in the Inner Chambers felt the need to return before the Entrance of the Seventh Hour was locked.

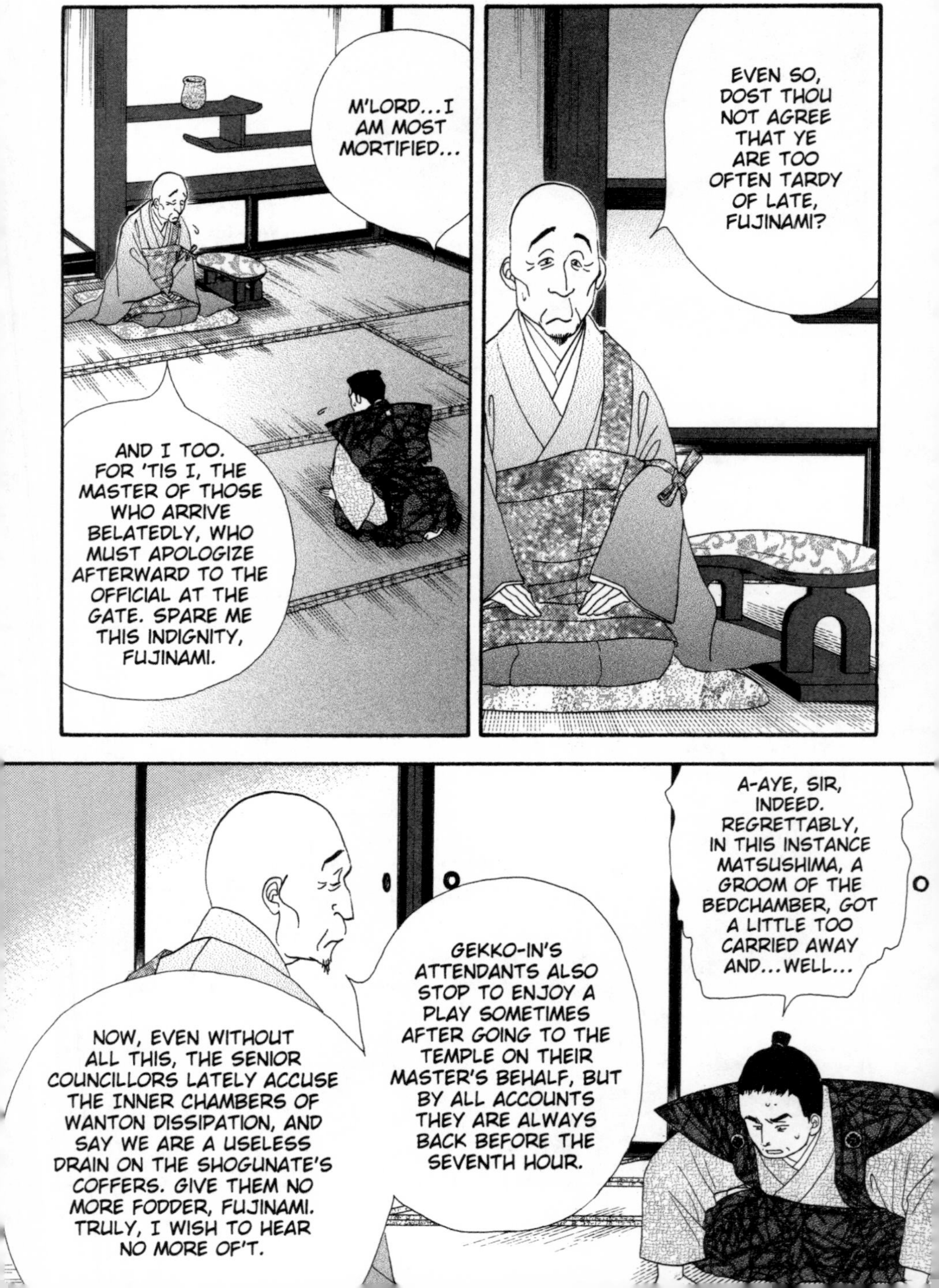
EVEN SO, DOST THOU NOT AGREE THAT YE ARE TOO OFTEN TARDY OF LATE, FUJINAMI?
M'LORD...I AM MOST MORTIFIED...
AND I TOO. FOR 'TIS I, THE MASTER OF THOSE WHO ARRIVE BELATEDLY, WHO MUST APOLOGIZE AFTERWARD TO THE OFFICIAL AT THE GATE. SPARE ME THIS INDIGNITY, FUJINAMI.
A-AYE, SIR, INDEED. REGRETTABLY, IN THIS INSTANCE MATSUSHIMA, A GROOM OF THE BEDCHAMBER, GOT A LITTLE TOO CARRIED AWAY AND...WELL...
GEKKO-IN'S ATTENDANTS ALSO STOP TO ENJOY A PLAY SOMETIMES AFTER GOING TO THE TEMPLE ON THEIR MASTER'S BEHALF, BUT BY ALL ACCOUNTS THEY ARE ALWAYS BACK BEFORE THE SEVENTH HOUR.
NOW, EVEN WITHOUT ALL THIS, THE SENIOR COUNCILLORS LATELY ACCUSE THE INNER CHAMBERS OF WANTON DISSIPATION, AND SAY WE ARE A USELESS DRAIN ON THE SHOGUNATE'S COFFERS. GIVE THEM NO MORE FODDER, FUJINAMI. TRULY, I WISH TO HEAR NO MORE OF'T.

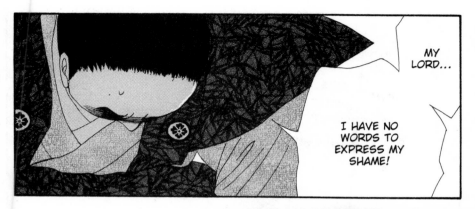

MY LORD...
I HAVE NO WORDS TO EXPRESS MY SHAME!
SIR MATSUSHIMA. YOU OUGHT TO BE A LITTLE MORE CAUTIOUS.
THEY HAVE TURNED A BLIND EYE SO FAR TO YOUR WENCHING IN THE TEAHOUSES, BUT DO IT TOO OFTEN AND ONE DAY IT MAY LEAD TO YOUR DOWNFALL.
LEAD TO MY DOWNFALL? *HMPH.*
THERE IS NO FALLING DOWN IF ONE IS LOW TO BEGIN WITH, KASHIWAGI. WORDS LIKE "DOWNFALL" ARE MORE SUITED TO THOSE WHO ARE RIDING HIGH, LIKE THE FELLOWS IN GEKKO-IN'S CHAMBERS.

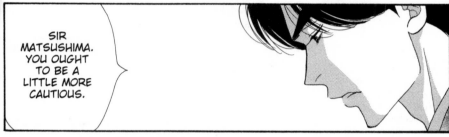

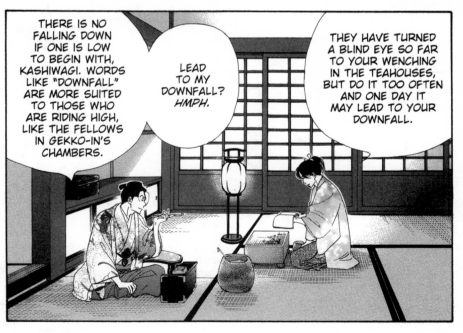

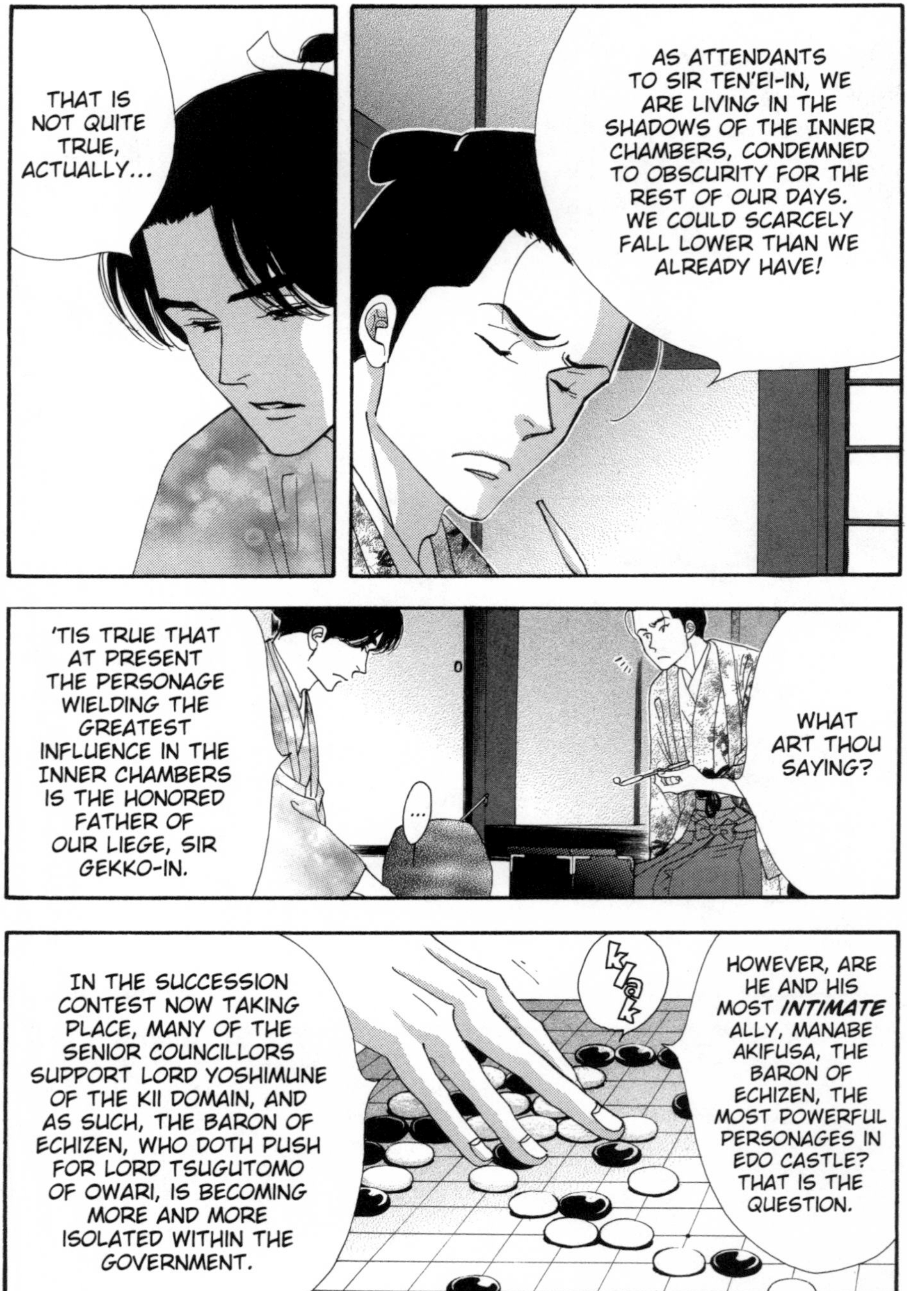
AS ATTENDANTS TO SIR TEN'EI-IN, WE ARE LIVING IN THE SHADOWS OF THE INNER CHAMBERS, CONDEMNED TO OBSCURITY FOR THE REST OF OUR DAYS. WE COULD SCARCELY FALL LOWER THAN WE ALREADY HAVE!
THAT IS NOT QUITE TRUE, ACTUALLY...
WHAT ART THOU SAYING?
...
'TIS TRUE THAT AT PRESENT THE PERSONAGE WIELDING THE GREATEST INFLUENCE IN THE INNER CHAMBERS IS THE HONORED FATHER OF OUR LIEGE, SIR GEKKO-IN.
IN THE SUCCESSION CONTEST NOW TAKING PLACE, MANY OF THE SENIOR COUNCILLORS SUPPORT LORD YOSHIMUNE OF THE KII DOMAIN, AND AS SUCH, THE BARON OF ECHIZEN, WHO DOTH PUSH FOR LORD TSUGUTOMO OF OWARI, IS BECOMING MORE AND MORE ISOLATED WITHIN THE GOVERNMENT.
klak
HOWEVER, ARE HE AND HIS MOST ***INTIMATE*** ALLY, MANABE AKIFUSA, THE BARON OF ECHIZEN, THE MOST POWERFUL PERSONAGES IN EDO CASTLE? THAT IS THE QUESTION.

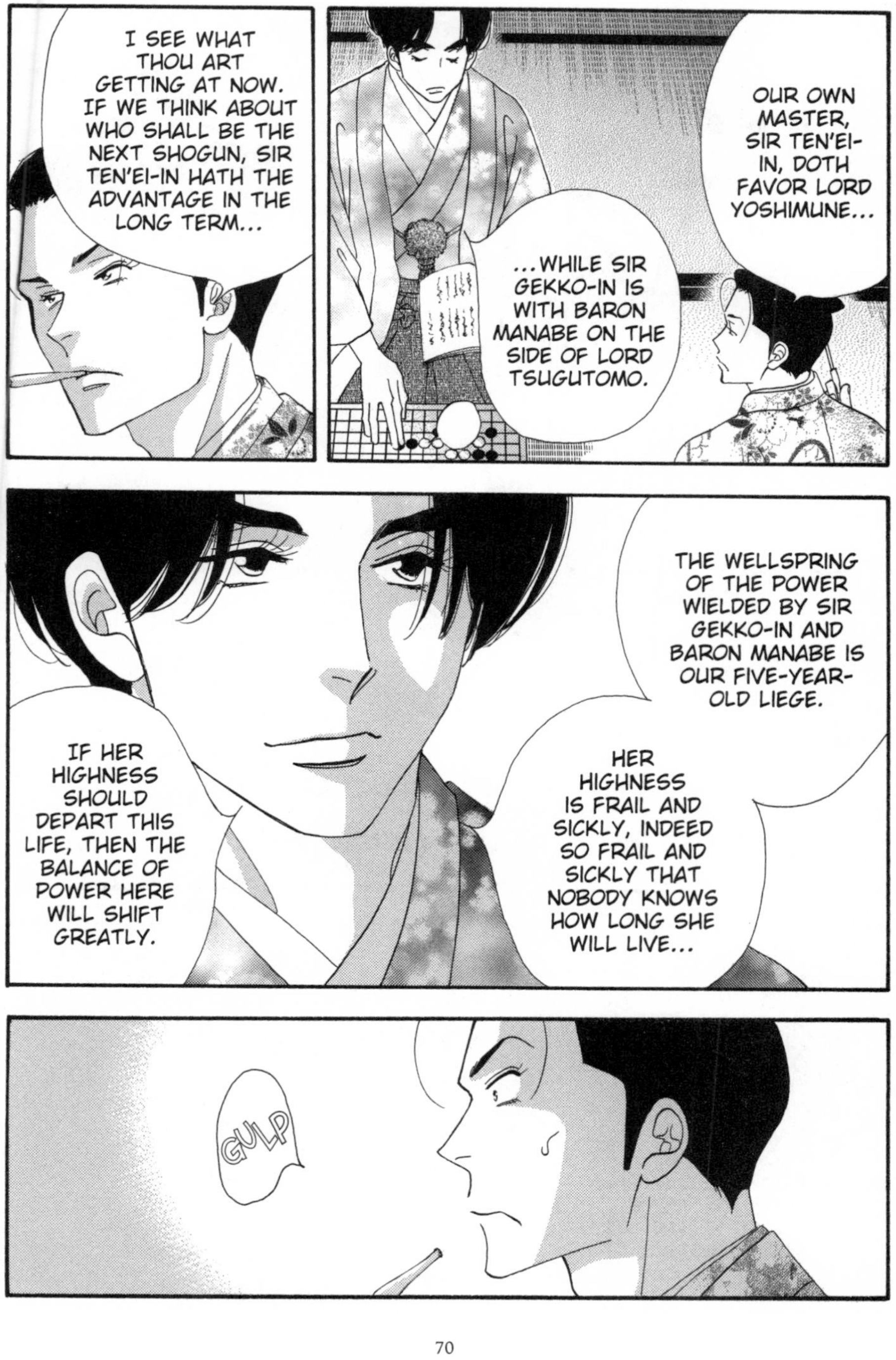
OUR OWN MASTER, SIR TEN'EI-IN, DOTH FAVOR LORD YOSHIMUNE...
...WHILE SIR GEKKO-IN IS WITH BARON MANABE ON THE SIDE OF LORD TSUGUTOMO.
I SEE WHAT THOU ART GETTING AT NOW. IF WE THINK ABOUT WHO SHALL BE THE NEXT SHOGUN, SIR TEN'EI-IN HATH THE ADVANTAGE IN THE LONG TERM...
THE WELLSPRING OF THE POWER WIELDED BY SIR GEKKO-IN AND BARON MANABE IS OUR FIVE-YEAR-OLD LIEGE.
HER HIGHNESS IS FRAIL AND SICKLY, INDEED SO FRAIL AND SICKLY THAT NOBODY KNOWS HOW LONG SHE WILL LIVE...
IF HER HIGHNESS SHOULD DEPART THIS LIFE, THEN THE BALANCE OF POWER HERE WILL SHIFT GREATLY.
GULP

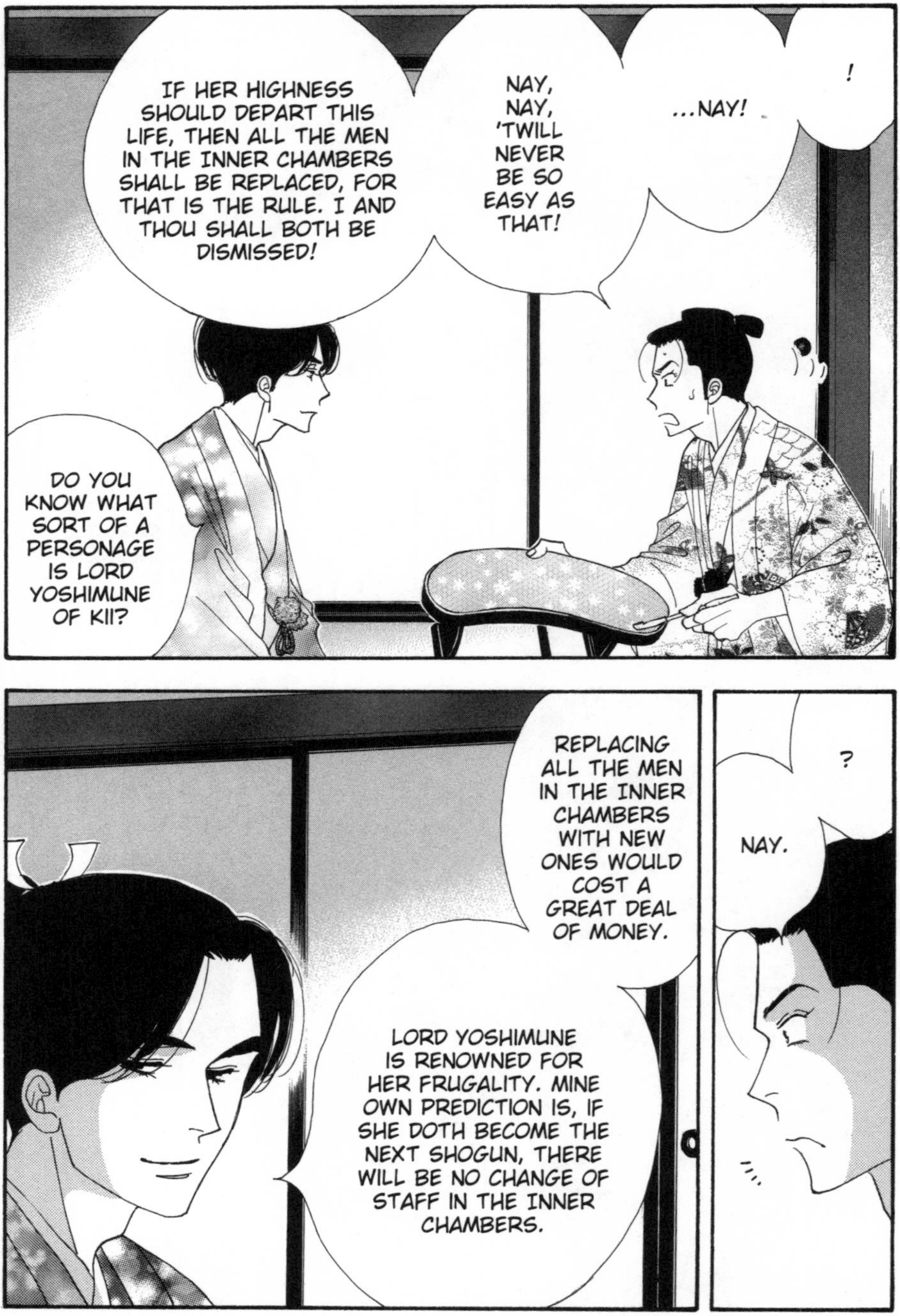
!
...NAY!
NAY, NAY, 'TWILL NEVER BE SO EASY AS THAT!
IF HER HIGHNESS SHOULD DEPART THIS LIFE, THEN ALL THE MEN IN THE INNER CHAMBERS SHALL BE REPLACED, FOR THAT IS THE RULE. I AND THOU SHALL BOTH BE DISMISSED!
DO YOU KNOW WHAT SORT OF A PERSONAGE IS LORD YOSHIMUNE OF KII?
?
NAY.
REPLACING ALL THE MEN IN THE INNER CHAMBERS WITH NEW ONES WOULD COST A GREAT DEAL OF MONEY.
LORD YOSHIMUNE IS RENOWNED FOR HER FRUGALITY. MINE OWN PREDICTION IS, IF SHE DOTH BECOME THE NEXT SHOGUN, THERE WILL BE NO CHANGE OF STAFF IN THE INNER CHAMBERS.

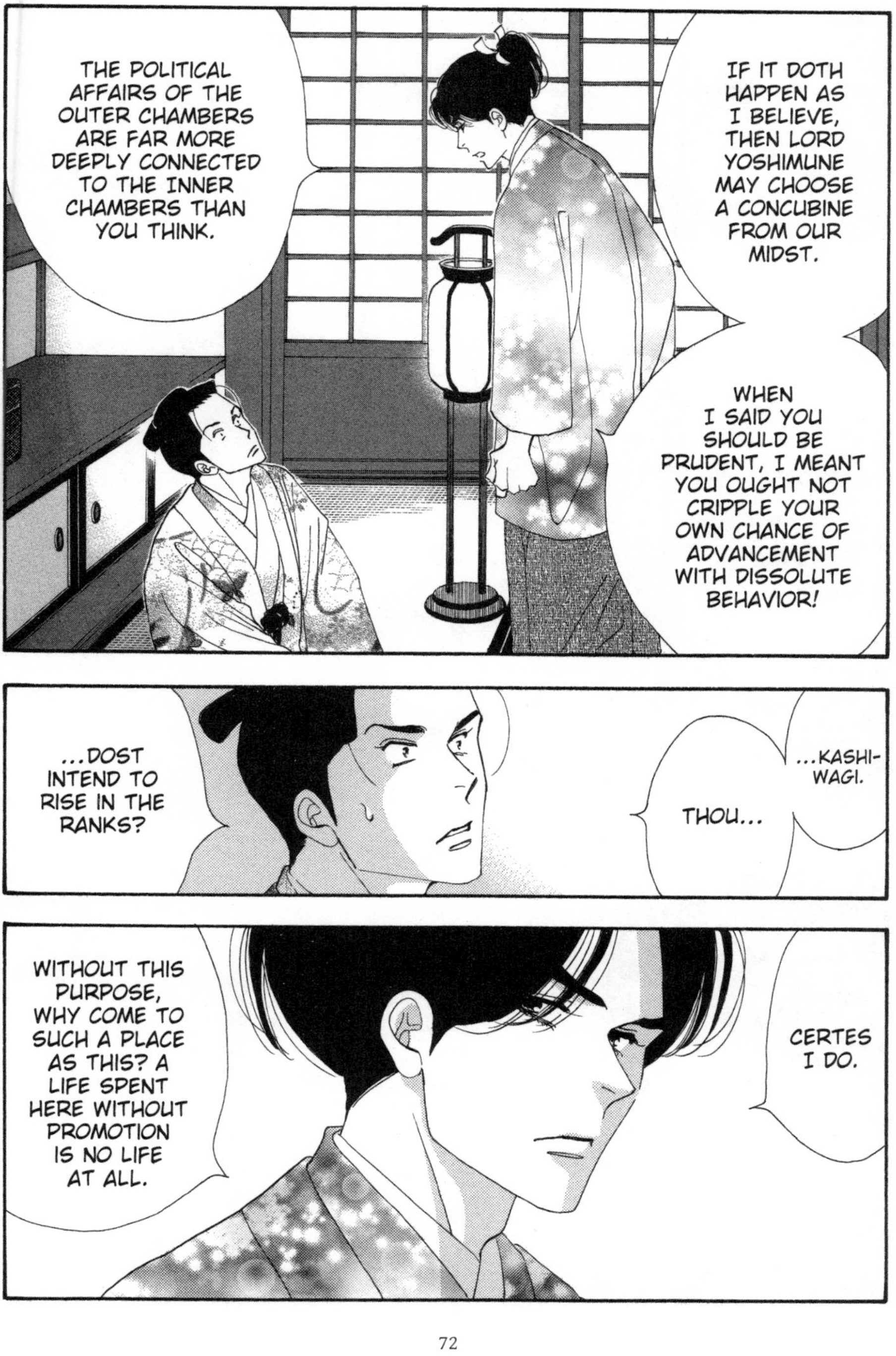
IF IT DOTH HAPPEN AS I BELIEVE, THEN LORD YOSHIMUNE MAY CHOOSE A CONCUBINE FROM OUR MIDST.
THE POLITICAL AFFAIRS OF THE OUTER CHAMBERS ARE FAR MORE DEEPLY CONNECTED TO THE INNER CHAMBERS THAN YOU THINK.
WHEN I SAID YOU SHOULD BE PRUDENT, I MEANT YOU OUGHT NOT CRIPPLE YOUR OWN CHANCE OF ADVANCEMENT WITH DISSOLUTE BEHAVIOR!
...KASHI-WAGI.
THOU...
...DOST INTEND TO RISE IN THE RANKS?
CERTES I DO.
WITHOUT THIS PURPOSE, WHY COME TO SUCH A PLACE AS THIS? A LIFE SPENT HERE WITHOUT PROMOTION IS NO LIFE AT ALL.

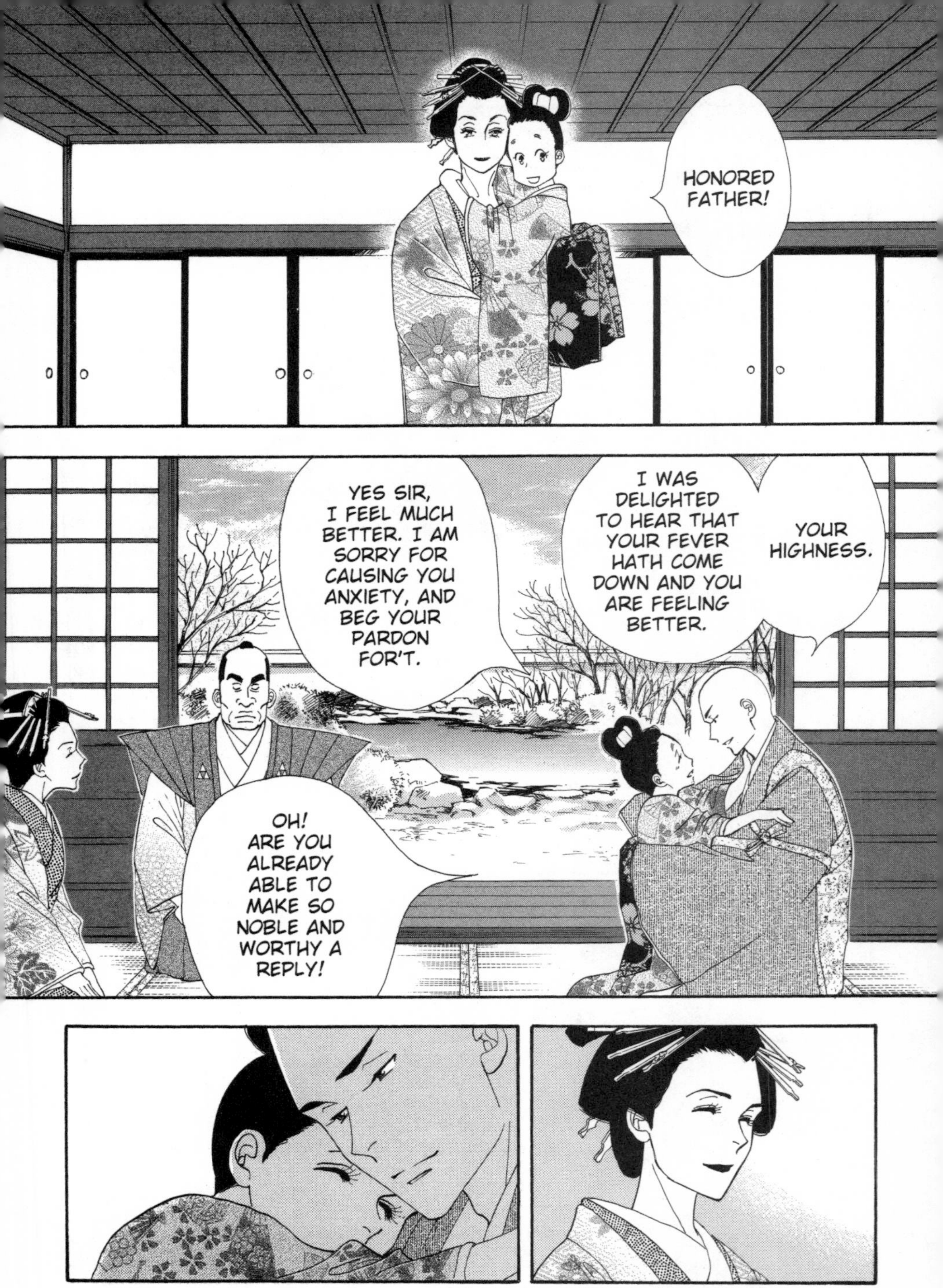
HONORED FATHER!
YOUR HIGHNESS.
I WAS DELIGHTED TO HEAR THAT YOUR FEVER HATH COME DOWN AND YOU ARE FEELING BETTER.
YES SIR, I FEEL MUCH BETTER. I AM SORRY FOR CAUSING YOU ANXIETY, AND BEG YOUR PARDON FOR'T.
OH! ARE YOU ALREADY ABLE TO MAKE SO NOBLE AND WORTHY A REPLY!

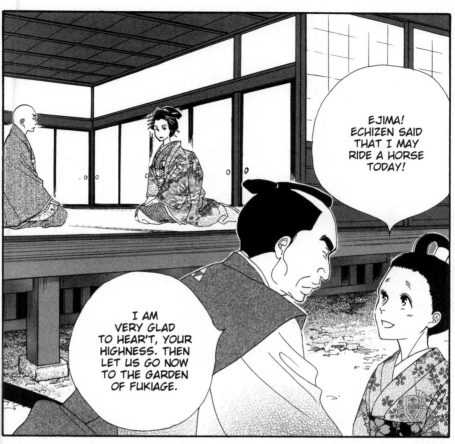

EJIMA! ECHIZEN SAID THAT I MAY RIDE A HORSE TODAY!
I AM VERY GLAD TO HEAR'T, YOUR HIGHNESS. THEN LET US GO NOW TO THE GARDEN OF FUKIAGE.
LADY MANABE.
'TIS REPORTED THAT BARON TSUCHIYA OF SAGAMI AND OTHER GOVERNMENT MINISTERS ARE FREQUENTLY SEEN TO BE CALLING ON SIR TEN'EI-IN IN HIS CHAMBERS.
AYE...
AND I CAN WELL GUESS THE TENOR OF THEIR CONVER-SATIONS.

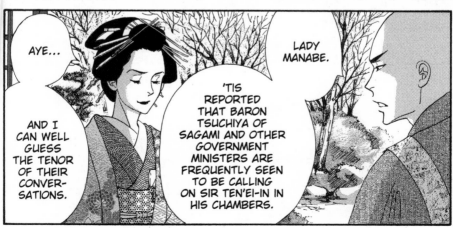

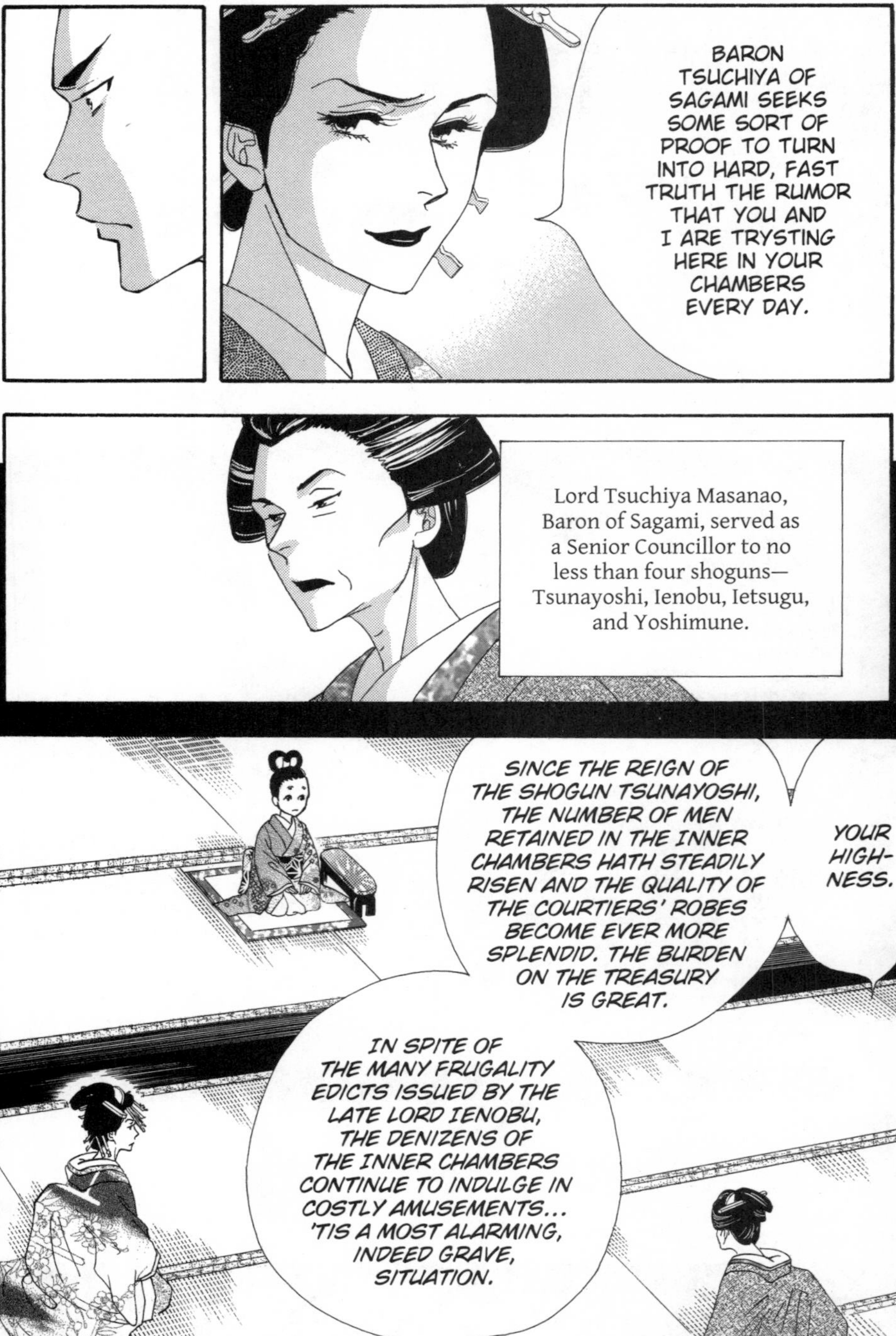
BARON TSUCHIYA OF SAGAMI SEEKS SOME SORT OF PROOF TO TURN INTO HARD, FAST TRUTH THE RUMOR THAT YOU AND I ARE TRYSTING HERE IN YOUR CHAMBERS EVERY DAY.
Lord Tsuchiya Masanao, Baron of Sagami, served as a Senior Councillor to no less than four shoguns—Tsunayoshi, Ienobu, Ietsugu, and Yoshimune.
YOUR HIGHNESS.
SINCE THE REIGN OF THE SHOGUN TSUNAYOSHI, THE NUMBER OF MEN RETAINED IN THE INNER CHAMBERS HATH STEADILY RISEN AND THE QUALITY OF THE COURTIERS' ROBES BECOME EVER MORE SPLENDID. THE BURDEN ON THE TREASURY IS GREAT.
IN SPITE OF THE MANY FRUGALITY EDICTS ISSUED BY THE LATE LORD IENOBU, THE DENIZENS OF THE INNER CHAMBERS CONTINUE TO INDULGE IN COSTLY AMUSEMENTS... 'TIS A MOST ALARMING, INDEED GRAVE, SITUATION.

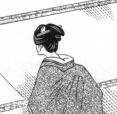

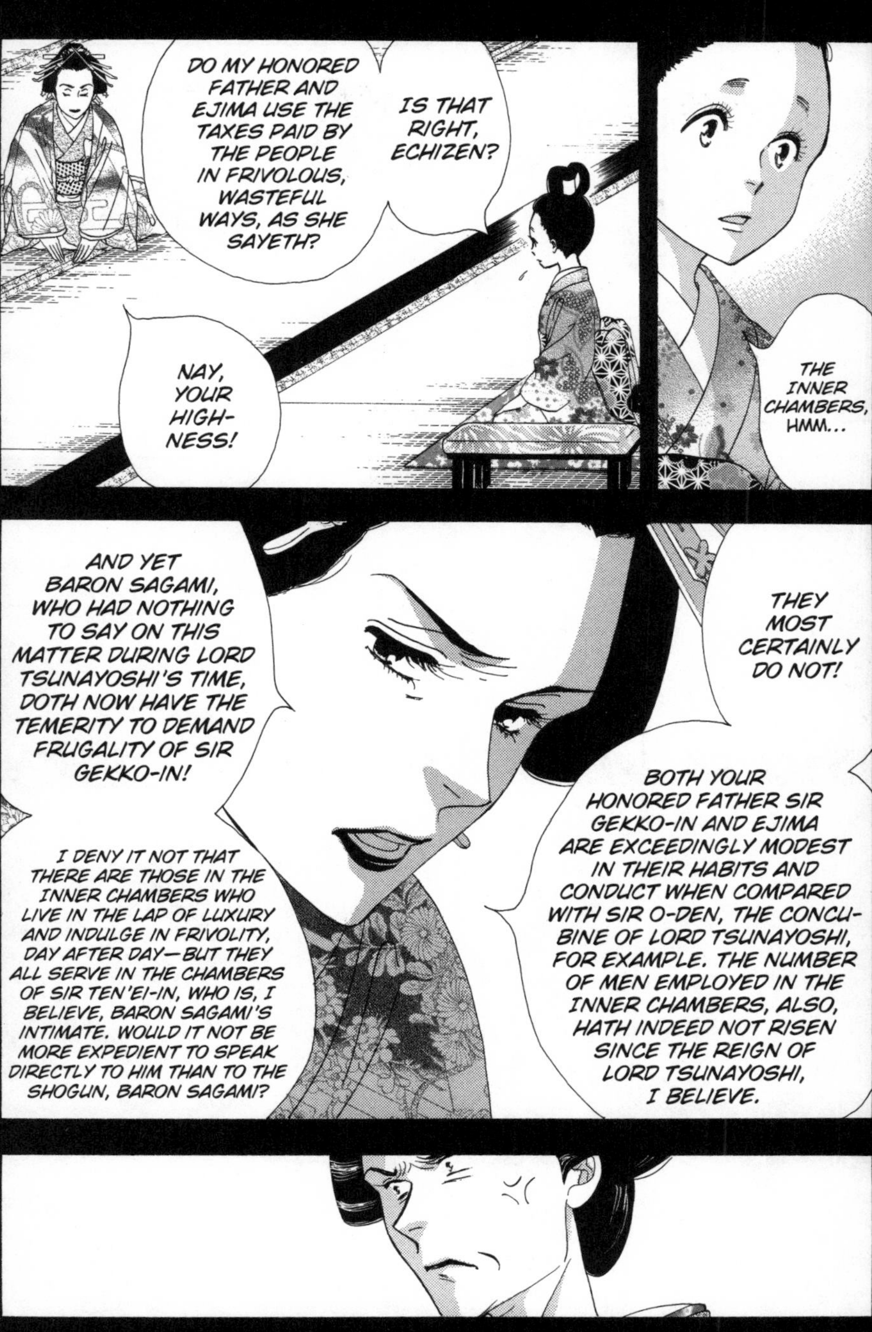
THE INNER CHAMBERS, HMM...
DO MY HONORED FATHER AND EJIMA USE THE TAXES PAID BY THE PEOPLE IN FRIVOLOUS, WASTEFUL WAYS, AS SHE SAYETH?
IS THAT RIGHT, ECHIZEN?
NAY, YOUR HIGH-NESS!
THEY MOST CERTAINLY DO NOT!
BOTH YOUR HONORED FATHER SIR GEKKO-IN AND EJIMA ARE EXCEEDINGLY MODEST IN THEIR HABITS AND CONDUCT WHEN COMPARED WITH SIR O-DEN, THE CONCU-BINE OF LORD TSUNAYOSHI, FOR EXAMPLE. THE NUMBER OF MEN EMPLOYED IN THE INNER CHAMBERS, ALSO, HATH INDEED NOT RISEN SINCE THE REIGN OF LORD TSUNAYOSHI, I BELIEVE.
AND YET BARON SAGAMI, WHO HAD NOTHING TO SAY ON THIS MATTER DURING LORD TSUNAYOSHI'S TIME, DOTH NOW HAVE THE TEMERITY TO DEMAND FRUGALITY OF SIR GEKKO-IN!
I DENY IT NOT THAT THERE ARE THOSE IN THE INNER CHAMBERS WHO LIVE IN THE LAP OF LUXURY AND INDULGE IN FRIVOLITY, DAY AFTER DAY—BUT THEY ALL SERVE IN THE CHAMBERS OF SIR TEN'EI-IN, WHO IS, I BELIEVE, BARON SAGAMI'S INTIMATE. WOULD IT NOT BE MORE EXPEDIENT TO SPEAK DIRECTLY TO HIM THAN TO THE SHOGUN, BARON SAGAMI?

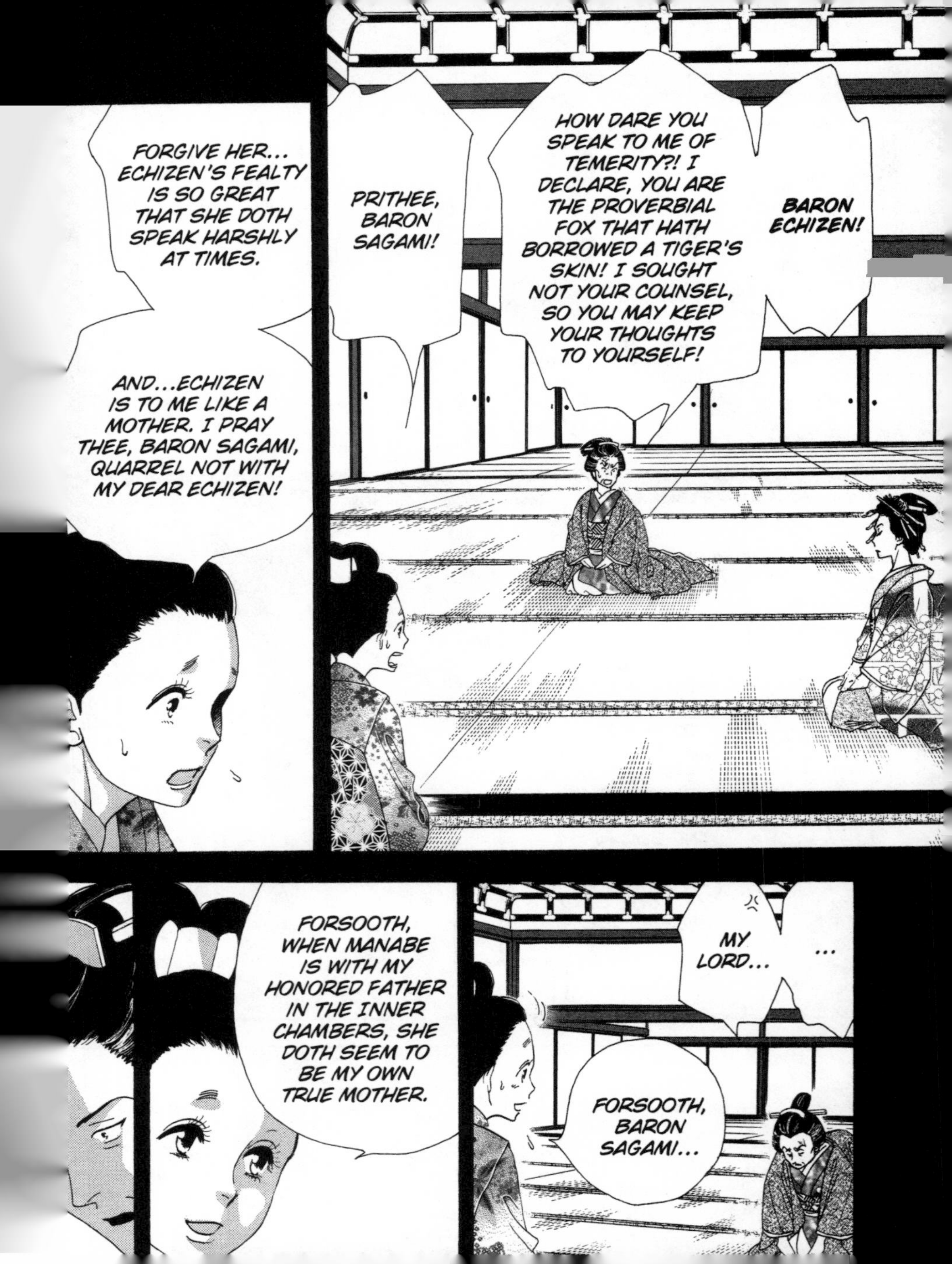
BARON ECHIZEN!
HOW DARE YOU SPEAK TO ME OF TEMERITY?! I DECLARE, YOU ARE THE PROVERBIAL FOX THAT HATH BORROWED A TIGER'S SKIN! I SOUGHT NOT YOUR COUNSEL, SO YOU MAY KEEP YOUR THOUGHTS TO YOURSELF!
PRITHEE, BARON SAGAMI!
FORGIVE HER... ECHIZEN'S FEALTY IS SO GREAT THAT SHE DOTH SPEAK HARSHLY AT TIMES.
AND...ECHIZEN IS TO ME LIKE A MOTHER. I PRAY THEE, BARON SAGAMI, QUARREL NOT WITH MY DEAR ECHIZEN!
...
MY LORD...
FORSOOTH, BARON SAGAMI...
FORSOOTH, WHEN MANABE IS WITH MY HONORED FATHER IN THE INNER CHAMBERS, SHE DOTH SEEM TO BE MY OWN TRUE MOTHER.

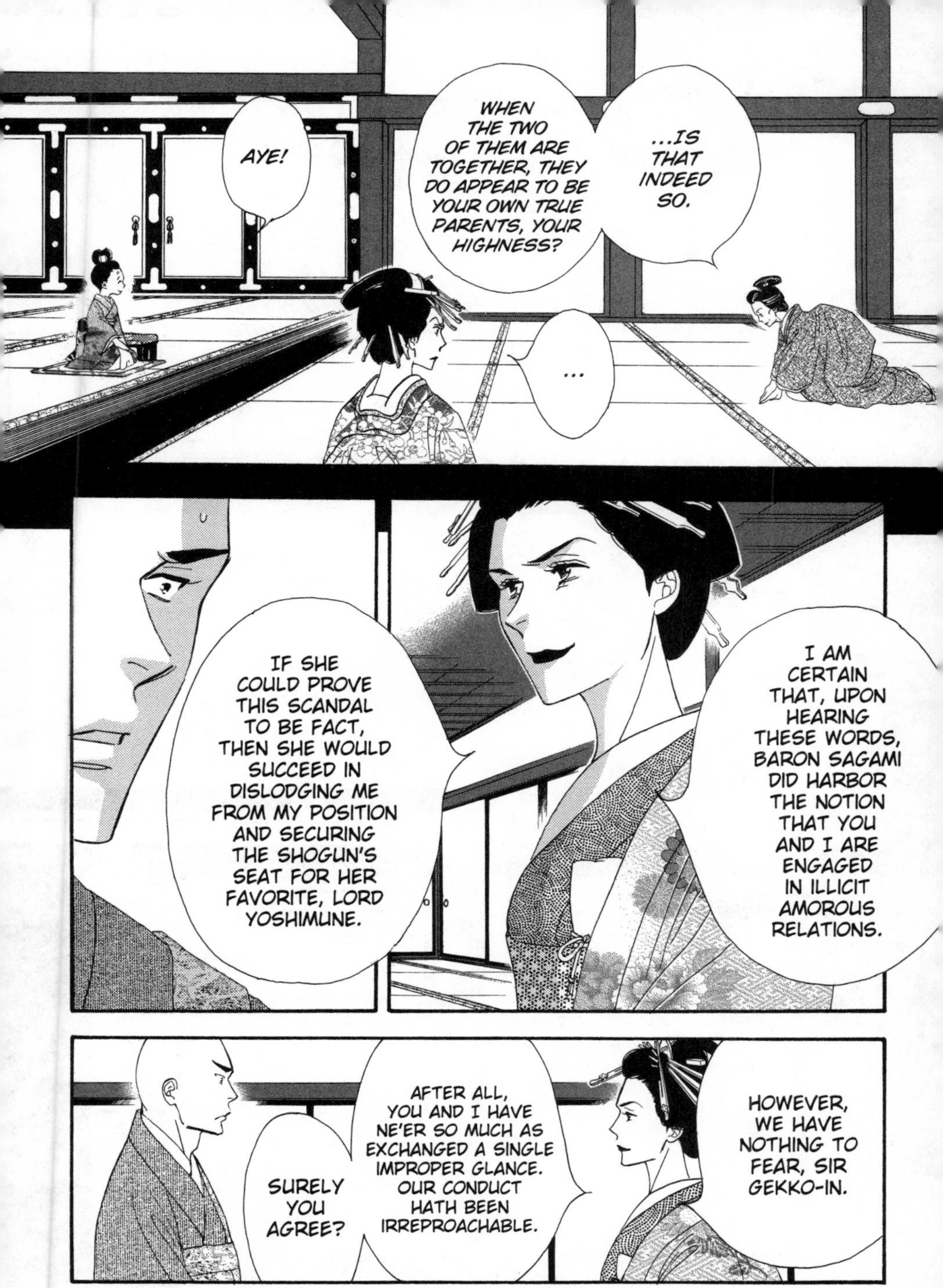
...IS THAT INDEED SO.
WHEN THE TWO OF THEM ARE TOGETHER, THEY DO APPEAR TO BE YOUR OWN TRUE PARENTS, YOUR HIGHNESS?
AYE!
...
I AM CERTAIN THAT, UPON HEARING THESE WORDS, BARON SAGAMI DID HARBOR THE NOTION THAT YOU AND I ARE ENGAGED IN ILLICIT AMOROUS RELATIONS.
IF SHE COULD PROVE THIS SCANDAL TO BE FACT, THEN SHE WOULD SUCCEED IN DISLODGING ME FROM MY POSITION AND SECURING THE SHOGUN'S SEAT FOR HER FAVORITE, LORD YOSHIMUNE.
HOWEVER, WE HAVE NOTHING TO FEAR, SIR GEKKO-IN.
AFTER ALL, YOU AND I HAVE NE'ER SO MUCH AS EXCHANGED A SINGLE IMPROPER GLANCE. OUR CONDUCT HATH BEEN IRREPROACHABLE.
SURELY YOU AGREE?

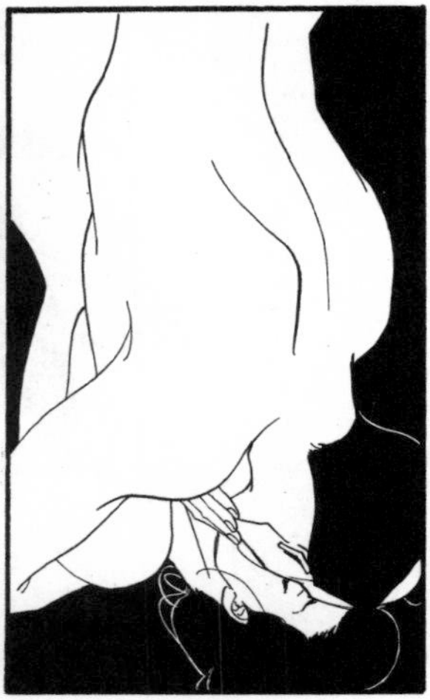
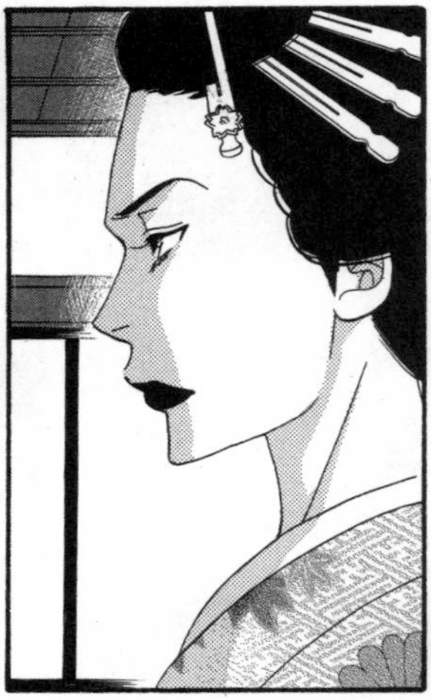
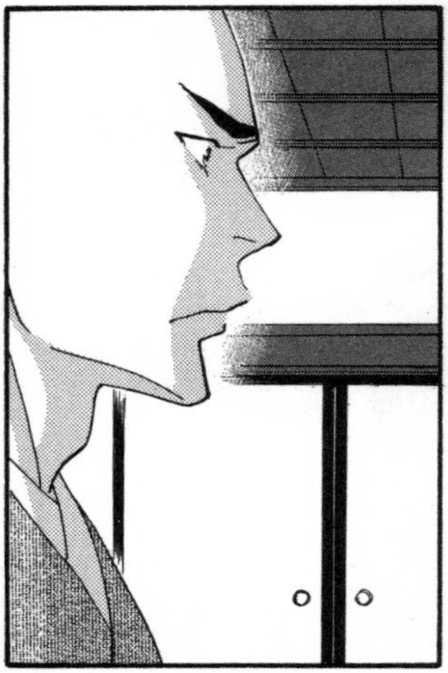
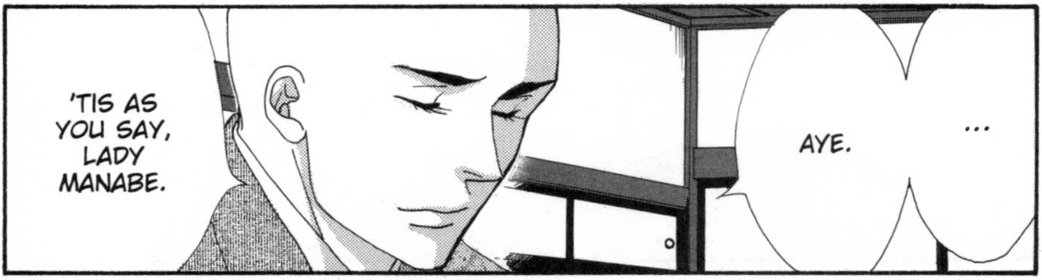
...
AYE.
'TIS AS YOU SAY, LADY MANABE.
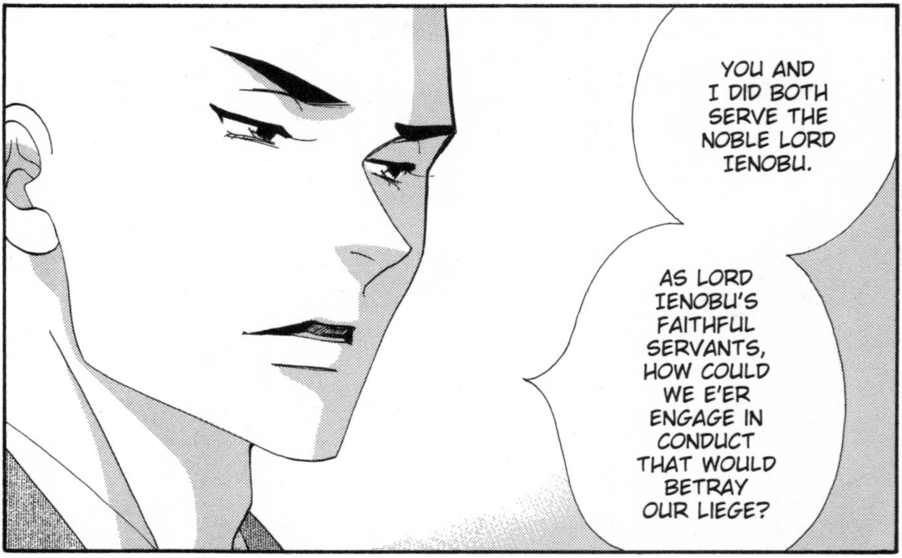
YOU AND I DID BOTH SERVE THE NOBLE LORD IENOBU.
AS LORD IENOBU'S FAITHFUL SERVANTS, HOW COULD WE E'ER ENGAGE IN CONDUCT THAT WOULD BETRAY OUR LIEGE?

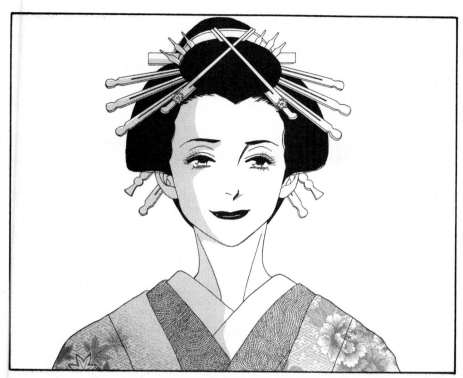

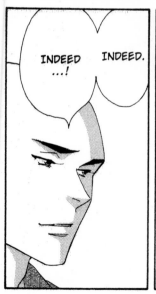

...
AYE, SIR GEKKO-IN. YOU HAVE SPOKEN TRUE.
...
I, AKIFUSA, AM MOST GRATIFIED, INDEED GRATEFUL, THAT YOU AND I ARE IN COMPLETE AGREEMENT...
INDEED.
INDEED ...!

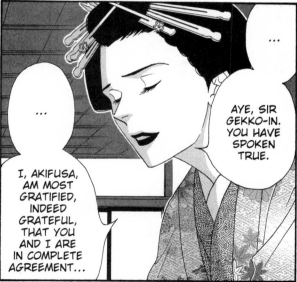

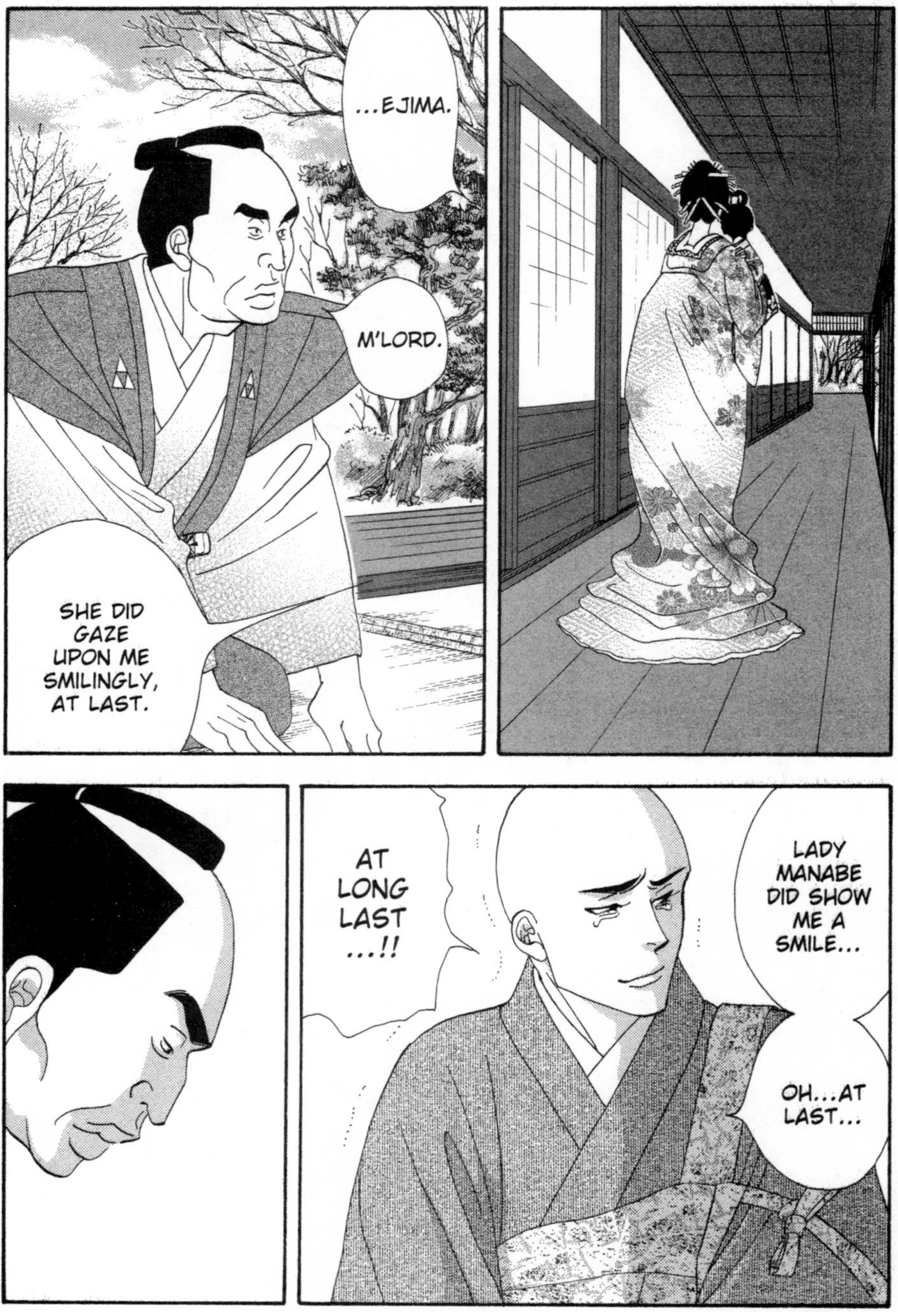
...EJIMA.
M'LORD.
SHE DID GAZE UPON ME SMILINGLY, AT LAST.
LADY MANABE DID SHOW ME A SMILE...
OH...AT LAST...
AT LONG LAST ...!!

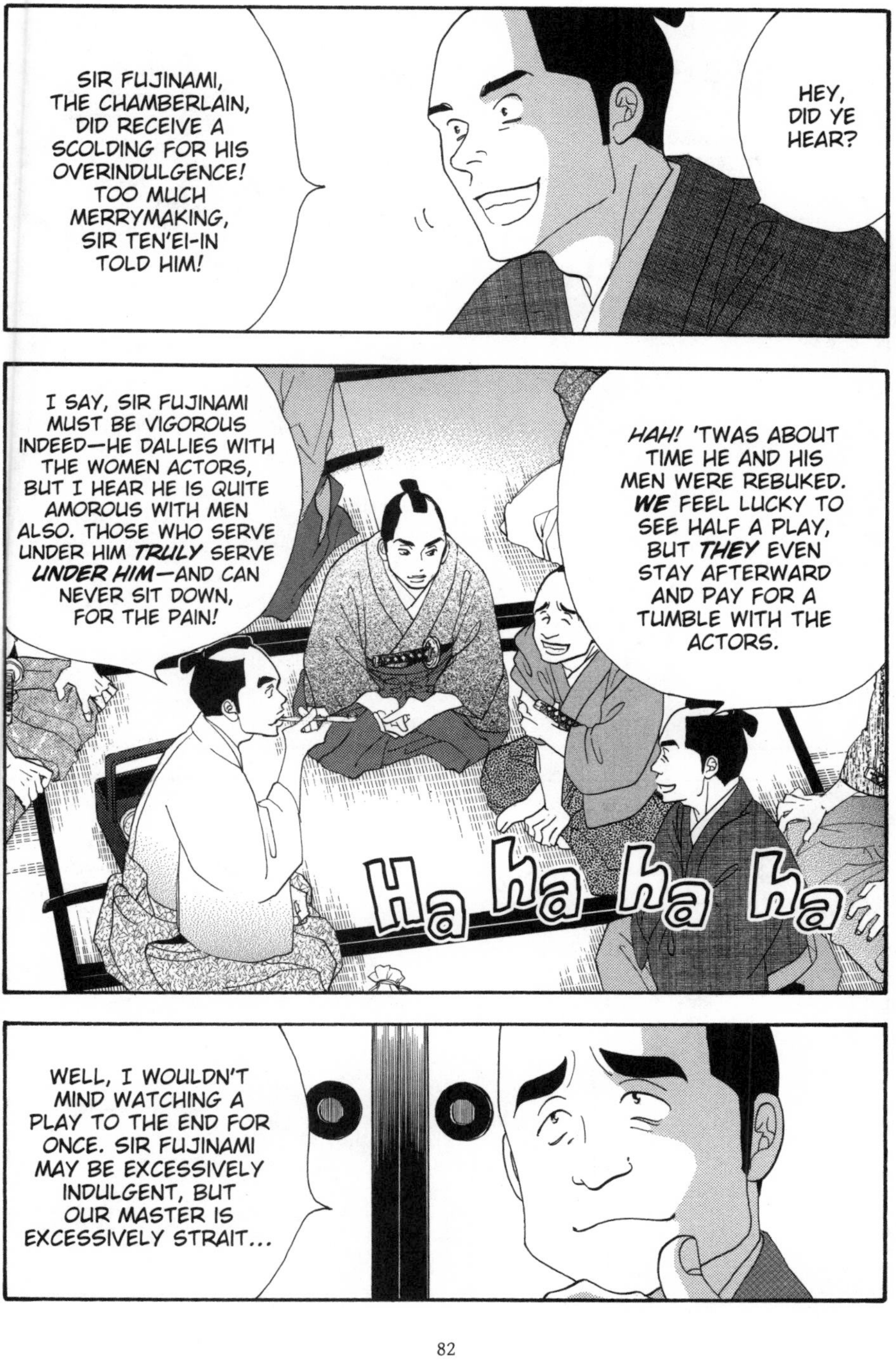
HEY, DID YE HEAR?
SIR FUJINAMI, THE CHAMBERLAIN, DID RECEIVE A SCOLDING FOR HIS OVERINDULGENCE! TOO MUCH MERRYMAKING, SIR TEN'EI-IN TOLD HIM!
HAH! 'TWAS ABOUT TIME HE AND HIS MEN WERE REBUKED. ***WE*** FEEL LUCKY TO SEE HALF A PLAY, BUT ***THEY*** EVEN STAY AFTERWARD AND PAY FOR A TUMBLE WITH THE ACTORS.
I SAY, SIR FUJINAMI MUST BE VIGOROUS INDEED—HE DALLIES WITH THE WOMEN ACTORS, BUT I HEAR HE IS QUITE AMOROUS WITH MEN ALSO. THOSE WHO SERVE UNDER HIM ***TRULY*** SERVE ***UNDER HIM***—AND CAN NEVER SIT DOWN, FOR THE PAIN!
Ha ha ha ha
WELL, I WOULDN'T MIND WATCHING A PLAY TO THE END FOR ONCE. SIR FUJINAMI MAY BE EXCESSIVELY INDULGENT, BUT OUR MASTER IS EXCESSIVELY STRAIT...

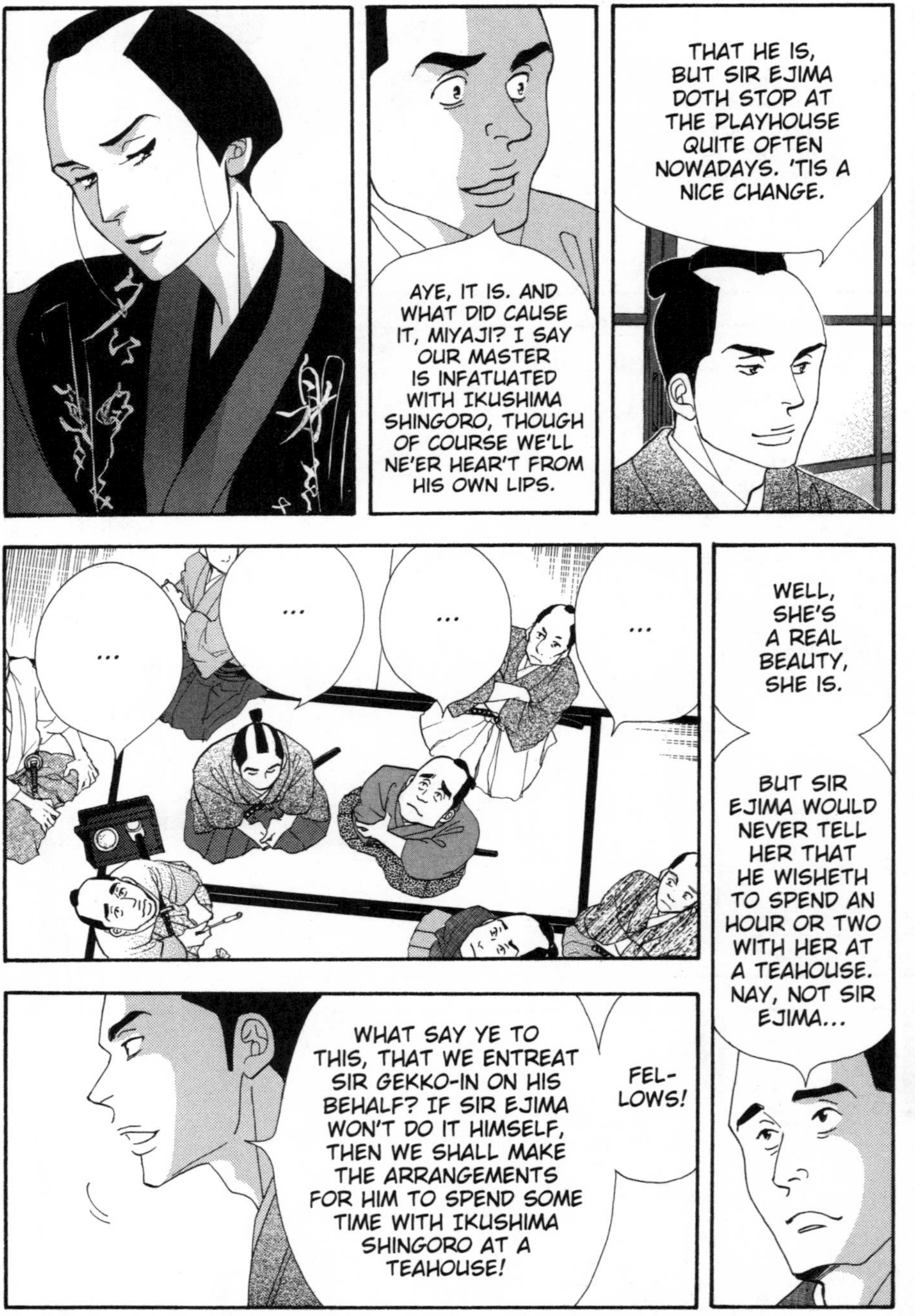
THAT HE IS, BUT SIR EJIMA DOTH STOP AT THE PLAYHOUSE QUITE OFTEN NOWADAYS. 'TIS A NICE CHANGE.
AYE, IT IS. AND WHAT DID CAUSE IT, MIYAJI? I SAY OUR MASTER IS INFATUATED WITH IKUSHIMA SHINGORO, THOUGH OF COURSE WE'LL NE'ER HEAR'T FROM HIS OWN LIPS.
WELL, SHE'S A REAL BEAUTY, SHE IS.
BUT SIR EJIMA WOULD NEVER TELL HER THAT HE WISHETH TO SPEND AN HOUR OR TWO WITH HER AT A TEAHOUSE. NAY, NOT SIR EJIMA...
...
...
...
...
FEL-LOWS!
WHAT SAY YE TO THIS, THAT WE ENTREAT SIR GEKKO-IN ON HIS BEHALF? IF SIR EJIMA WON'T DO IT HIMSELF, THEN WE SHALL MAKE THE ARRANGEMENTS FOR HIM TO SPEND SOME TIME WITH IKUSHIMA SHINGORO AT A TEAHOUSE!

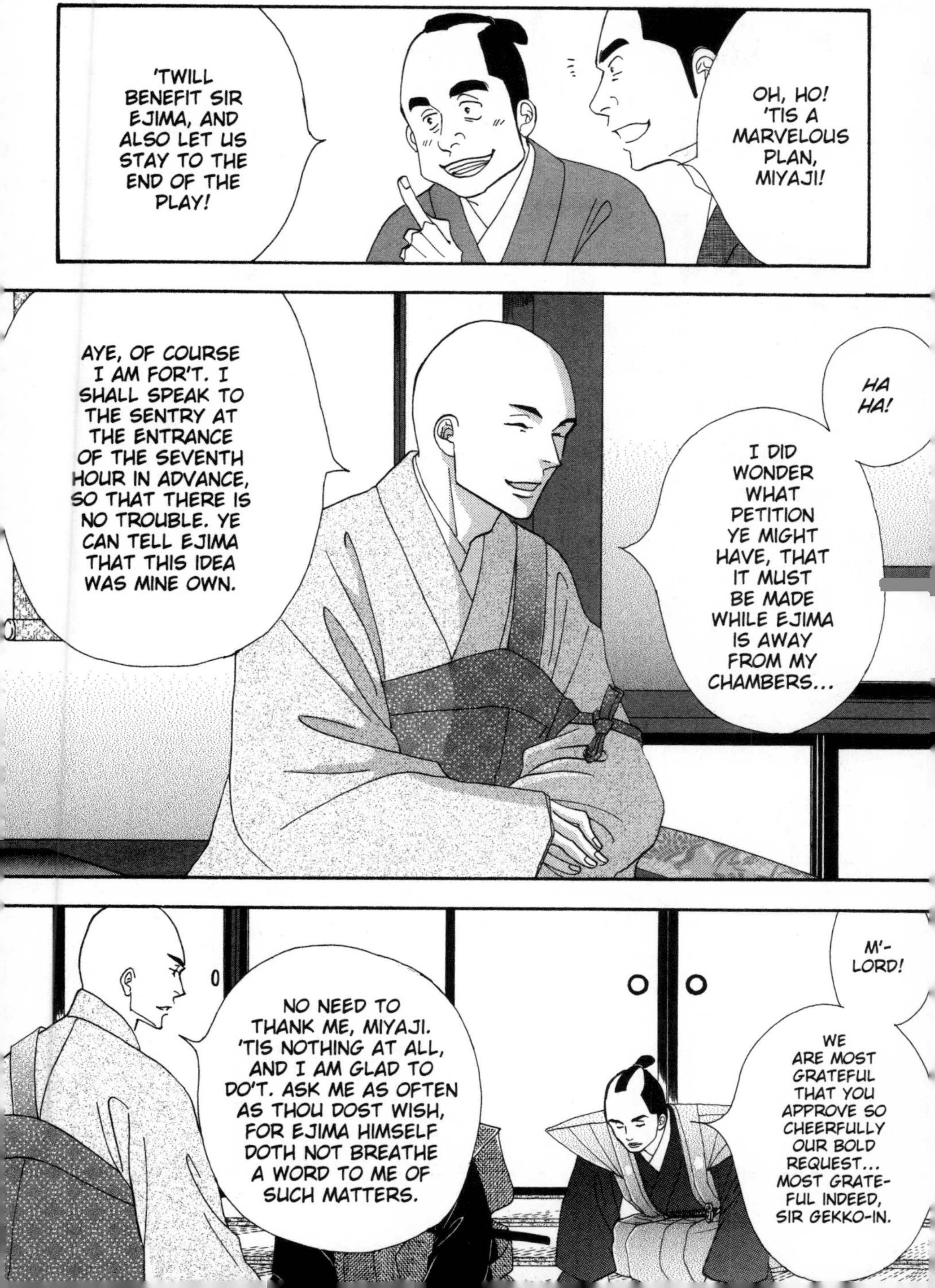
OH, HO! 'TIS A MARVELOUS PLAN, MIYAJI!
'TWILL BENEFIT SIR EJIMA, AND ALSO LET US STAY TO THE END OF THE PLAY!
HA HA!
I DID WONDER WHAT PETITION YE MIGHT HAVE, THAT IT MUST BE MADE WHILE EJIMA IS AWAY FROM MY CHAMBERS...
AYE, OF COURSE I AM FOR'T. I SHALL SPEAK TO THE SENTRY AT THE ENTRANCE OF THE SEVENTH HOUR IN ADVANCE, SO THAT THERE IS NO TROUBLE. YE CAN TELL EJIMA THAT THIS IDEA WAS MINE OWN.
M'-LORD!
WE ARE MOST GRATEFUL THAT YOU APPROVE SO CHEERFULLY OUR BOLD REQUEST... MOST GRATE-FUL INDEED, SIR GEKKO-IN.
NO NEED TO THANK ME, MIYAJI. 'TIS NOTHING AT ALL, AND I AM GLAD TO DO'T. ASK ME AS OFTEN AS THOU DOST WISH, FOR EJIMA HIMSELF DOTH NOT BREATHE A WORD TO ME OF SUCH MATTERS.

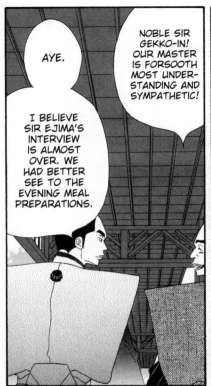

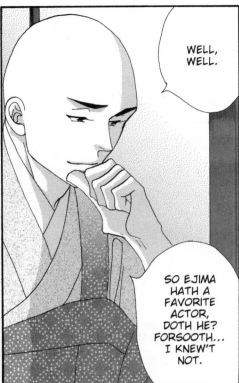

WELL, WELL.
SO EJIMA HATH A FAVORITE ACTOR, DOTH HE? FORSOOTH... I KNEW'T NOT.
NOBLE SIR GEKKO-IN! OUR MASTER IS FORSOOTH MOST UNDER-STANDING AND SYMPATHETIC!
AYE.
I BELIEVE SIR EJIMA'S INTERVIEW IS ALMOST OVER. WE HAD BETTER SEE TO THE EVENING MEAL PREPARATIONS.
SPLISH

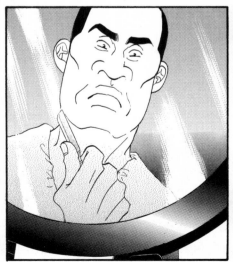

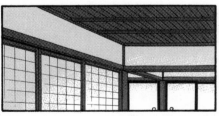

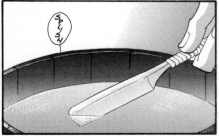

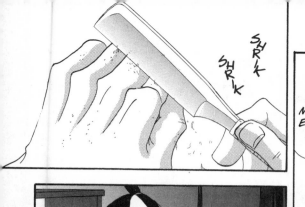

SHRIK

SHRIK

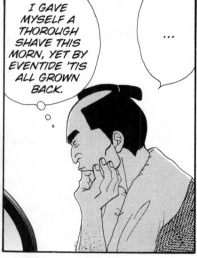

I GAVE MYSELF A THOROUGH SHAVE THIS MORN, YET BY EVENTIDE 'TIS ALL GROWN BACK.

...

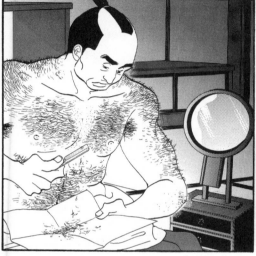

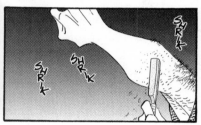

SHRIK

SHRIK

SHRIK

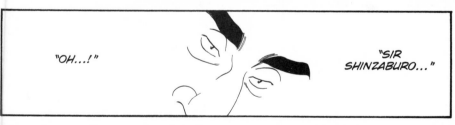

"OH...!"

"SIR SHINZABURO..."

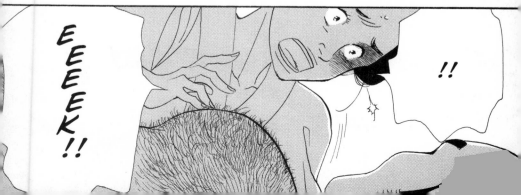

EEEEK!!

!!

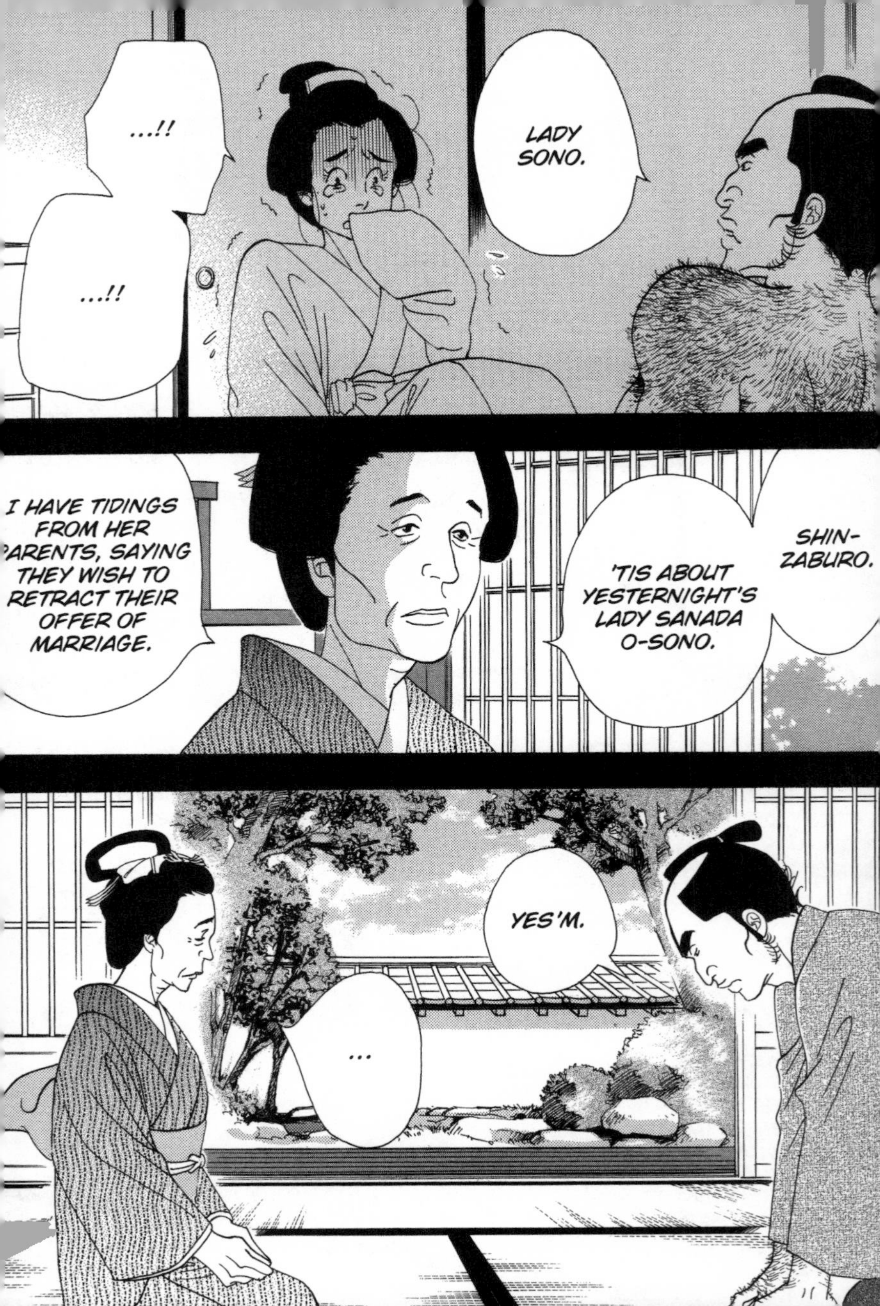

LADY SONO.
...!!
...!!
SHIN-ZABURO.
'TIS ABOUT YESTERNIGHT'S LADY SANADA O-SONO.
I HAVE TIDINGS FROM HER PARENTS, SAYING THEY WISH TO RETRACT THEIR OFFER OF MARRIAGE.
YES'M.
...

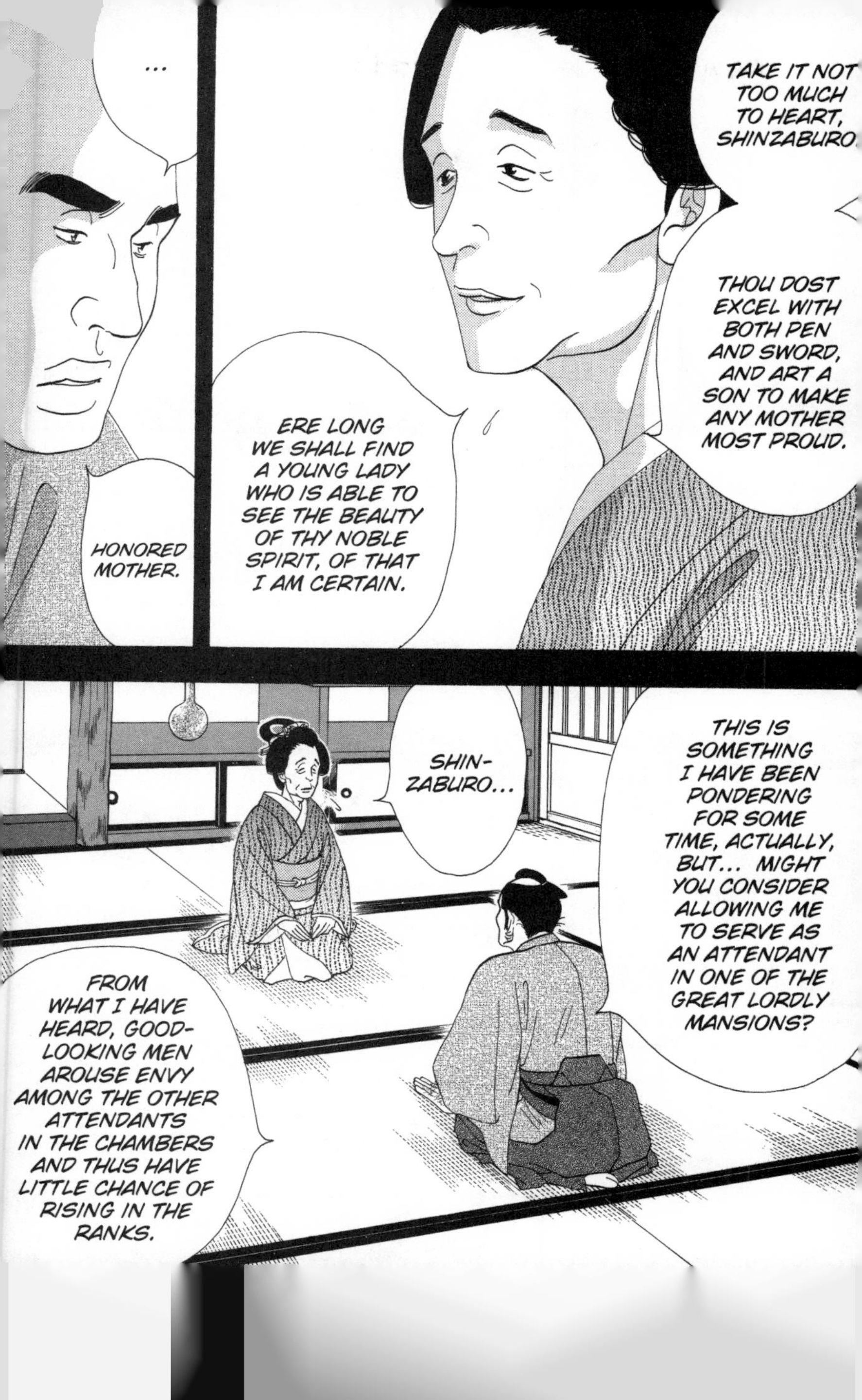
TAKE IT NOT TOO MUCH TO HEART, SHINZABURO.
THOU DOST EXCEL WITH BOTH PEN AND SWORD, AND ART A SON TO MAKE ANY MOTHER MOST PROUD.
ERE LONG WE SHALL FIND A YOUNG LADY WHO IS ABLE TO SEE THE BEAUTY OF THY NOBLE SPIRIT, OF THAT I AM CERTAIN.
...
HONORED MOTHER.
THIS IS SOMETHING I HAVE BEEN PONDERING FOR SOME TIME, ACTUALLY, BUT... MIGHT YOU CONSIDER ALLOWING ME TO SERVE AS AN ATTENDANT IN ONE OF THE GREAT LORDLY MANSIONS?
SHIN-ZABURO...
FROM WHAT I HAVE HEARD, GOOD-LOOKING MEN AROUSE ENVY AMONG THE OTHER ATTENDANTS IN THE CHAMBERS AND THUS HAVE LITTLE CHANCE OF RISING IN THE RANKS.

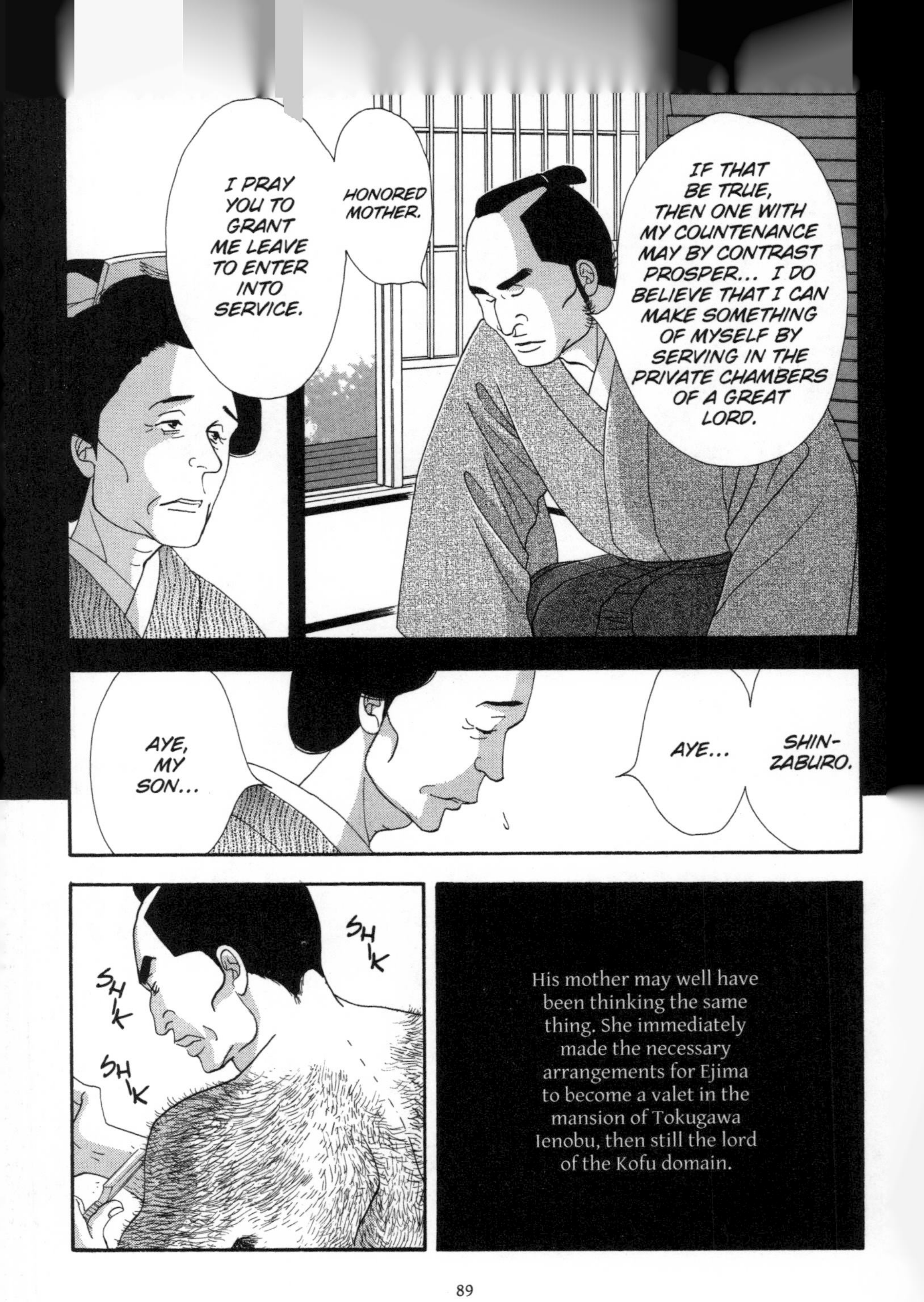
IF THAT BE TRUE, THEN ONE WITH MY COUNTENANCE MAY BY CONTRAST PROSPER... I DO BELIEVE THAT I CAN MAKE SOMETHING OF MYSELF BY SERVING IN THE PRIVATE CHAMBERS OF A GREAT LORD.
HONORED MOTHER.
I PRAY YOU TO GRANT ME LEAVE TO ENTER INTO SERVICE.
SHIN-ZABURO.
AYE...
AYE, MY SON...
His mother may well have been thinking the same thing. She immediately made the necessary arrangements for Ejima to become a valet in the mansion of Tokugawa Ienobu, then still the lord of the Kofu domain.
SHIK
SHIK
SHIK

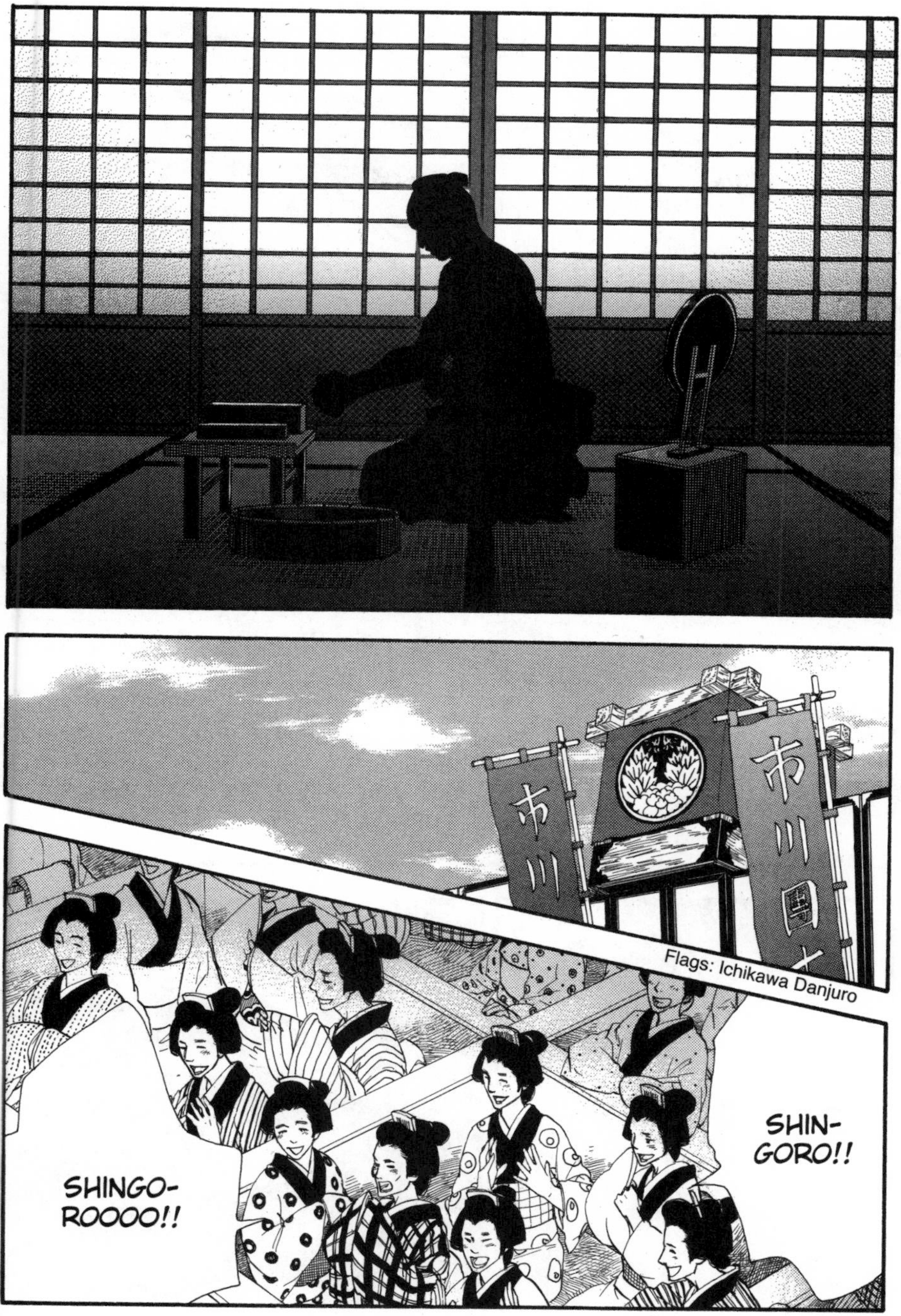
市川
市川
Flags: Ichikawa Danjuro
SHIN-GORO!!
SHINGO-ROOOO!!

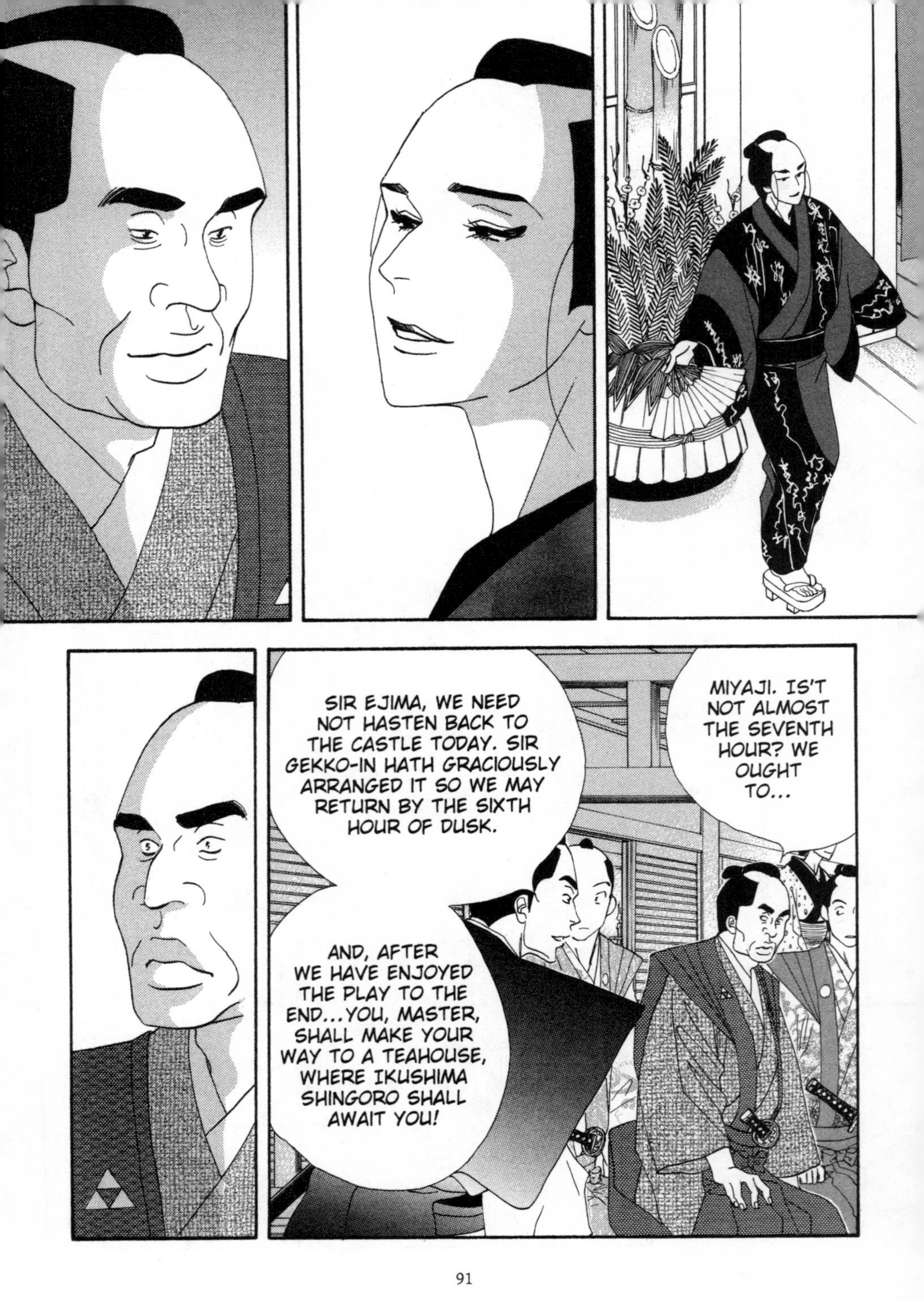
MIYAJI. IS'T NOT ALMOST THE SEVENTH HOUR? WE OUGHT TO...
SIR EJIMA, WE NEED NOT HASTEN BACK TO THE CASTLE TODAY. SIR GEKKO-IN HATH GRACIOUSLY ARRANGED IT SO WE MAY RETURN BY THE SIXTH HOUR OF DUSK.
AND, AFTER WE HAVE ENJOYED THE PLAY TO THE END...YOU, MASTER, SHALL MAKE YOUR WAY TO A TEAHOUSE, WHERE IKUSHIMA SHINGORO SHALL AWAIT YOU!

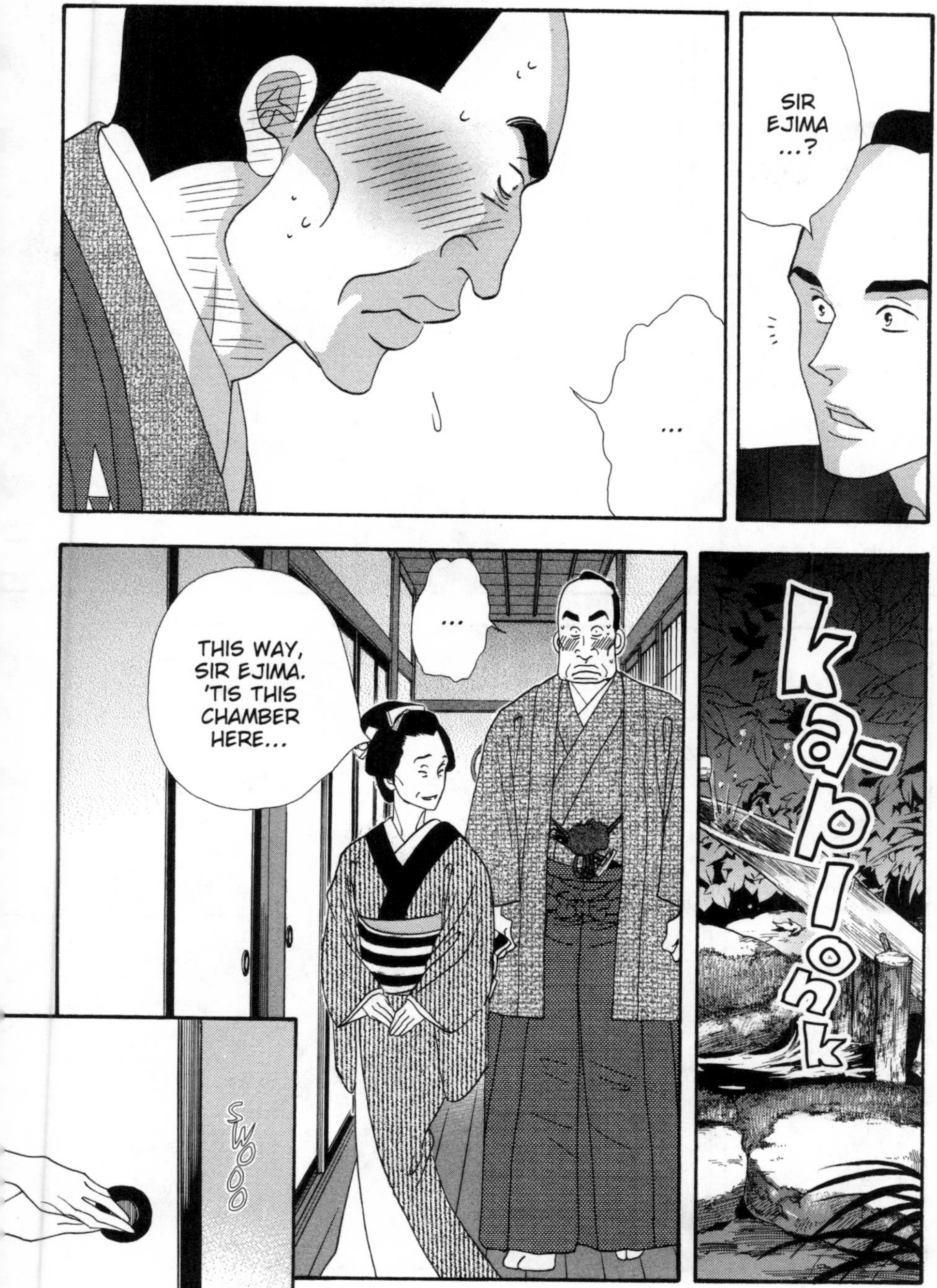
SIR EJIMA ...?
...
ka-plonk
...
THIS WAY, SIR EJIMA. 'TIS THIS CHAMBER HERE...
SWOOO

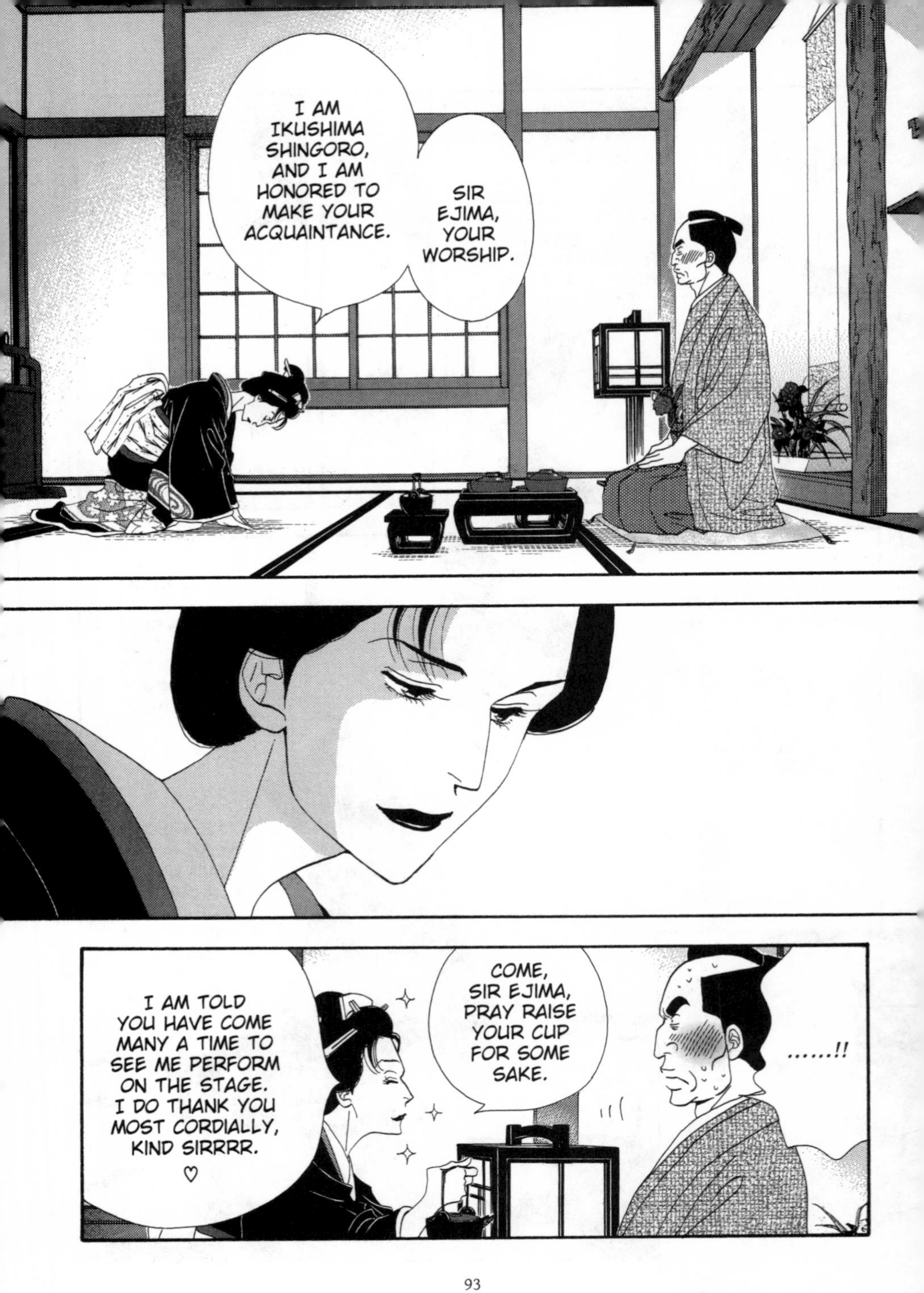
SIR EJIMA, YOUR WORSHIP.
I AM IKUSHIMA SHINGORO, AND I AM HONORED TO MAKE YOUR ACQUAINTANCE.
......!!
COME, SIR EJIMA, PRAY RAISE YOUR CUP FOR SOME SAKE.
I AM TOLD YOU HAVE COME MANY A TIME TO SEE ME PERFORM ON THE STAGE. I DO THANK YOU MOST CORDIALLY, KIND SIRRRR. ♡

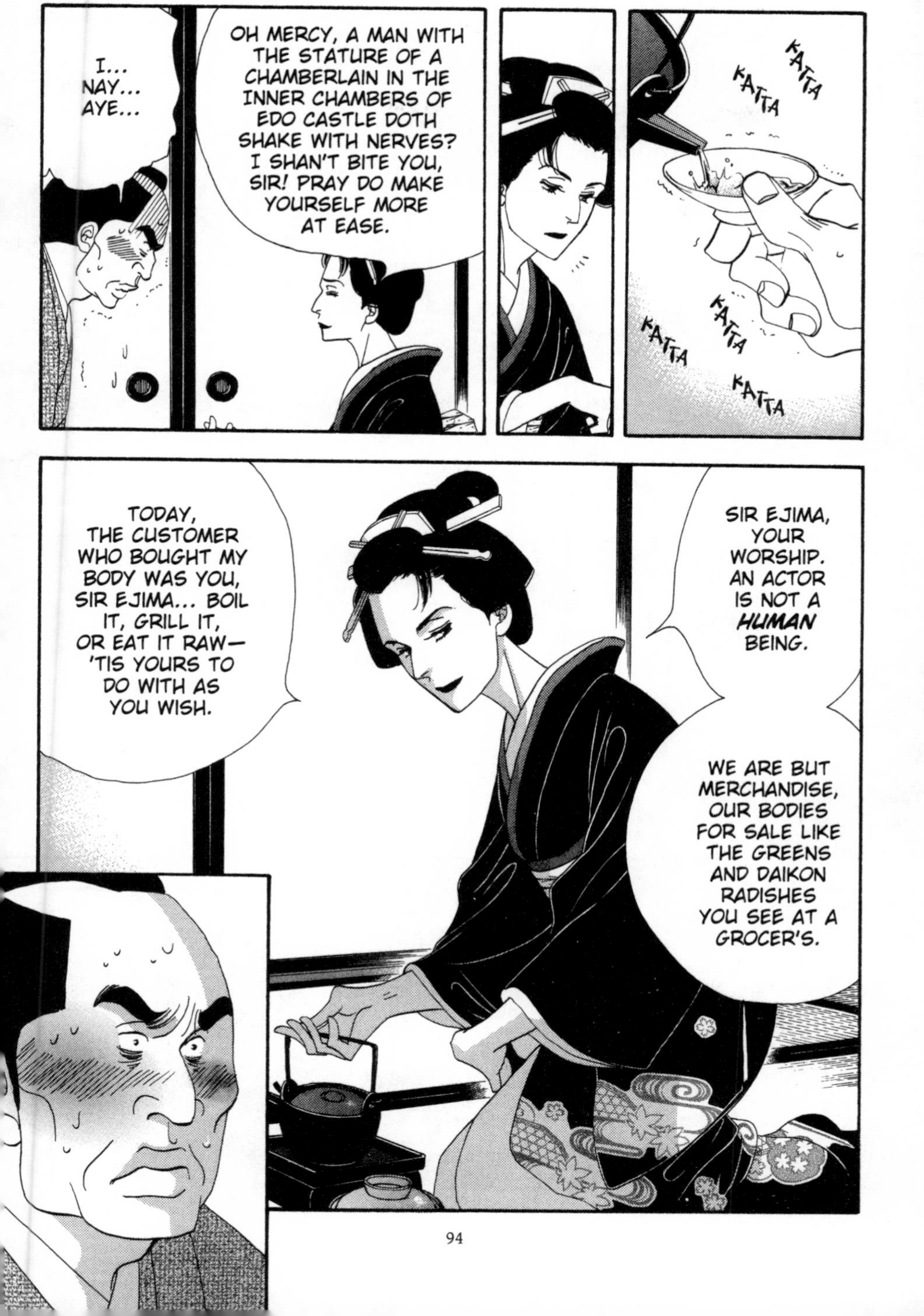
KATTA
KATTA
KATTA
KATTA
KATTA
OH MERCY, A MAN WITH THE STATURE OF A CHAMBERLAIN IN THE INNER CHAMBERS OF EDO CASTLE DOTH SHAKE WITH NERVES? I SHAN'T BITE YOU, SIR! PRAY DO MAKE YOURSELF MORE AT EASE.
I... NAY... AYE...
SIR EJIMA, YOUR WORSHIP. AN ACTOR IS NOT A HUMAN BEING.
WE ARE BUT MERCHANDISE, OUR BODIES FOR SALE LIKE THE GREENS AND DAIKON RADISHES YOU SEE AT A GROCER'S.
TODAY, THE CUSTOMER WHO BOUGHT MY BODY WAS YOU, SIR EJIMA... BOIL IT, GRILL IT, OR EAT IT RAW—'TIS YOURS TO DO WITH AS YOU WISH.

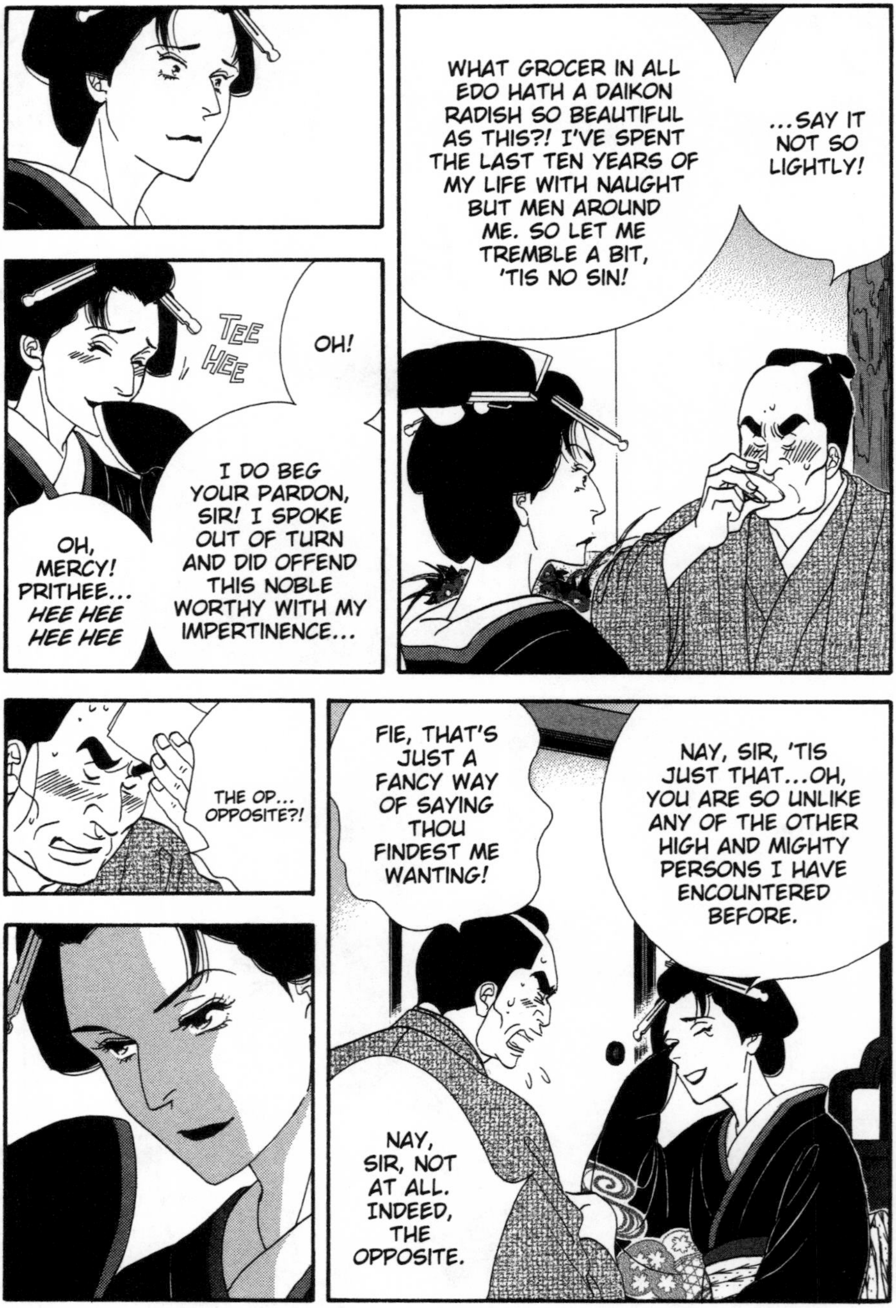
...SAY IT NOT SO LIGHTLY!
WHAT GROCER IN ALL EDO HATH A DAIKON RADISH SO BEAUTIFUL AS THIS?! I'VE SPENT THE LAST TEN YEARS OF MY LIFE WITH NAUGHT BUT MEN AROUND ME. SO LET ME TREMBLE A BIT, 'TIS NO SIN!
OH!
TEE HEE
I DO BEG YOUR PARDON, SIR! I SPOKE OUT OF TURN AND DID OFFEND THIS NOBLE WORTHY WITH MY IMPERTINENCE...
OH, MERCY! PRITHEE... *HEE HEE HEE HEE*
NAY, SIR, 'TIS JUST THAT...OH, YOU ARE SO UNLIKE ANY OF THE OTHER HIGH AND MIGHTY PERSONS I HAVE ENCOUNTERED BEFORE.
FIE, THAT'S JUST A FANCY WAY OF SAYING THOU FINDEST ME WANTING!
NAY, SIR, NOT AT ALL. INDEED, THE OPPOSITE.
THE OP... OPPOSITE?!

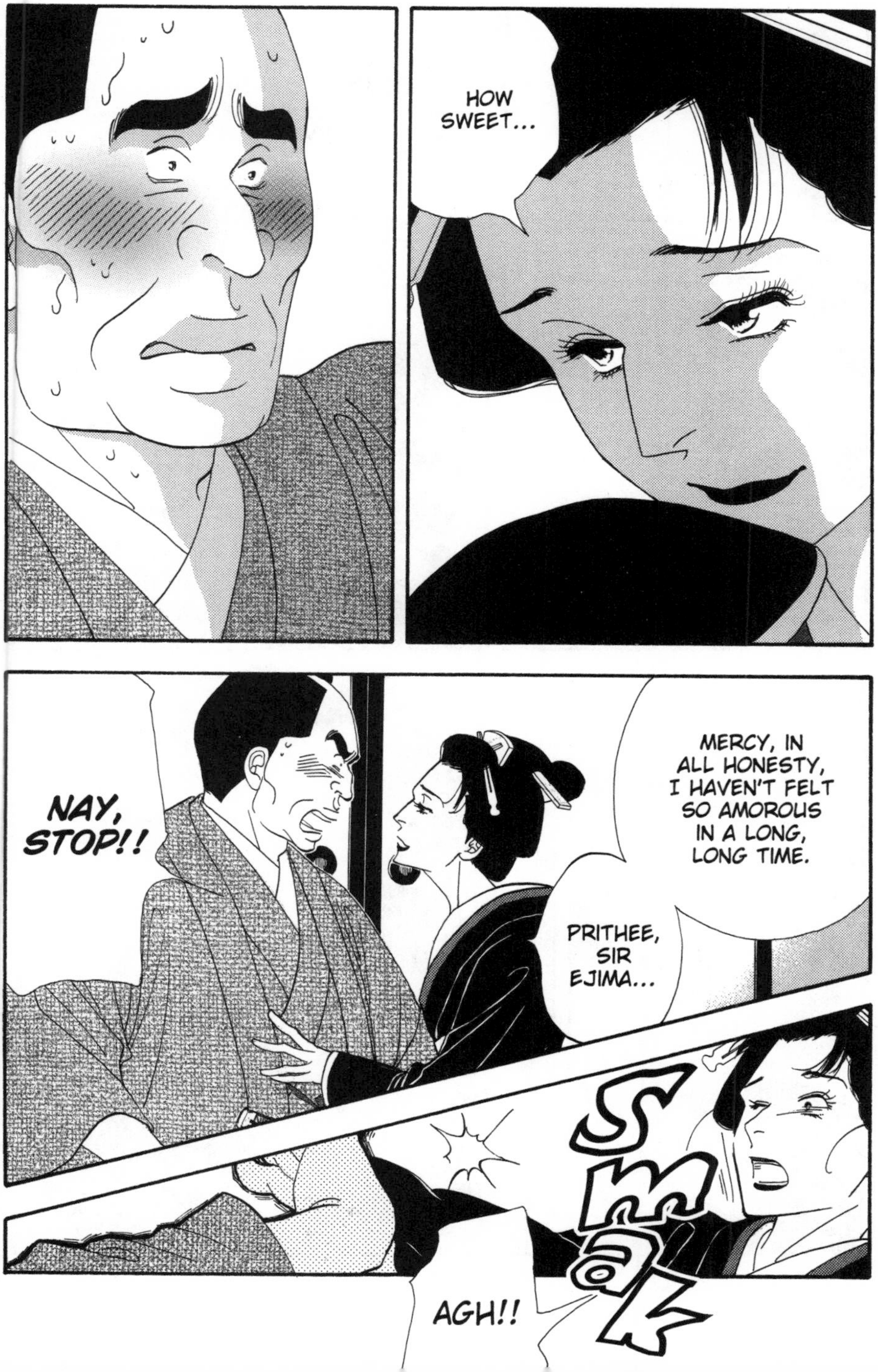
HOW SWEET...
MERCY, IN ALL HONESTY, I HAVEN'T FELT SO AMOROUS IN A LONG, LONG TIME.
PRITHEE, SIR EJIMA...
NAY, STOP!!
Smak
AGH!!

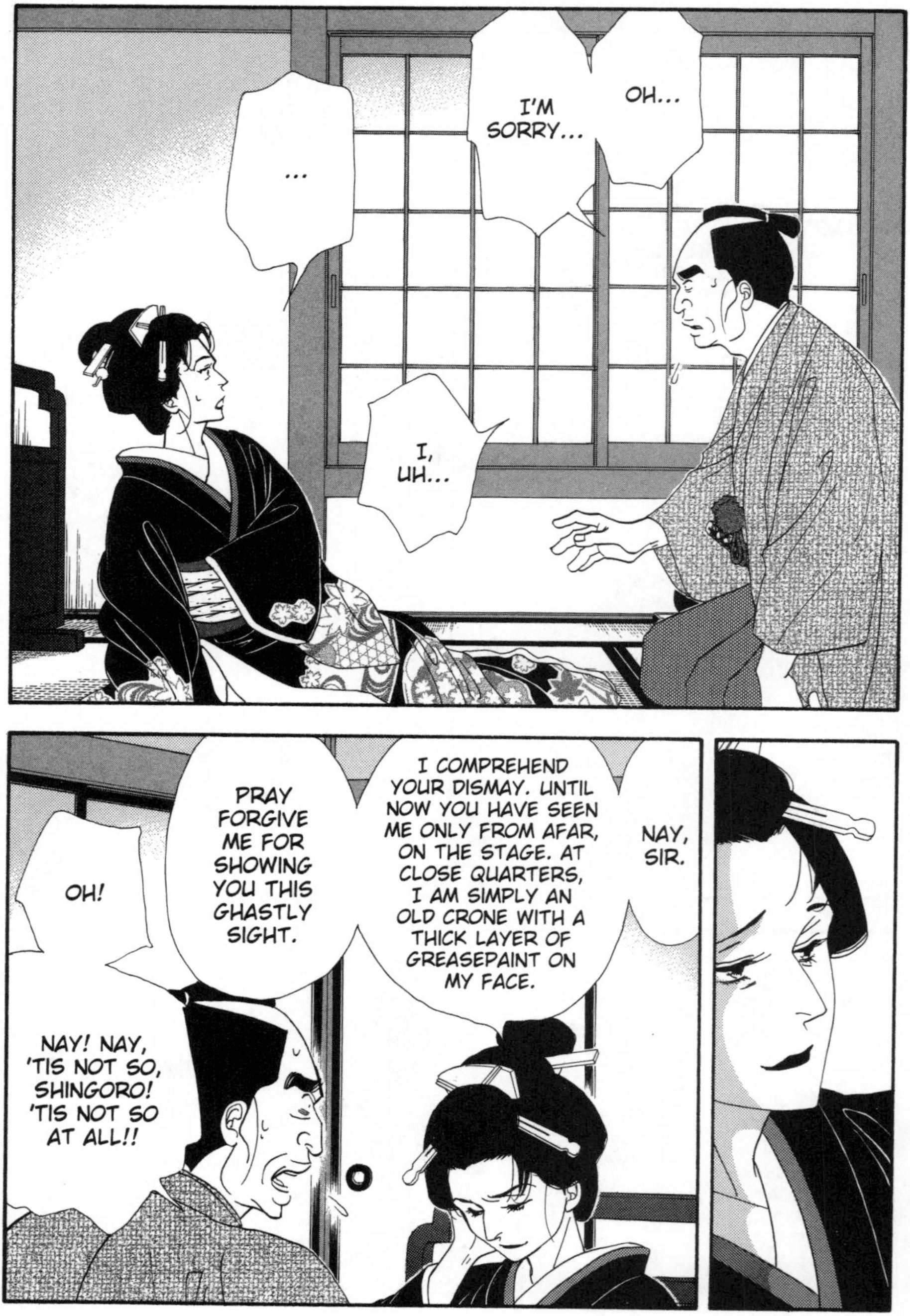
OH...
I'M SORRY...
...
I, UH...
NAY, SIR.
I COMPREHEND YOUR DISMAY. UNTIL NOW YOU HAVE SEEN ME ONLY FROM AFAR, ON THE STAGE. AT CLOSE QUARTERS, I AM SIMPLY AN OLD CRONE WITH A THICK LAYER OF GREASEPAINT ON MY FACE.
PRAY FORGIVE ME FOR SHOWING YOU THIS GHASTLY SIGHT.
OH!
NAY! NAY, 'TIS NOT SO, SHINGORO! 'TIS NOT SO AT ALL!!

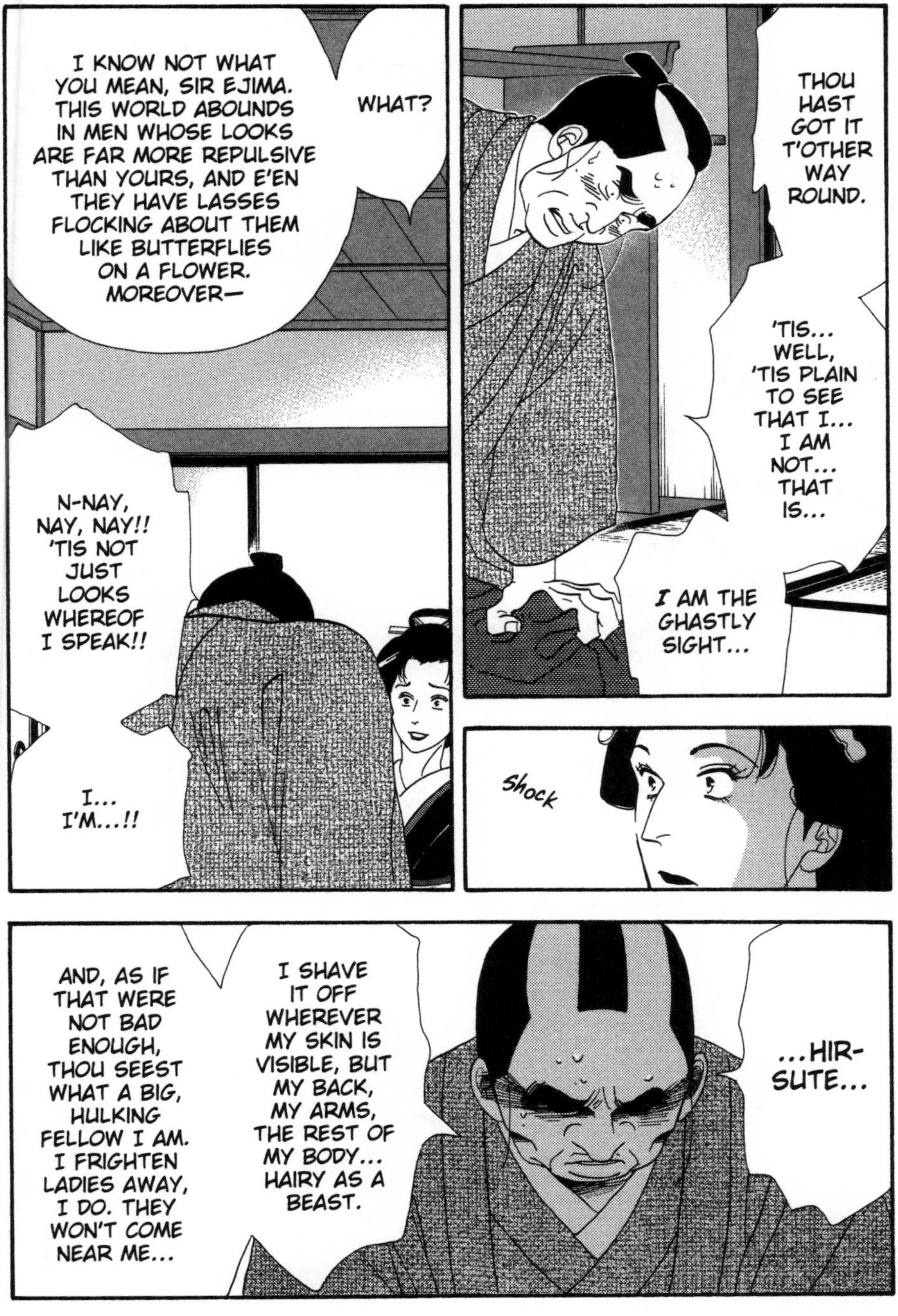
THOU HAST GOT IT T'OTHER WAY ROUND.
'TIS... WELL, 'TIS PLAIN TO SEE THAT I... I AM NOT... THAT IS...
I AM THE GHASTLY SIGHT...
Shock
WHAT?
I KNOW NOT WHAT YOU MEAN, SIR EJIMA. THIS WORLD ABOUNDS IN MEN WHOSE LOOKS ARE FAR MORE REPULSIVE THAN YOURS, AND E'EN THEY HAVE LASSES FLOCKING ABOUT THEM LIKE BUTTERFLIES ON A FLOWER. MOREOVER—
N-NAY, NAY, NAY!! 'TIS NOT JUST LOOKS WHEREOF I SPEAK!!
I... I'M...!!
...HIR-SUTE...
I SHAVE IT OFF WHEREVER MY SKIN IS VISIBLE, BUT MY BACK, MY ARMS, THE REST OF MY BODY... HAIRY AS A BEAST.
AND, AS IF THAT WERE NOT BAD ENOUGH, THOU SEEST WHAT A BIG, HULKING FELLOW I AM. I FRIGHTEN LADIES AWAY, I DO. THEY WON'T COME NEAR ME...

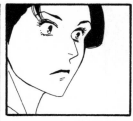

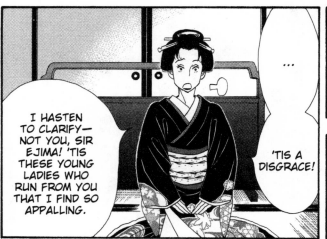

...
'TIS A DISGRACE!
I HASTEN TO CLARIFY— NOT YOU, SIR EJIMA! 'TIS THESE YOUNG LADIES WHO RUN FROM YOU THAT I FIND SO APPALLING.
WITH RESPECT, SIR, ONE LOOK AT THE DARK SHADOW OF YOUR BEARD GIVETH A GOOD IDEA ABOUT THE AMOUNT OF HAIR ON THE REST OF YOUR BODY.
BUT WHAT OF IT? MENFOLK ARE HIRSUTE— EVERYBODY KNOWS THAT, OR OUGHT TO!
ALLOW ME TO CONJECTURE THAT THESE LADIES WHO DID RECOIL FROM YOU WERE ALL HIGH-BORN MAIDS FROM THE WARRIOR CLASS?
AND HOW MANY SUCH MAIDENS DID FLEE FROM YOUR BED, SIR EJIMA, ANYWAY? I VENTURE 'TWERE NO MORE THAN FIVE OR SIX, AM I RIGHT? WELL, YOU CAN SCARCELY DRAW CONCLUSIONS ABOUT ALL WOMANKIND FROM SUCH A SAMPLE!
THEY'D NE'ER SEEN A REAL MAN'S BODY BEFORE THEY SAW YOURS, I RECKON. I DARESAY THEY HAD THE MISTAKEN BELIEF THAT ALL MEN RESEMBLE THE PALE, SMOOTH-SKINNED FOPS YOU SEE IN UKIYO-E.

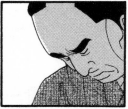

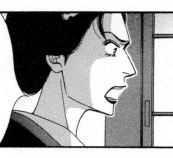

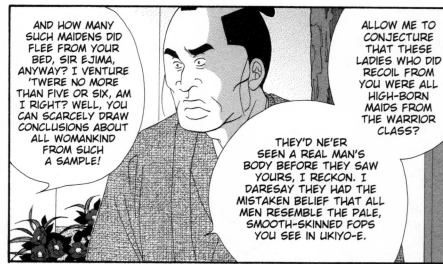

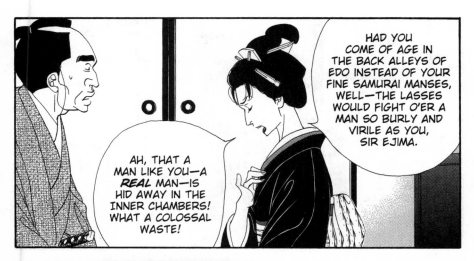

HAD YOU COME OF AGE IN THE BACK ALLEYS OF EDO INSTEAD OF YOUR FINE SAMURAI MANSES, WELL—THE LASSES WOULD FIGHT O'ER A MAN SO BURLY AND VIRILE AS YOU, SIR EJIMA.

AH, THAT A MAN LIKE YOU—A **REAL** MAN—IS HID AWAY IN THE INNER CHAMBERS! WHAT A COLOSSAL WASTE!

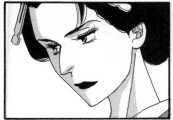

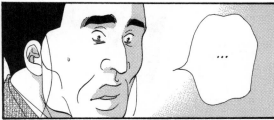

...

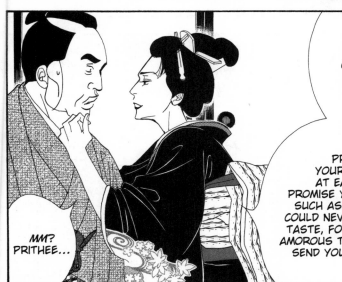

COME, SWEET SIR EJIMA. I CARE NOT A BIT ABOUT THESE CONCERNS OF YOURS.

PRAY LET YOURSELF FEEL AT EASE. I CAN PROMISE YOU PLEASURES SUCH AS A VIRGIN MAID COULD NEVER GIVE YOU TO TASTE, FOR I KNOW MANY AMOROUS TRICKS THAT WILL SEND YOU TO PARADISE.

MM? PRITHEE...

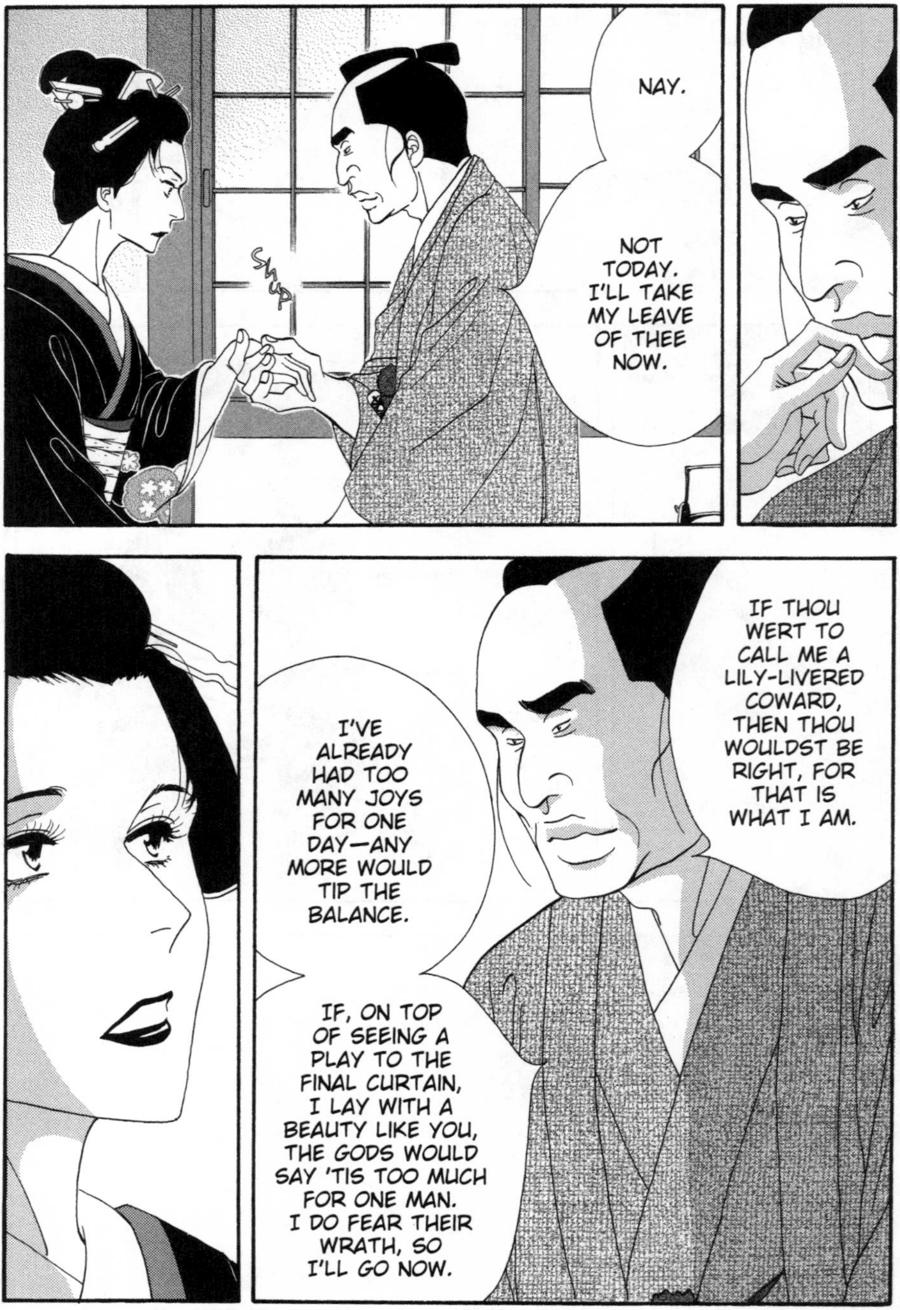
NAY.
NOT TODAY. I'LL TAKE MY LEAVE OF THEE NOW.
SMUP
IF THOU WERT TO CALL ME A LILY-LIVERED COWARD, THEN THOU WOULDST BE RIGHT, FOR THAT IS WHAT I AM.
I'VE ALREADY HAD TOO MANY JOYS FOR ONE DAY—ANY MORE WOULD TIP THE BALANCE.
IF, ON TOP OF SEEING A PLAY TO THE FINAL CURTAIN, I LAY WITH A BEAUTY LIKE YOU, THE GODS WOULD SAY 'TIS TOO MUCH FOR ONE MAN. I DO FEAR THEIR WRATH, SO I'LL GO NOW.

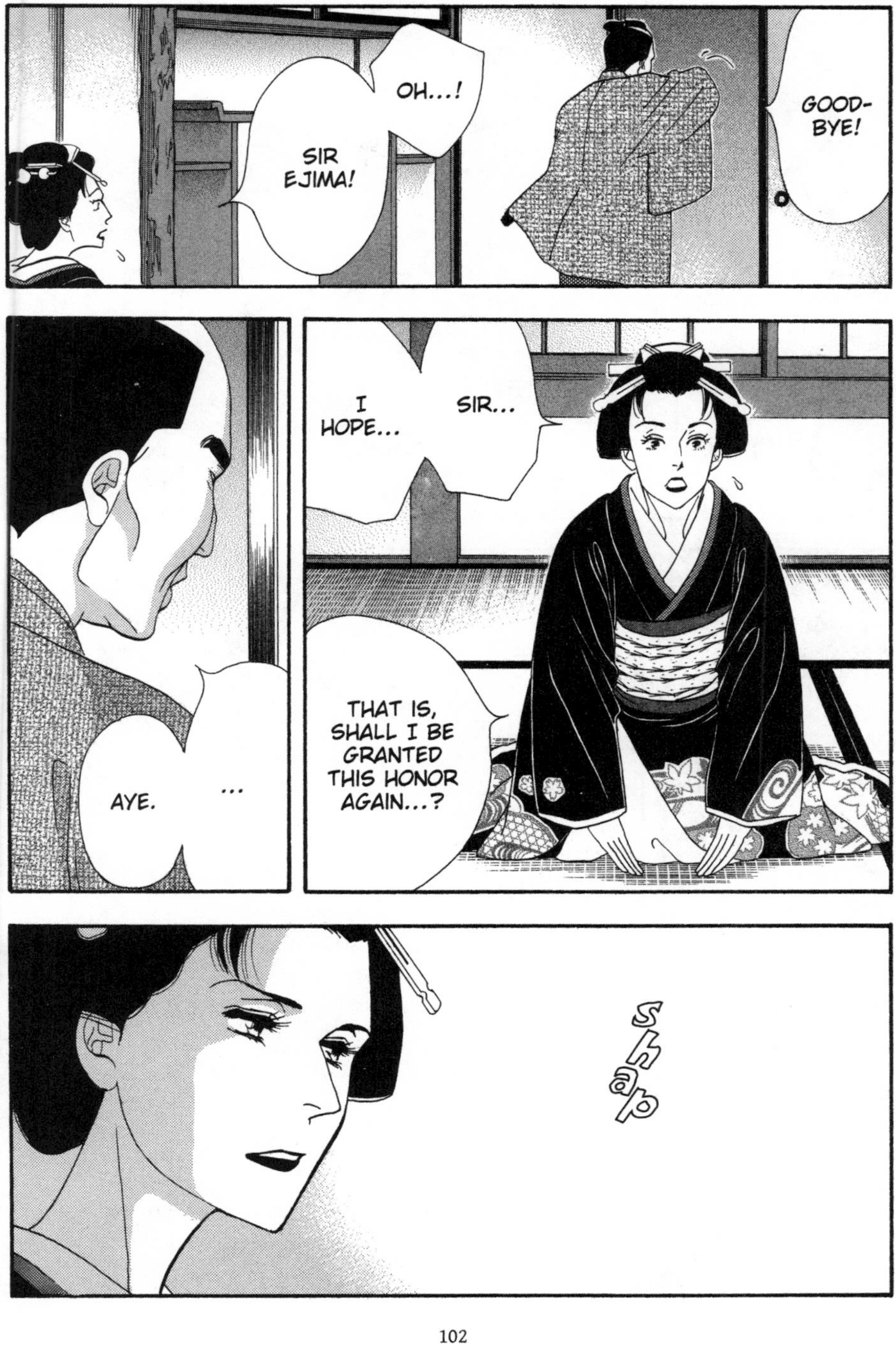

GOOD-BYE!
OH...! SIR EJIMA!
SIR...
I HOPE...
THAT IS, SHALL I BE GRANTED THIS HONOR AGAIN...?
...
AYE.
Shap

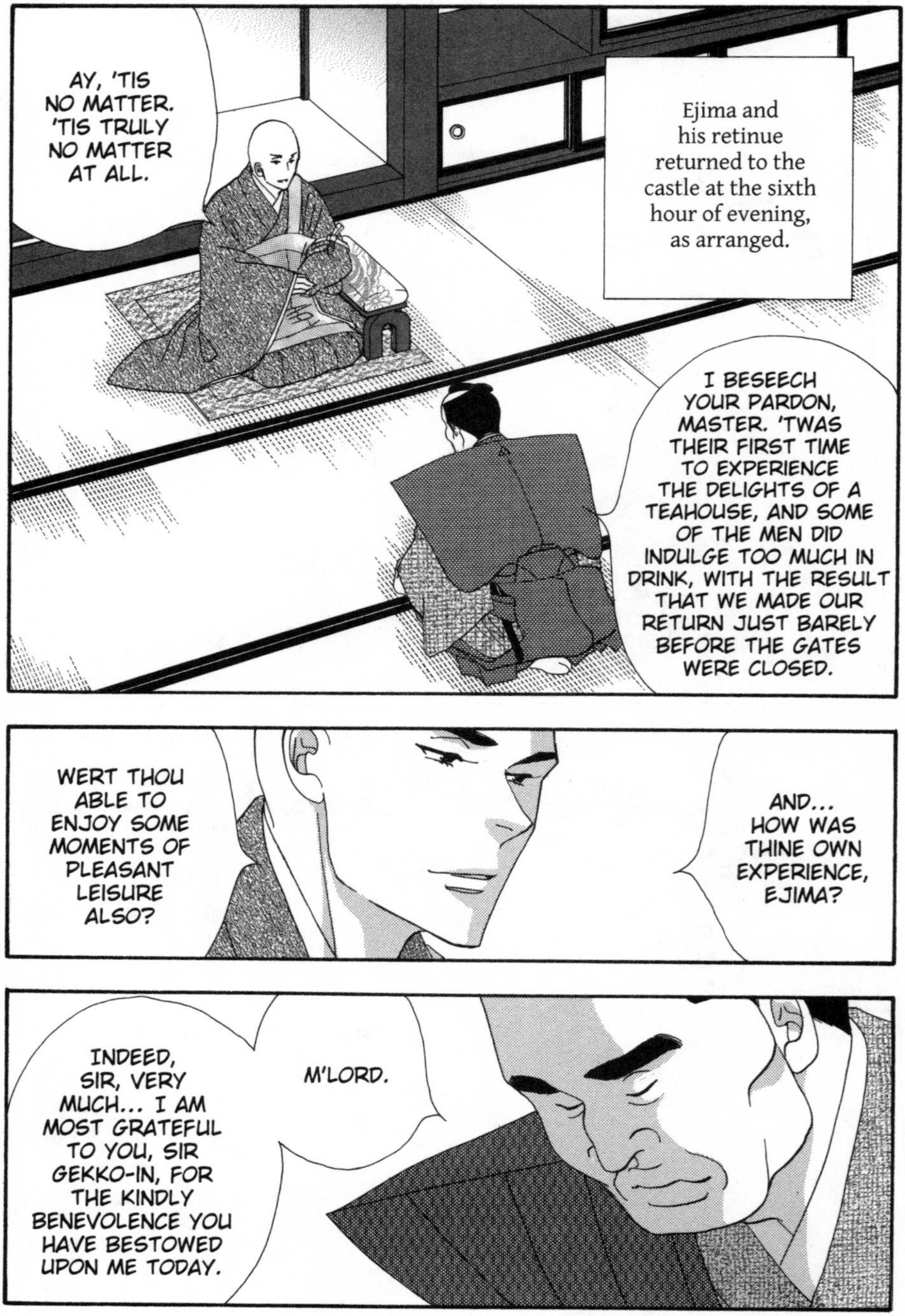
Ejima and his retinue returned to the castle at the sixth hour of evening, as arranged.
I BESEECH YOUR PARDON, MASTER. 'TWAS THEIR FIRST TIME TO EXPERIENCE THE DELIGHTS OF A TEAHOUSE, AND SOME OF THE MEN DID INDULGE TOO MUCH IN DRINK, WITH THE RESULT THAT WE MADE OUR RETURN JUST BARELY BEFORE THE GATES WERE CLOSED.
AY, 'TIS NO MATTER. 'TIS TRULY NO MATTER AT ALL.
AND... HOW WAS THINE OWN EXPERIENCE, EJIMA?
WERT THOU ABLE TO ENJOY SOME MOMENTS OF PLEASANT LEISURE ALSO?
M'LORD.
INDEED, SIR, VERY MUCH... I AM MOST GRATEFUL TO YOU, SIR GEKKO-IN, FOR THE KINDLY BENEVOLENCE YOU HAVE BESTOWED UPON ME TODAY.

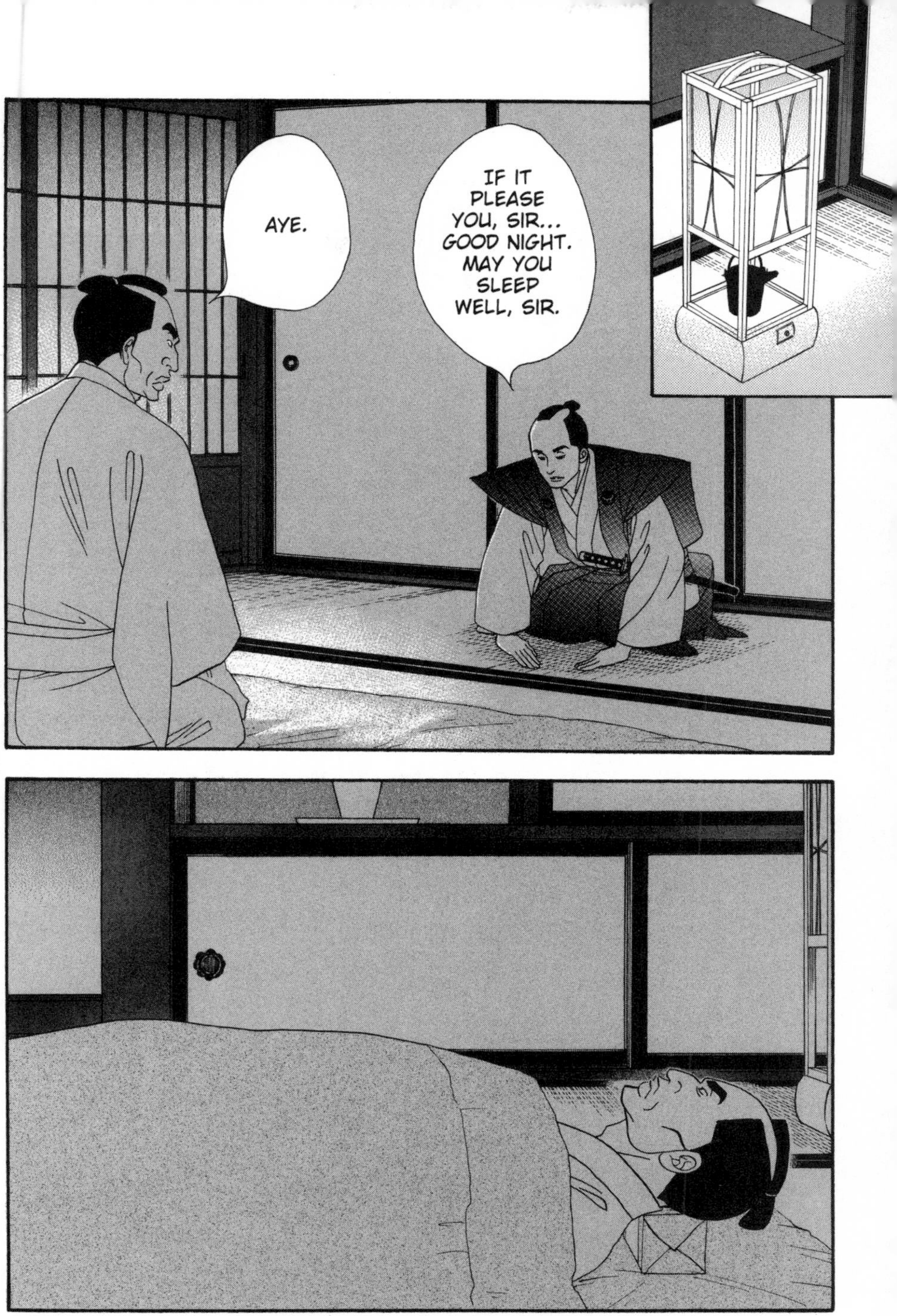
IF IT PLEASE YOU, SIR... GOOD NIGHT. MAY YOU SLEEP WELL, SIR.
AYE.

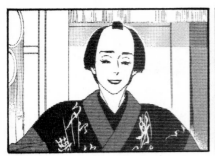
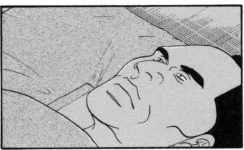
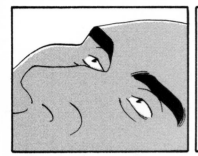
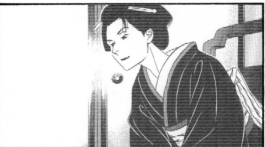
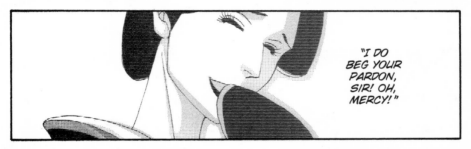

"I DO BEG YOUR PARDON, SIR! OH, MERCY!"

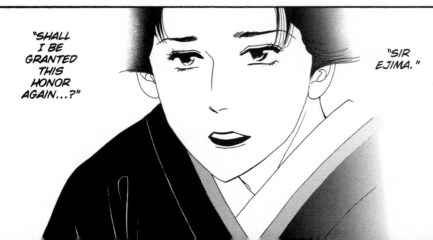

"SHALL I BE GRANTED THIS HONOR AGAIN...?"

"SIR EJIMA."

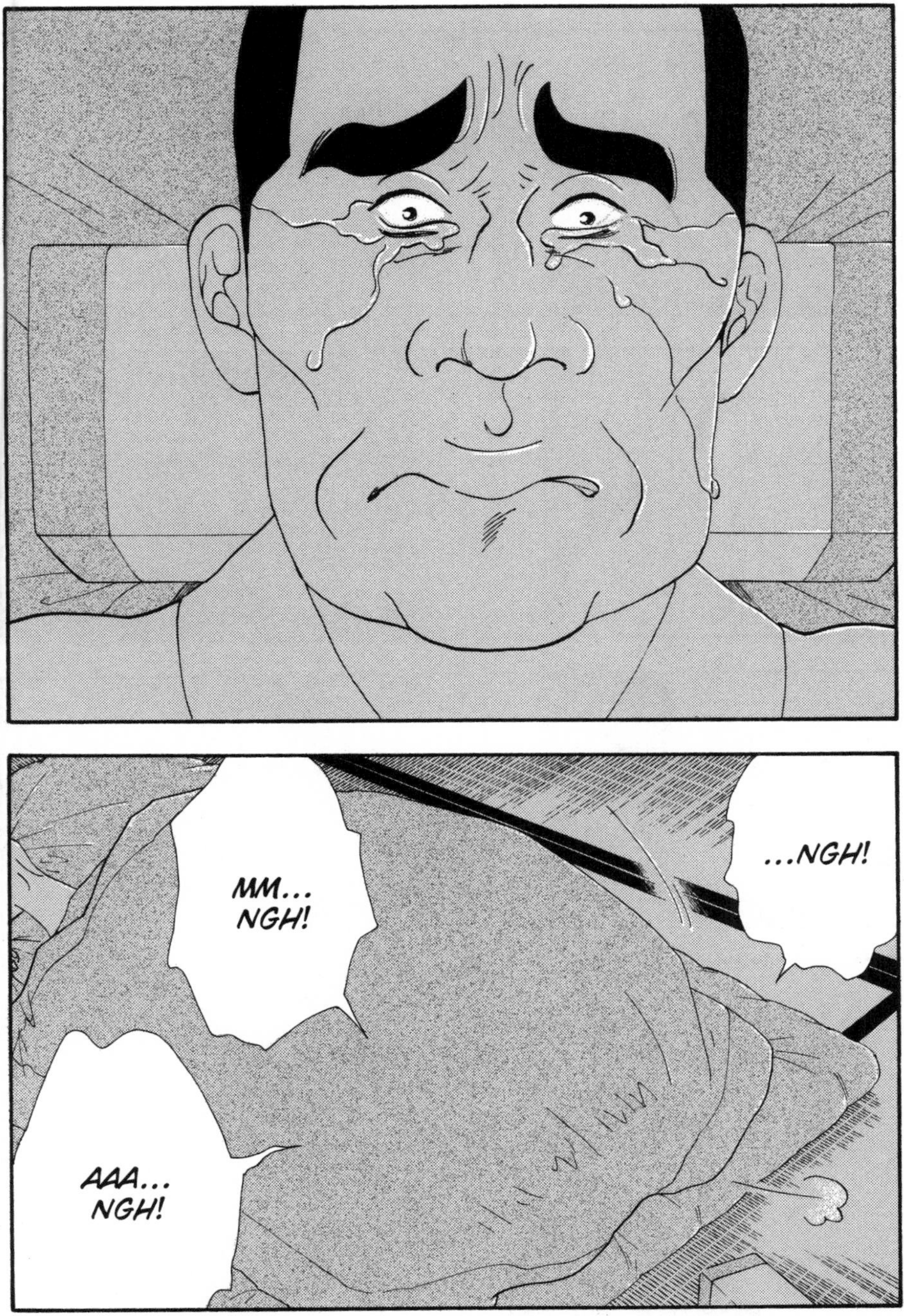
...NGH!
MM... NGH!
AAA... NGH!

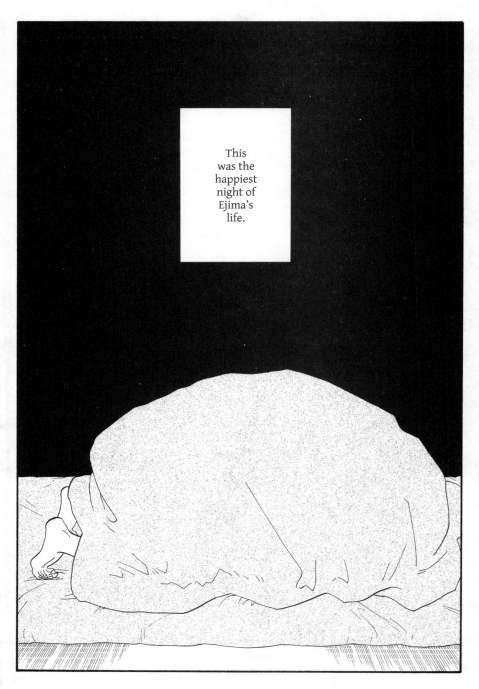

This
was the
happiest
night of
Ejima's
life.

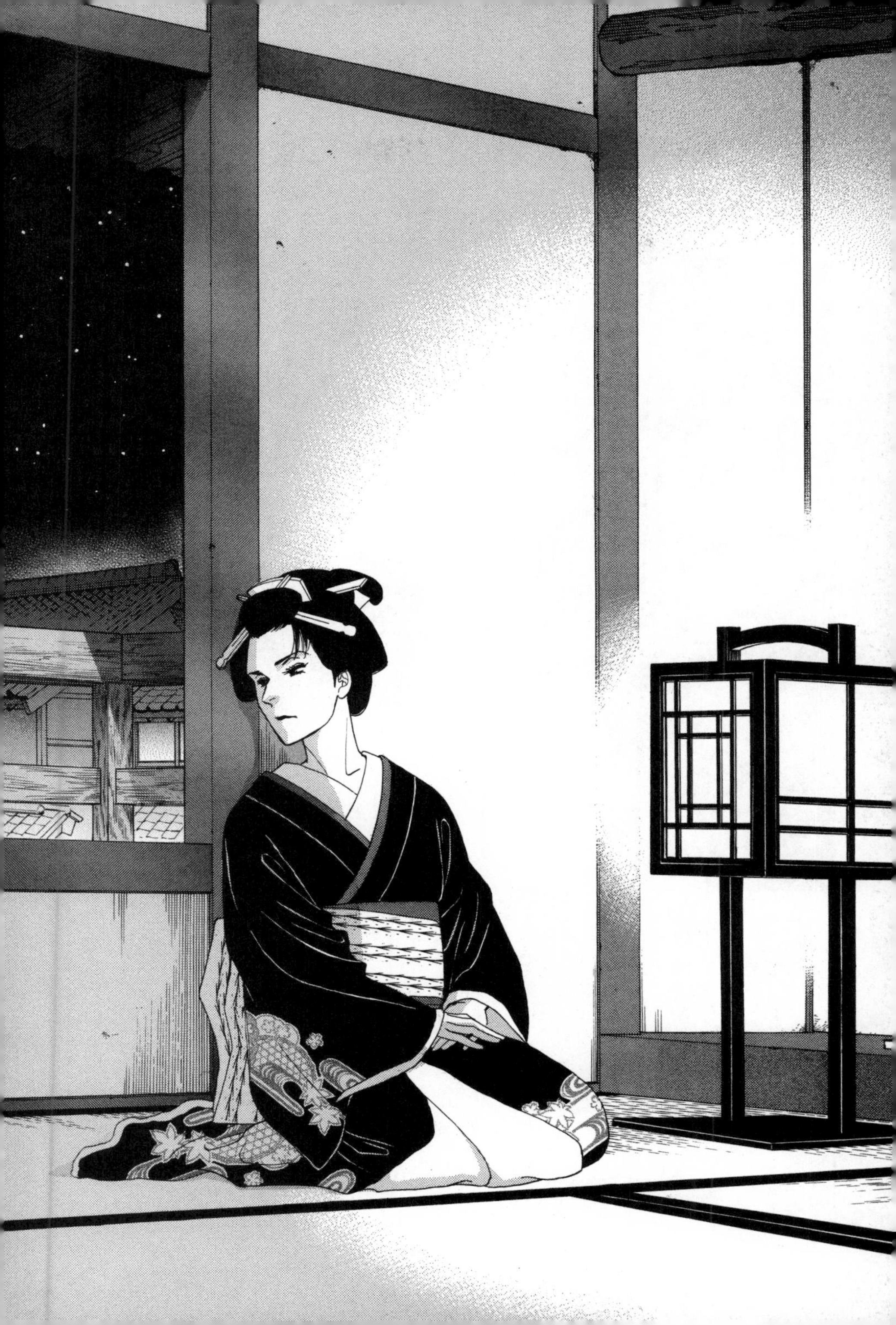

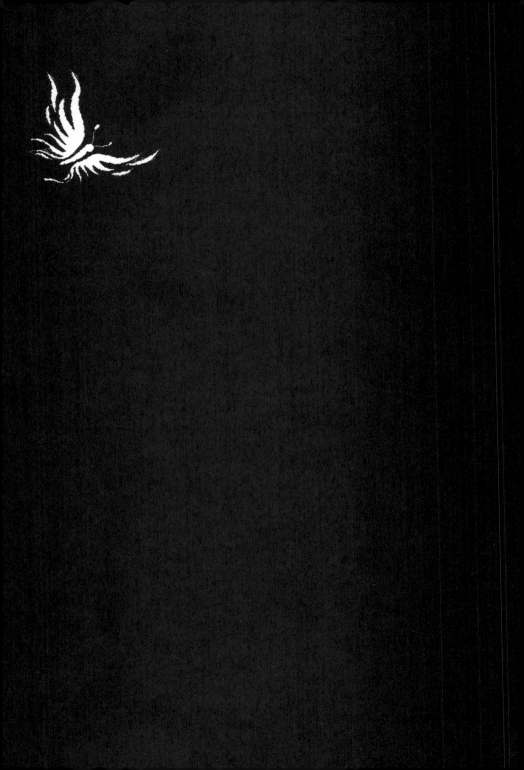

Ōoku

❀ THE INNER CHAMBERS

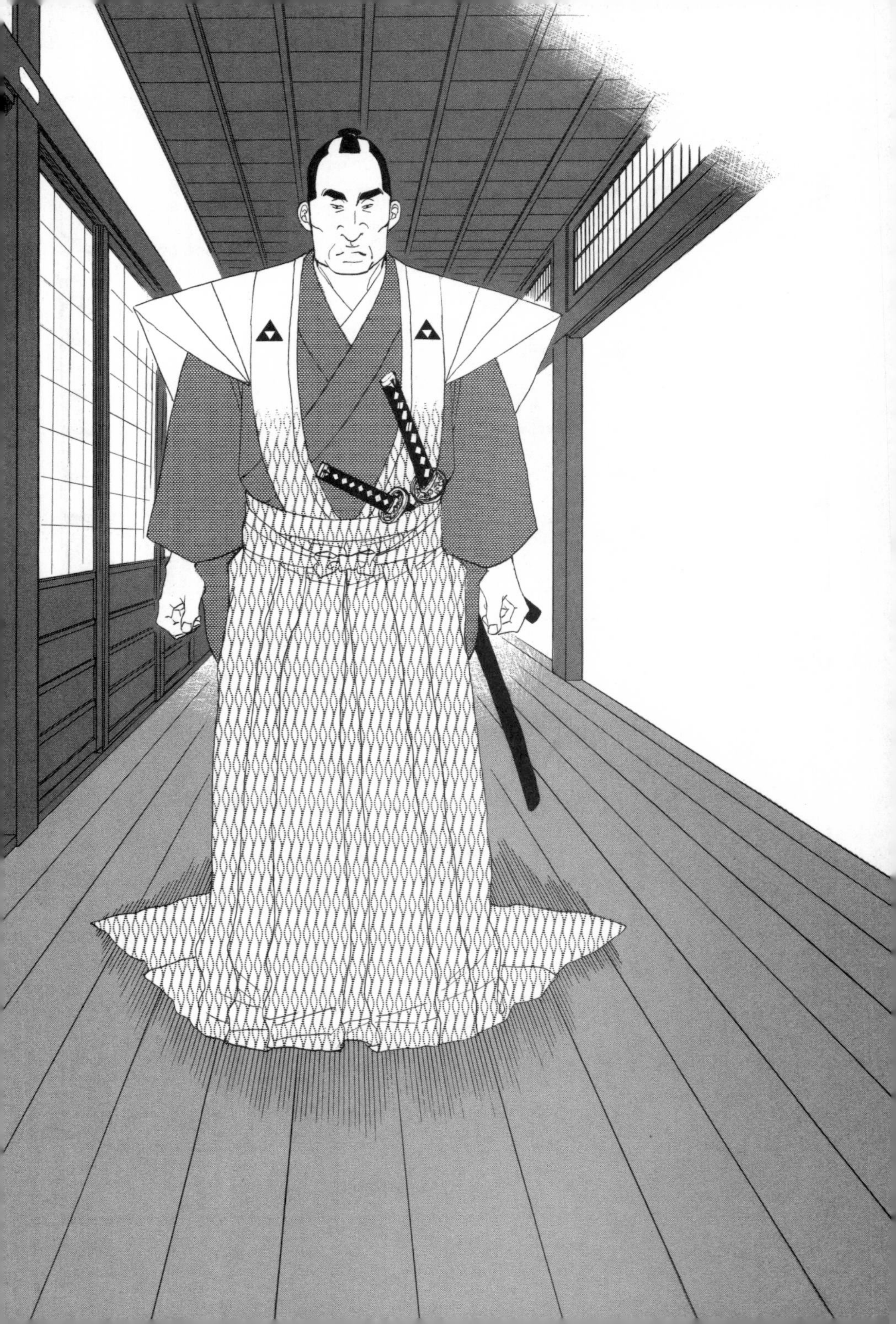

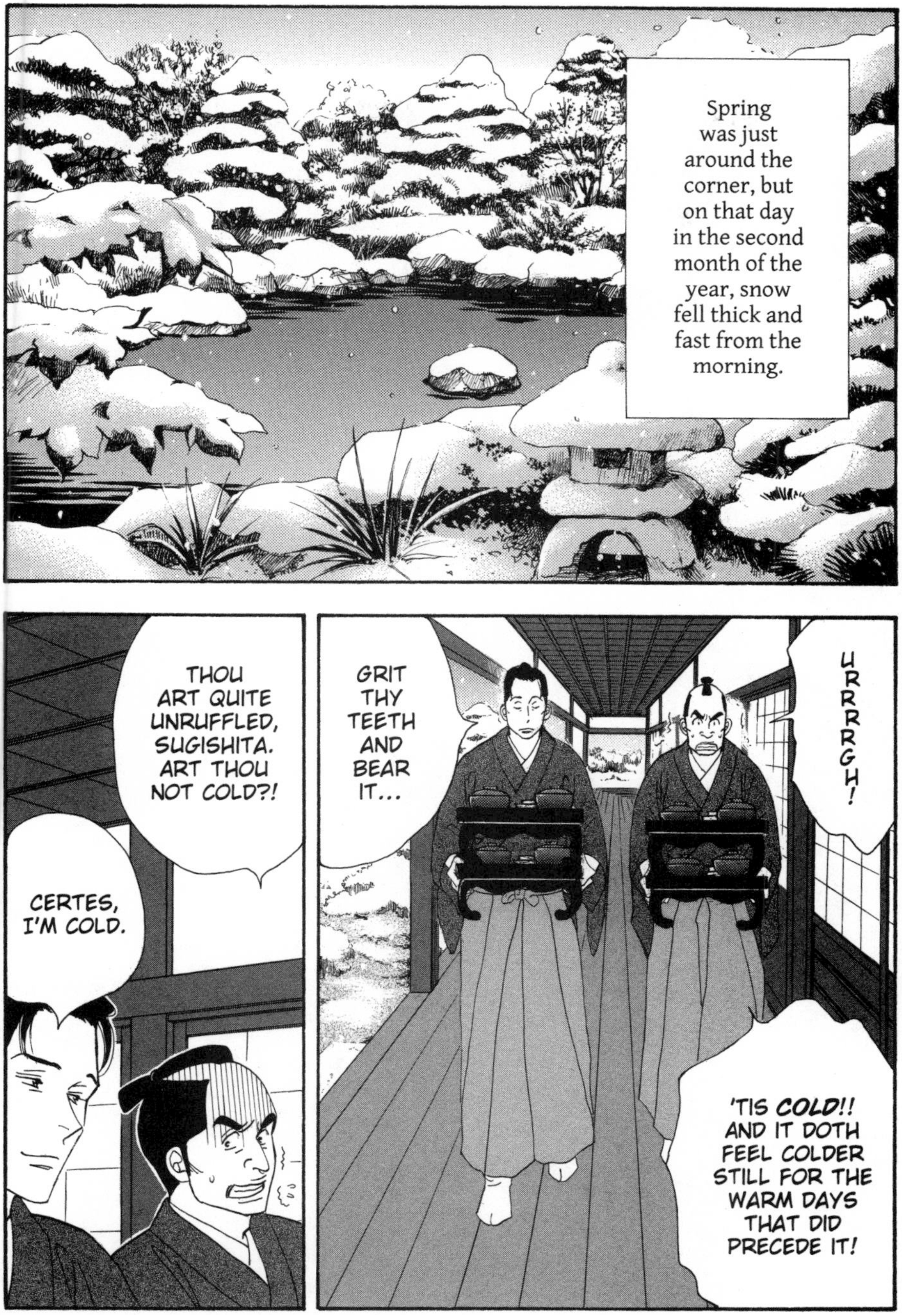
Spring was just around the corner, but on that day in the second month of the year, snow fell thick and fast from the morning.
URRRGH!
'TIS *COLD*!! AND IT DOTH FEEL COLDER STILL FOR THE WARM DAYS THAT DID PRECEDE IT!
GRIT THY TEETH AND BEAR IT...
THOU ART QUITE UNRUFFLED, SUGISHITA. ART THOU NOT COLD?!
CERTES, I'M COLD.

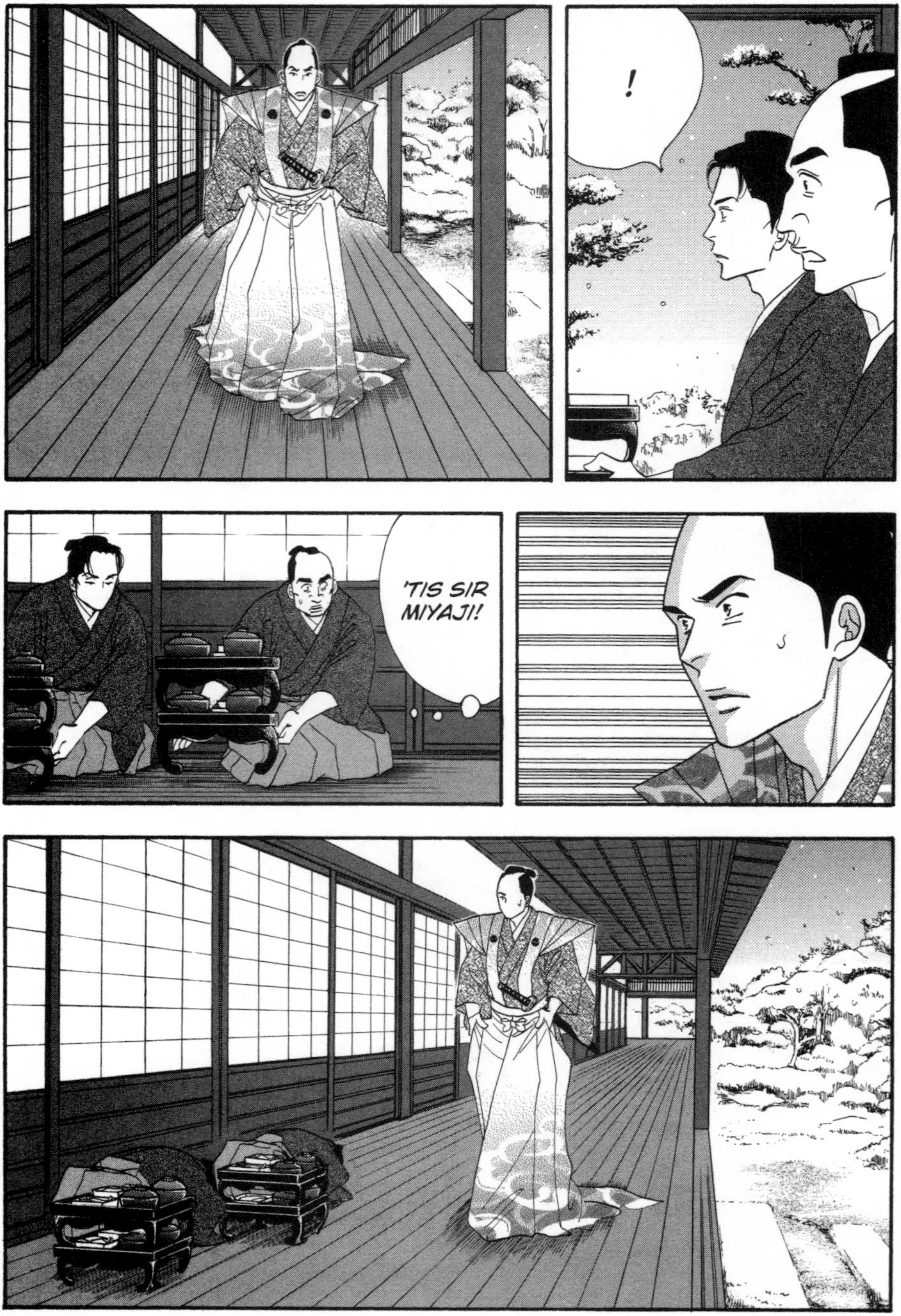
!
'TIS SIR MIYAJI!

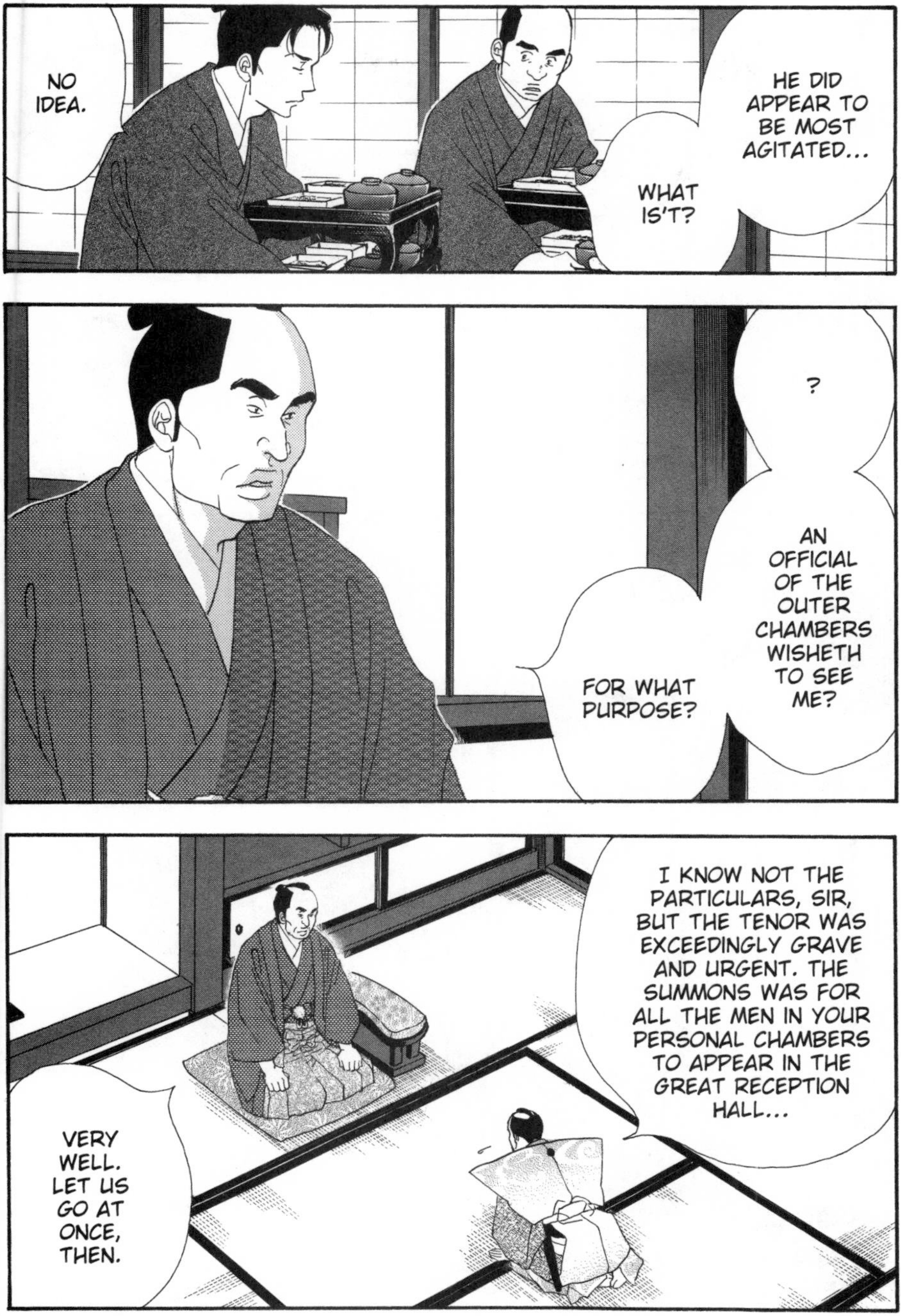
HE DID APPEAR TO BE MOST AGITATED...
WHAT IS'T?
NO IDEA.
?
AN OFFICIAL OF THE OUTER CHAMBERS WISHETH TO SEE ME?
FOR WHAT PURPOSE?
I KNOW NOT THE PARTICULARS, SIR, BUT THE TENOR WAS EXCEEDINGLY GRAVE AND URGENT. THE SUMMONS WAS FOR ALL THE MEN IN YOUR PERSONAL CHAMBERS TO APPEAR IN THE GREAT RECEPTION HALL...
VERY WELL. LET US GO AT ONCE, THEN.

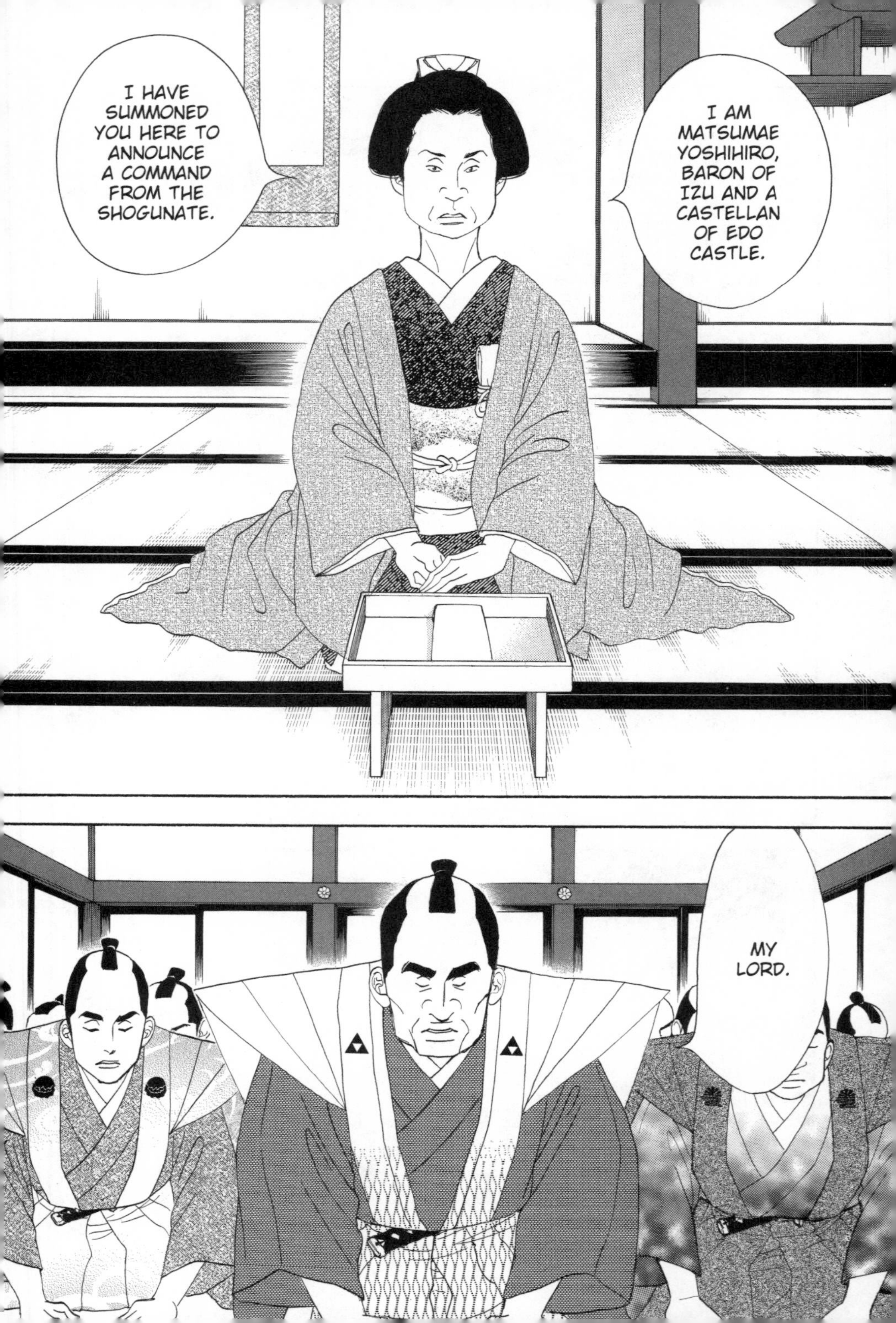
I AM MATSUMAE YOSHIHIRO, BARON OF IZU AND A CASTELLAN OF EDO CASTLE.
I HAVE SUMMONED YOU HERE TO ANNOUNCE A COMMAND FROM THE SHOGUNATE.
MY LORD.

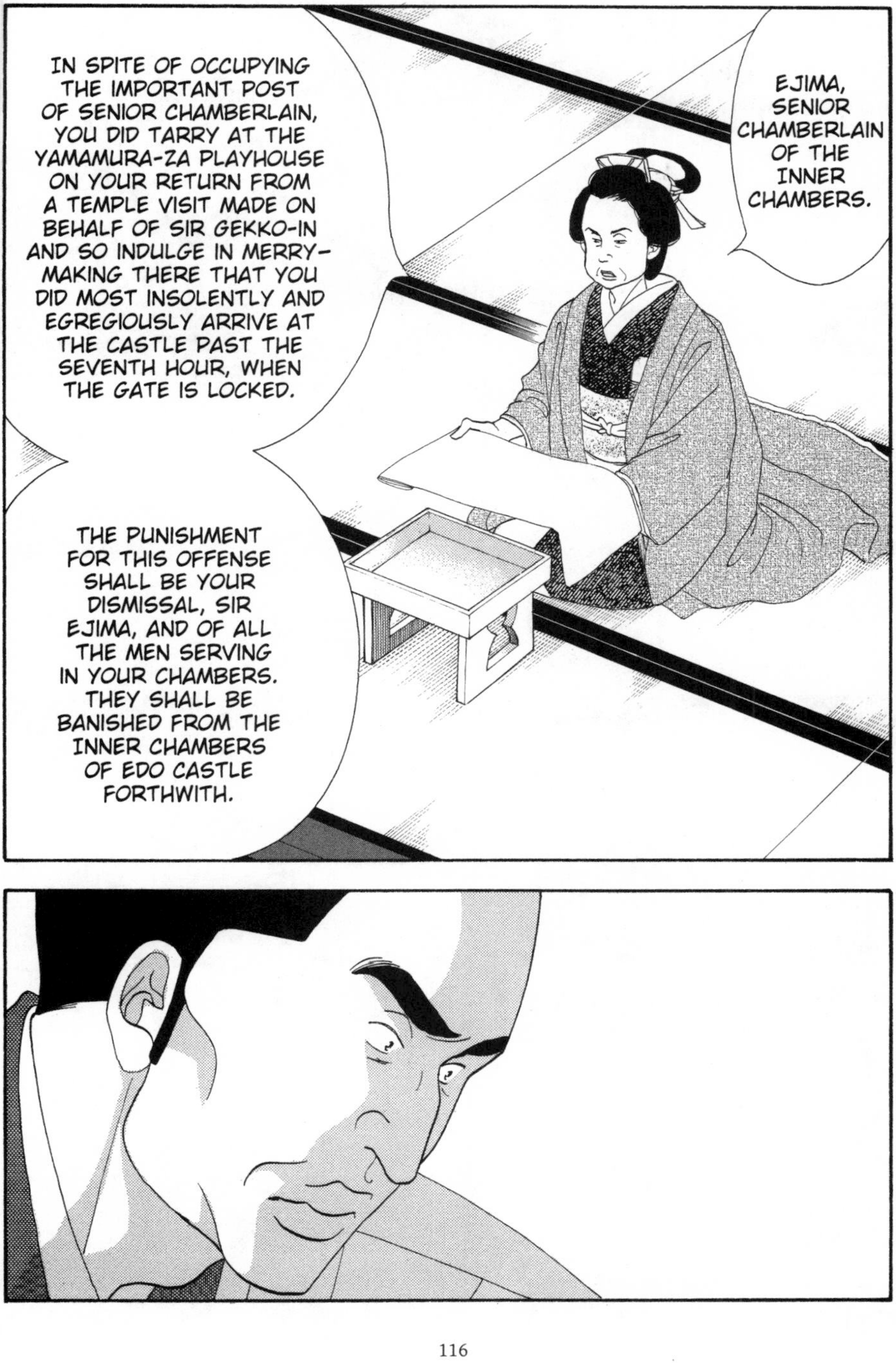
EJIMA, SENIOR CHAMBERLAIN OF THE INNER CHAMBERS.
IN SPITE OF OCCUPYING THE IMPORTANT POST OF SENIOR CHAMBERLAIN, YOU DID TARRY AT THE YAMAMURA-ZA PLAYHOUSE ON YOUR RETURN FROM A TEMPLE VISIT MADE ON BEHALF OF SIR GEKKO-IN AND SO INDULGE IN MERRY-MAKING THERE THAT YOU DID MOST INSOLENTLY AND EGREGIOUSLY ARRIVE AT THE CASTLE PAST THE SEVENTH HOUR, WHEN THE GATE IS LOCKED.
THE PUNISHMENT FOR THIS OFFENSE SHALL BE YOUR DISMISSAL, SIR EJIMA, AND OF ALL THE MEN SERVING IN YOUR CHAMBERS. THEY SHALL BE BANISHED FROM THE INNER CHAMBERS OF EDO CASTLE FORTHWITH.

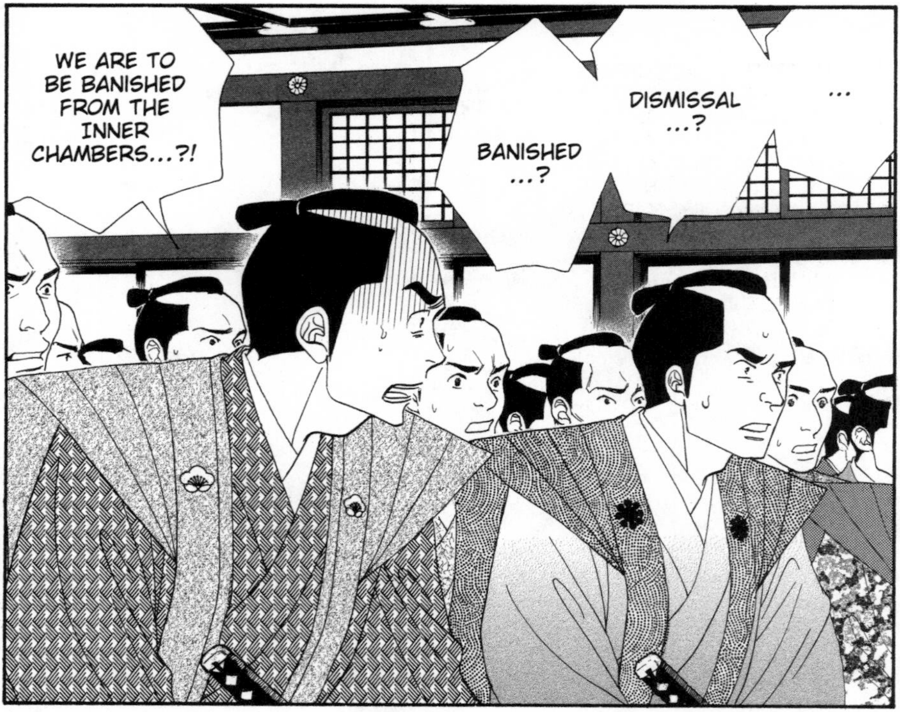
...
DISMISSAL ...?
BANISHED ...?
WE ARE TO BE BANISHED FROM THE INNER CHAMBERS...?!

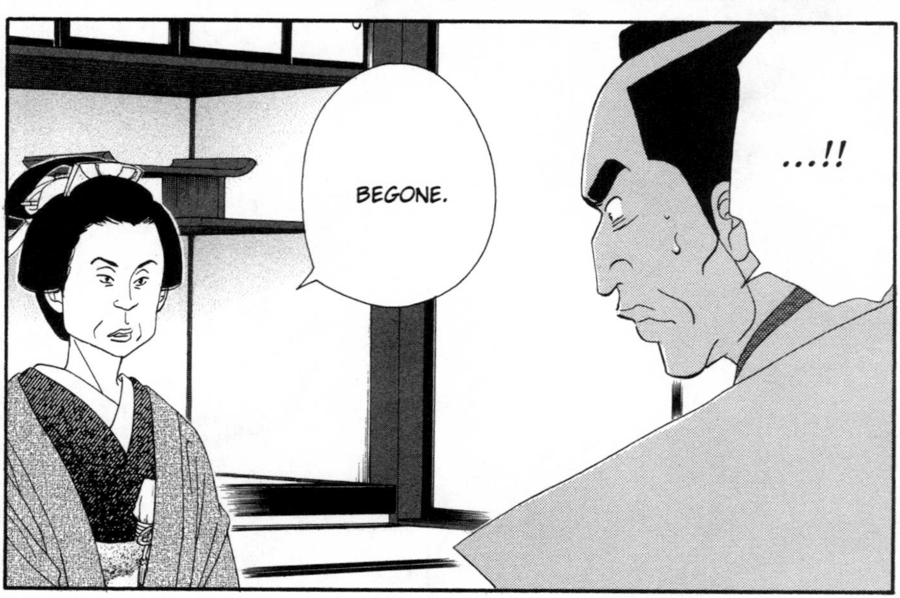
...!!
BEGONE.

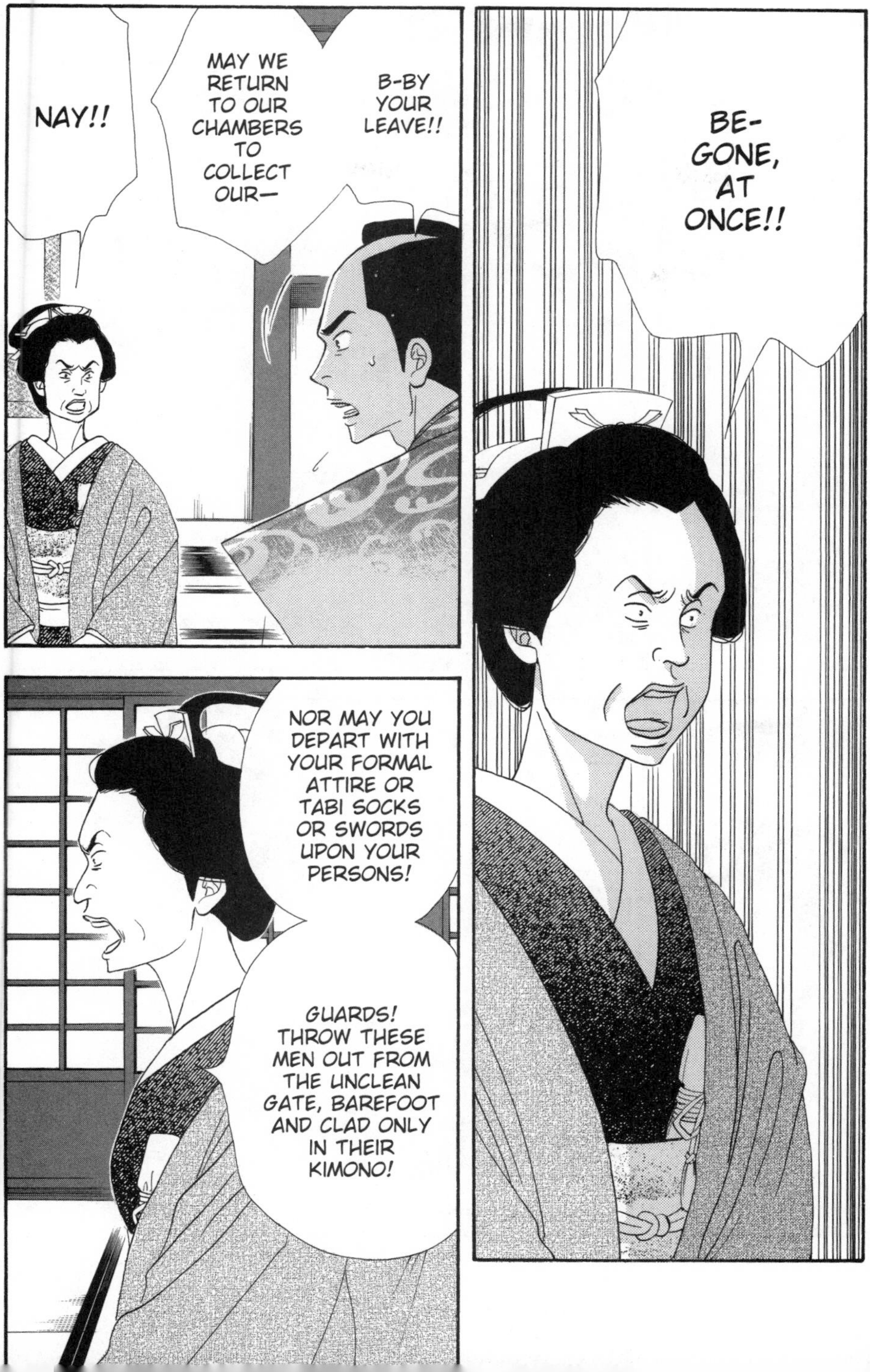
BE-GONE, AT ONCE!!
B-BY YOUR LEAVE!!
MAY WE RETURN TO OUR CHAMBERS TO COLLECT OUR—
NAY!!
NOR MAY YOU DEPART WITH YOUR FORMAL ATTIRE OR TABI SOCKS OR SWORDS UPON YOUR PERSONS!
GUARDS! THROW THESE MEN OUT FROM THE UNCLEAN GATE, BAREFOOT AND CLAD ONLY IN THEIR KIMONO!

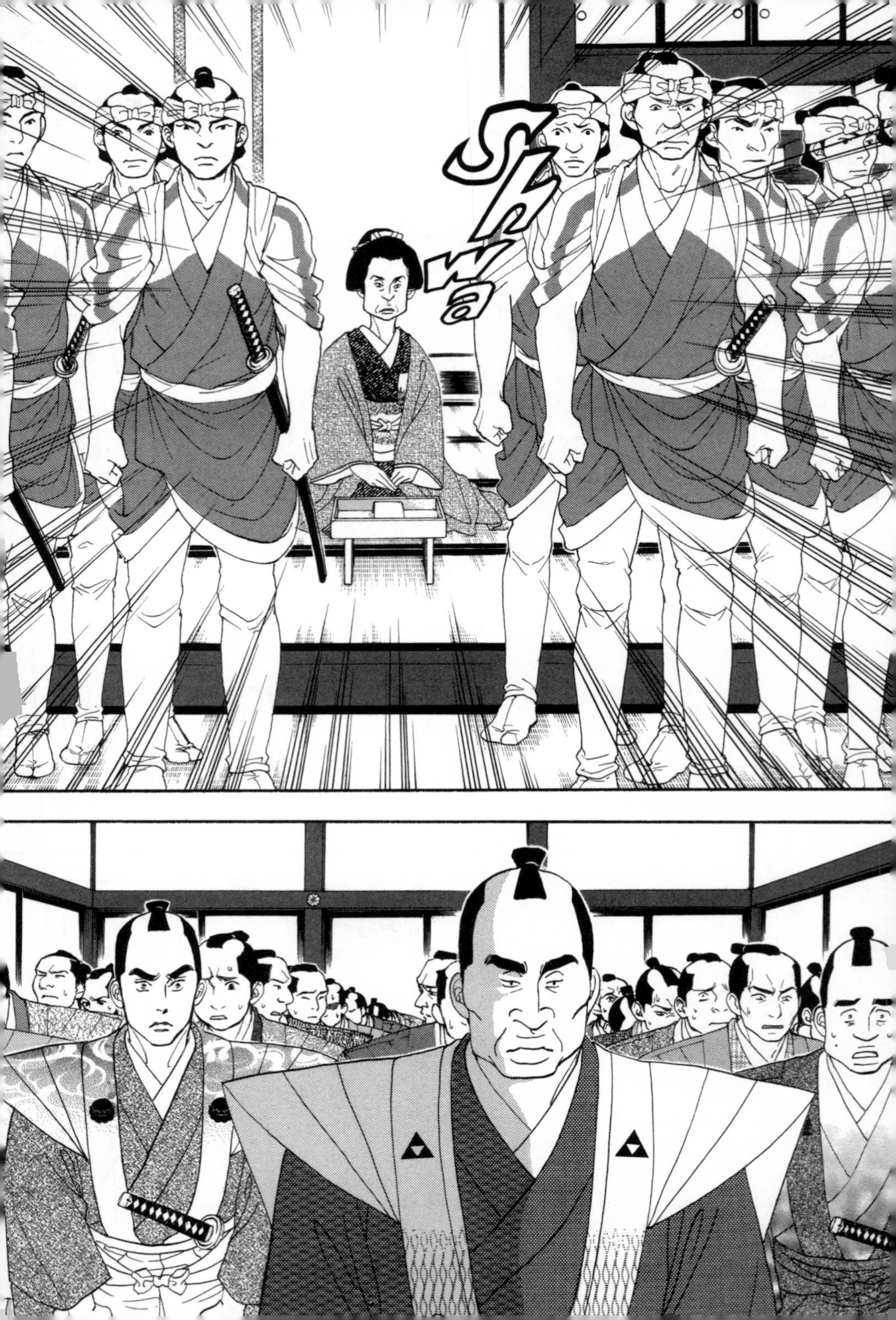
Shwa

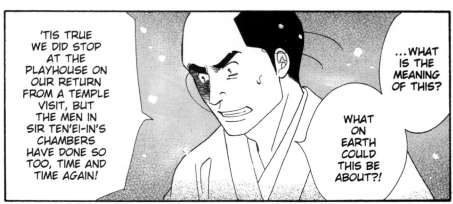

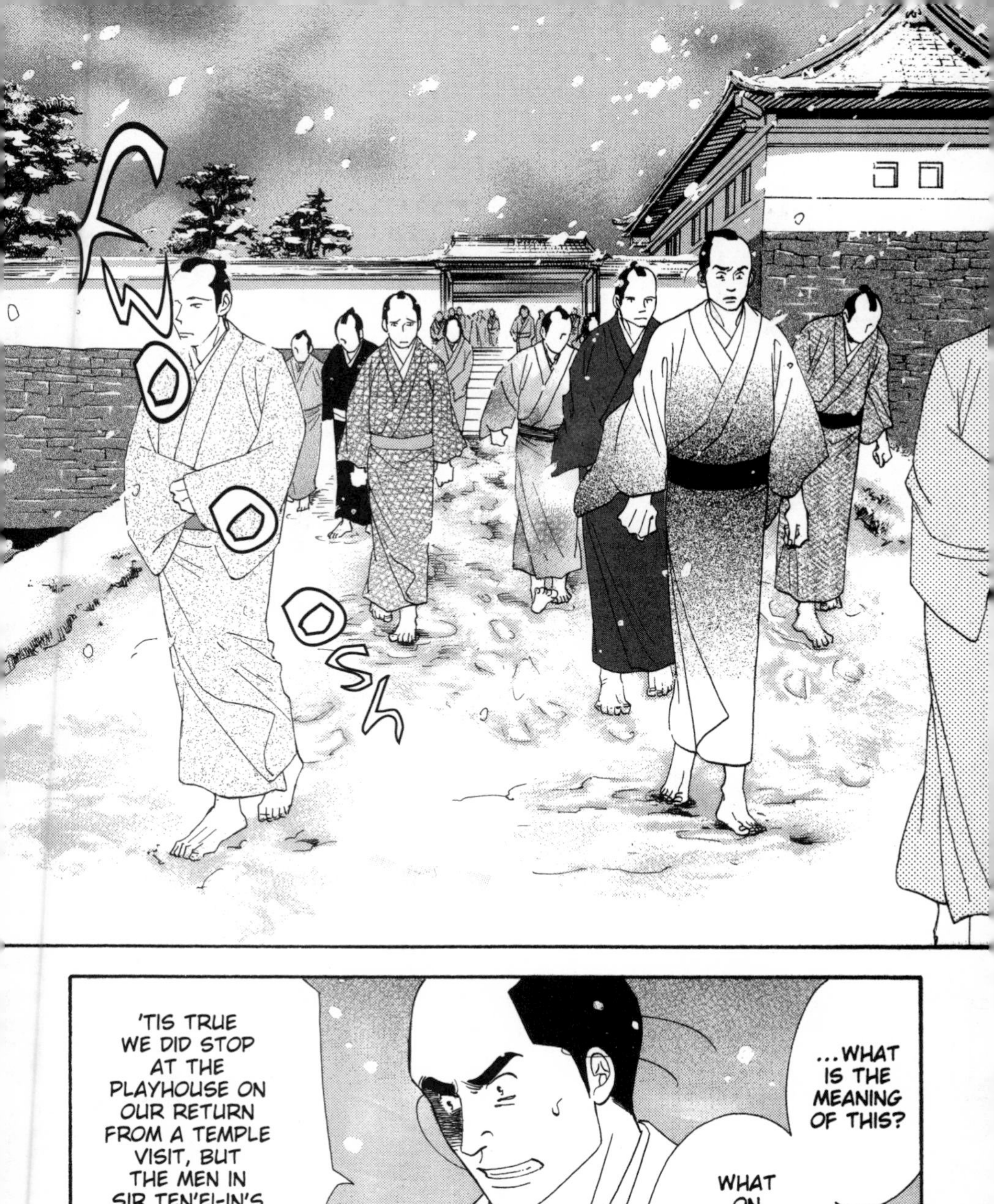
FWOOOSH
...WHAT IS THE MEANING OF THIS?
WHAT ON EARTH COULD THIS BE ABOUT?!
'TIS TRUE WE DID STOP AT THE PLAYHOUSE ON OUR RETURN FROM A TEMPLE VISIT, BUT THE MEN IN SIR TEN'EI-IN'S CHAMBERS HAVE DONE SO TOO, TIME AND TIME AGAIN!

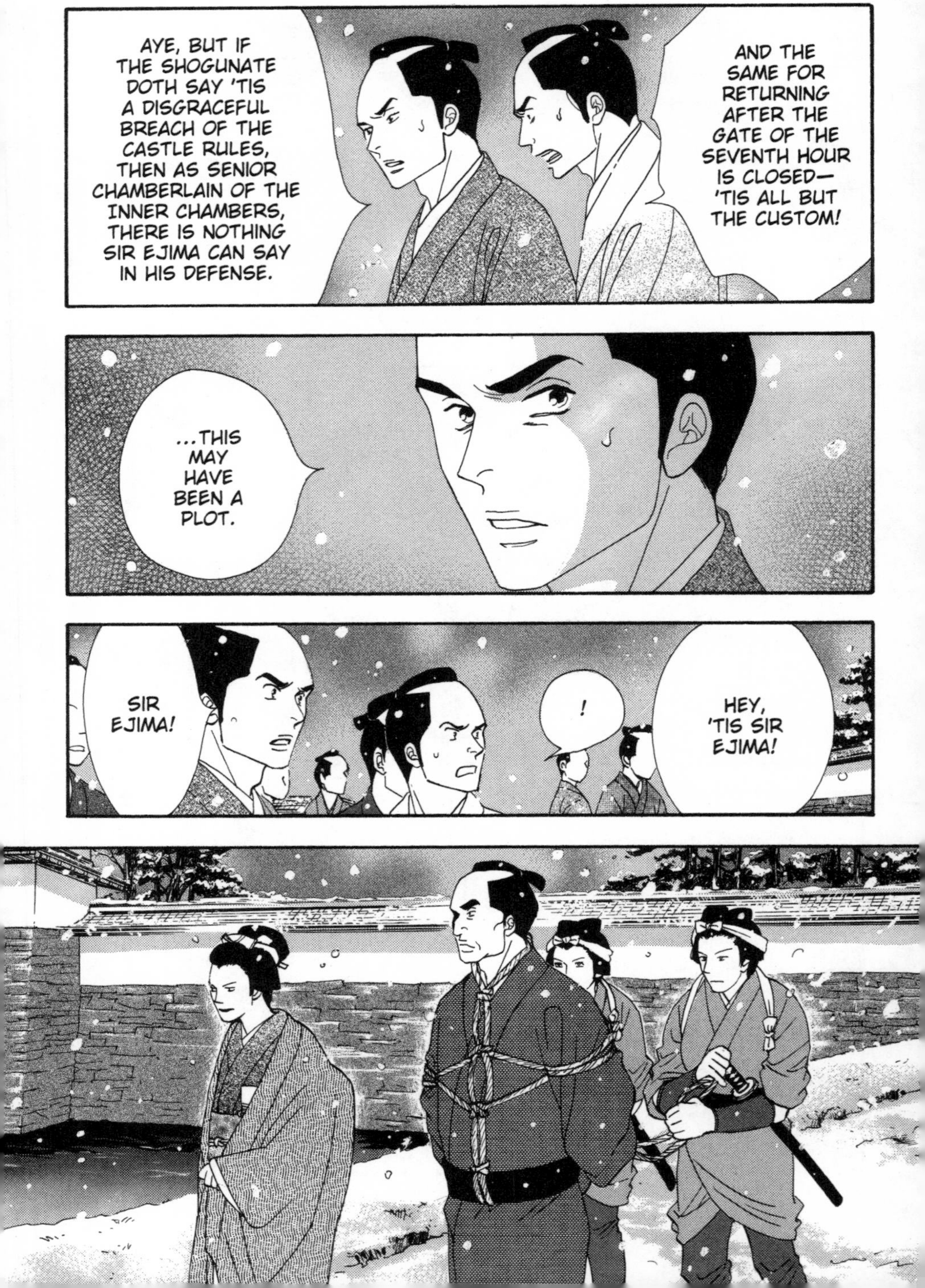
AND THE SAME FOR RETURNING AFTER THE GATE OF THE SEVENTH HOUR IS CLOSED— 'TIS ALL BUT THE CUSTOM!
AYE, BUT IF THE SHOGUNATE DOTH SAY 'TIS A DISGRACEFUL BREACH OF THE CASTLE RULES, THEN AS SENIOR CHAMBERLAIN OF THE INNER CHAMBERS, THERE IS NOTHING SIR EJIMA CAN SAY IN HIS DEFENSE.
...THIS MAY HAVE BEEN A PLOT.
HEY, 'TIS SIR EJIMA!
!
SIR EJIMA!

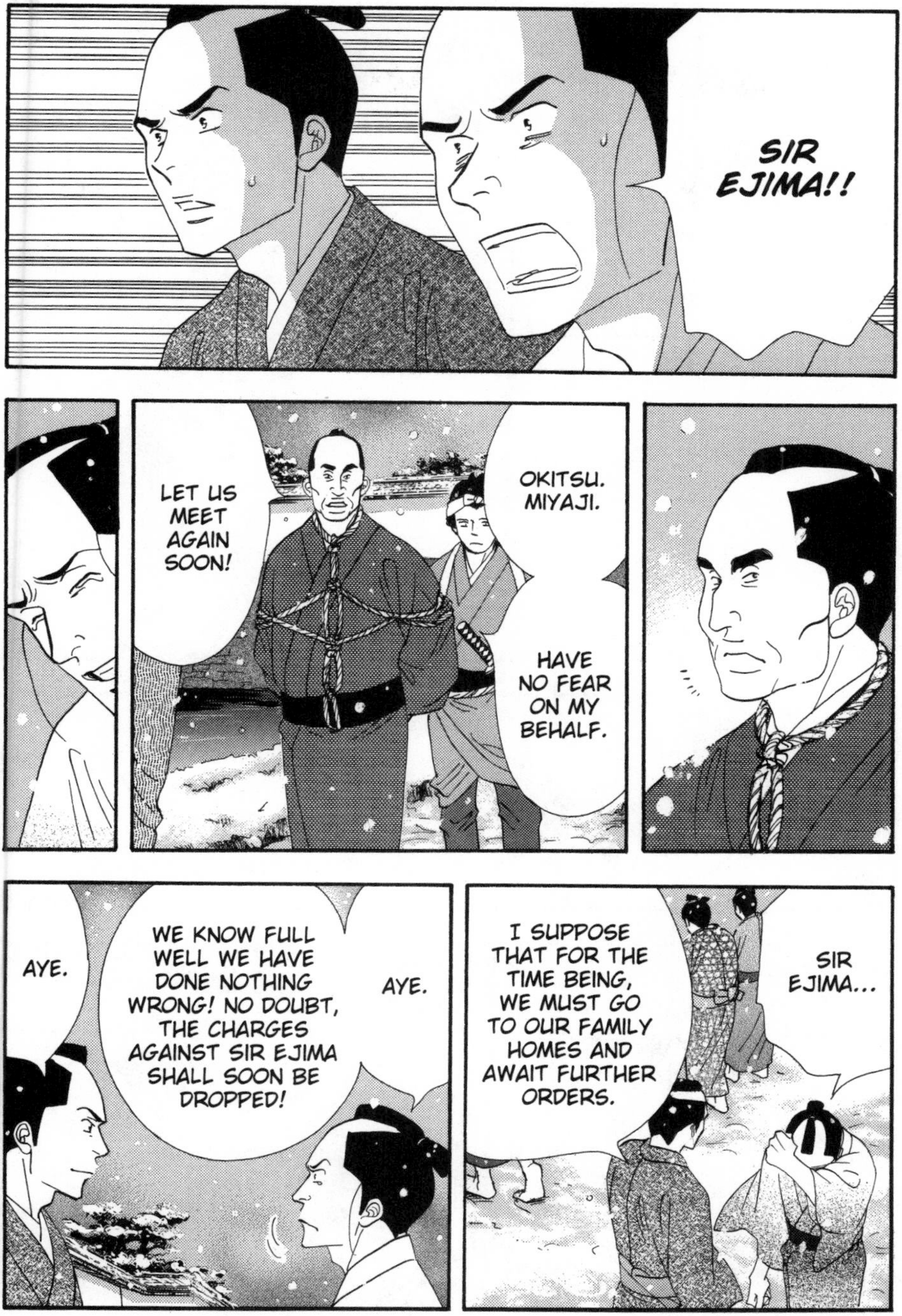
SIR EJIMA!!
OKITSU. MIYAJI.
HAVE NO FEAR ON MY BEHALF.
LET US MEET AGAIN SOON!
SIR EJIMA...
I SUPPOSE THAT FOR THE TIME BEING, WE MUST GO TO OUR FAMILY HOMES AND AWAIT FURTHER ORDERS.
AYE.
WE KNOW FULL WELL WE HAVE DONE NOTHING WRONG! NO DOUBT, THE CHARGES AGAINST SIR EJIMA SHALL SOON BE DROPPED!
AYE.

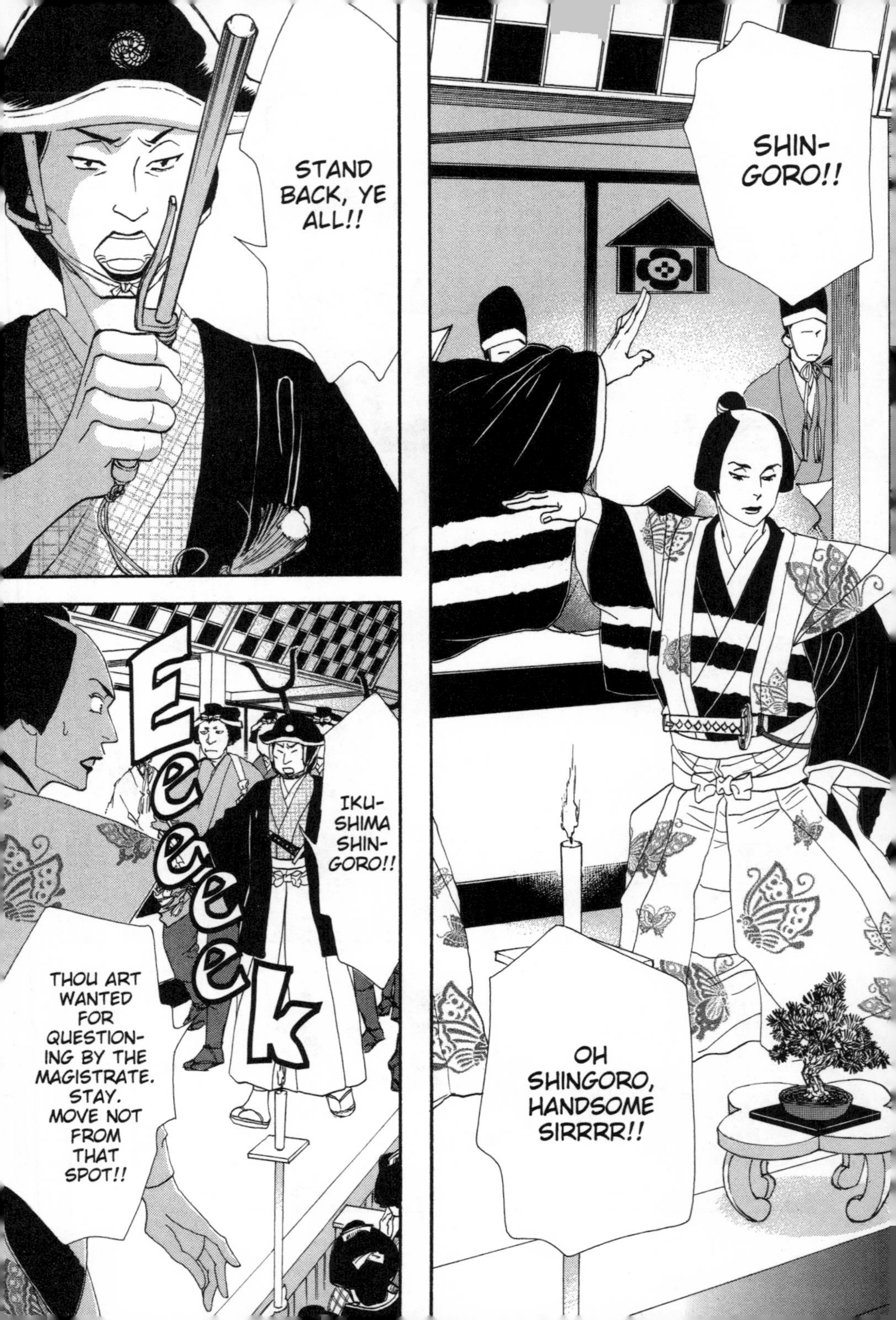
SHIN-GORO!!
OH SHINGORO, HANDSOME SIRRRR!!
STAND BACK, YE ALL!!
IKU-SHIMA SHIN-GORO!!
Eeeeek
THOU ART WANTED FOR QUESTIONING BY THE MAGISTRATE. STAY. MOVE NOT FROM THAT SPOT!!

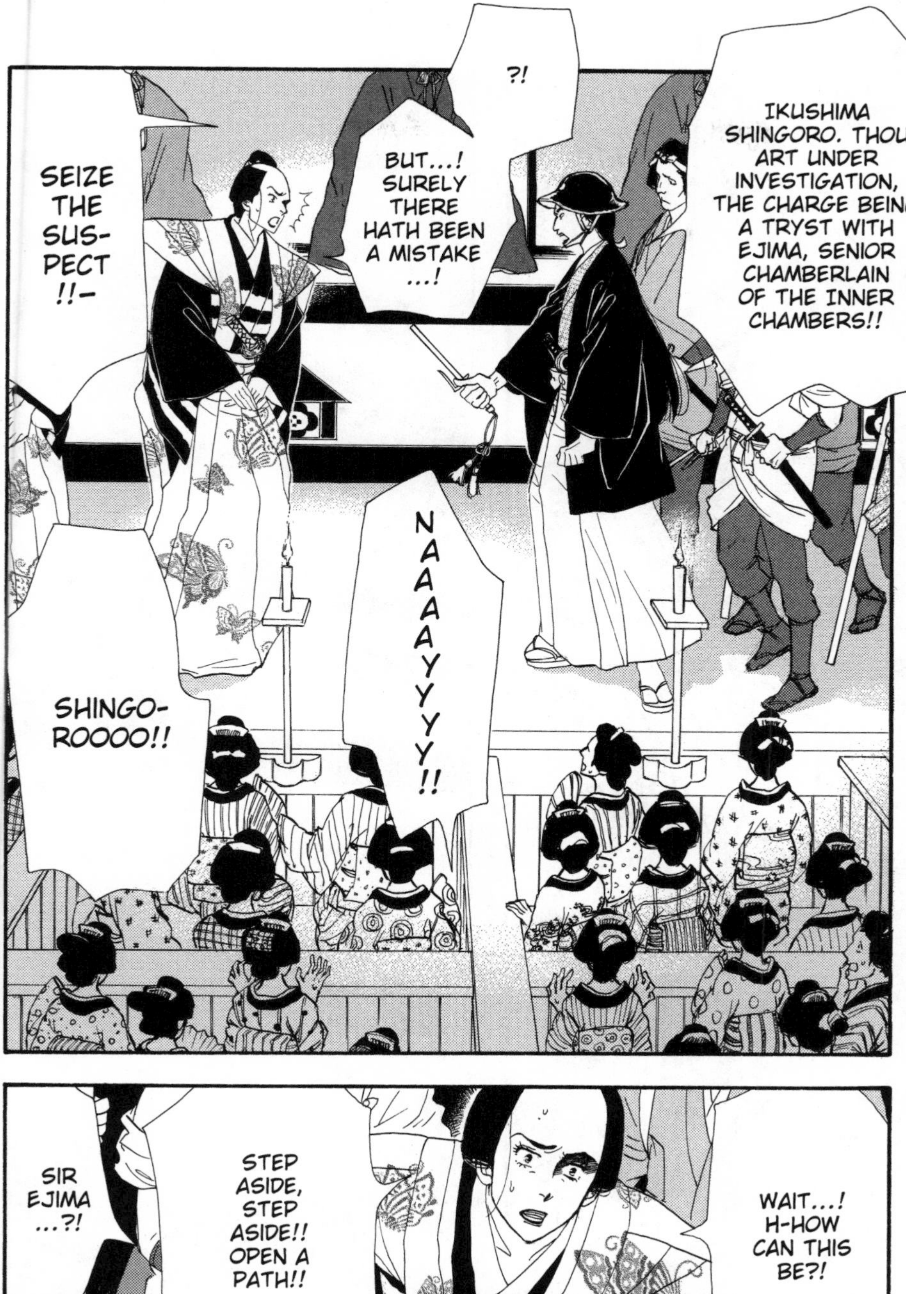
IKUSHIMA SHINGORO. THOU ART UNDER INVESTIGATION, THE CHARGE BEING A TRYST WITH EJIMA, SENIOR CHAMBERLAIN OF THE INNER CHAMBERS!!
?!
BUT...! SURELY THERE HATH BEEN A MISTAKE ...!
SEIZE THE SUS-PECT !!–
NAAAAYYYY!!
SHINGO-ROOOO!!
WAIT...! H-HOW CAN THIS BE?!
STEP ASIDE, STEP ASIDE!! OPEN A PATH!!
SIR EJIMA ...?!

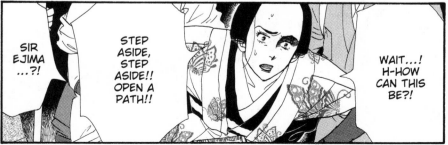

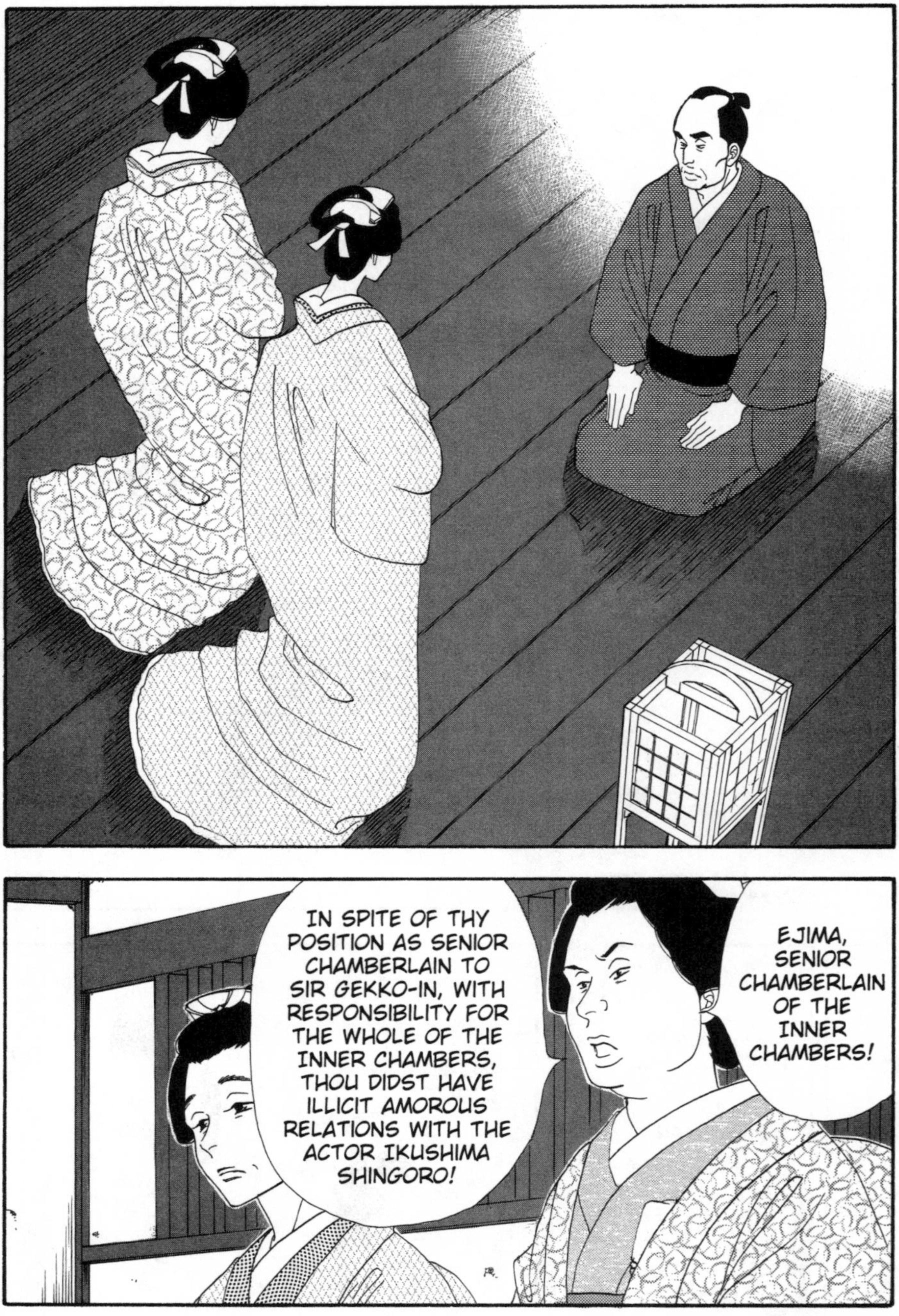
EJIMA, SENIOR CHAMBERLAIN OF THE INNER CHAMBERS!
IN SPITE OF THY POSITION AS SENIOR CHAMBERLAIN TO SIR GEKKO-IN, WITH RESPONSIBILITY FOR THE WHOLE OF THE INNER CHAMBERS, THOU DIDST HAVE ILLICIT AMOROUS RELATIONS WITH THE ACTOR IKUSHIMA SHINGORO!

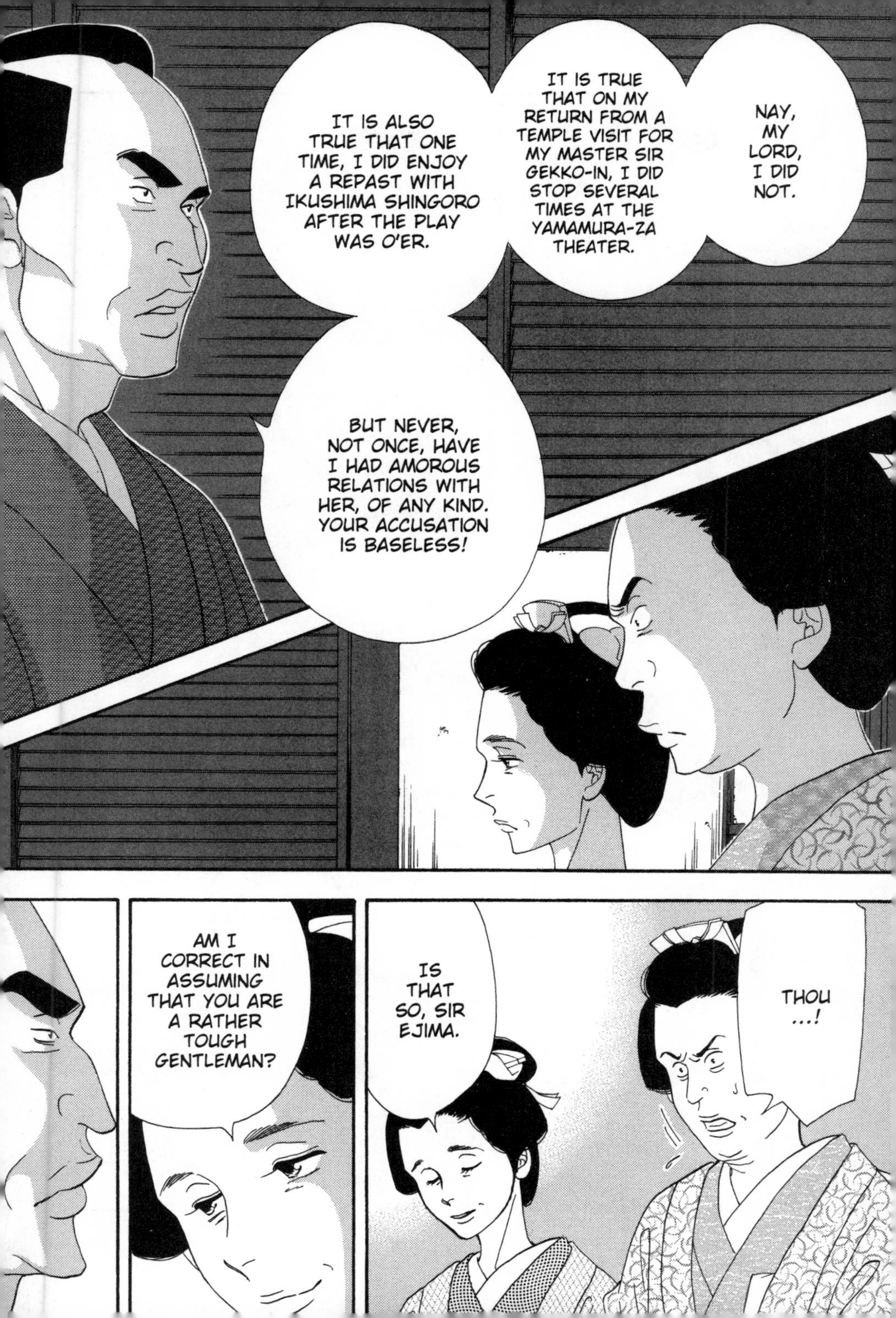
NAY, MY LORD, I DID NOT.
IT IS TRUE THAT ON MY RETURN FROM A TEMPLE VISIT FOR MY MASTER SIR GEKKO-IN, I DID STOP SEVERAL TIMES AT THE YAMAMURA-ZA THEATER.
IT IS ALSO TRUE THAT ONE TIME, I DID ENJOY A REPAST WITH IKUSHIMA SHINGORO AFTER THE PLAY WAS O'ER.
BUT NEVER, NOT ONCE, HAVE I HAD AMOROUS RELATIONS WITH HER, OF ANY KIND. YOUR ACCUSATION IS BASELESS!
THOU ...!
IS THAT SO, SIR EJIMA.
AM I CORRECT IN ASSUMING THAT YOU ARE A RATHER TOUGH GENTLEMAN?

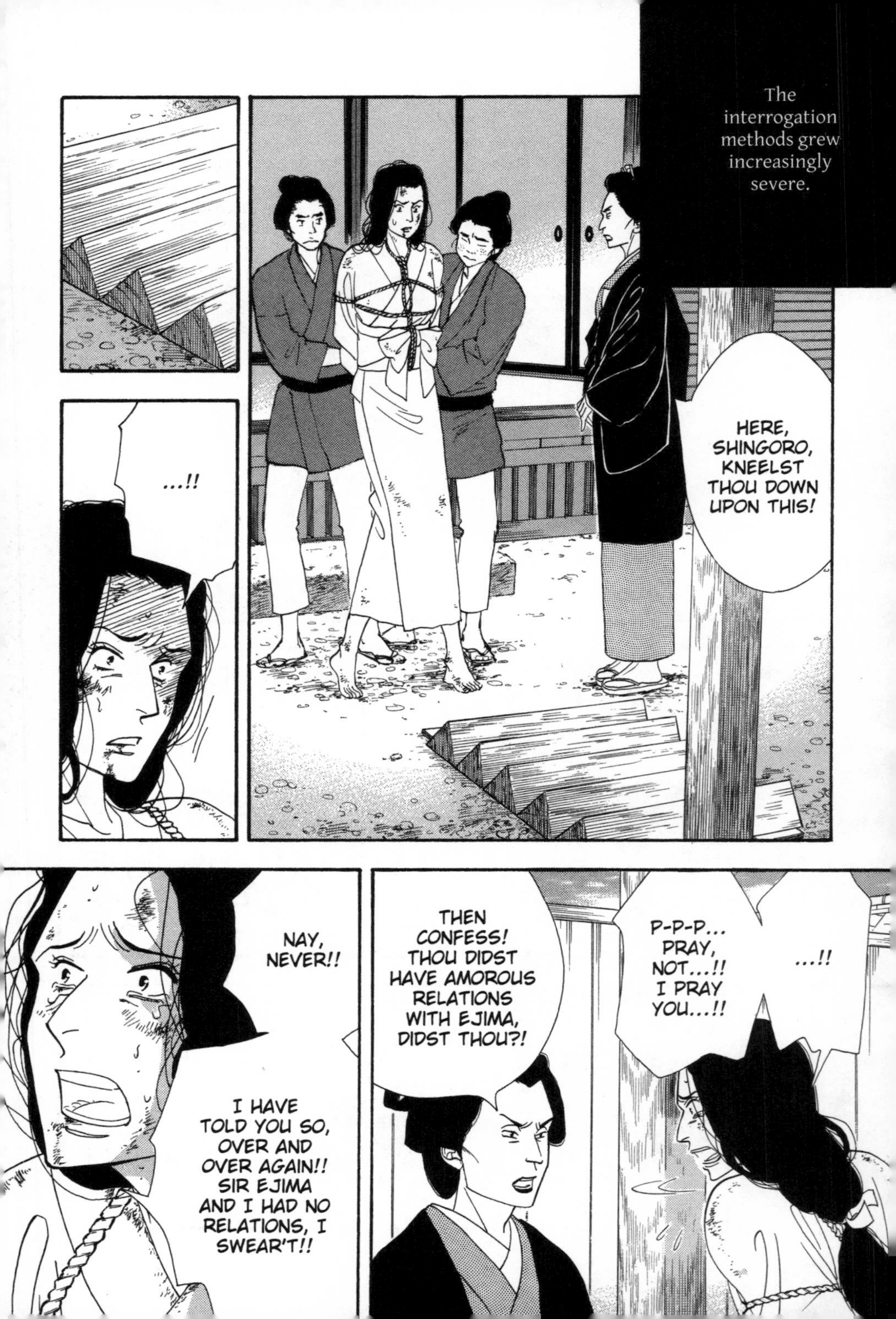
The interrogation methods grew increasingly severe.
HERE, SHINGORO, KNEELST THOU DOWN UPON THIS!
...!!
...!!
P-P-P... PRAY, NOT...!! I PRAY YOU...!!
THEN CONFESS! THOU DIDST HAVE AMOROUS RELATIONS WITH EJIMA, DIDST THOU?!
NAY, NEVER!!
I HAVE TOLD YOU SO, OVER AND OVER AGAIN!! SIR EJIMA AND I HAD NO RELATIONS, I SWEAR'T!!

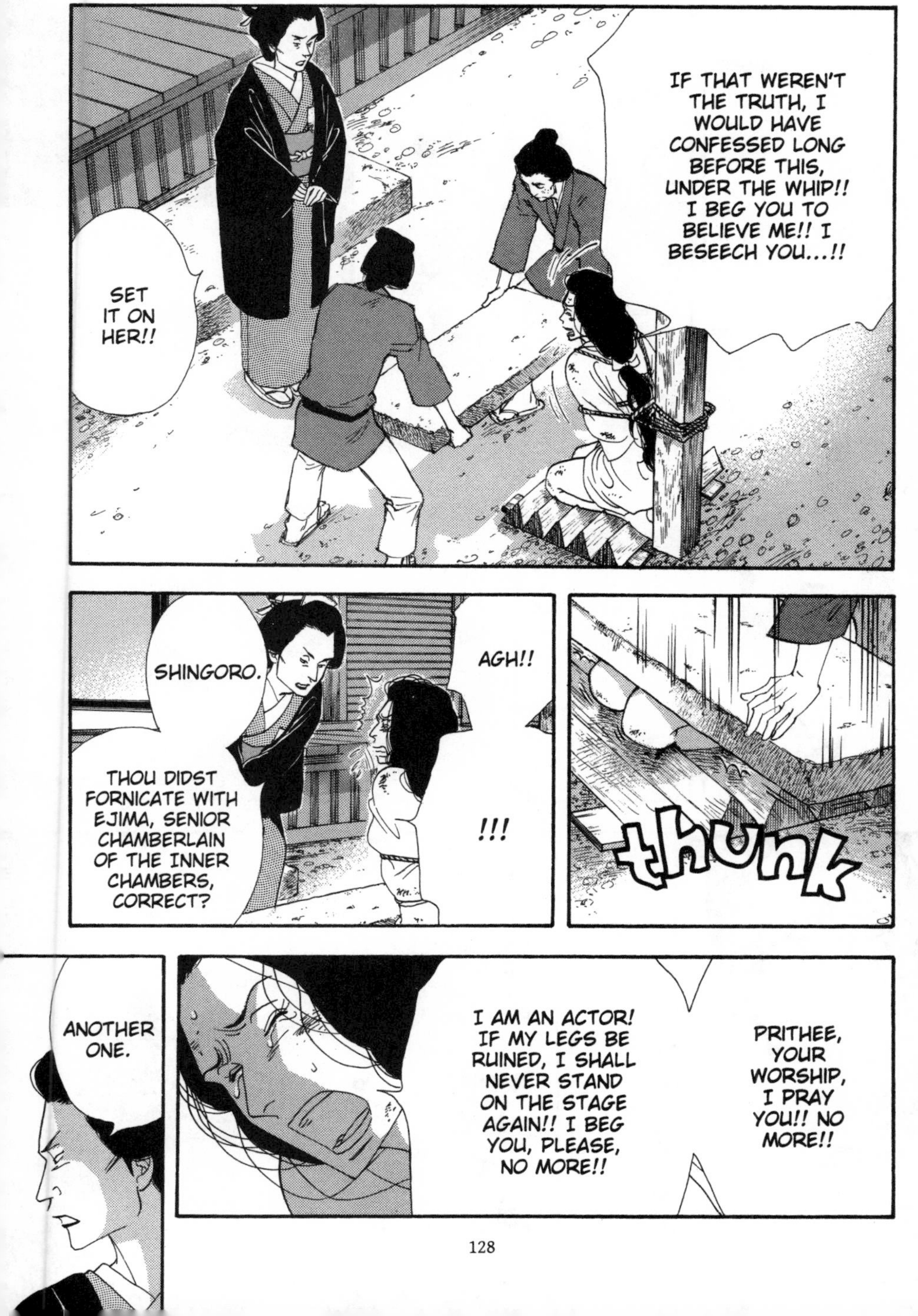
IF THAT WEREN'T THE TRUTH, I WOULD HAVE CONFESSED LONG BEFORE THIS, UNDER THE WHIP!! I BEG YOU TO BELIEVE ME!! I BESEECH YOU...!!
SET IT ON HER!!
thunk
AGH!!
!!!
SHINGORO.
THOU DIDST FORNICATE WITH EJIMA, SENIOR CHAMBERLAIN OF THE INNER CHAMBERS, CORRECT?
PRITHEE, YOUR WORSHIP, I PRAY YOU!! NO MORE!!
I AM AN ACTOR! IF MY LEGS BE RUINED, I SHALL NEVER STAND ON THE STAGE AGAIN!! I BEG YOU, PLEASE, NO MORE!!
ANOTHER ONE.

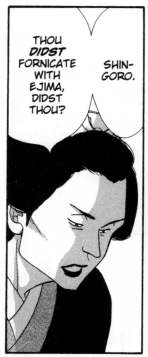

thunk
GYAAA-AAAAA-AGH!!
SHIN-GORO.
THOU *DIDST* FORNICATE WITH EJIMA, DIDST THOU?
AGH!! AWGH!!
A-AYE, I DID!!
I CONFESS...
...THAT I DID FORNICATE WITH SIR EJIMA, AYE...!!

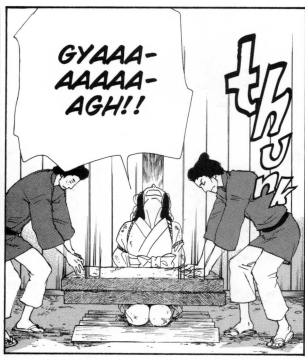

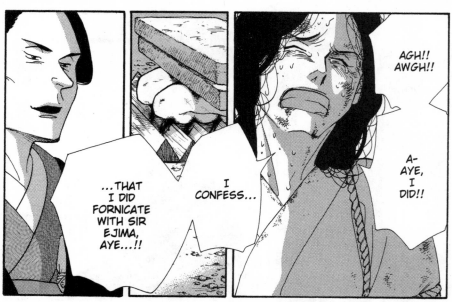

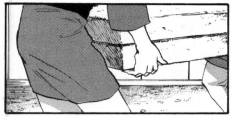

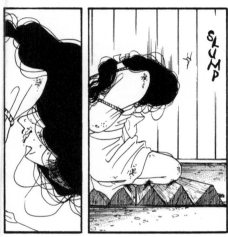

VERY WELL.
I DID HEAR IT WITH MINE OWN EARS, SHINGORO.
REMOVE THE SLABS.
SLUMP
FOOLISH WENCH...
SHE DOTH BELIEVE SHE CAN RETURN TO THE STAGE!
WHIP HIM AGAIN.

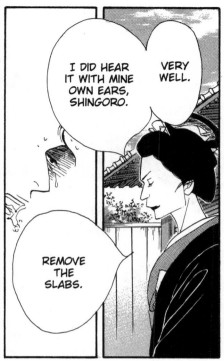

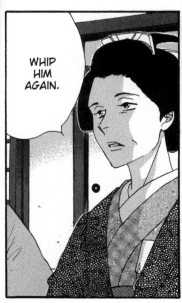

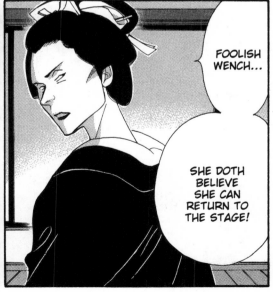

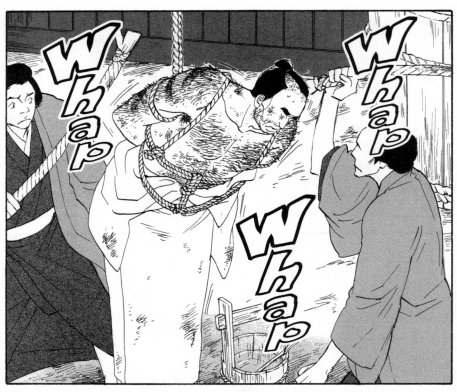

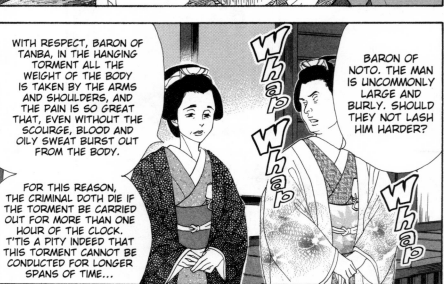

Whap
Whap
Whap
Whap
BARON OF NOTO. THE MAN IS UNCOMMONLY LARGE AND BURLY. SHOULD THEY NOT LASH HIM HARDER?
Whap
Whap
Whap
WITH RESPECT, BARON OF TANBA, IN THE HANGING TORMENT ALL THE WEIGHT OF THE BODY IS TAKEN BY THE ARMS AND SHOULDERS, AND THE PAIN IS SO GREAT THAT, EVEN WITHOUT THE SCOURGE, BLOOD AND OILY SWEAT BURST OUT FROM THE BODY.
FOR THIS REASON, THE CRIMINAL DOTH DIE IF THE TORMENT BE CARRIED OUT FOR MORE THAN ONE HOUR OF THE CLOCK. T'TIS A PITY INDEED THAT THIS TORMENT CANNOT BE CONDUCTED FOR LONGER SPANS OF TIME...

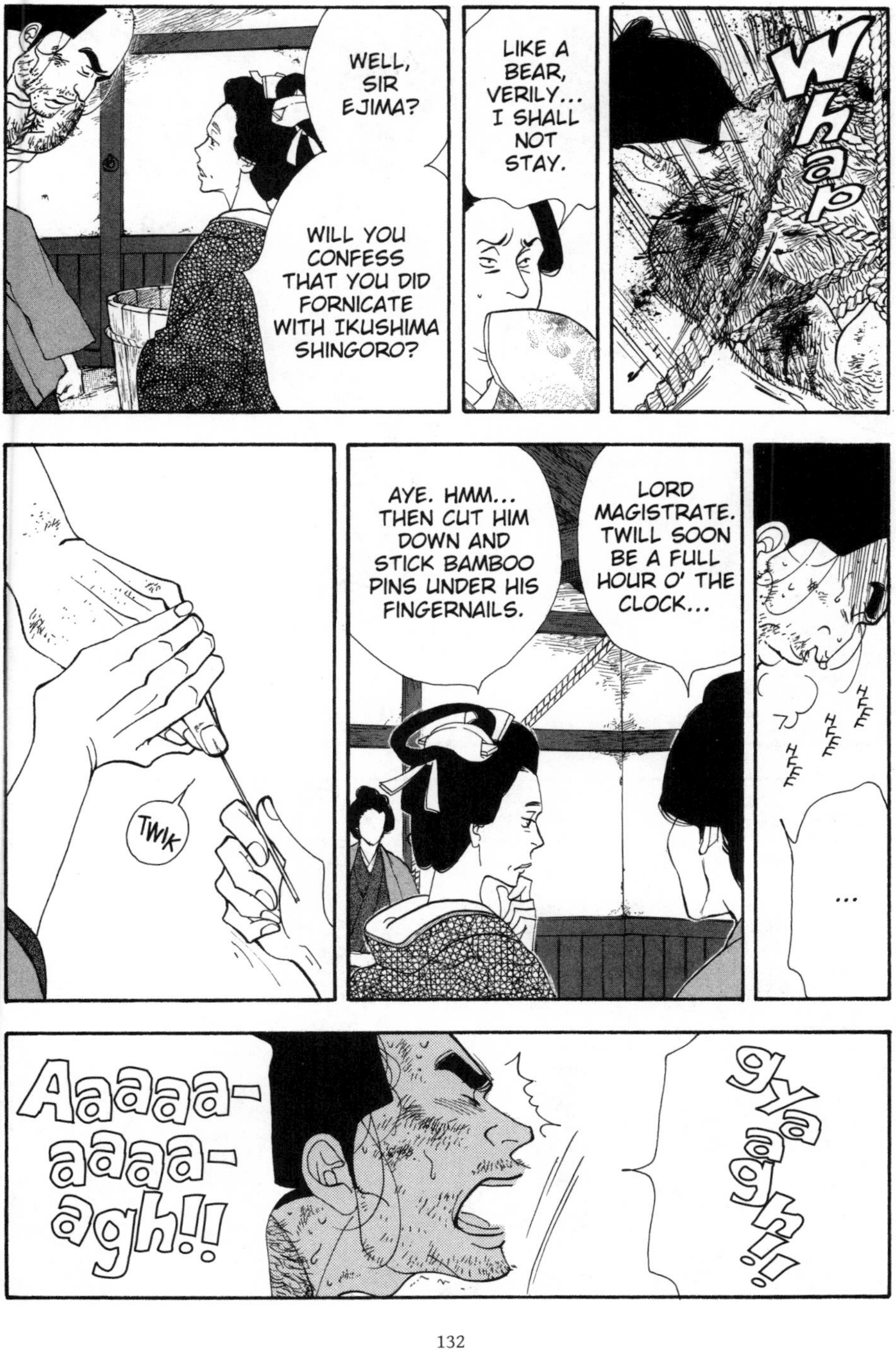
Whap
LIKE A BEAR, VERILY... I SHALL NOT STAY.
WELL, SIR EJIMA?
WILL YOU CONFESS THAT YOU DID FORNICATE WITH IKUSHIMA SHINGORO?
HFFF
HFFF
HFFF
...
LORD MAGISTRATE. TWILL SOON BE A FULL HOUR O' THE CLOCK...
AYE. HMM... THEN CUT HIM DOWN AND STICK BAMBOO PINS UNDER HIS FINGERNAILS.
TWIK
gyaagh!!
Aaaaa-aaaaa-agh!!

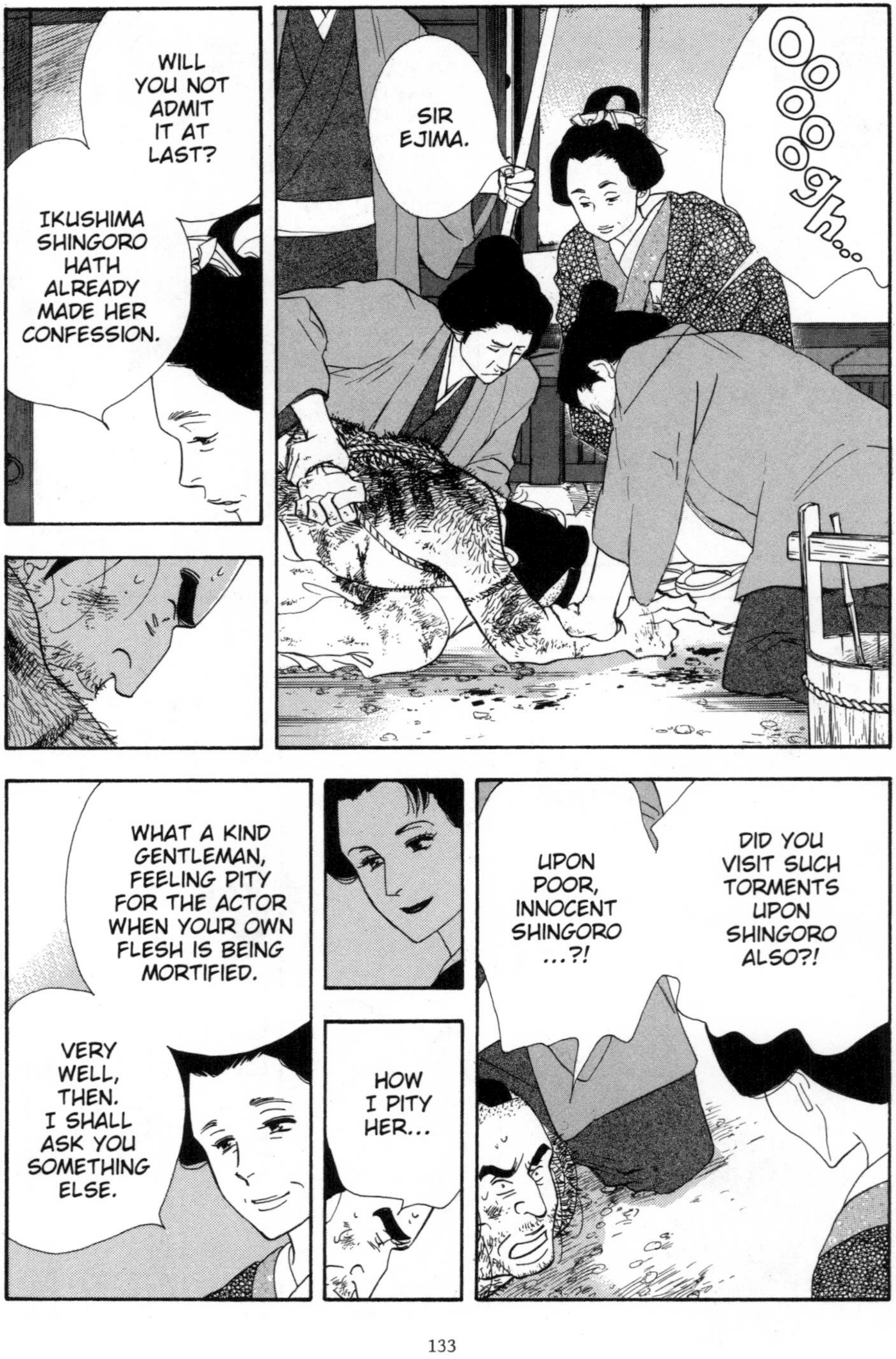
Ooooogh...
SIR EJIMA.
WILL YOU NOT ADMIT IT AT LAST?
IKUSHIMA SHINGORO HATH ALREADY MADE HER CONFESSION.
DID YOU VISIT SUCH TORMENTS UPON SHINGORO ALSO?!
UPON POOR, INNOCENT SHINGORO ...?!
HOW I PITY HER...
WHAT A KIND GENTLEMAN, FEELING PITY FOR THE ACTOR WHEN YOUR OWN FLESH IS BEING MORTIFIED.
VERY WELL, THEN. I SHALL ASK YOU SOMETHING ELSE.

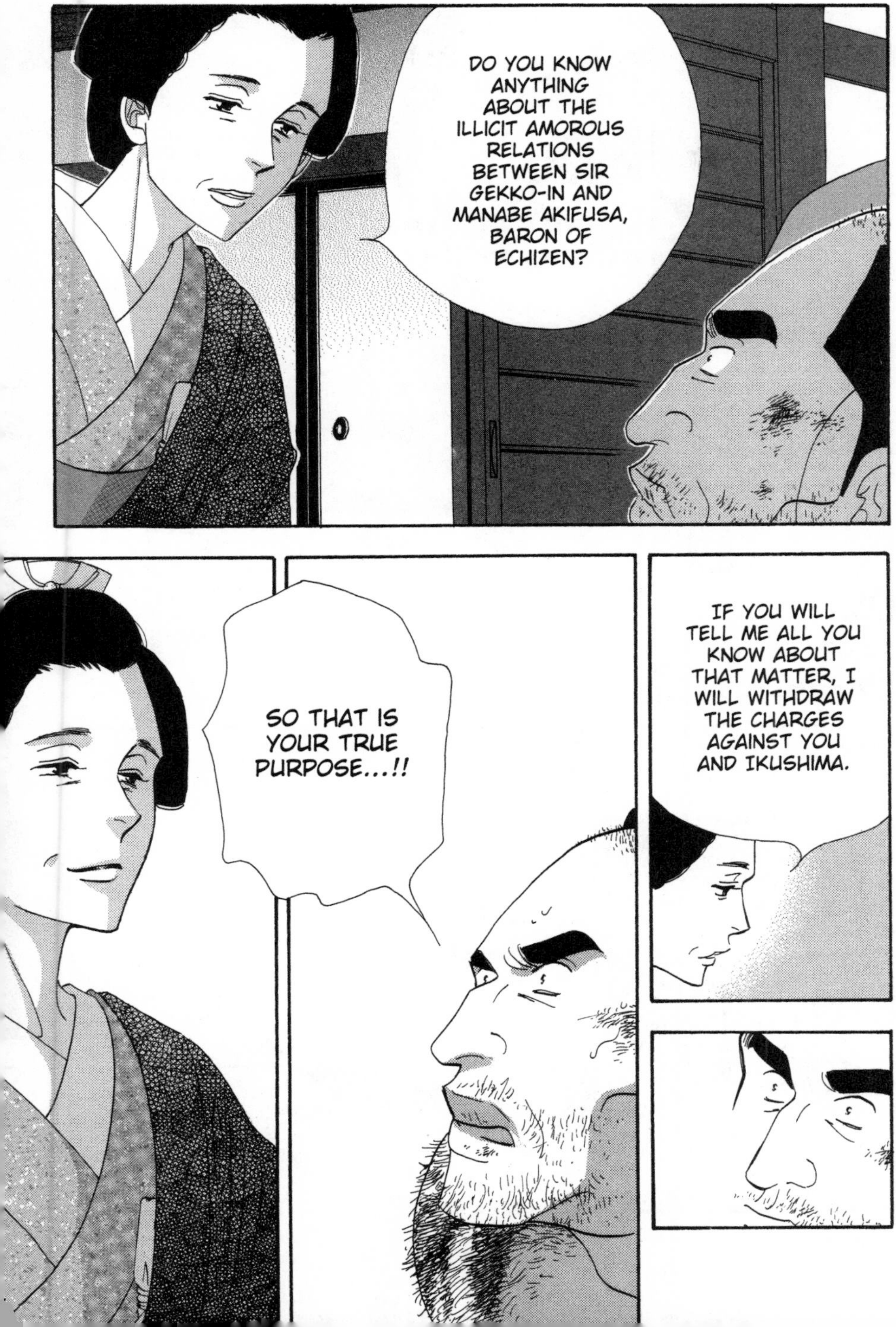
DO YOU KNOW ANYTHING ABOUT THE ILLICIT AMOROUS RELATIONS BETWEEN SIR GEKKO-IN AND MANABE AKIFUSA, BARON OF ECHIZEN?
IF YOU WILL TELL ME ALL YOU KNOW ABOUT THAT MATTER, I WILL WITHDRAW THE CHARGES AGAINST YOU AND IKUSHIMA.
SO THAT IS YOUR TRUE PURPOSE...!!

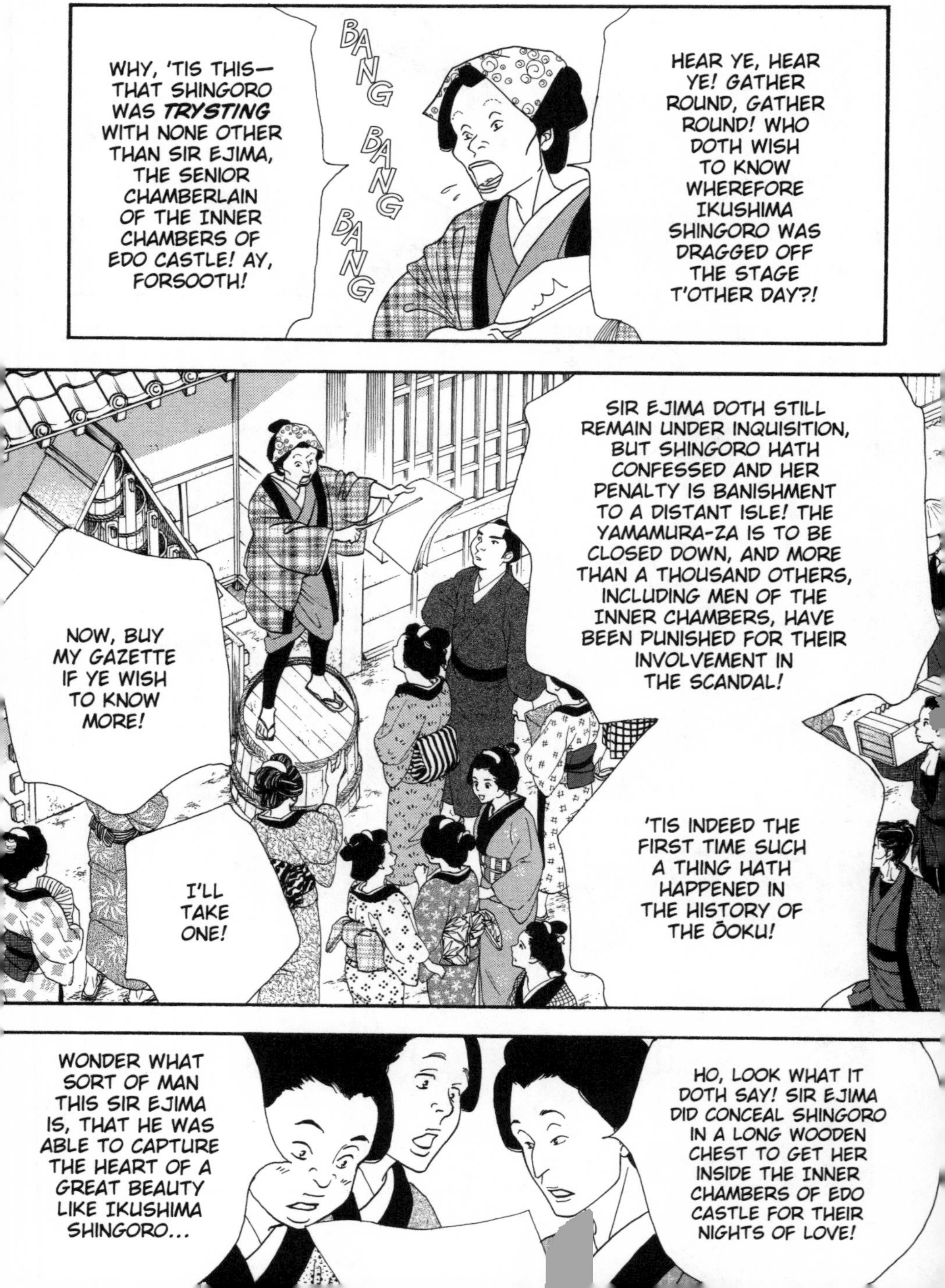
HEAR YE, HEAR YE! GATHER ROUND, GATHER ROUND! WHO DOTH WISH TO KNOW WHEREFORE IKUSHIMA SHINGORO WAS DRAGGED OFF THE STAGE T'OTHER DAY?!
BANG BANG BANG
WHY, 'TIS THIS—THAT SHINGORO WAS *TRYSTING* WITH NONE OTHER THAN SIR EJIMA, THE SENIOR CHAMBERLAIN OF THE INNER CHAMBERS OF EDO CASTLE! AY, FORSOOTH!
SIR EJIMA DOTH STILL REMAIN UNDER INQUISITION, BUT SHINGORO HATH CONFESSED AND HER PENALTY IS BANISHMENT TO A DISTANT ISLE! THE YAMAMURA-ZA IS TO BE CLOSED DOWN, AND MORE THAN A THOUSAND OTHERS, INCLUDING MEN OF THE INNER CHAMBERS, HAVE BEEN PUNISHED FOR THEIR INVOLVEMENT IN THE SCANDAL!
'TIS INDEED THE FIRST TIME SUCH A THING HATH HAPPENED IN THE HISTORY OF THE ŌOKU!
NOW, BUY MY GAZETTE IF YE WISH TO KNOW MORE!
I'LL TAKE ONE!
HO, LOOK WHAT IT DOTH SAY! SIR EJIMA DID CONCEAL SHINGORO IN A LONG WOODEN CHEST TO GET HER INSIDE THE INNER CHAMBERS OF EDO CASTLE FOR THEIR NIGHTS OF LOVE!
WONDER WHAT SORT OF MAN THIS SIR EJIMA IS, THAT HE WAS ABLE TO CAPTURE THE HEART OF A GREAT BEAUTY LIKE IKUSHIMA SHINGORO...

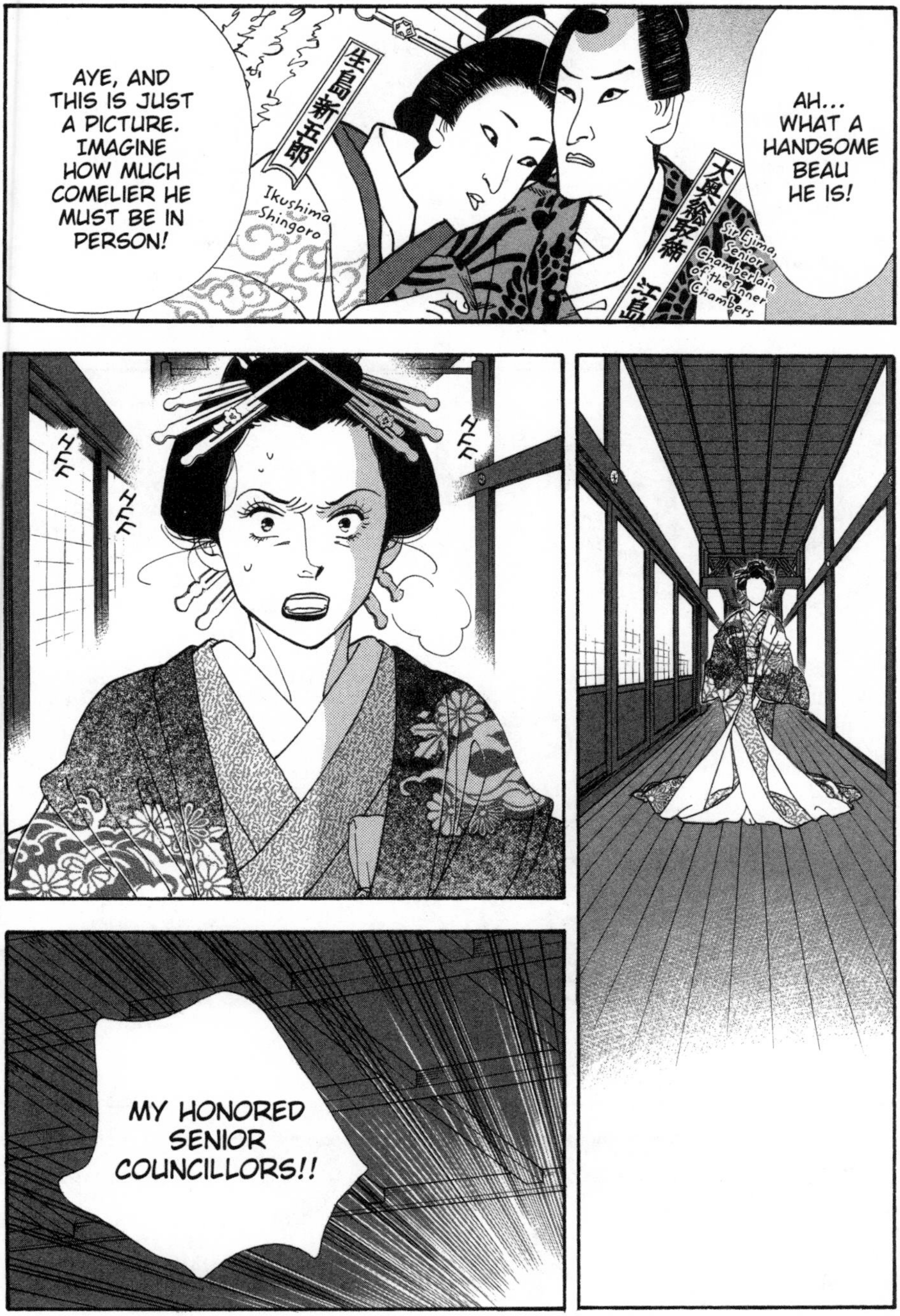
AH... WHAT A HANDSOME BEAU HE IS!
大奥総取締 江島
Sir Ejima, Senior Chamberlain of the Inner Chambers
生島新五郎
Ikushima Shingoro
AYE, AND THIS IS JUST A PICTURE. IMAGINE HOW MUCH COMELIER HE MUST BE IN PERSON!
HFF
HFF
HFF
MY HONORED SENIOR COUNCILLORS!!

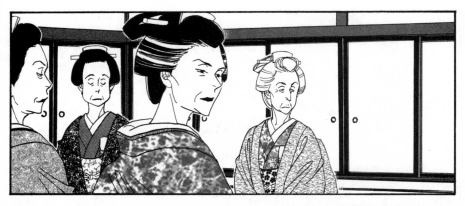

THE RECENT ARRESTS...
WHAT IS THIS ALL ABOUT?! WHEREFORE HAVE YOU DISMISSED EJIMA?! THE MAN HATH DONE NOTHING WRONG...!!
HATH DONE NOTHING WRONG?
HOW CAN YOU SAY THAT? HE HATH STOPPED MANY A TIME AT A PLAYHOUSE ON HIS RETURN FROM A TEMPLE VISIT FOR SIR GEKKO-IN! THE RECENT DECLINE OF MORALS IN THE INNER CHAMBERS WAS GROSS AND INTOLERABLE.
THAT BEING THE CASE, WE MADE AN EXAMPLE OF SIR EJIMA, WHO WAS THE SENIOR CHAMBERLAIN, IN ORDER TO ENFORCE DISCIPLINE AMONG THE MEN.

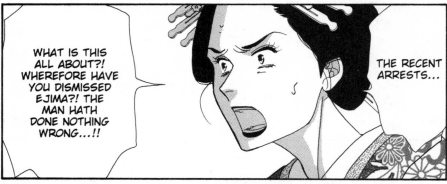

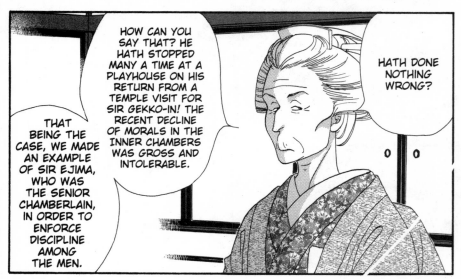

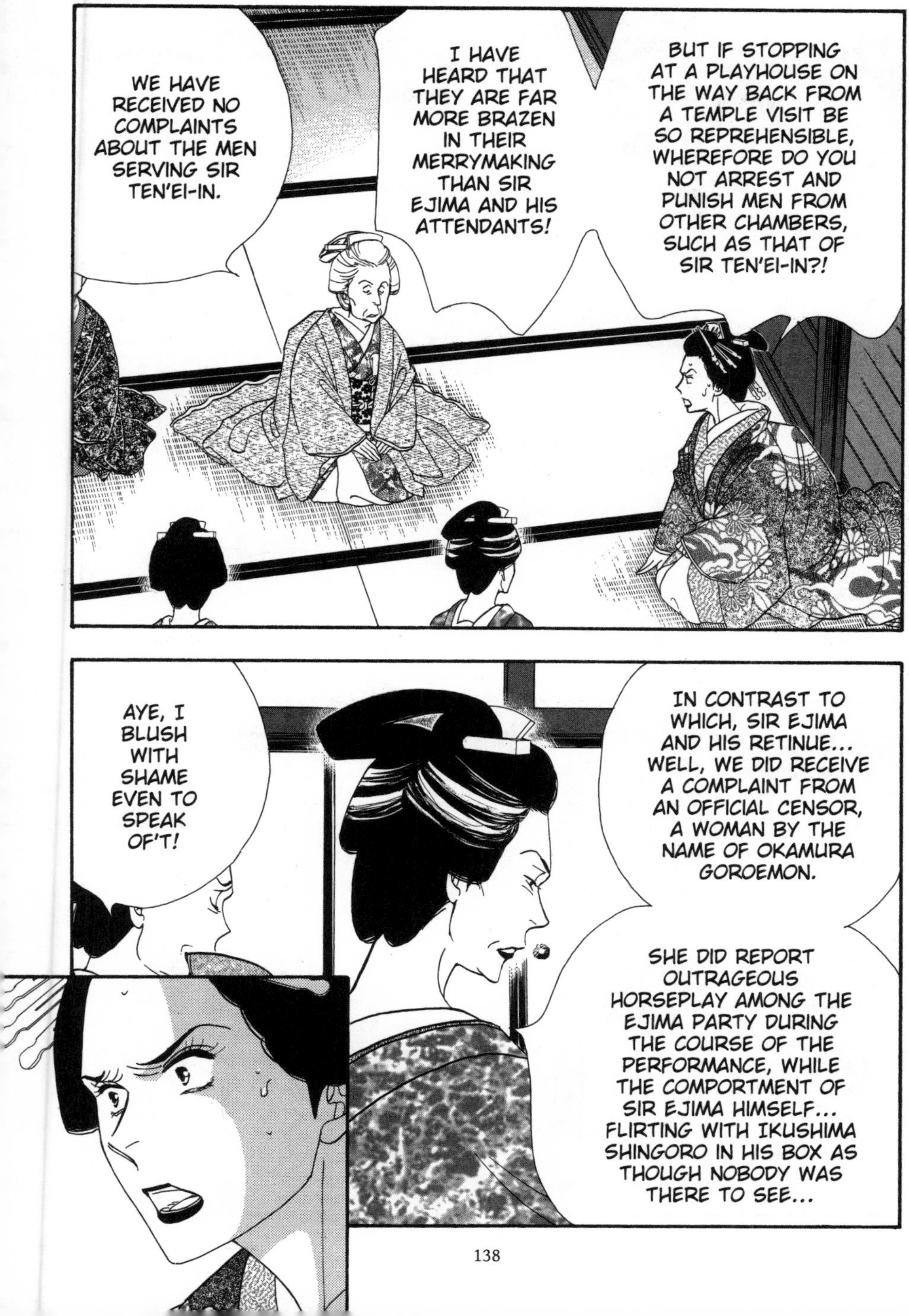
BUT IF STOPPING AT A PLAYHOUSE ON THE WAY BACK FROM A TEMPLE VISIT BE SO REPREHENSIBLE, WHEREFORE DO YOU NOT ARREST AND PUNISH MEN FROM OTHER CHAMBERS, SUCH AS THAT OF SIR TEN'EI-IN?!
I HAVE HEARD THAT THEY ARE FAR MORE BRAZEN IN THEIR MERRYMAKING THAN SIR EJIMA AND HIS ATTENDANTS!
WE HAVE RECEIVED NO COMPLAINTS ABOUT THE MEN SERVING SIR TEN'EI-IN.
IN CONTRAST TO WHICH, SIR EJIMA AND HIS RETINUE... WELL, WE DID RECEIVE A COMPLAINT FROM AN OFFICIAL CENSOR, A WOMAN BY THE NAME OF OKAMURA GOROEMON.
SHE DID REPORT OUTRAGEOUS HORSEPLAY AMONG THE EJIMA PARTY DURING THE COURSE OF THE PERFORMANCE, WHILE THE COMPORTMENT OF SIR EJIMA HIMSELF... FLIRTING WITH IKUSHIMA SHINGORO IN HIS BOX AS THOUGH NOBODY WAS THERE TO SEE...
AYE, I BLUSH WITH SHAME EVEN TO SPEAK OF'T!

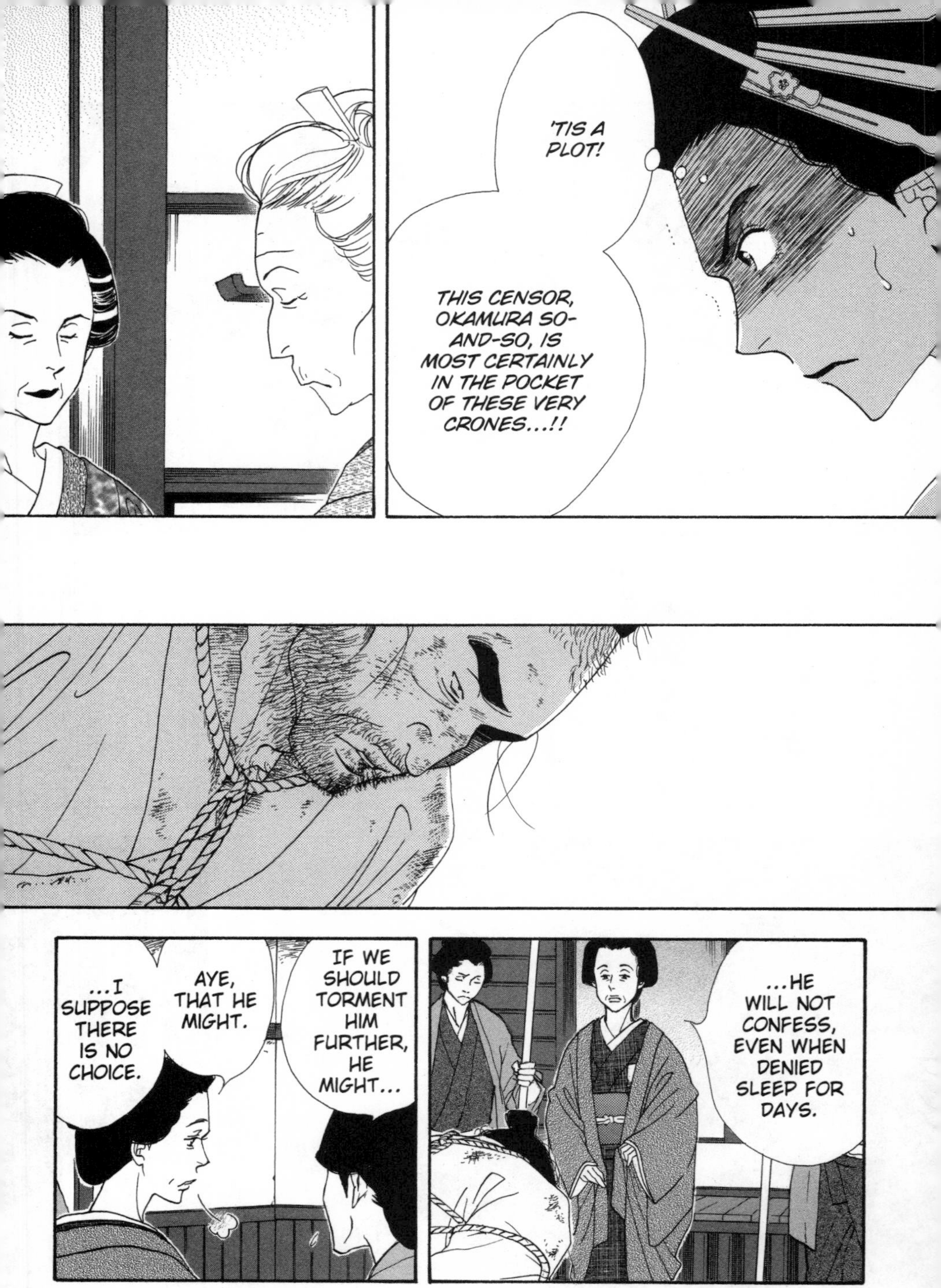
'TIS A PLOT!
THIS CENSOR, OKAMURA SO-AND-SO, IS MOST CERTAINLY IN THE POCKET OF THESE VERY CRONES...!!
...HE WILL NOT CONFESS, EVEN WHEN DENIED SLEEP FOR DAYS.
IF WE SHOULD TORMENT HIM FURTHER, HE MIGHT...
AYE, THAT HE MIGHT.
...I SUPPOSE THERE IS NO CHOICE.

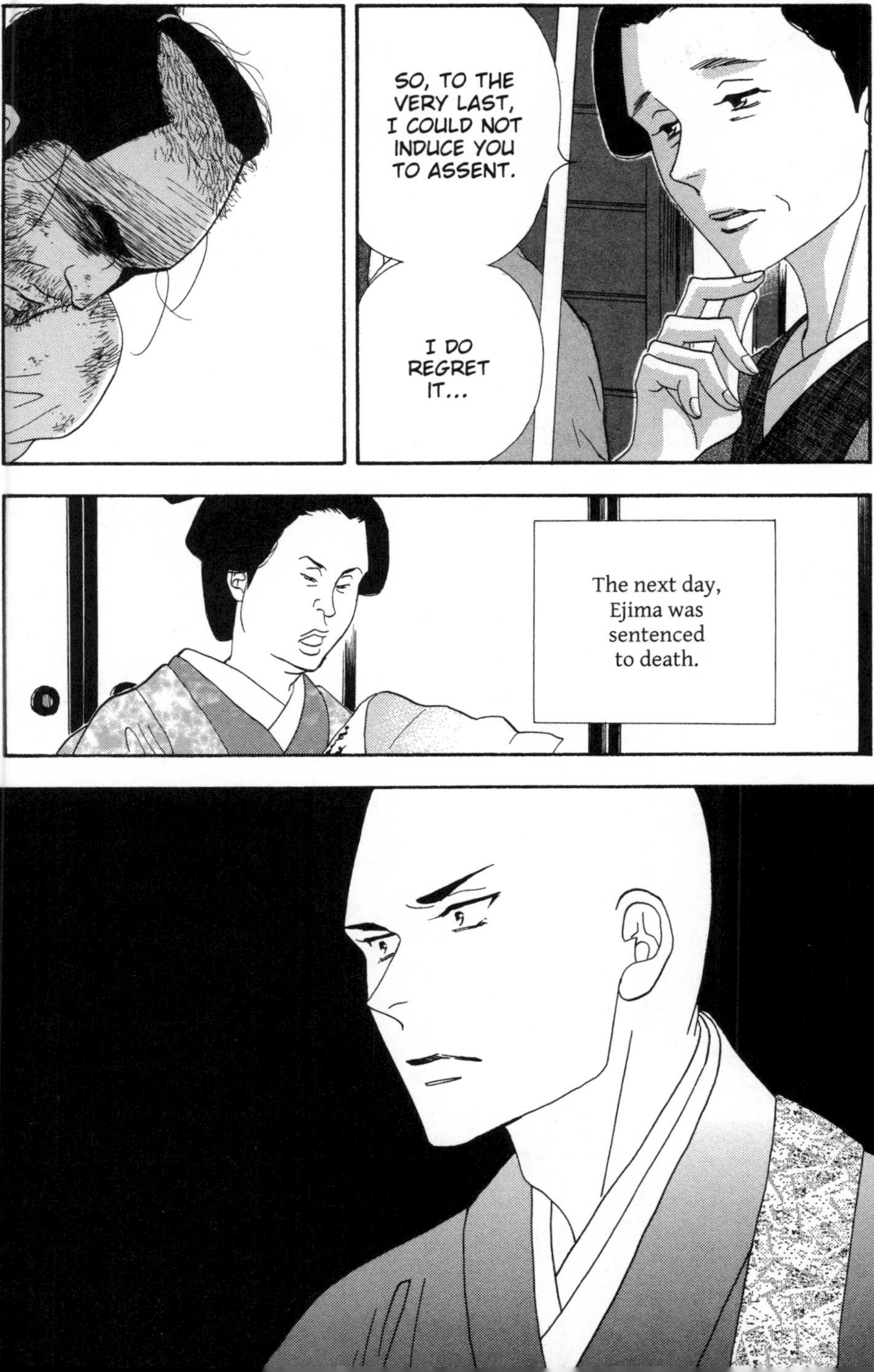
SO, TO THE VERY LAST, I COULD NOT INDUCE YOU TO ASSENT.
I DO REGRET IT...
The next day, Ejima was sentenced to death.

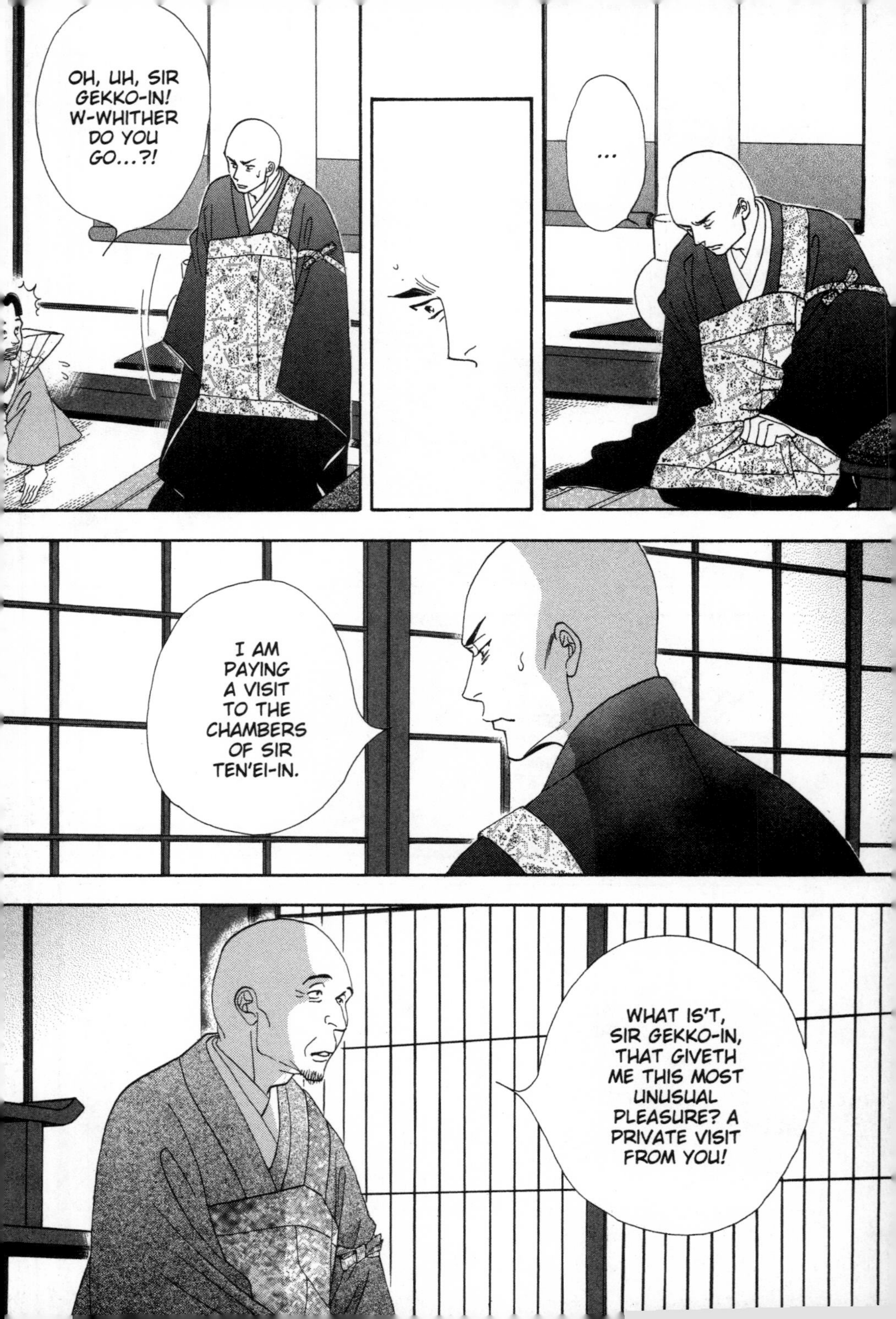
...
OH, UH, SIR GEKKO-IN! W-WHITHER DO YOU GO...?!
I AM PAYING A VISIT TO THE CHAMBERS OF SIR TEN'EI-IN.
WHAT IS'T, SIR GEKKO-IN, THAT GIVETH ME THIS MOST UNUSUAL PLEASURE? A PRIVATE VISIT FROM YOU!

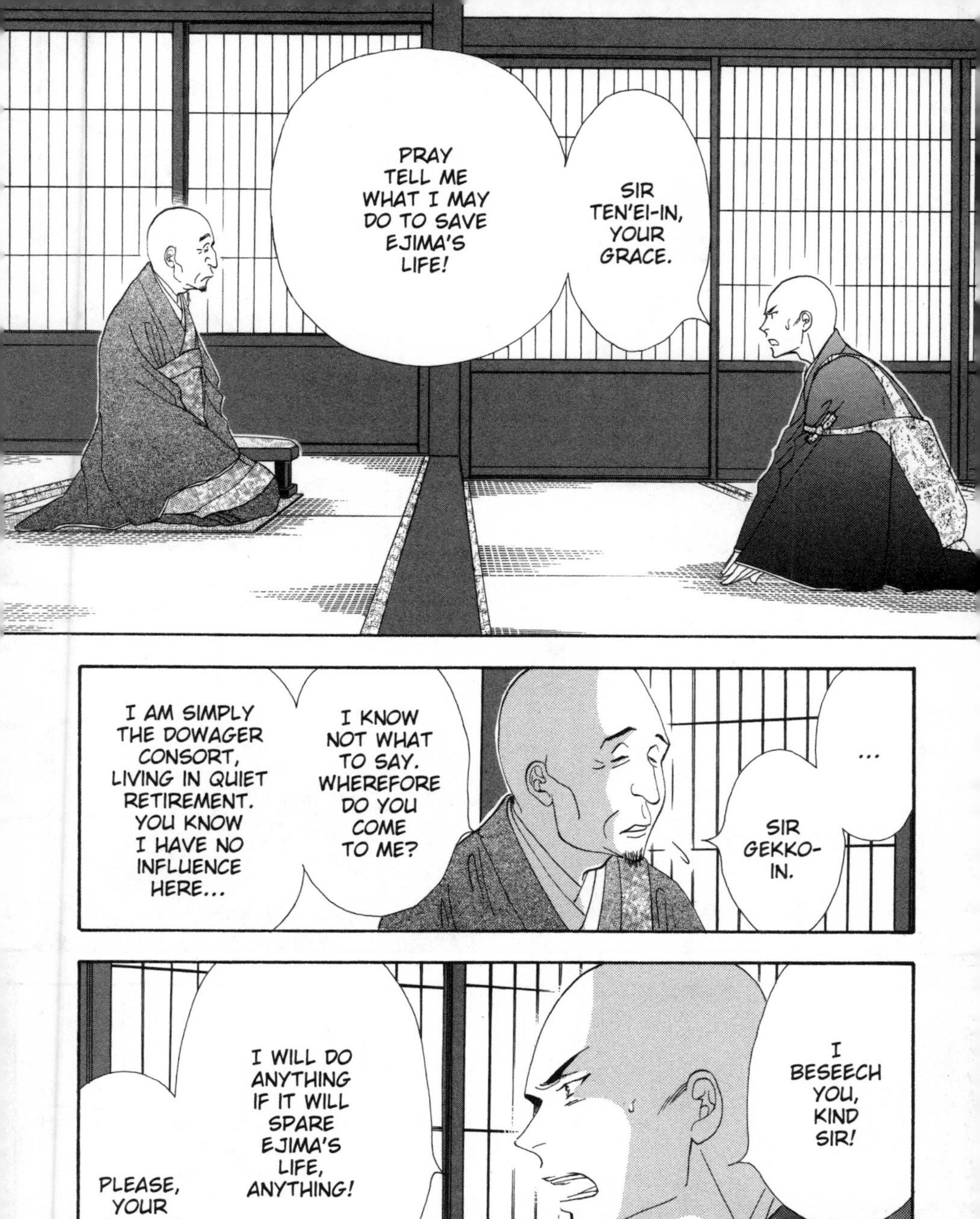
SIR TEN'EI-IN, YOUR GRACE.
PRAY TELL ME WHAT I MAY DO TO SAVE EJIMA'S LIFE!
...
SIR GEKKO-IN.
I KNOW NOT WHAT TO SAY. WHEREFORE DO YOU COME TO ME?
I AM SIMPLY THE DOWAGER CONSORT, LIVING IN QUIET RETIREMENT. YOU KNOW I HAVE NO INFLUENCE HERE...
I BESEECH YOU, KIND SIR!
I WILL DO ANYTHING IF IT WILL SPARE EJIMA'S LIFE, ANYTHING!
PLEASE, YOUR GRACE!!

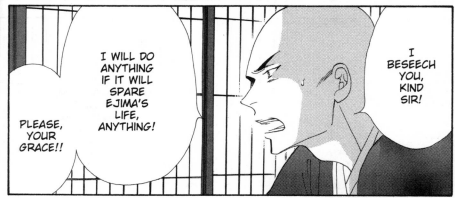

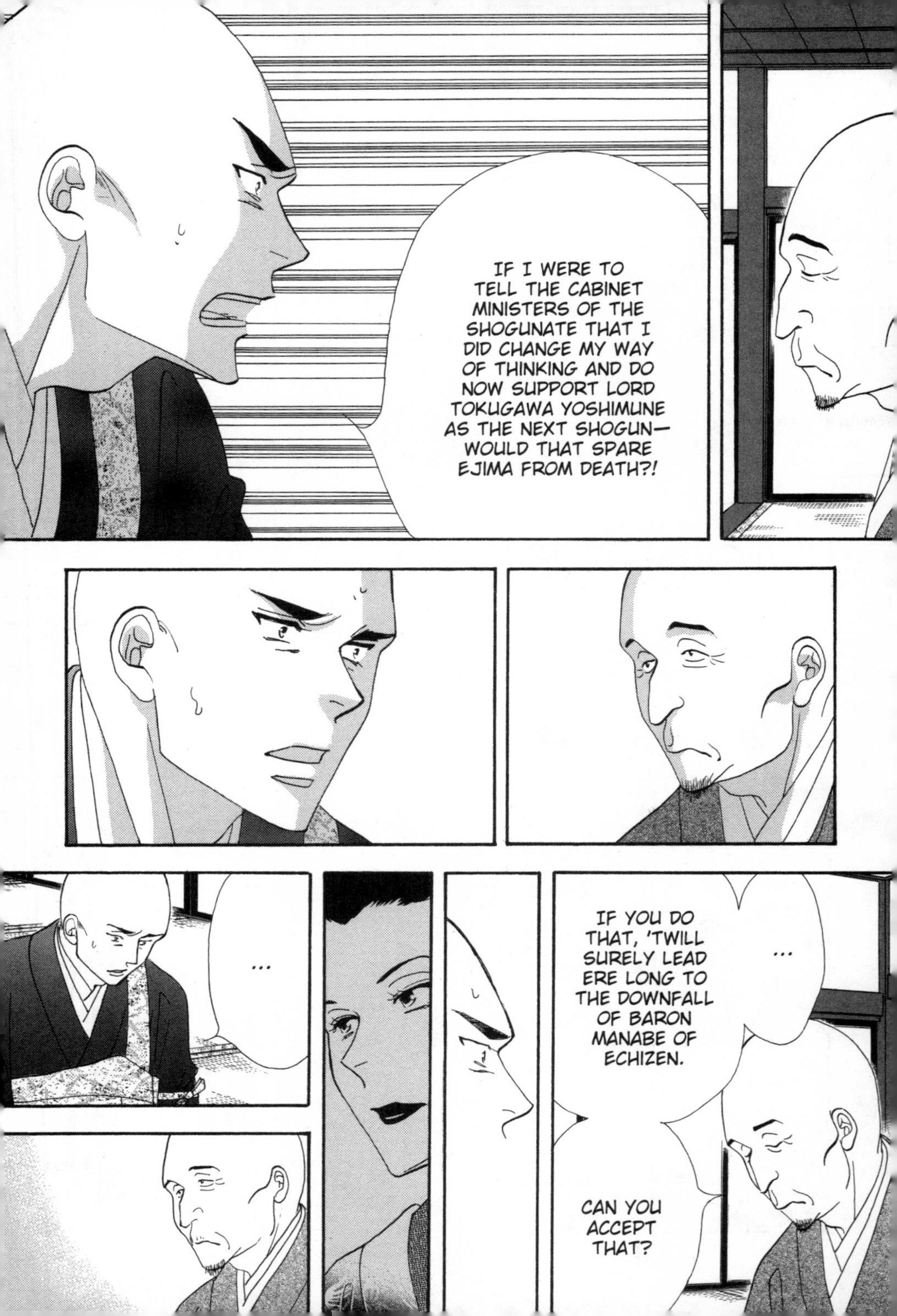
IF I WERE TO TELL THE CABINET MINISTERS OF THE SHOGUNATE THAT I DID CHANGE MY WAY OF THINKING AND DO NOW SUPPORT LORD TOKUGAWA YOSHIMUNE AS THE NEXT SHOGUN—WOULD THAT SPARE EJIMA FROM DEATH?!
...
IF YOU DO THAT, 'TWILL SURELY LEAD ERE LONG TO THE DOWNFALL OF BARON MANABE OF ECHIZEN.
CAN YOU ACCEPT THAT?
...

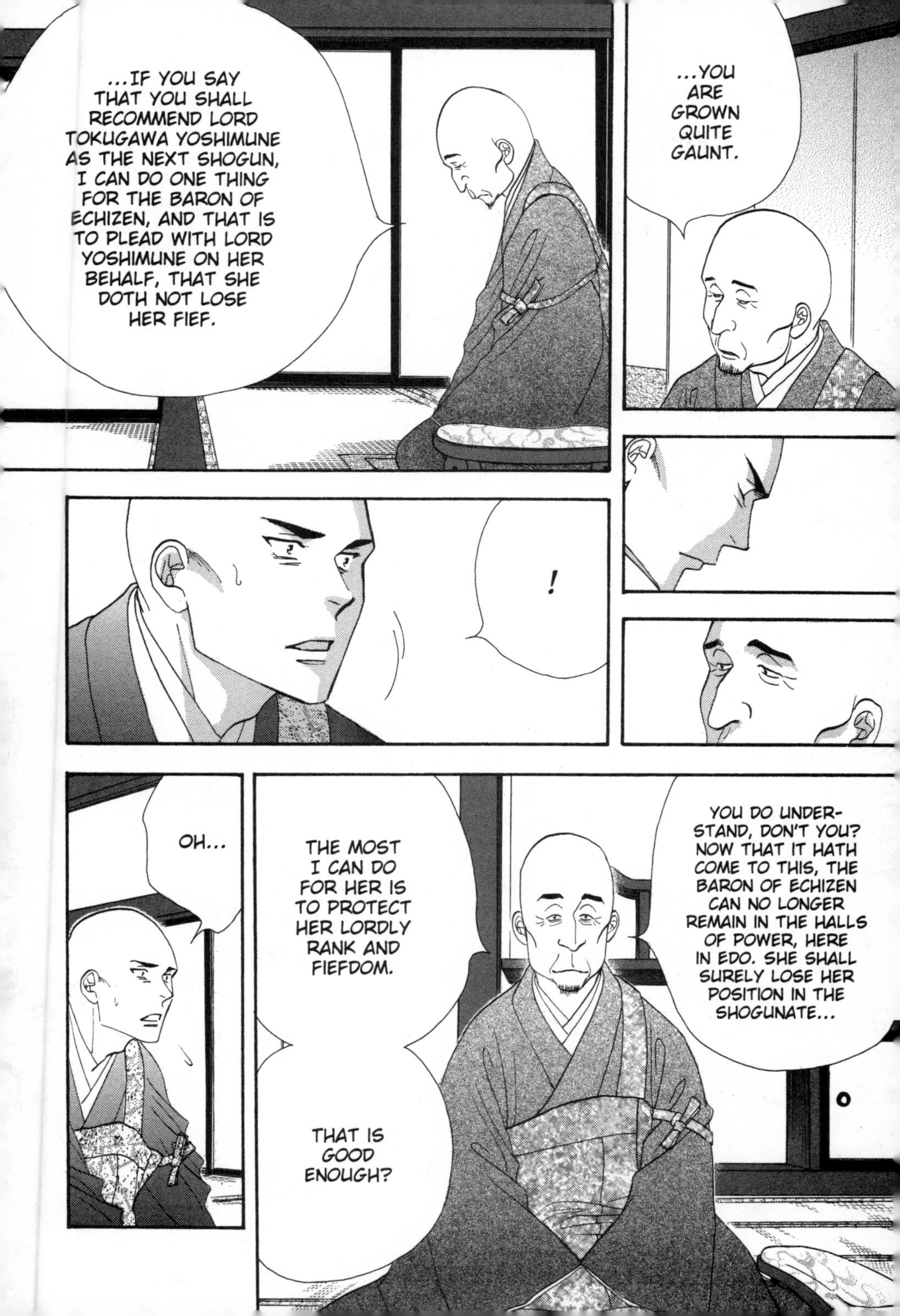
...YOU ARE GROWN QUITE GAUNT.
...IF YOU SAY THAT YOU SHALL RECOMMEND LORD TOKUGAWA YOSHIMUNE AS THE NEXT SHOGUN, I CAN DO ONE THING FOR THE BARON OF ECHIZEN, AND THAT IS TO PLEAD WITH LORD YOSHIMUNE ON HER BEHALF, THAT SHE DOTH NOT LOSE HER FIEF.
!
YOU DO UNDER-STAND, DON'T YOU? NOW THAT IT HATH COME TO THIS, THE BARON OF ECHIZEN CAN NO LONGER REMAIN IN THE HALLS OF POWER, HERE IN EDO. SHE SHALL SURELY LOSE HER POSITION IN THE SHOGUNATE...
THE MOST I CAN DO FOR HER IS TO PROTECT HER LORDLY RANK AND FIEFDOM.
THAT IS GOOD ENOUGH?
OH...

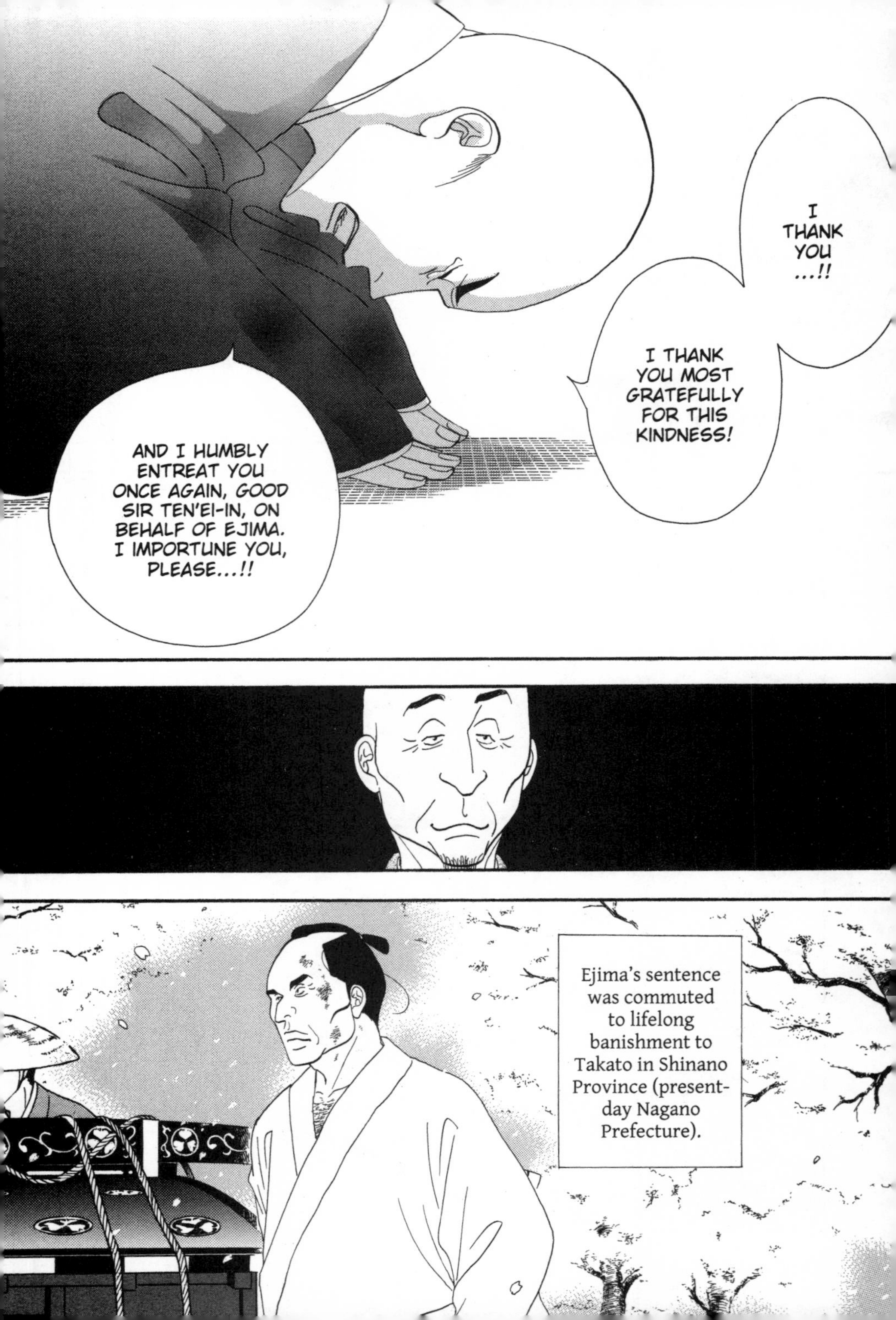
I THANK YOU ...!!
I THANK YOU MOST GRATEFULLY FOR THIS KINDNESS!
AND I HUMBLY ENTREAT YOU ONCE AGAIN, GOOD SIR TEN'EI-IN, ON BEHALF OF EJIMA. I IMPORTUNE YOU, PLEASE...!!
Ejima's sentence was commuted to lifelong banishment to Takato in Shinano Province (present-day Nagano Prefecture).

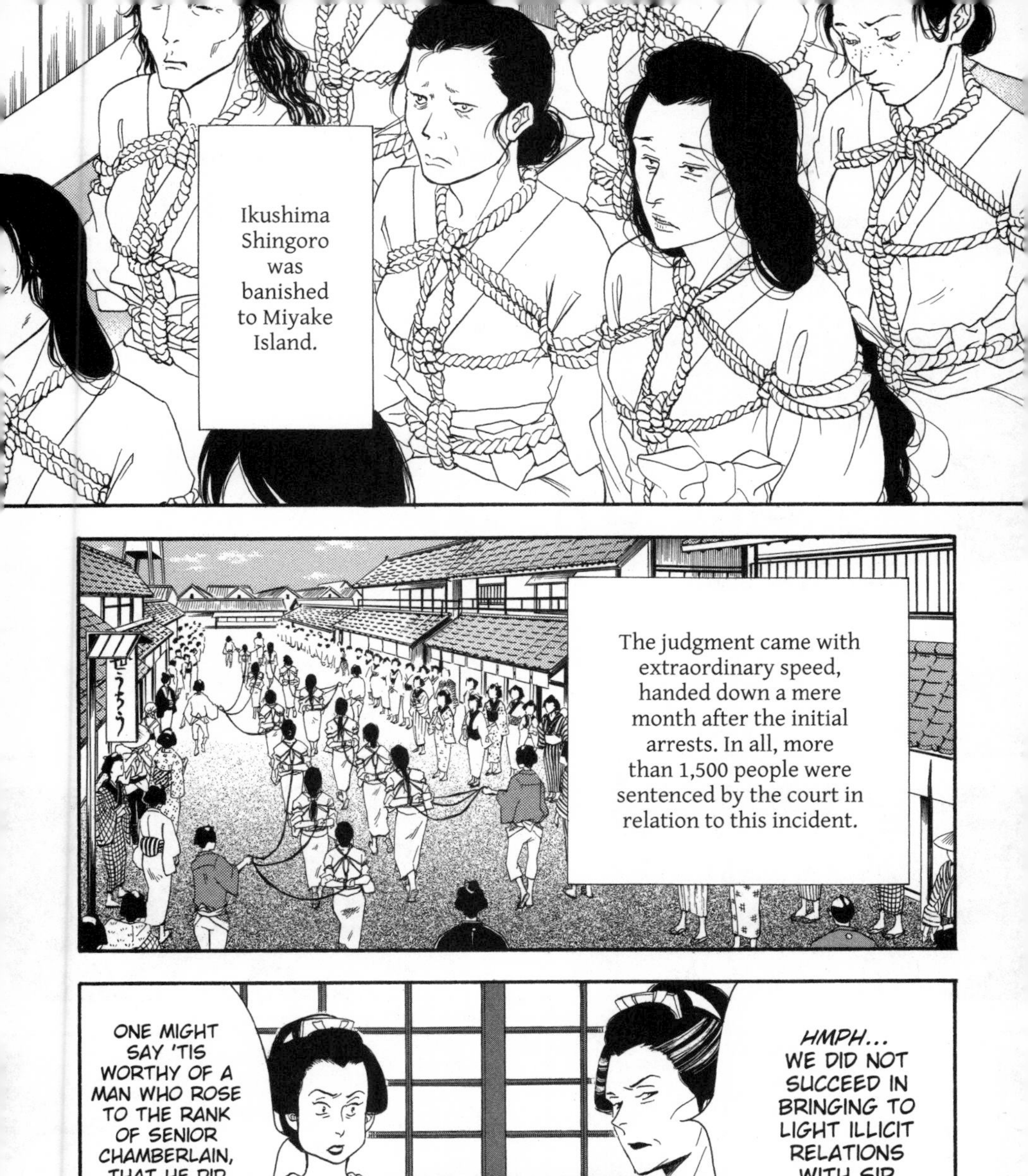
Ikushima Shingoro was banished to Miyake Island.
The judgment came with extraordinary speed, handed down a mere month after the initial arrests. In all, more than 1,500 people were sentenced by the court in relation to this incident.
HMPH... WE DID NOT SUCCEED IN BRINGING TO LIGHT ILLICIT RELATIONS WITH SIR GEKKO-IN, SO WERE UNABLE TO OUST THE BARON OF ECHIZEN.
ONE MIGHT SAY 'TIS WORTHY OF A MAN WHO ROSE TO THE RANK OF SENIOR CHAMBERLAIN, THAT HE DID REMAIN FIRMLY LOYAL TO HIS MASTER TO THE LAST.

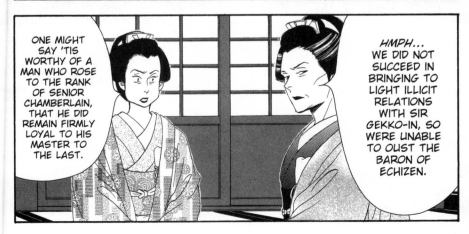

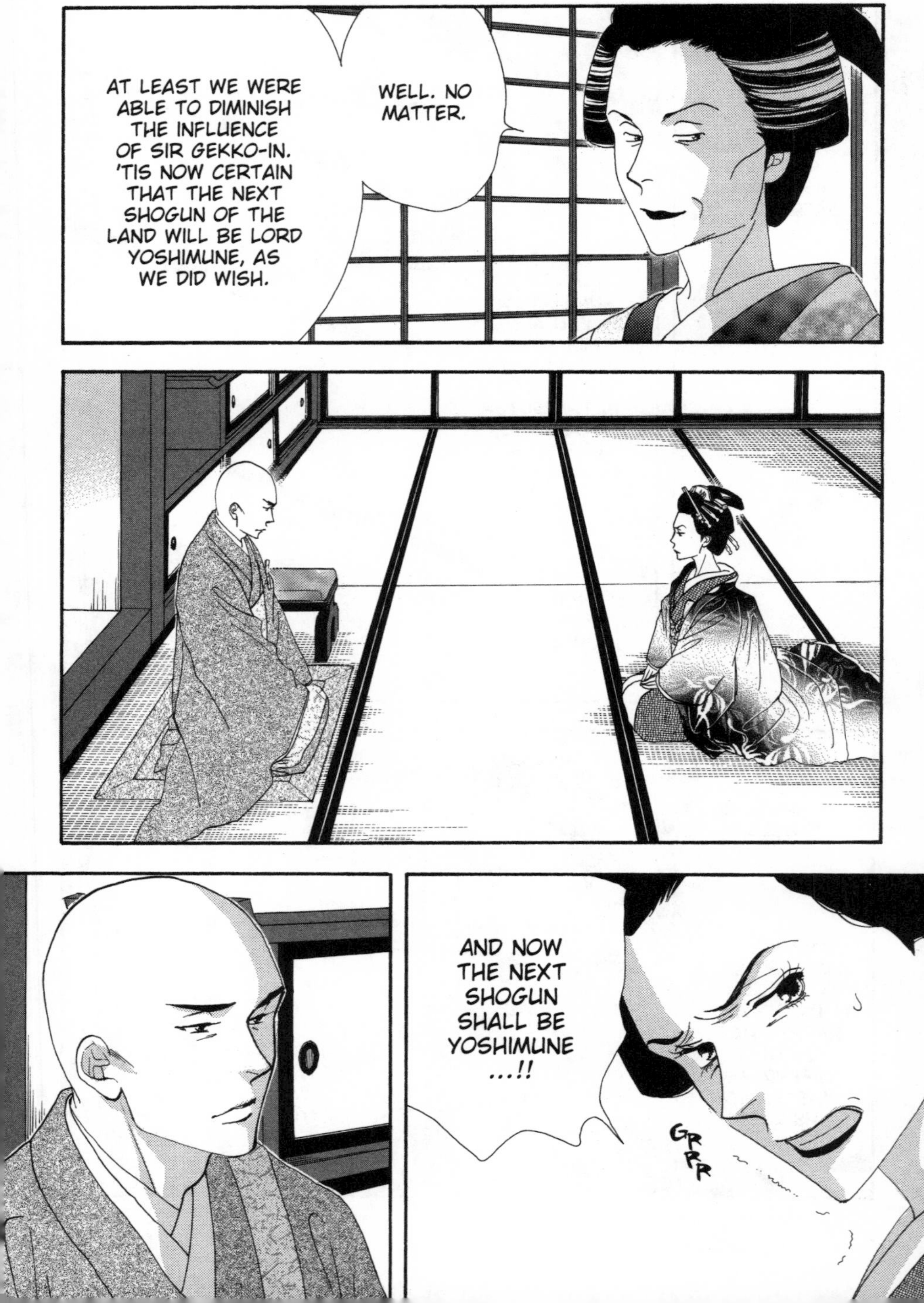
WELL. NO MATTER.
AT LEAST WE WERE ABLE TO DIMINISH THE INFLUENCE OF SIR GEKKO-IN. 'TIS NOW CERTAIN THAT THE NEXT SHOGUN OF THE LAND WILL BE LORD YOSHIMUNE, AS WE DID WISH.
AND NOW THE NEXT SHOGUN SHALL BE YOSHIMUNE ...!!
GRRR

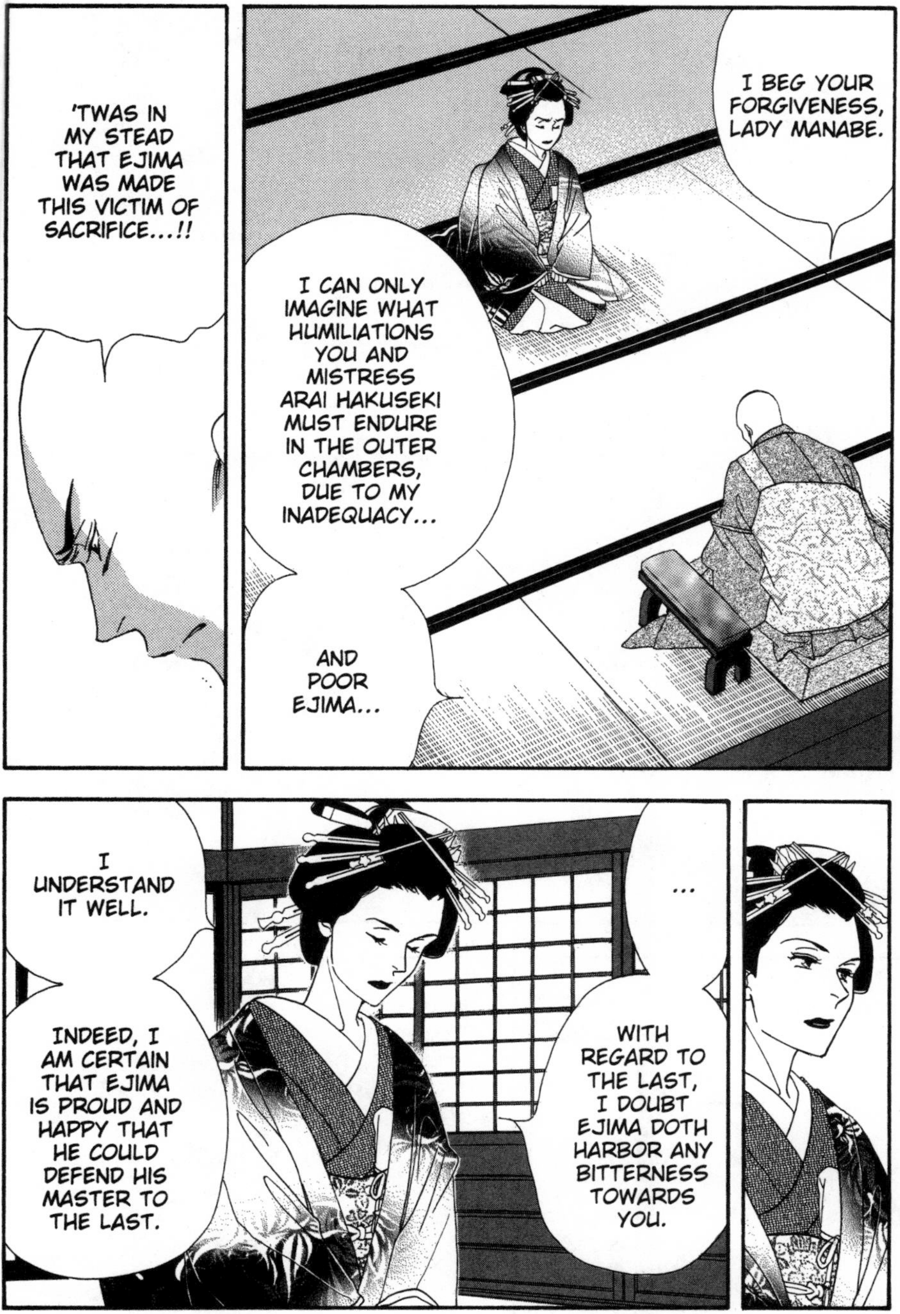
I BEG YOUR FORGIVENESS, LADY MANABE.
I CAN ONLY IMAGINE WHAT HUMILIATIONS YOU AND MISTRESS ARAI HAKUSEKI MUST ENDURE IN THE OUTER CHAMBERS, DUE TO MY INADEQUACY...
AND POOR EJIMA...
'TWAS IN MY STEAD THAT EJIMA WAS MADE THIS VICTIM OF SACRIFICE...!!
I UNDERSTAND IT WELL.
INDEED, I AM CERTAIN THAT EJIMA IS PROUD AND HAPPY THAT HE COULD DEFEND HIS MASTER TO THE LAST.
...
WITH REGARD TO THE LAST, I DOUBT EJIMA DOTH HARBOR ANY BITTERNESS TOWARDS YOU.

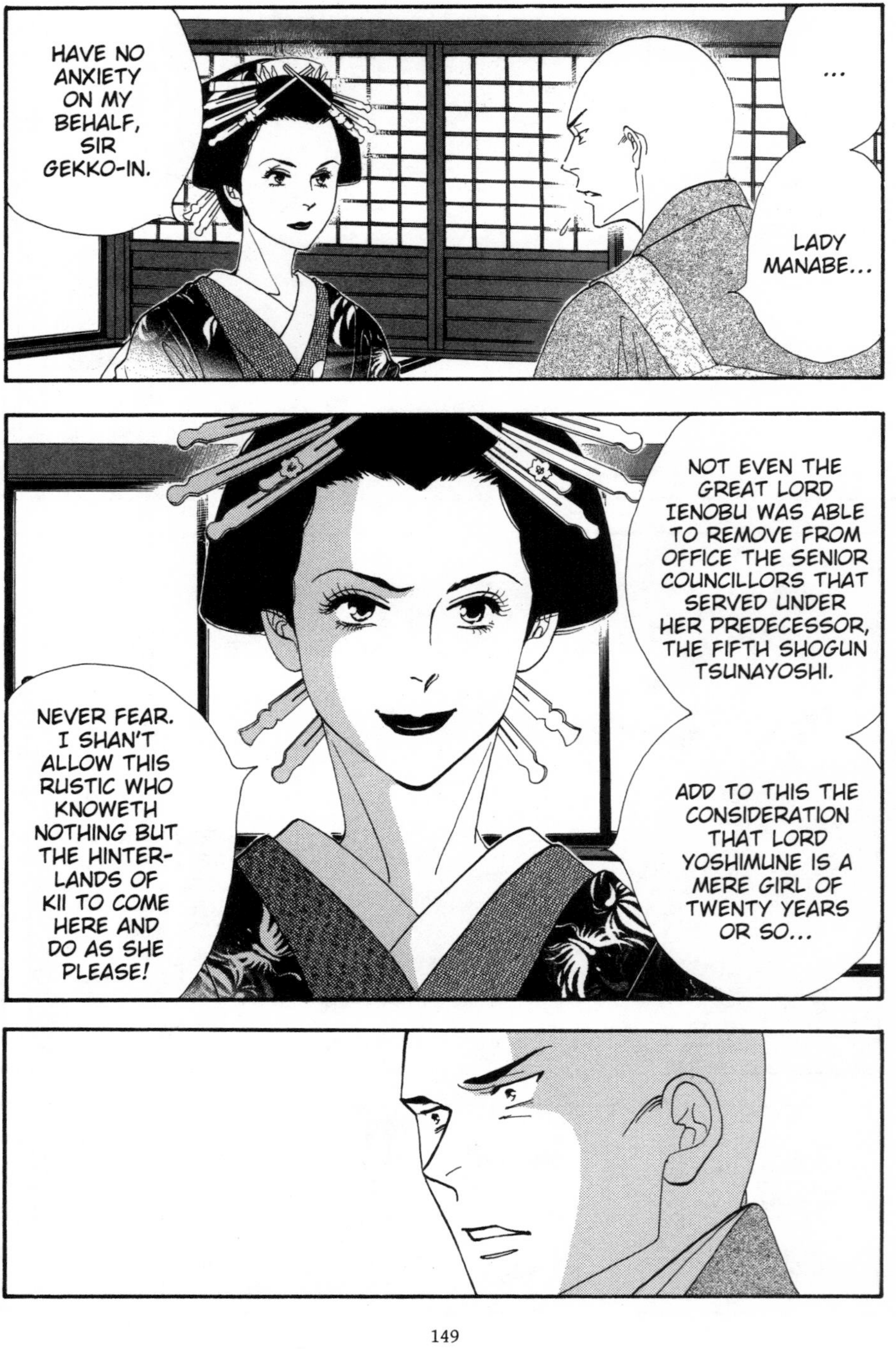
...
LADY MANABE...
HAVE NO ANXIETY ON MY BEHALF, SIR GEKKO-IN.
NOT EVEN THE GREAT LORD IENOBU WAS ABLE TO REMOVE FROM OFFICE THE SENIOR COUNCILLORS THAT SERVED UNDER HER PREDECESSOR, THE FIFTH SHOGUN TSUNAYOSHI.
ADD TO THIS THE CONSIDERATION THAT LORD YOSHIMUNE IS A MERE GIRL OF TWENTY YEARS OR SO...
NEVER FEAR. I SHAN'T ALLOW THIS RUSTIC WHO KNOWETH NOTHING BUT THE HINTER-LANDS OF KII TO COME HERE AND DO AS SHE PLEASE!

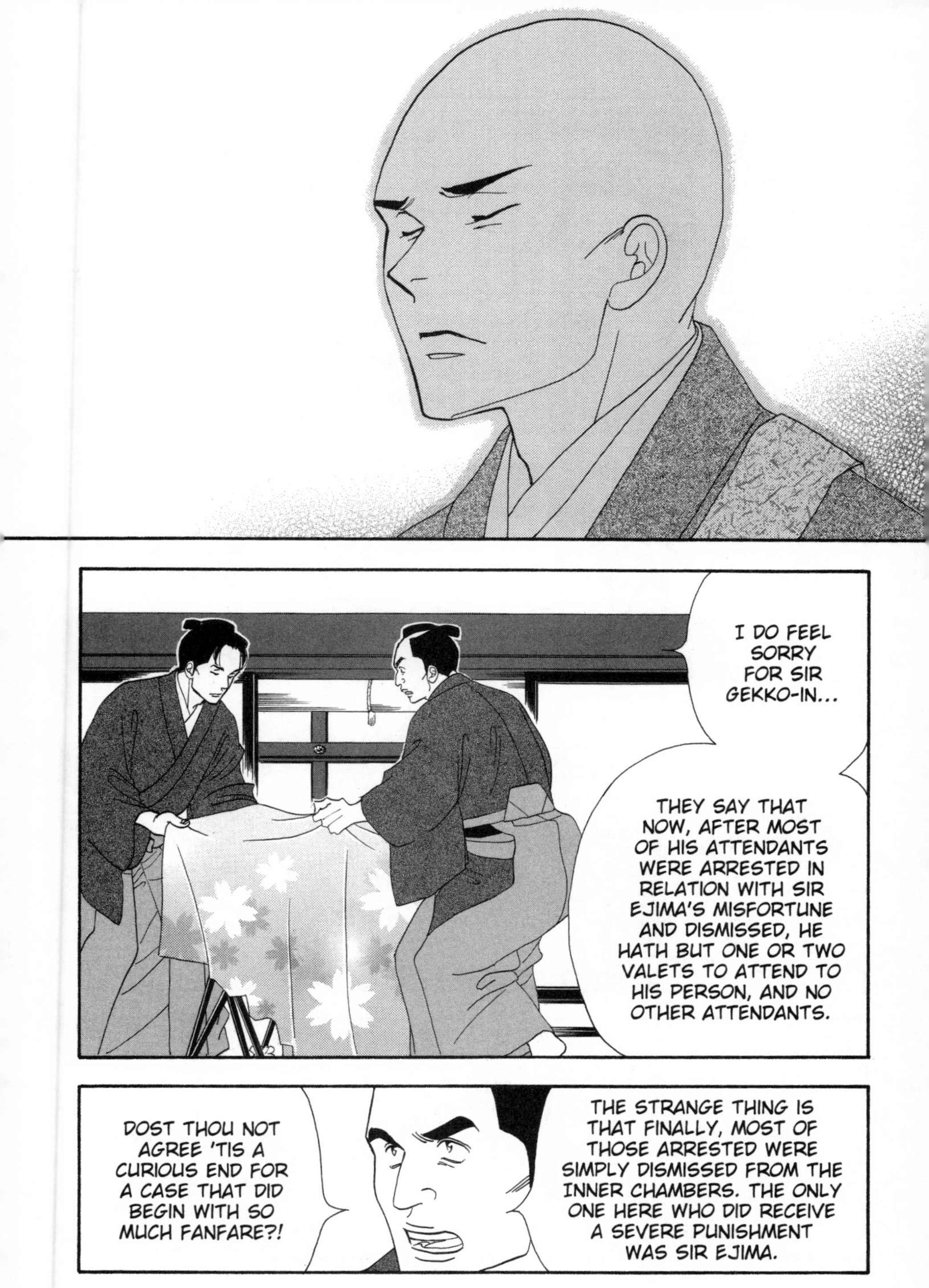
I DO FEEL SORRY FOR SIR GEKKO-IN...
THEY SAY THAT NOW, AFTER MOST OF HIS ATTENDANTS WERE ARRESTED IN RELATION WITH SIR EJIMA'S MISFORTUNE AND DISMISSED, HE HATH BUT ONE OR TWO VALETS TO ATTEND TO HIS PERSON, AND NO OTHER ATTENDANTS.
THE STRANGE THING IS THAT FINALLY, MOST OF THOSE ARRESTED WERE SIMPLY DISMISSED FROM THE INNER CHAMBERS. THE ONLY ONE HERE WHO DID RECEIVE A SEVERE PUNISHMENT WAS SIR EJIMA.
DOST THOU NOT AGREE 'TIS A CURIOUS END FOR A CASE THAT DID BEGIN WITH SO MUCH FANFARE?!

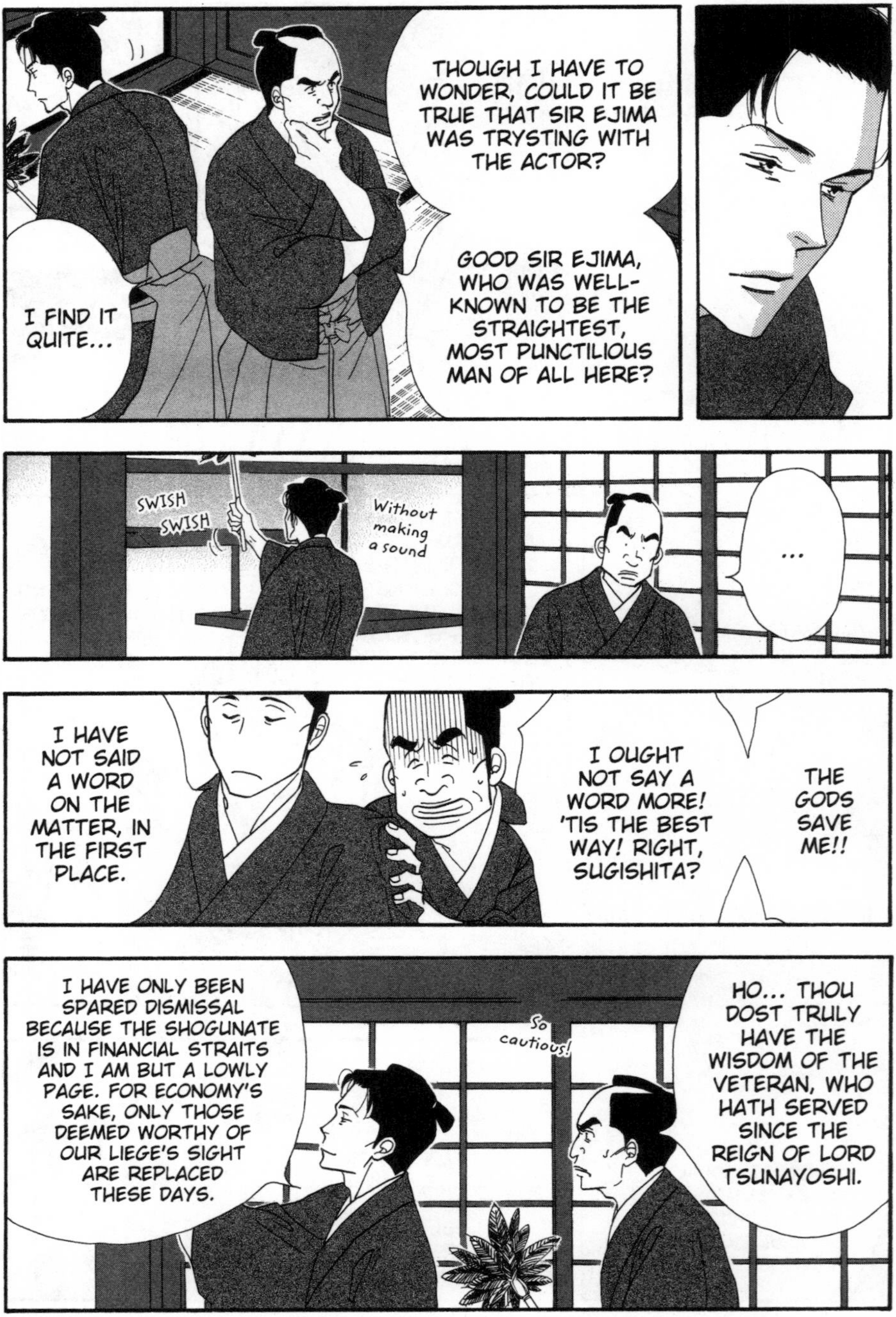
THOUGH I HAVE TO WONDER, COULD IT BE TRUE THAT SIR EJIMA WAS TRYSTING WITH THE ACTOR?
GOOD SIR EJIMA, WHO WAS WELL-KNOWN TO BE THE STRAIGHTEST, MOST PUNCTILIOUS MAN OF ALL HERE?
I FIND IT QUITE...
...
Without making a sound
SWISH SWISH
THE GODS SAVE ME!!
I OUGHT NOT SAY A WORD MORE! 'TIS THE BEST WAY! RIGHT, SUGISHITA?
I HAVE NOT SAID A WORD ON THE MATTER, IN THE FIRST PLACE.
HO... THOU DOST TRULY HAVE THE WISDOM OF THE VETERAN, WHO HATH SERVED SINCE THE REIGN OF LORD TSUNAYOSHI.
So cautious!
I HAVE ONLY BEEN SPARED DISMISSAL BECAUSE THE SHOGUNATE IS IN FINANCIAL STRAITS AND I AM BUT A LOWLY PAGE. FOR ECONOMY'S SAKE, ONLY THOSE DEEMED WORTHY OF OUR LIEGE'S SIGHT ARE REPLACED THESE DAYS.

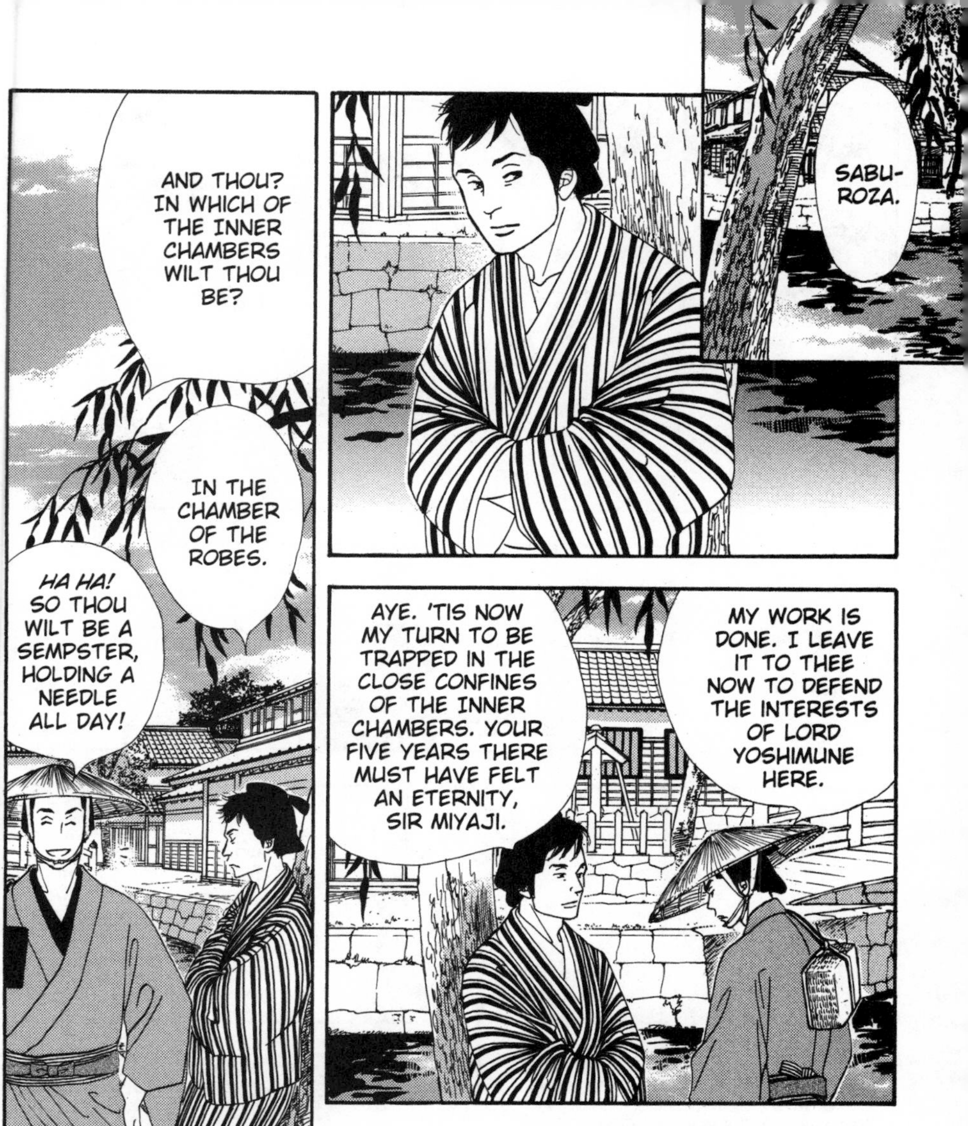
SABU-ROZA.
MY WORK IS DONE. I LEAVE IT TO THEE NOW TO DEFEND THE INTERESTS OF LORD YOSHIMUNE HERE.
AYE. 'TIS NOW MY TURN TO BE TRAPPED IN THE CLOSE CONFINES OF THE INNER CHAMBERS. YOUR FIVE YEARS THERE MUST HAVE FELT AN ETERNITY, SIR MIYAJI.
QUIT THE "SIR MIYAJI." HENCEFORTH I'M YASUKE THE SCOUT ONCE MORE. FOR THE NONCE, I SHALL LEAVE EDO TO COOL MY HEELS UNTIL THIS STORM HATH BLOWN OVER.
AND THOU? IN WHICH OF THE INNER CHAMBERS WILT THOU BE?
IN THE CHAMBER OF THE ROBES.
HA HA! SO THOU WILT BE A SEMPSTER, HOLDING A NEEDLE ALL DAY!
SO BE IT. I AM WILLING TO DO ANYTHING, IF IT BE FOR MY WORK.

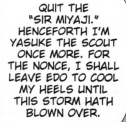

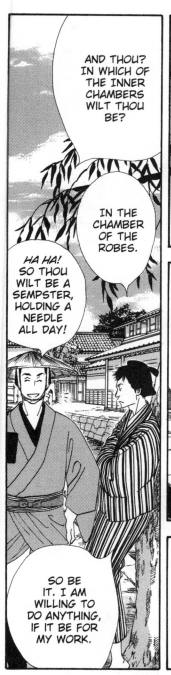

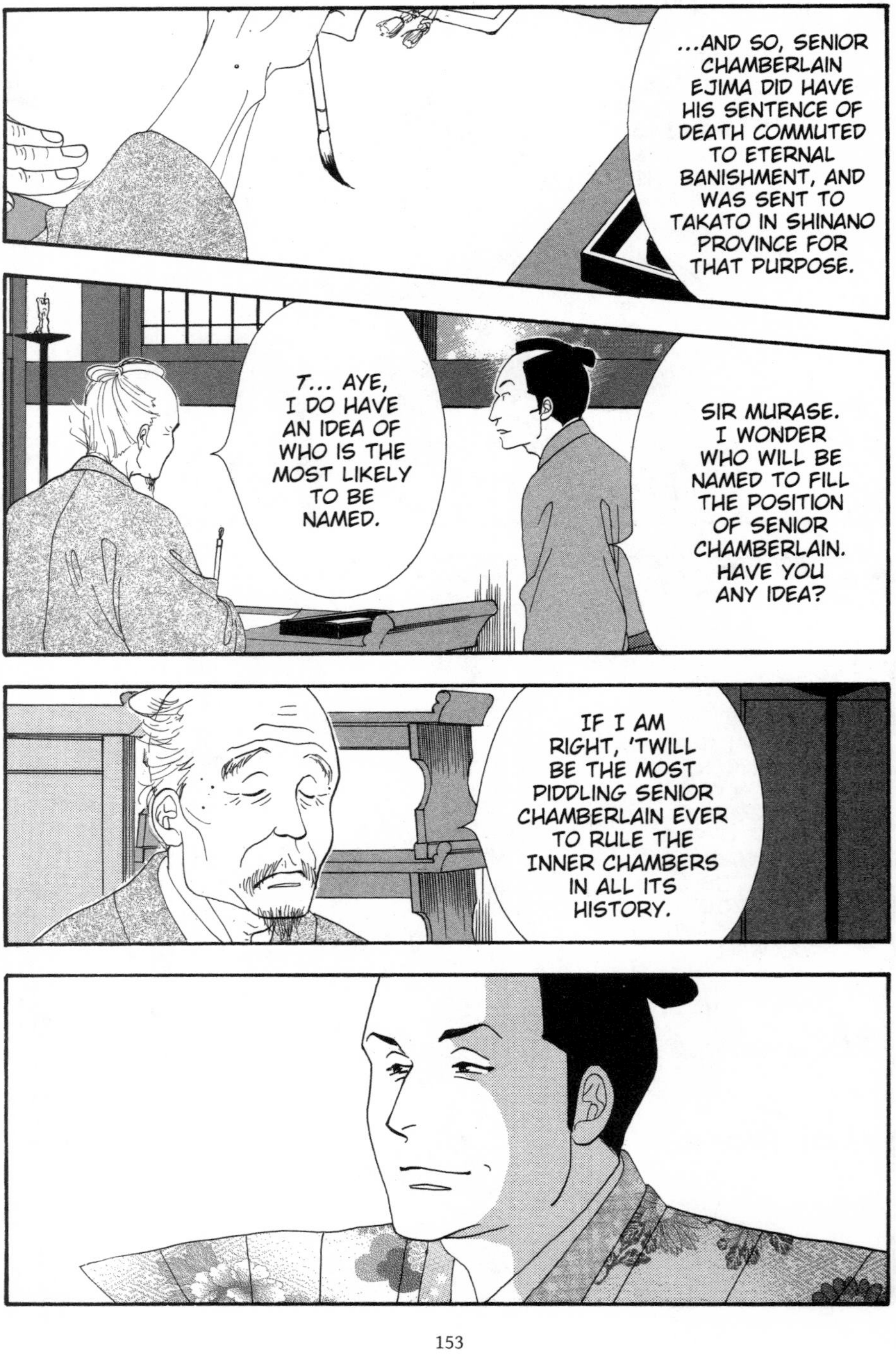
...AND SO, SENIOR CHAMBERLAIN EJIMA DID HAVE HIS SENTENCE OF DEATH COMMUTED TO ETERNAL BANISHMENT, AND WAS SENT TO TAKATO IN SHINANO PROVINCE FOR THAT PURPOSE.
SIR MURASE. I WONDER WHO WILL BE NAMED TO FILL THE POSITION OF SENIOR CHAMBERLAIN. HAVE YOU ANY IDEA?
T... AYE, I DO HAVE AN IDEA OF WHO IS THE MOST LIKELY TO BE NAMED.
IF I AM RIGHT, 'TWILL BE THE MOST PIDDLING SENIOR CHAMBERLAIN EVER TO RULE THE INNER CHAMBERS IN ALL ITS HISTORY.

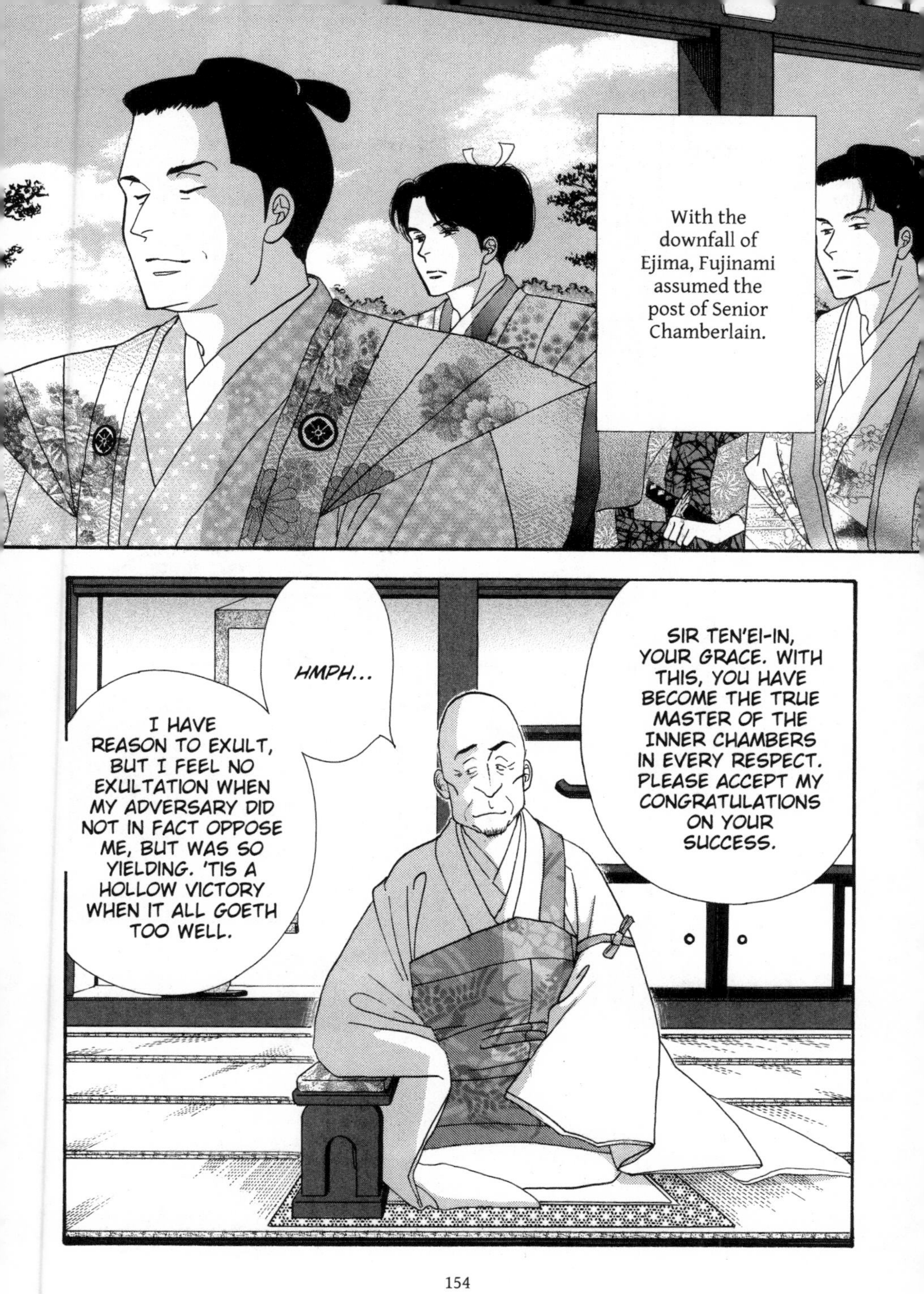
With the downfall of Ejima, Fujinami assumed the post of Senior Chamberlain.
SIR TEN'EI-IN, YOUR GRACE. WITH THIS, YOU HAVE BECOME THE TRUE MASTER OF THE INNER CHAMBERS IN EVERY RESPECT. PLEASE ACCEPT MY CONGRATULATIONS ON YOUR SUCCESS.
HMPH...
I HAVE REASON TO EXULT, BUT I FEEL NO EXULTATION WHEN MY ADVERSARY DID NOT IN FACT OPPOSE ME, BUT WAS SO YIELDING. 'TIS A HOLLOW VICTORY WHEN IT ALL GOETH TOO WELL.

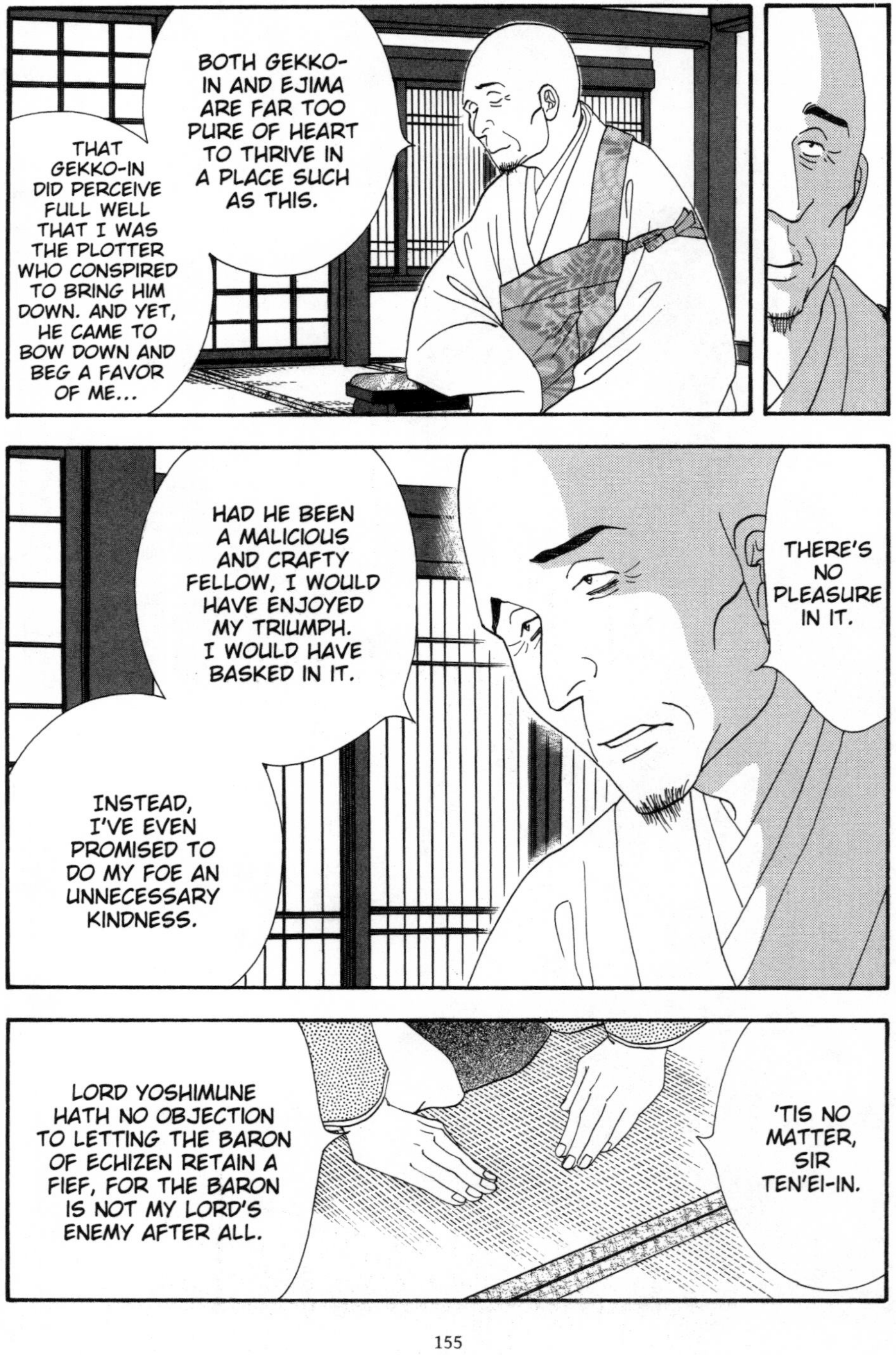
BOTH GEKKO-IN AND EJIMA ARE FAR TOO PURE OF HEART TO THRIVE IN A PLACE SUCH AS THIS.
THAT GEKKO-IN DID PERCEIVE FULL WELL THAT I WAS THE PLOTTER WHO CONSPIRED TO BRING HIM DOWN. AND YET, HE CAME TO BOW DOWN AND BEG A FAVOR OF ME...
THERE'S NO PLEASURE IN IT.
HAD HE BEEN A MALICIOUS AND CRAFTY FELLOW, I WOULD HAVE ENJOYED MY TRIUMPH. I WOULD HAVE BASKED IN IT.
INSTEAD, I'VE EVEN PROMISED TO DO MY FOE AN UNNECESSARY KINDNESS.
'TIS NO MATTER, SIR TEN'EI-IN.
LORD YOSHIMUNE HATH NO OBJECTION TO LETTING THE BARON OF ECHIZEN RETAIN A FIEF, FOR THE BARON IS NOT MY LORD'S ENEMY AFTER ALL.

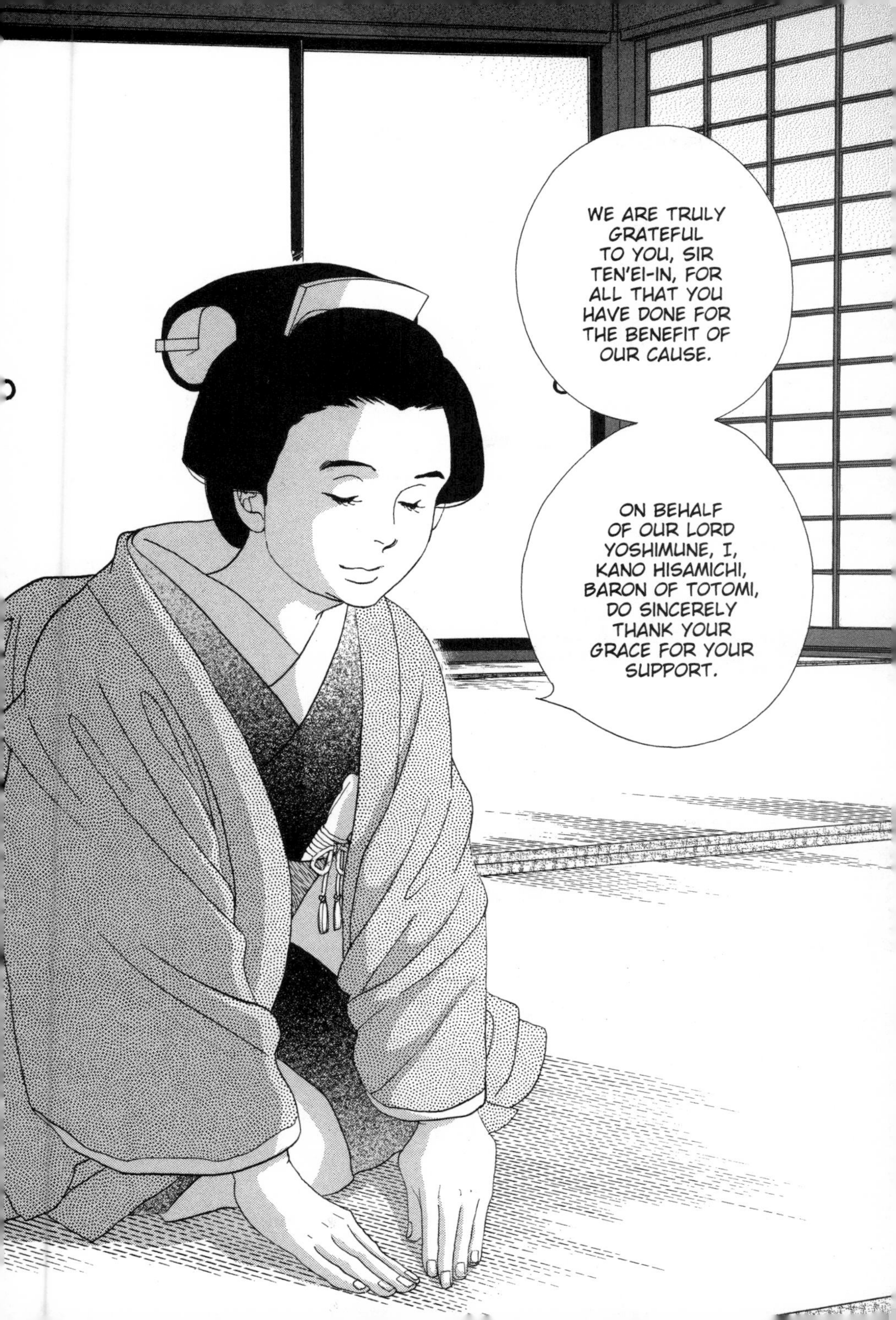
WE ARE TRULY GRATEFUL TO YOU, SIR TEN'EI-IN, FOR ALL THAT YOU HAVE DONE FOR THE BENEFIT OF OUR CAUSE.
ON BEHALF OF OUR LORD YOSHIMUNE, I, KANO HISAMICHI, BARON OF TOTOMI, DO SINCERELY THANK YOUR GRACE FOR YOUR SUPPORT.

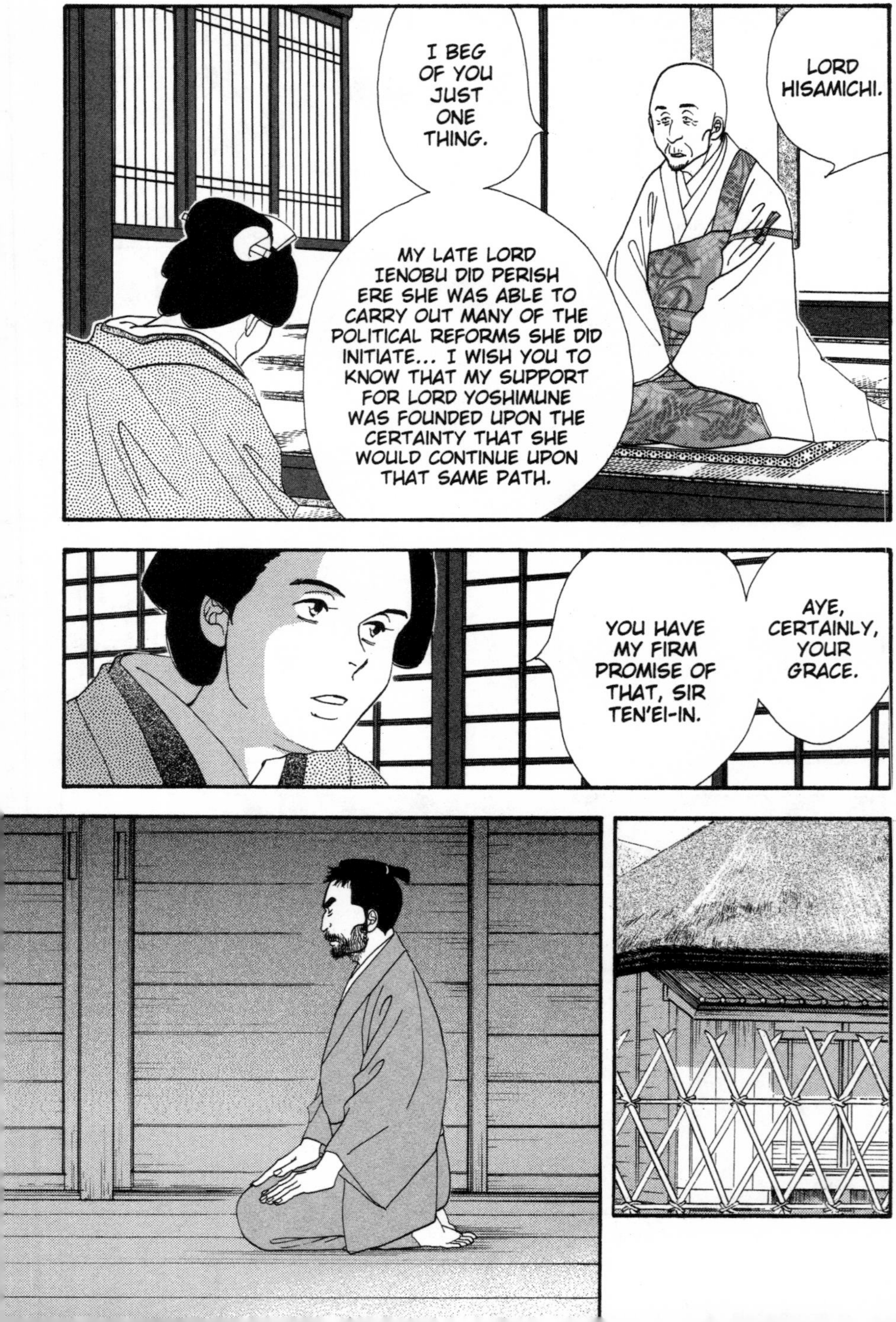
LORD HISAMICHI.
I BEG OF YOU JUST ONE THING.
MY LATE LORD IENOBU DID PERISH ERE SHE WAS ABLE TO CARRY OUT MANY OF THE POLITICAL REFORMS SHE DID INITIATE... I WISH YOU TO KNOW THAT MY SUPPORT FOR LORD YOSHIMUNE WAS FOUNDED UPON THE CERTAINTY THAT SHE WOULD CONTINUE UPON THAT SAME PATH.
AYE, CERTAINLY, YOUR GRACE.
YOU HAVE MY FIRM PROMISE OF THAT, SIR TEN'EI-IN.

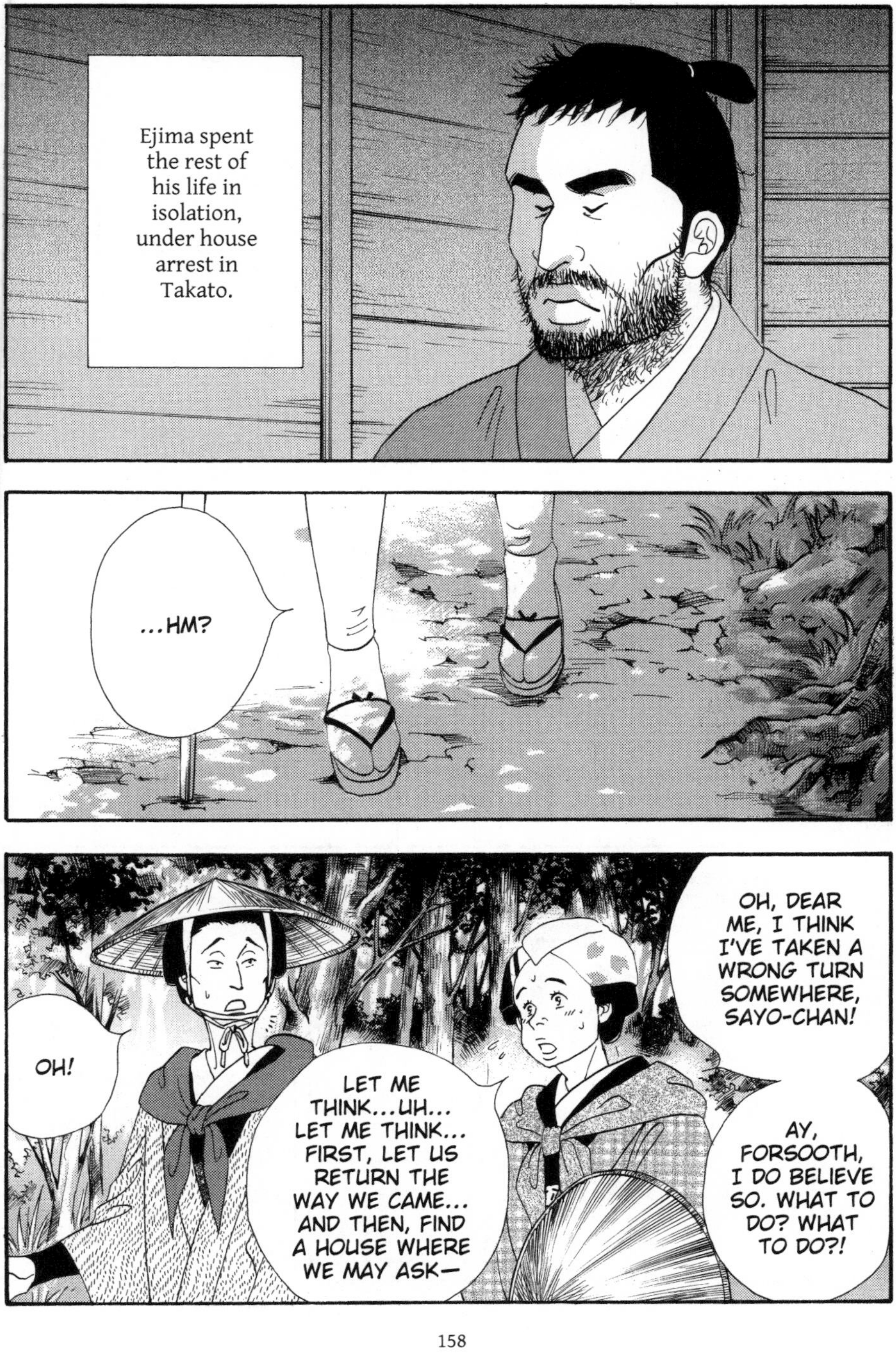
Ejima spent the rest of his life in isolation, under house arrest in Takato.
...HM?
OH, DEAR ME, I THINK I'VE TAKEN A WRONG TURN SOMEWHERE, SAYO-CHAN!
AY, FORSOOTH, I DO BELIEVE SO. WHAT TO DO? WHAT TO DO?!
LET ME THINK...UH... LET ME THINK... FIRST, LET US RETURN THE WAY WE CAME... AND THEN, FIND A HOUSE WHERE WE MAY ASK—
OH!

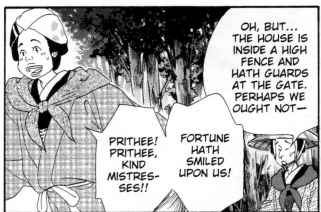

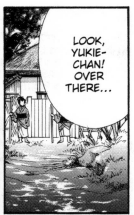

LOOK, YUKIE-CHAN! OVER THERE...
OH, BUT... THE HOUSE IS INSIDE A HIGH FENCE AND HATH GUARDS AT THE GATE. PERHAPS WE OUGHT NOT—
FORTUNE HATH SMILED UPON US!
PRITHEE! PRITHEE, KIND MISTRES-SES!!
SCOWL
HAVE YE LOST YOUR WAY?
RETURN TO THE RIVER AND TURN RIGHT. YE SHALL SOON REACH THE HIGHWAY.
OH, WE DO THANK YOU MOST GRATEFULLY!
TAKE HEED, AND GODSPEED.
...
ERRM...
MIGHT THIS... BE THE HOUSE WHERE THE NOBLE GENTLEMEN FROM THE INNER CHAMBERS IS SEQUESTERED...?
YUKIE-CHAN!!

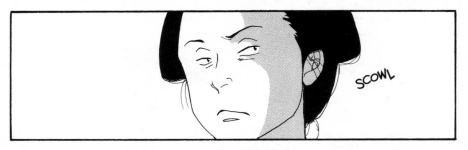

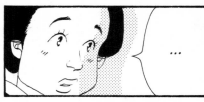

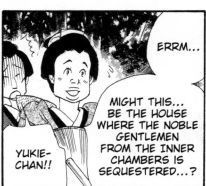

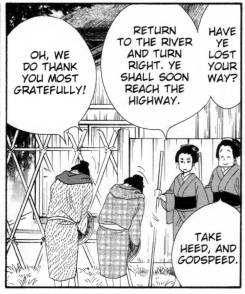

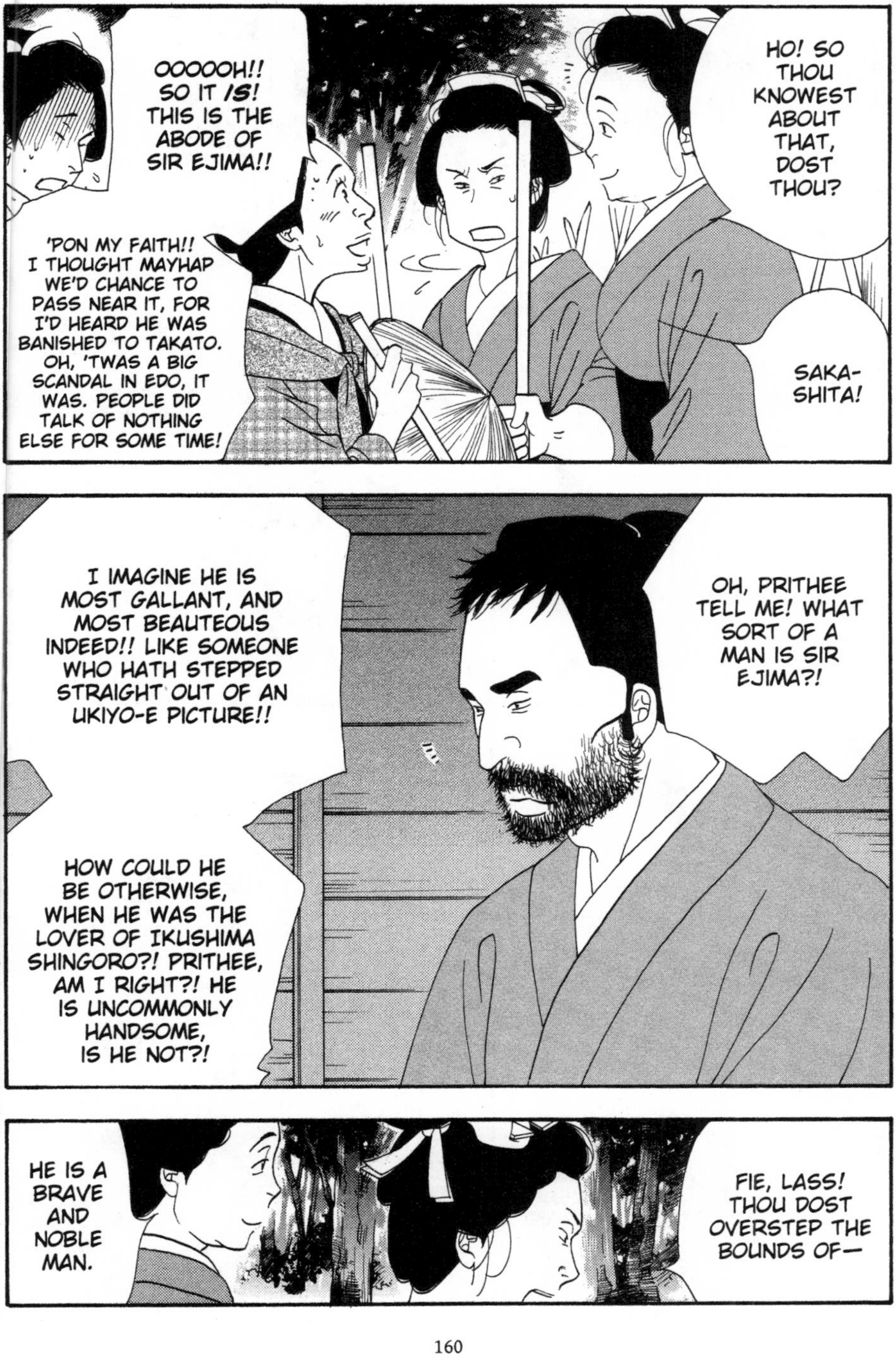
OOOOOH!! SO IT IS! THIS IS THE ABODE OF SIR EJIMA!!
'PON MY FAITH!! I THOUGHT MAYHAP WE'D CHANCE TO PASS NEAR IT, FOR I'D HEARD HE WAS BANISHED TO TAKATO. OH, 'TWAS A BIG SCANDAL IN EDO, IT WAS. PEOPLE DID TALK OF NOTHING ELSE FOR SOME TIME!
HO! SO THOU KNOWEST ABOUT THAT, DOST THOU?
SAKA-SHITA!
OH, PRITHEE TELL ME! WHAT SORT OF A MAN IS SIR EJIMA?!
I IMAGINE HE IS MOST GALLANT, AND MOST BEAUTEOUS INDEED!! LIKE SOMEONE WHO HATH STEPPED STRAIGHT OUT OF AN UKIYO-E PICTURE!!
HOW COULD HE BE OTHERWISE, WHEN HE WAS THE LOVER OF IKUSHIMA SHINGORO?! PRITHEE, AM I RIGHT?! HE IS UNCOMMONLY HANDSOME, IS HE NOT?!
FIE, LASS! THOU DOST OVERSTEP THE BOUNDS OF—
HE IS A BRAVE AND NOBLE MAN.

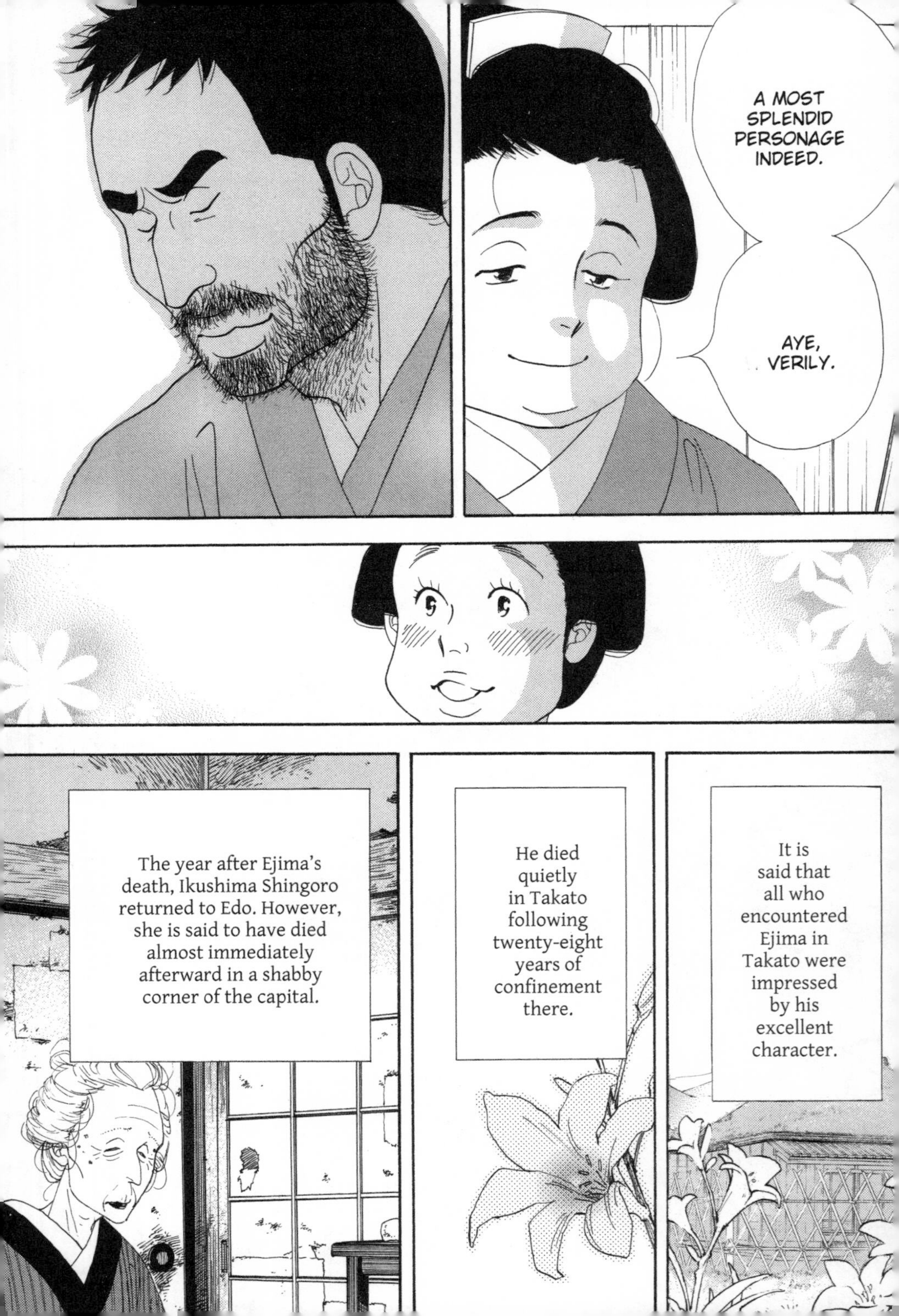
A MOST SPLENDID PERSONAGE INDEED.
AYE, VERILY.
It is said that all who encountered Ejima in Takato were impressed by his excellent character.
He died quietly in Takato following twenty-eight years of confinement there.
The year after Ejima's death, Ikushima Shingoro returned to Edo. However, she is said to have died almost immediately afterward in a shabby corner of the capital.

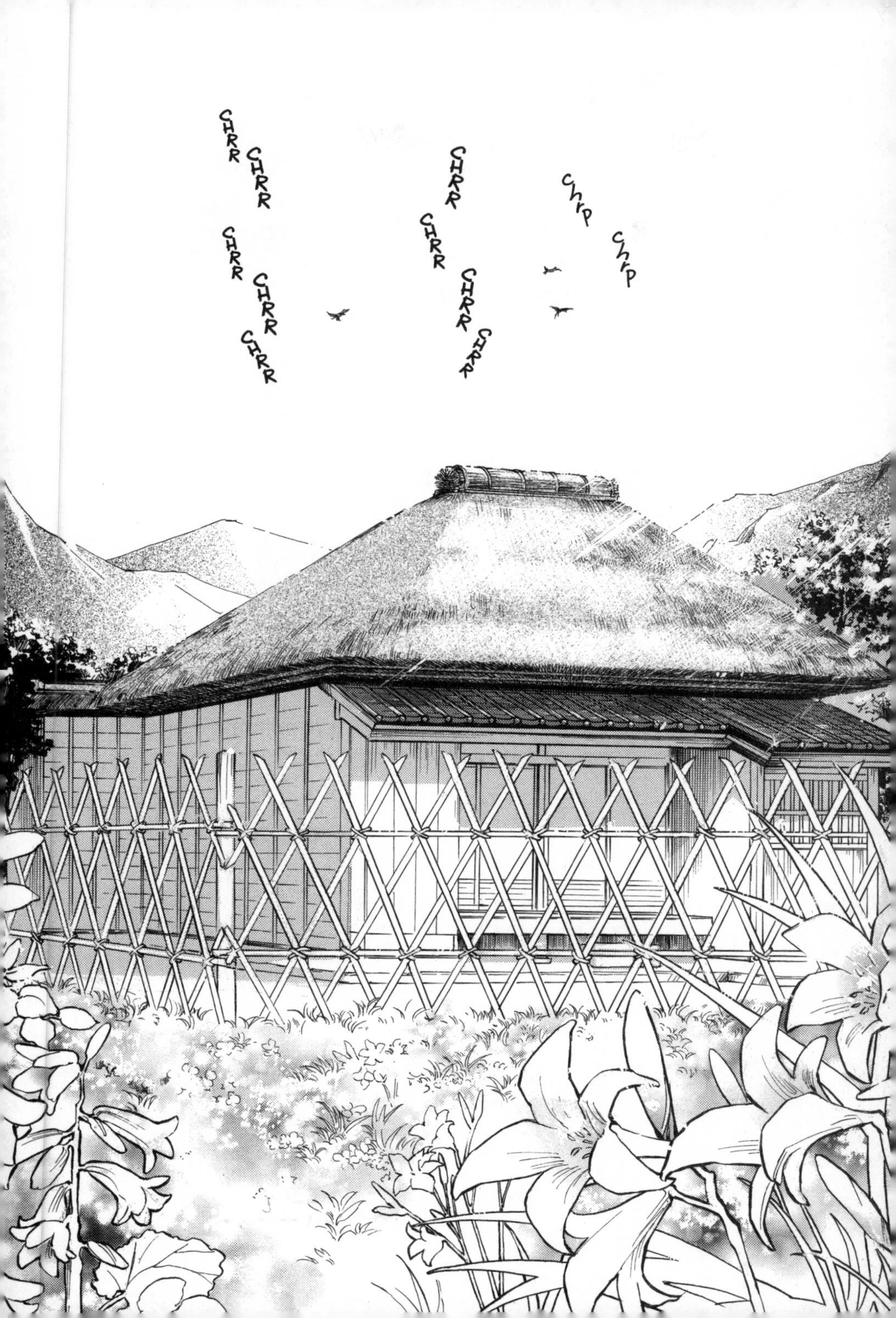
Chirp
Chirp
CHRR
CHRR
CHRR
CHRR
CHRR
CHRR
CHRR
CHRR
CHRR
CHRR

Ōoku

THE INNER CHAMBERS

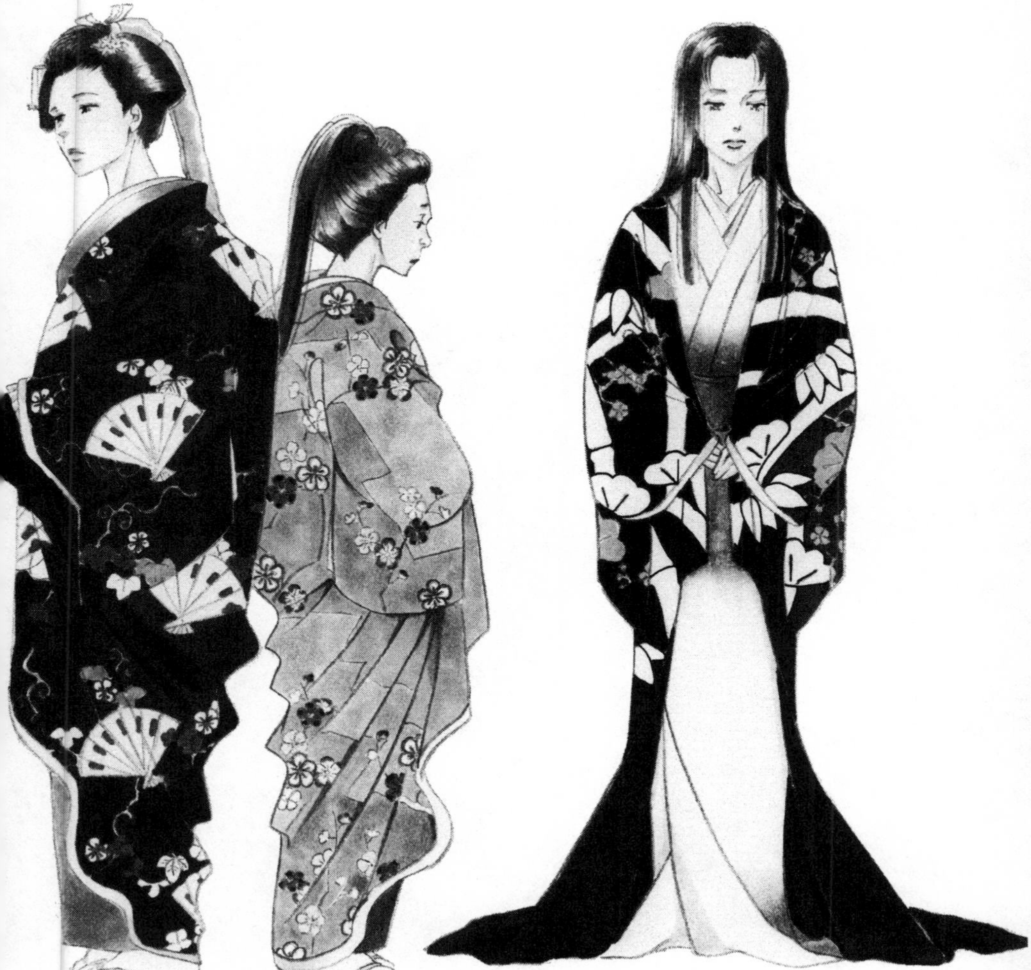

Ōoku

✿ THE INNER CHAMBERS

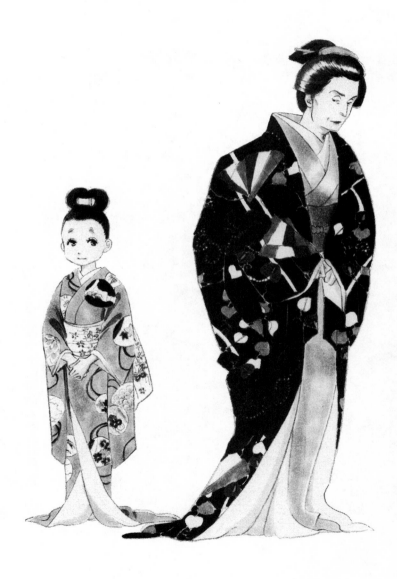

Ōoku

THE INNER CHAMBERS

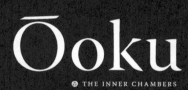

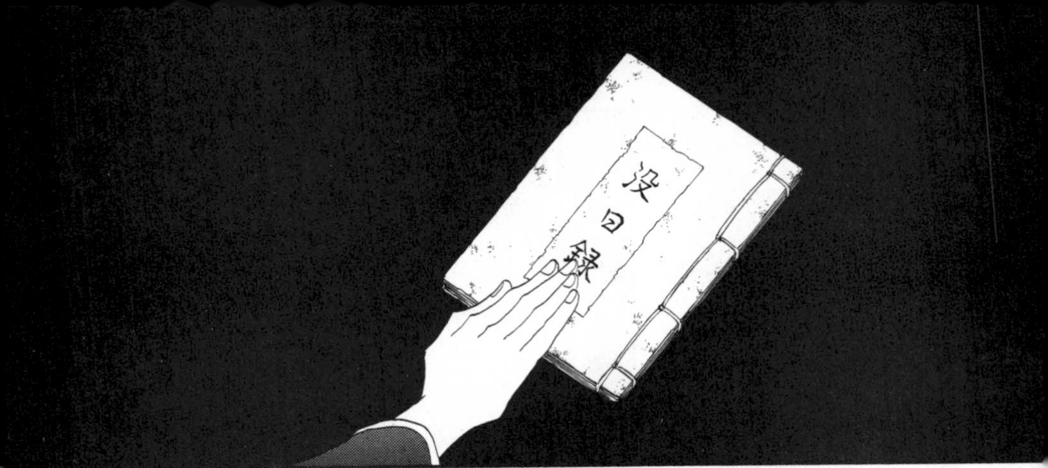
没日録

Book: Chronicle of a Dying Day

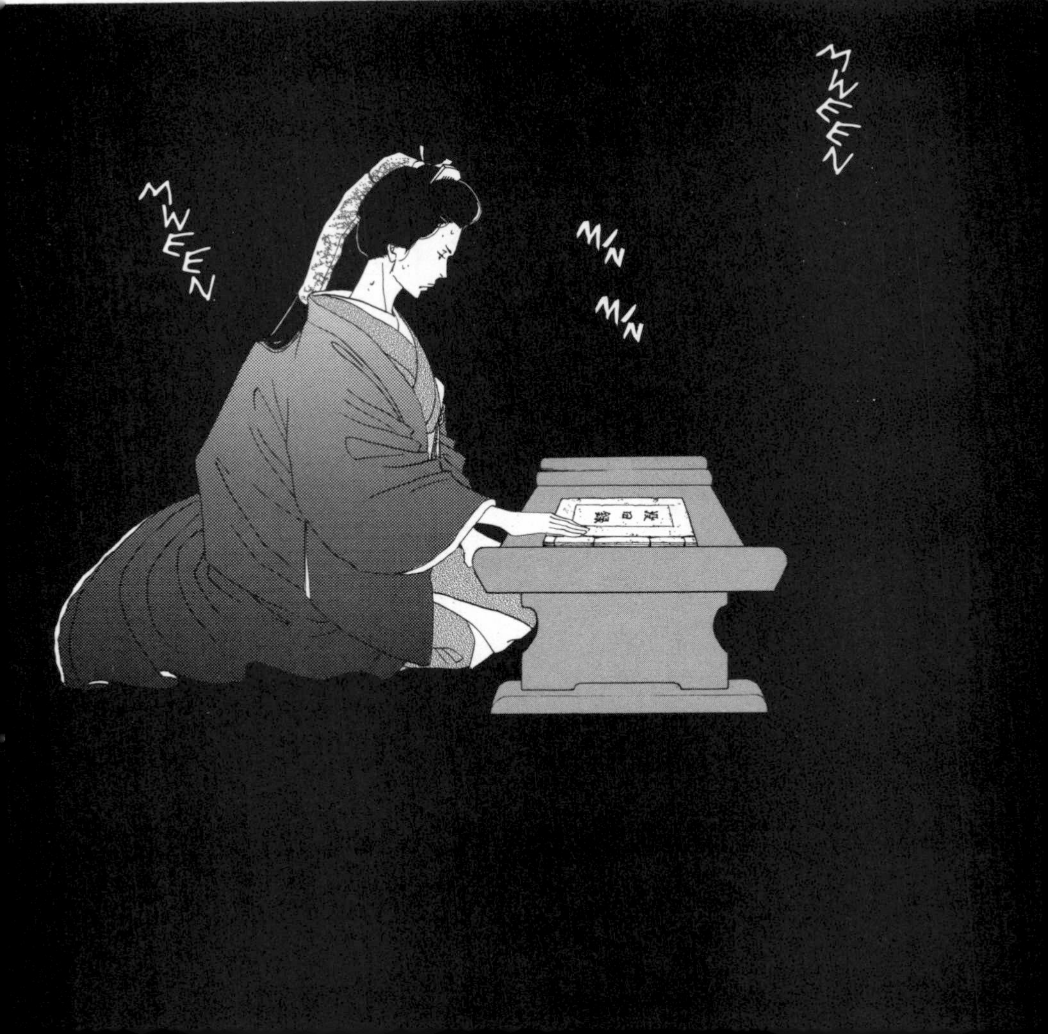
MWEEN
MIN MIN
MWEEN

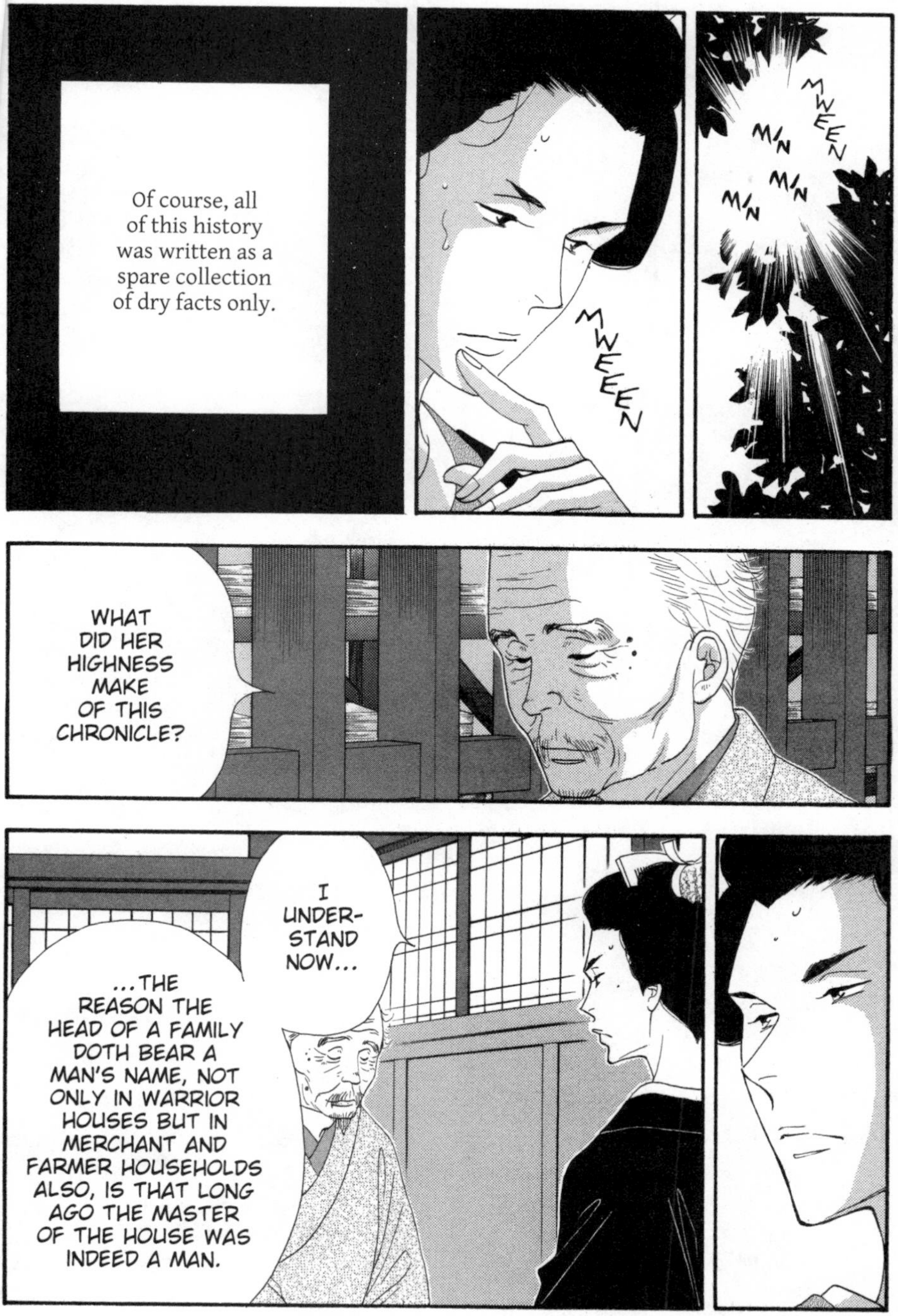
MWEEN
MIN
MIN
MIN
MWEEEN
Of course, all of this history was written as a spare collection of dry facts only.
WHAT DID HER HIGHNESS MAKE OF THIS CHRONICLE?
I UNDER-STAND NOW...
...THE REASON THE HEAD OF A FAMILY DOTH BEAR A MAN'S NAME, NOT ONLY IN WARRIOR HOUSES BUT IN MERCHANT AND FARMER HOUSEHOLDS ALSO, IS THAT LONG AGO THE MASTER OF THE HOUSE WAS INDEED A MAN.

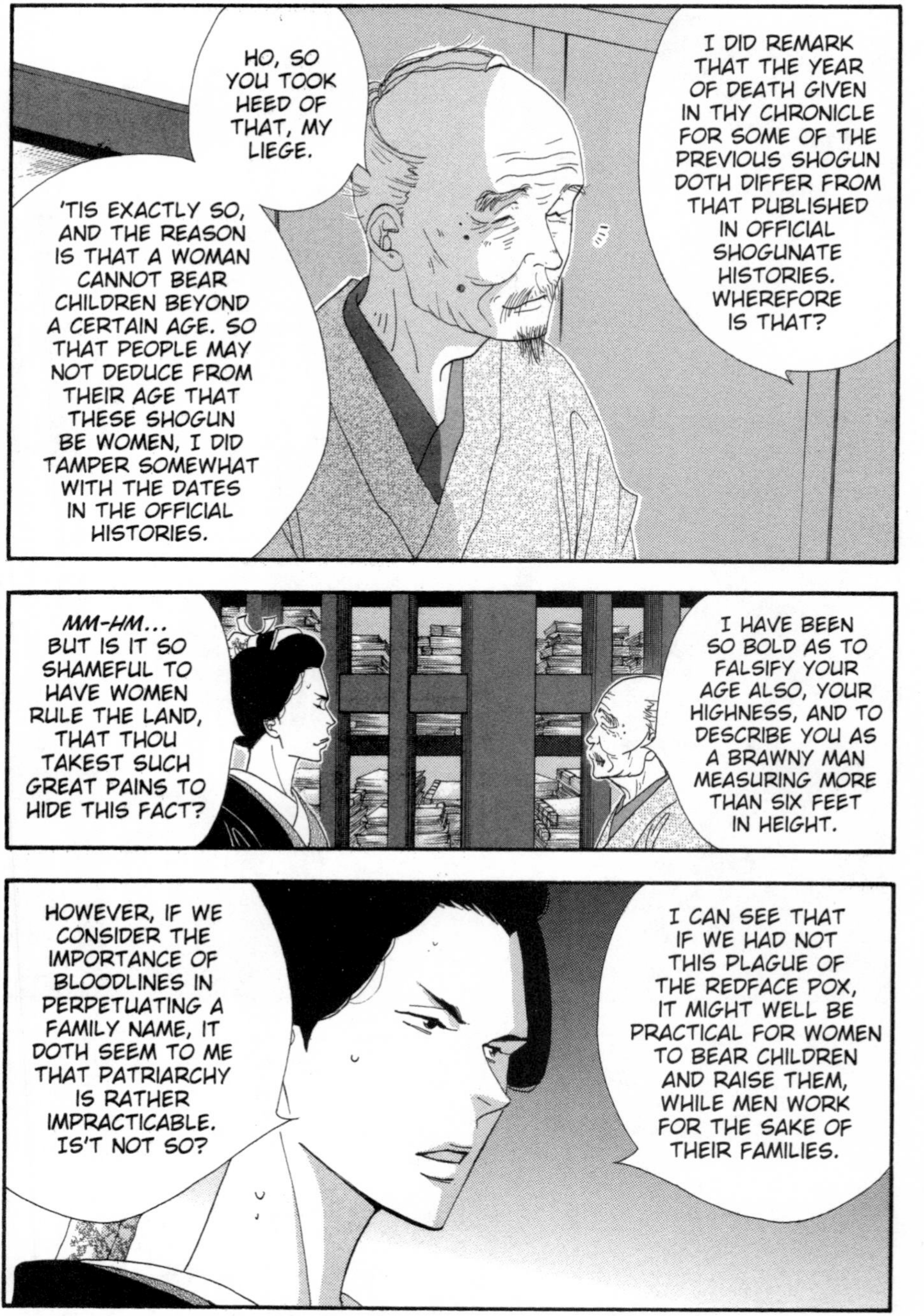
I DID REMARK THAT THE YEAR OF DEATH GIVEN IN THY CHRONICLE FOR SOME OF THE PREVIOUS SHOGUN DOTH DIFFER FROM THAT PUBLISHED IN OFFICIAL SHOGUNATE HISTORIES. WHEREFORE IS THAT?
HO, SO YOU TOOK HEED OF THAT, MY LIEGE.
'TIS EXACTLY SO, AND THE REASON IS THAT A WOMAN CANNOT BEAR CHILDREN BEYOND A CERTAIN AGE. SO THAT PEOPLE MAY NOT DEDUCE FROM THEIR AGE THAT THESE SHOGUN BE WOMEN, I DID TAMPER SOMEWHAT WITH THE DATES IN THE OFFICIAL HISTORIES.
I HAVE BEEN SO BOLD AS TO FALSIFY YOUR AGE ALSO, YOUR HIGHNESS, AND TO DESCRIBE YOU AS A BRAWNY MAN MEASURING MORE THAN SIX FEET IN HEIGHT.
MM-HM... BUT IS IT SO SHAMEFUL TO HAVE WOMEN RULE THE LAND, THAT THOU TAKEST SUCH GREAT PAINS TO HIDE THIS FACT?
I CAN SEE THAT IF WE HAD NOT THIS PLAGUE OF THE REDFACE POX, IT MIGHT WELL BE PRACTICAL FOR WOMEN TO BEAR CHILDREN AND RAISE THEM, WHILE MEN WORK FOR THE SAKE OF THEIR FAMILIES.
HOWEVER, IF WE CONSIDER THE IMPORTANCE OF BLOODLINES IN PERPETUATING A FAMILY NAME, IT DOTH SEEM TO ME THAT PATRIARCHY IS RATHER IMPRACTICABLE. IS'T NOT SO?

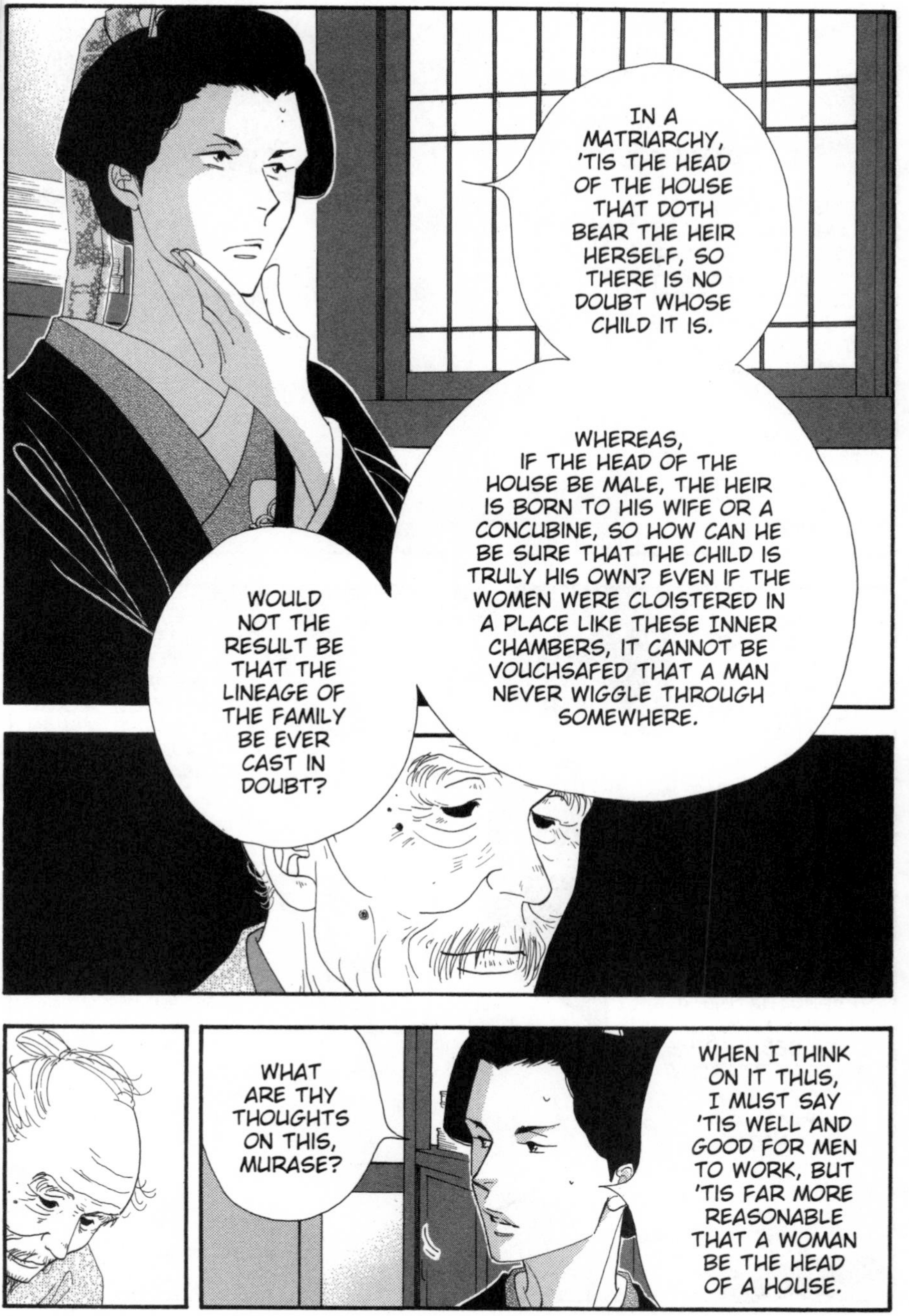
IN A MATRIARCHY, 'TIS THE HEAD OF THE HOUSE THAT DOTH BEAR THE HEIR HERSELF, SO THERE IS NO DOUBT WHOSE CHILD IT IS.
WHEREAS, IF THE HEAD OF THE HOUSE BE MALE, THE HEIR IS BORN TO HIS WIFE OR A CONCUBINE, SO HOW CAN HE BE SURE THAT THE CHILD IS TRULY HIS OWN? EVEN IF THE WOMEN WERE CLOISTERED IN A PLACE LIKE THESE INNER CHAMBERS, IT CANNOT BE VOUCHSAFED THAT A MAN NEVER WIGGLE THROUGH SOMEWHERE.
WOULD NOT THE RESULT BE THAT THE LINEAGE OF THE FAMILY BE EVER CAST IN DOUBT?
WHEN I THINK ON IT THUS, I MUST SAY 'TIS WELL AND GOOD FOR MEN TO WORK, BUT 'TIS FAR MORE REASONABLE THAT A WOMAN BE THE HEAD OF A HOUSE.
WHAT ARE THY THOUGHTS ON THIS, MURASE?

kttunk
MWEEN
MIN
MIN
...
HE'S DEAD.
SIR MURASE!!

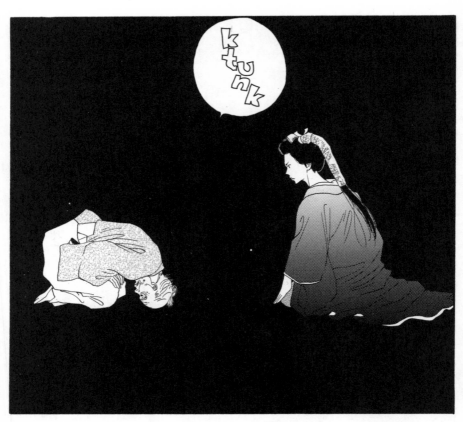

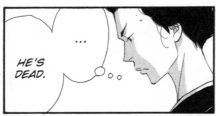

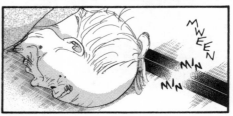

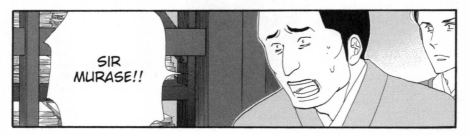

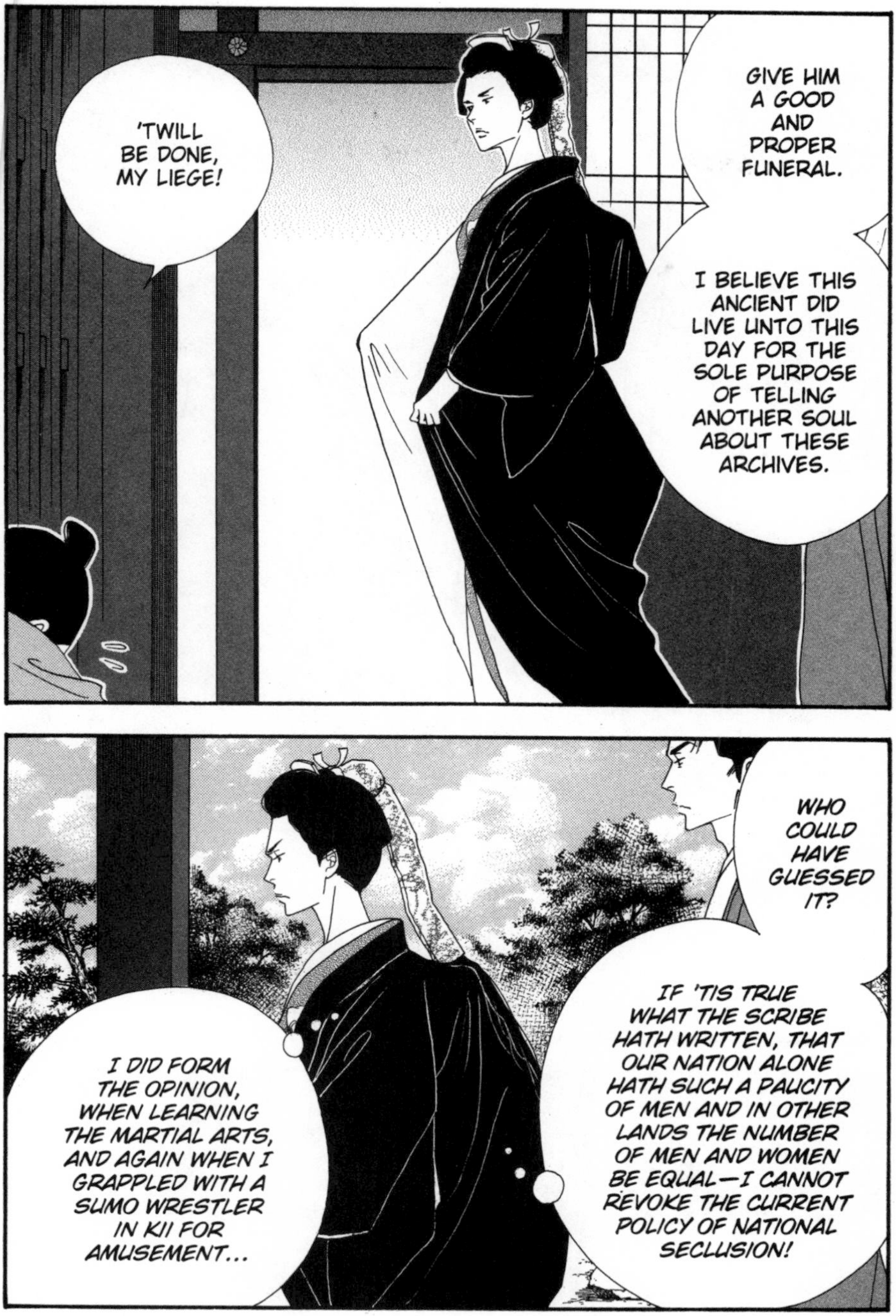
GIVE HIM A GOOD AND PROPER FUNERAL.
I BELIEVE THIS ANCIENT DID LIVE UNTO THIS DAY FOR THE SOLE PURPOSE OF TELLING ANOTHER SOUL ABOUT THESE ARCHIVES.
'TWILL BE DONE, MY LIEGE!
WHO COULD HAVE GUESSED IT?
IF 'TIS TRUE WHAT THE SCRIBE HATH WRITTEN, THAT OUR NATION ALONE HATH SUCH A PAUCITY OF MEN AND IN OTHER LANDS THE NUMBER OF MEN AND WOMEN BE EQUAL—I CANNOT REVOKE THE CURRENT POLICY OF NATIONAL SECLUSION!
I DID FORM THE OPINION, WHEN LEARNING THE MARTIAL ARTS, AND AGAIN WHEN I GRAPPLED WITH A SUMO WRESTLER IN KII FOR AMUSEMENT...

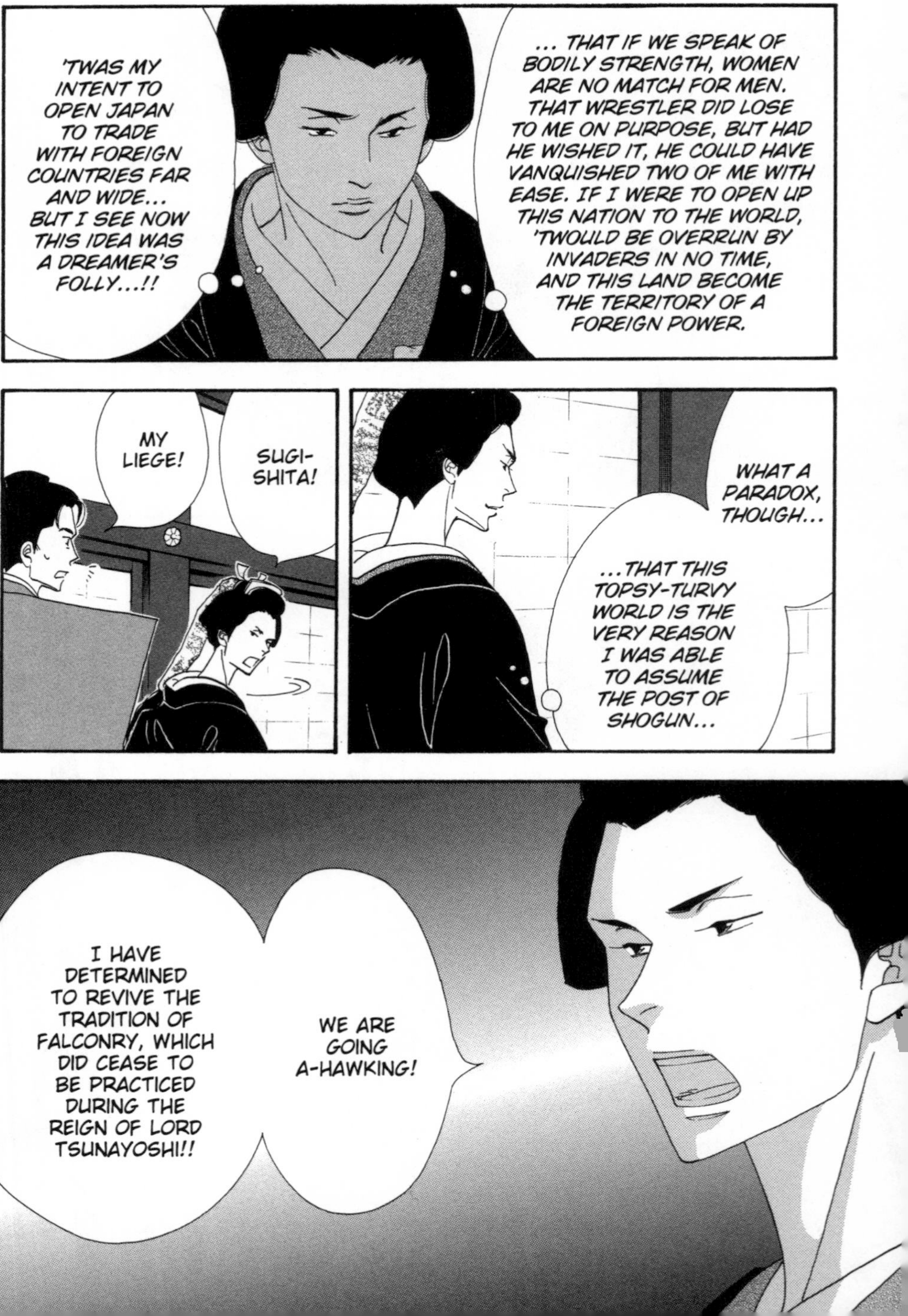
... THAT IF WE SPEAK OF BODILY STRENGTH, WOMEN ARE NO MATCH FOR MEN. THAT WRESTLER DID LOSE TO ME ON PURPOSE, BUT HAD HE WISHED IT, HE COULD HAVE VANQUISHED TWO OF ME WITH EASE. IF I WERE TO OPEN UP THIS NATION TO THE WORLD, 'TWOULD BE OVERRUN BY INVADERS IN NO TIME, AND THIS LAND BECOME THE TERRITORY OF A FOREIGN POWER.
'TWAS MY INTENT TO OPEN JAPAN TO TRADE WITH FOREIGN COUNTRIES FAR AND WIDE... BUT I SEE NOW THIS IDEA WAS A DREAMER'S FOLLY...!!
WHAT A PARADOX, THOUGH...
...THAT THIS TOPSY-TURVY WORLD IS THE VERY REASON I WAS ABLE TO ASSUME THE POST OF SHOGUN...
SUGI-SHITA!
MY LIEGE!
WE ARE GOING A-HAWKING!
I HAVE DETERMINED TO REVIVE THE TRADITION OF FALCONRY, WHICH DID CEASE TO BE PRACTICED DURING THE REIGN OF LORD TSUNAYOSHI!!

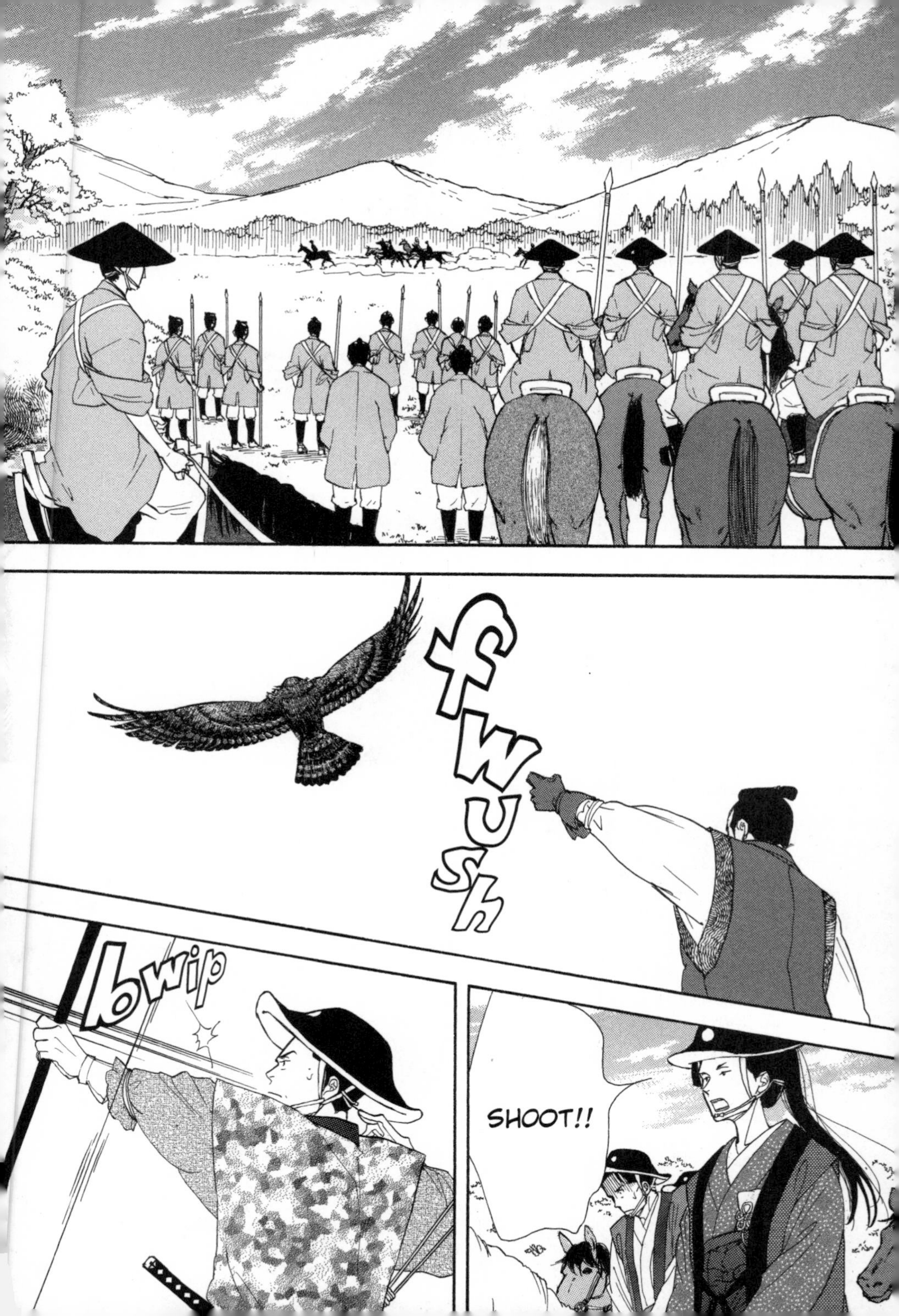
fwush
SHOOT!!
bwip

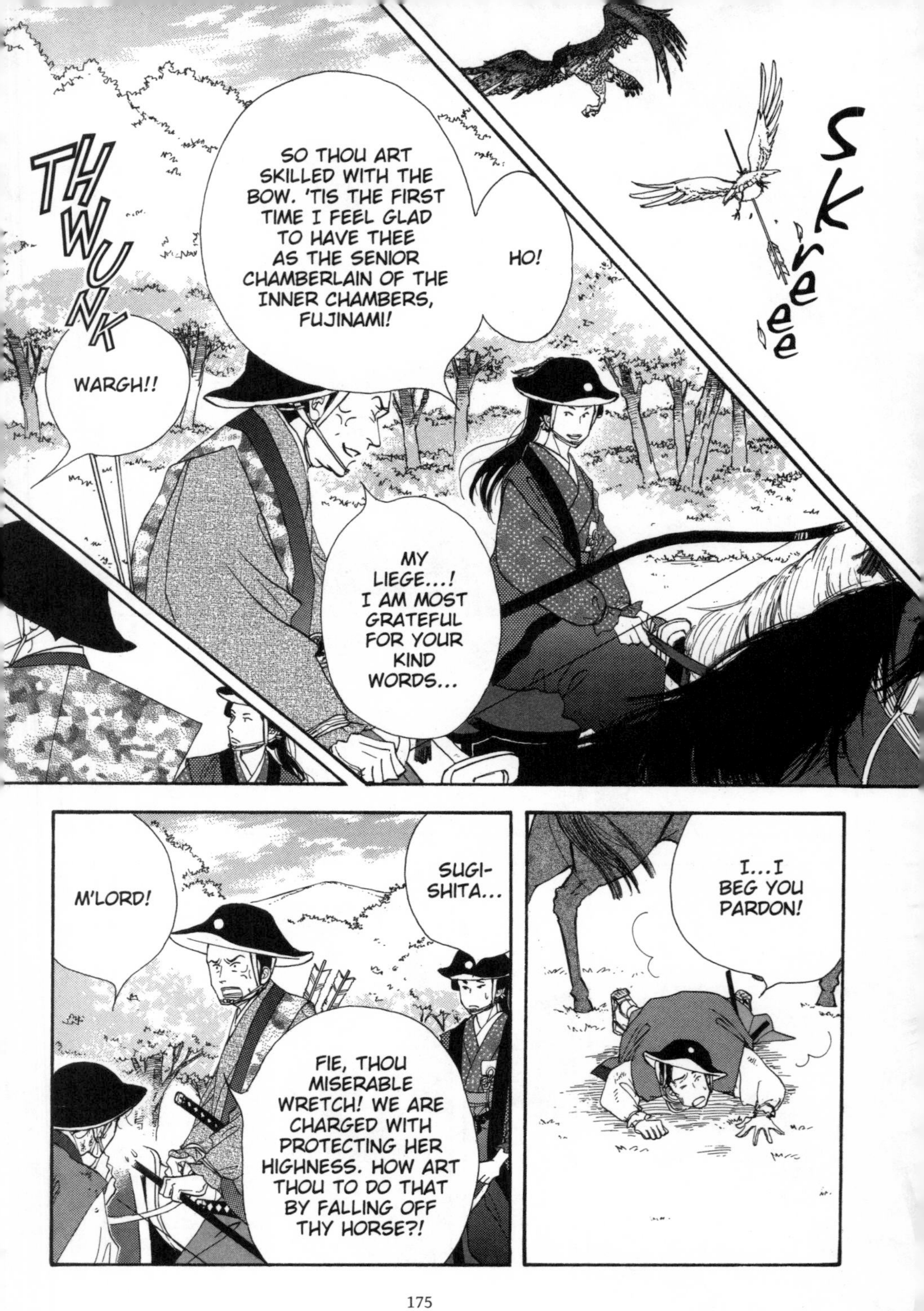
SKreeee
HO!
SO THOU ART SKILLED WITH THE BOW. 'TIS THE FIRST TIME I FEEL GLAD TO HAVE THEE AS THE SENIOR CHAMBERLAIN OF THE INNER CHAMBERS, FUJINAMI!
THWUNK
WARGH!!
MY LIEGE...! I AM MOST GRATEFUL FOR YOUR KIND WORDS...
I...I BEG YOU PARDON!
SUGI-SHITA...
M'LORD!
FIE, THOU MISERABLE WRETCH! WE ARE CHARGED WITH PROTECTING HER HIGHNESS. HOW ART THOU TO DO THAT BY FALLING OFF THY HORSE?!

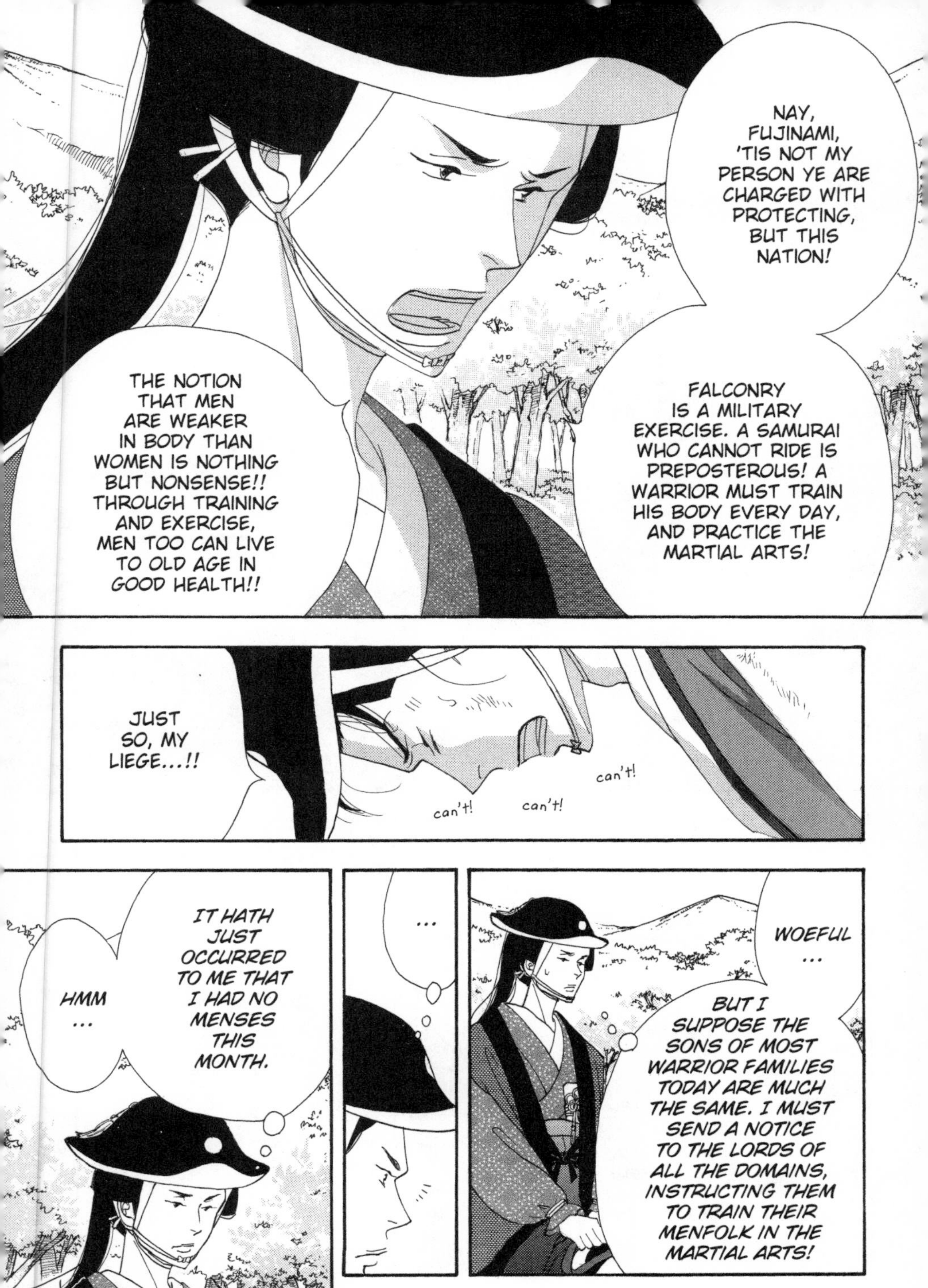
NAY, FUJINAMI, 'TIS NOT MY PERSON YE ARE CHARGED WITH PROTECTING, BUT THIS NATION!
FALCONRY IS A MILITARY EXERCISE. A SAMURAI WHO CANNOT RIDE IS PREPOSTEROUS! A WARRIOR MUST TRAIN HIS BODY EVERY DAY, AND PRACTICE THE MARTIAL ARTS!
THE NOTION THAT MEN ARE WEAKER IN BODY THAN WOMEN IS NOTHING BUT NONSENSE!! THROUGH TRAINING AND EXERCISE, MEN TOO CAN LIVE TO OLD AGE IN GOOD HEALTH!!
can't!
can't!
can't!
JUST SO, MY LIEGE...!!
WOEFUL...
BUT I SUPPOSE THE SONS OF MOST WARRIOR FAMILIES TODAY ARE MUCH THE SAME. I MUST SEND A NOTICE TO THE LORDS OF ALL THE DOMAINS, INSTRUCTING THEM TO TRAIN THEIR MENFOLK IN THE MARTIAL ARTS!
...
IT HATH JUST OCCURRED TO ME THAT I HAD NO MENSES THIS MONTH.
HMM...

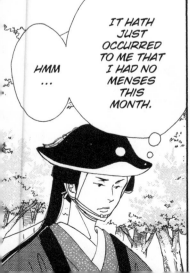

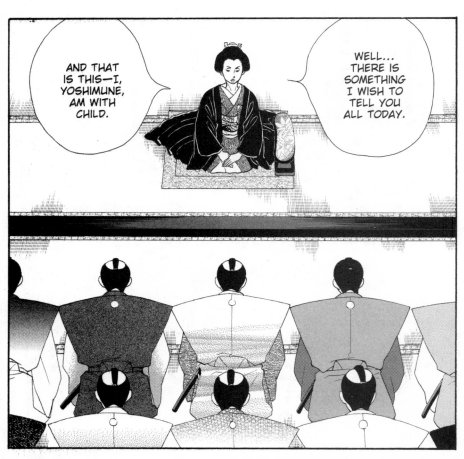

WELL... THERE IS SOMETHING I WISH TO TELL YOU ALL TODAY.

AND THAT IS THIS—I, YOSHIMUNE, AM WITH CHILD.

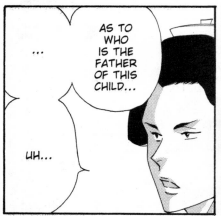

AS TO WHO IS THE FATHER OF THIS CHILD...

...

UH...

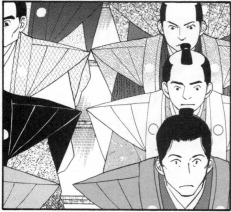

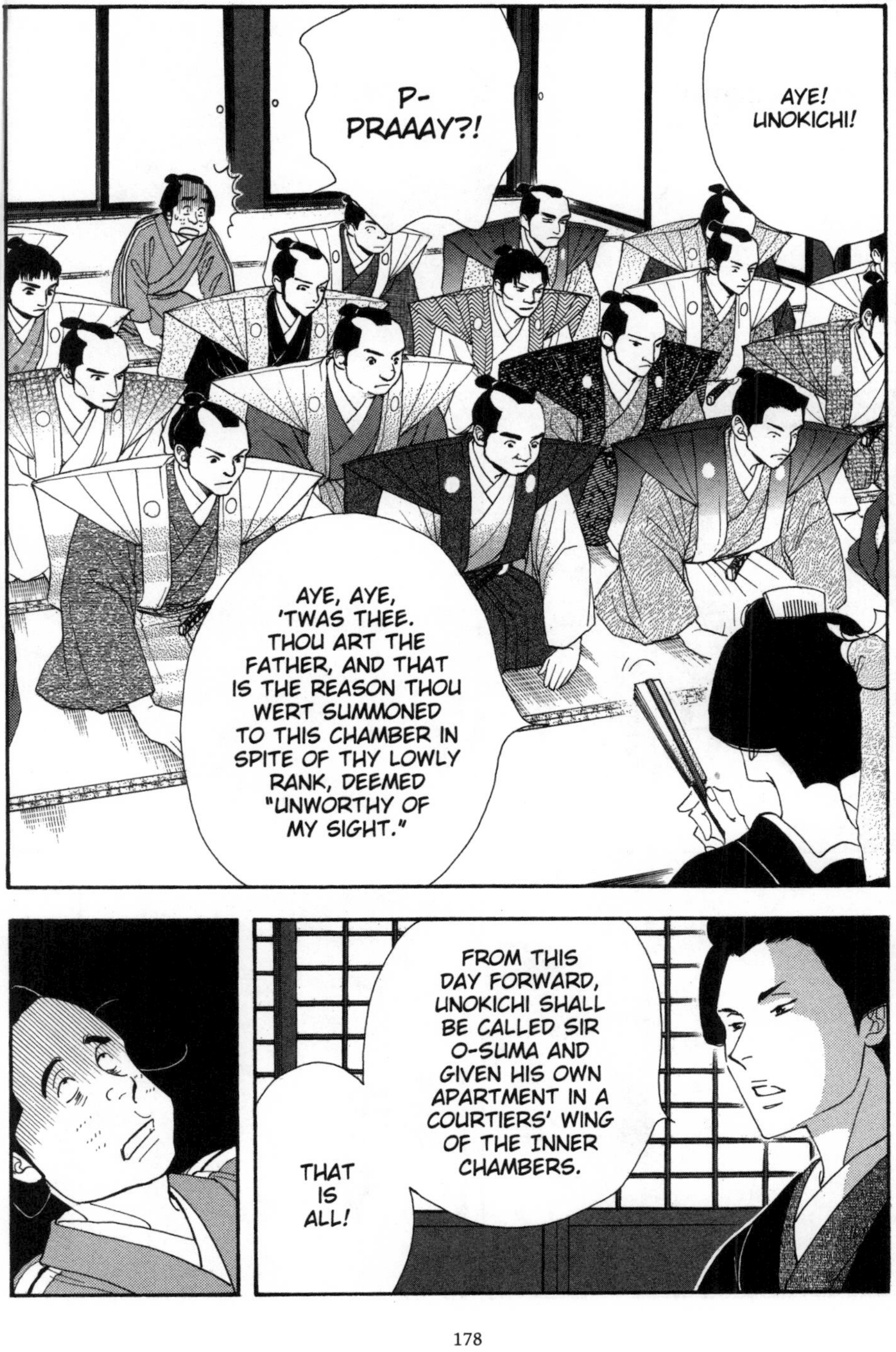
AYE! UNOKICHI!
P-PRAAAY?!
AYE, AYE, 'TWAS THEE. THOU ART THE FATHER, AND THAT IS THE REASON THOU WERT SUMMONED TO THIS CHAMBER IN SPITE OF THY LOWLY RANK, DEEMED "UNWORTHY OF MY SIGHT."
FROM THIS DAY FORWARD, UNOKICHI SHALL BE CALLED SIR O-SUMA AND GIVEN HIS OWN APARTMENT IN A COURTIERS' WING OF THE INNER CHAMBERS.
THAT IS ALL!

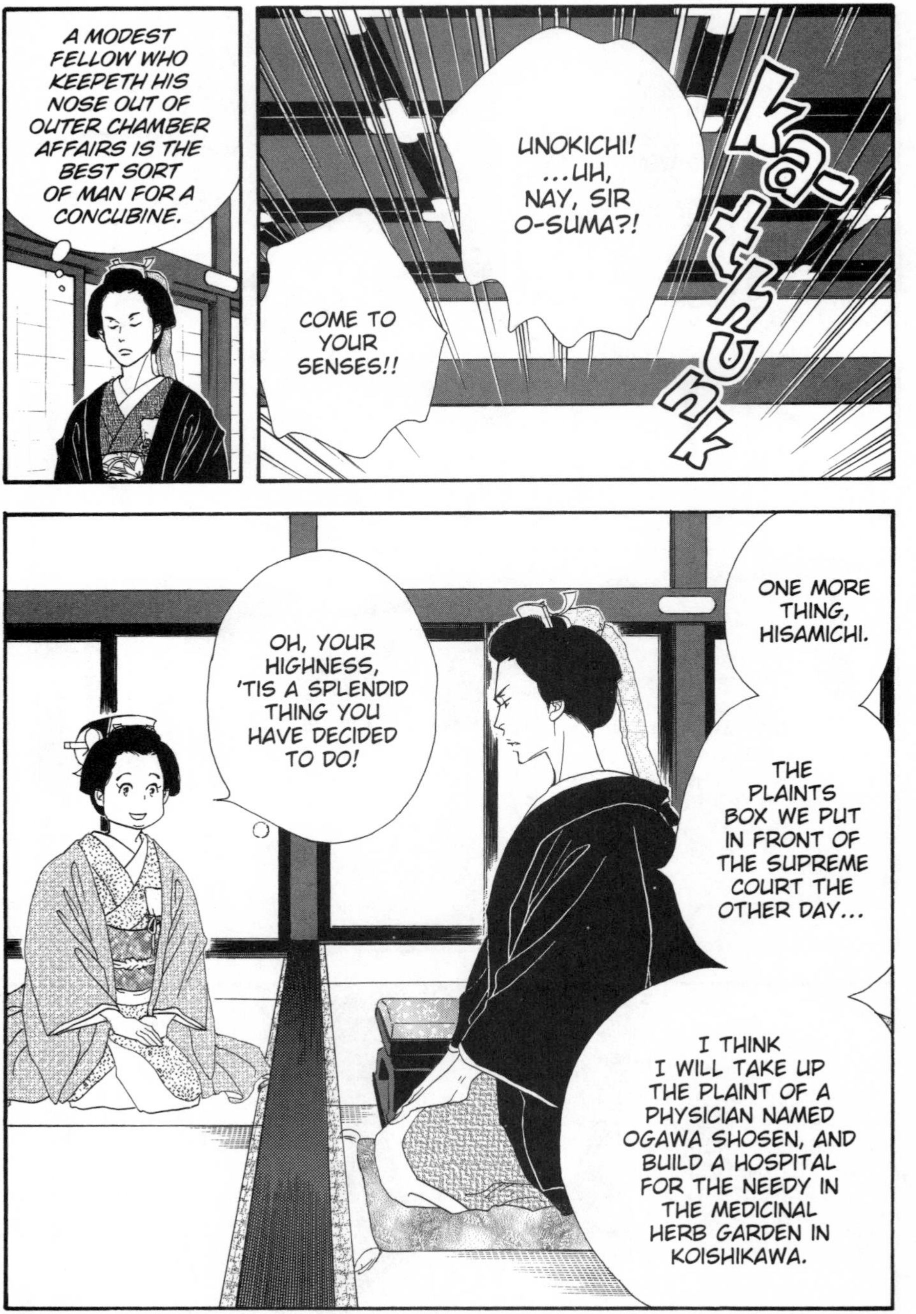
UNOKICHI! ...UH, NAY, SIR O-SUMA?!
COME TO YOUR SENSES!!
ka-thunk
A MODEST FELLOW WHO KEEPETH HIS NOSE OUT OF OUTER CHAMBER AFFAIRS IS THE BEST SORT OF MAN FOR A CONCUBINE.
ONE MORE THING, HISAMICHI.
THE PLAINTS BOX WE PUT IN FRONT OF THE SUPREME COURT THE OTHER DAY...
I THINK I WILL TAKE UP THE PLAINT OF A PHYSICIAN NAMED OGAWA SHOSEN, AND BUILD A HOSPITAL FOR THE NEEDY IN THE MEDICINAL HERB GARDEN IN KOISHIKAWA.
OH, YOUR HIGHNESS, 'TIS A SPLENDID THING YOU HAVE DECIDED TO DO!

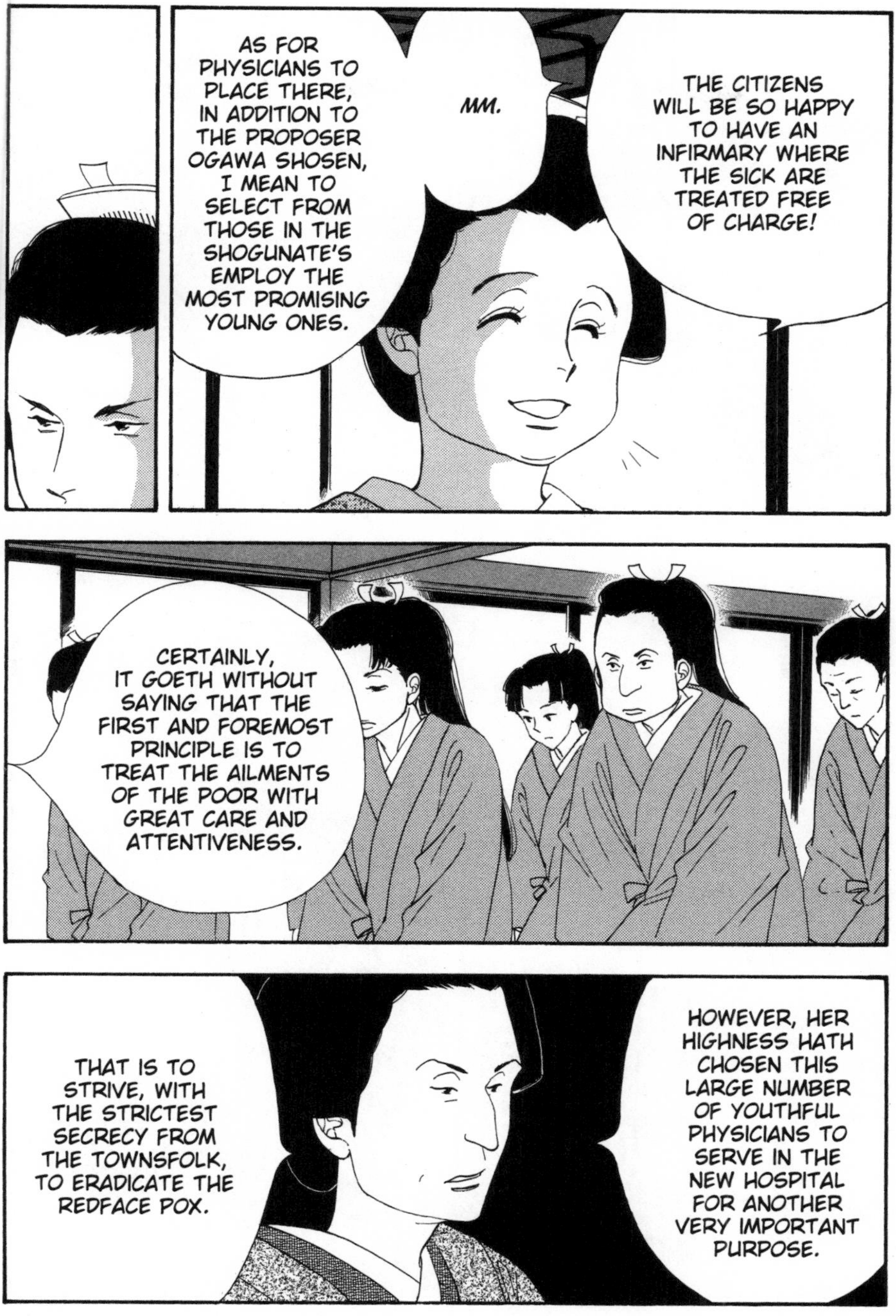
THE CITIZENS WILL BE SO HAPPY TO HAVE AN INFIRMARY WHERE THE SICK ARE TREATED FREE OF CHARGE!
MM.
AS FOR PHYSICIANS TO PLACE THERE, IN ADDITION TO THE PROPOSER OGAWA SHOSEN, I MEAN TO SELECT FROM THOSE IN THE SHOGUNATE'S EMPLOY THE MOST PROMISING YOUNG ONES.
CERTAINLY, IT GOETH WITHOUT SAYING THAT THE FIRST AND FOREMOST PRINCIPLE IS TO TREAT THE AILMENTS OF THE POOR WITH GREAT CARE AND ATTENTIVENESS.
HOWEVER, HER HIGHNESS HATH CHOSEN THIS LARGE NUMBER OF YOUTHFUL PHYSICIANS TO SERVE IN THE NEW HOSPITAL FOR ANOTHER VERY IMPORTANT PURPOSE.
THAT IS TO STRIVE, WITH THE STRICTEST SECRECY FROM THE TOWNSFOLK, TO ERADICATE THE REDFACE POX.

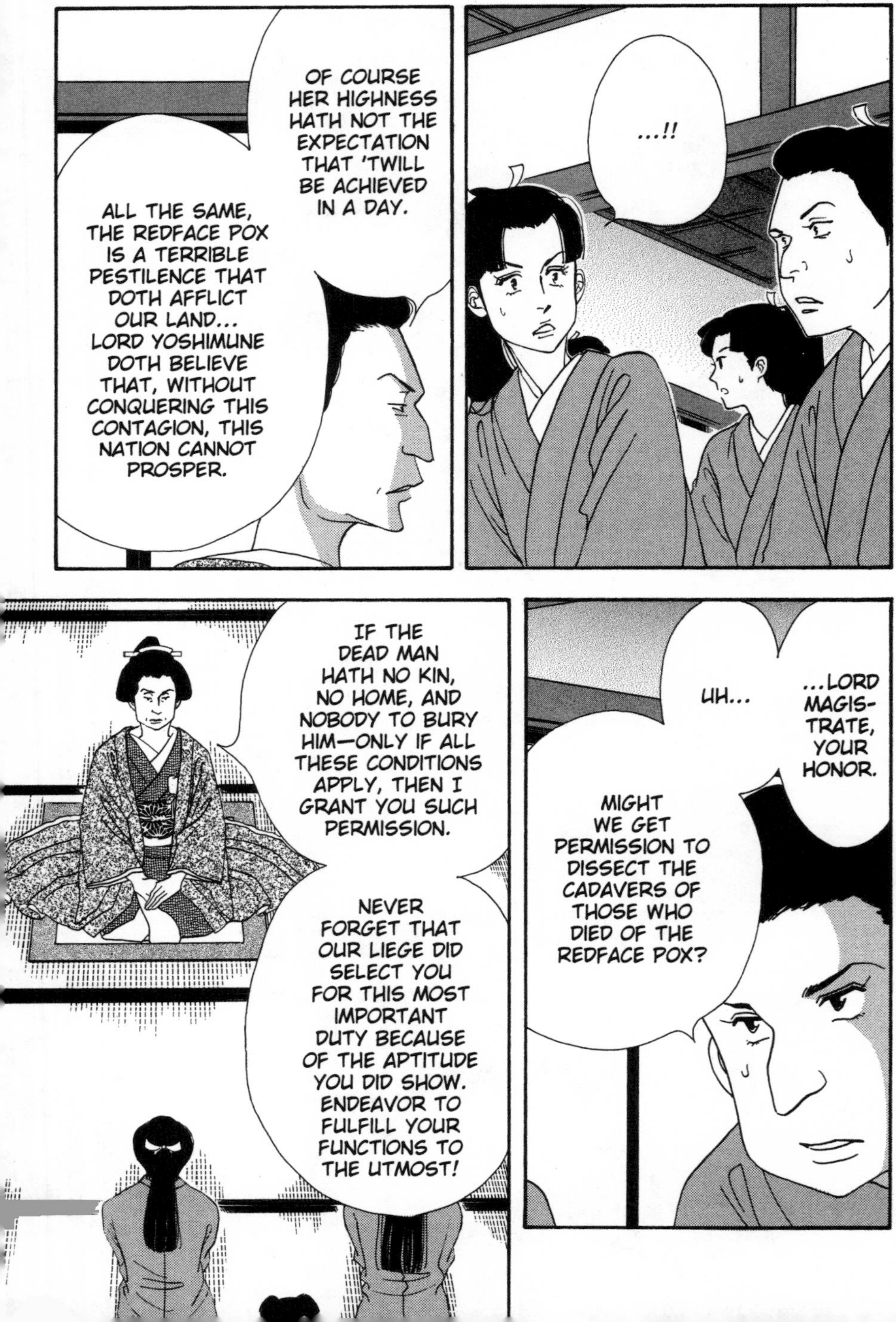
...!!
OF COURSE HER HIGHNESS HATH NOT THE EXPECTATION THAT 'TWILL BE ACHIEVED IN A DAY.
ALL THE SAME, THE REDFACE POX IS A TERRIBLE PESTILENCE THAT DOTH AFFLICT OUR LAND... LORD YOSHIMUNE DOTH BELIEVE THAT, WITHOUT CONQUERING THIS CONTAGION, THIS NATION CANNOT PROSPER.
UH... ...LORD MAGISTRATE, YOUR HONOR.
MIGHT WE GET PERMISSION TO DISSECT THE CADAVERS OF THOSE WHO DIED OF THE REDFACE POX?
IF THE DEAD MAN HATH NO KIN, NO HOME, AND NOBODY TO BURY HIM—ONLY IF ALL THESE CONDITIONS APPLY, THEN I GRANT YOU SUCH PERMISSION.
NEVER FORGET THAT OUR LIEGE DID SELECT YOU FOR THIS MOST IMPORTANT DUTY BECAUSE OF THE APTITUDE YOU DID SHOW. ENDEAVOR TO FULFILL YOUR FUNCTIONS TO THE UTMOST!

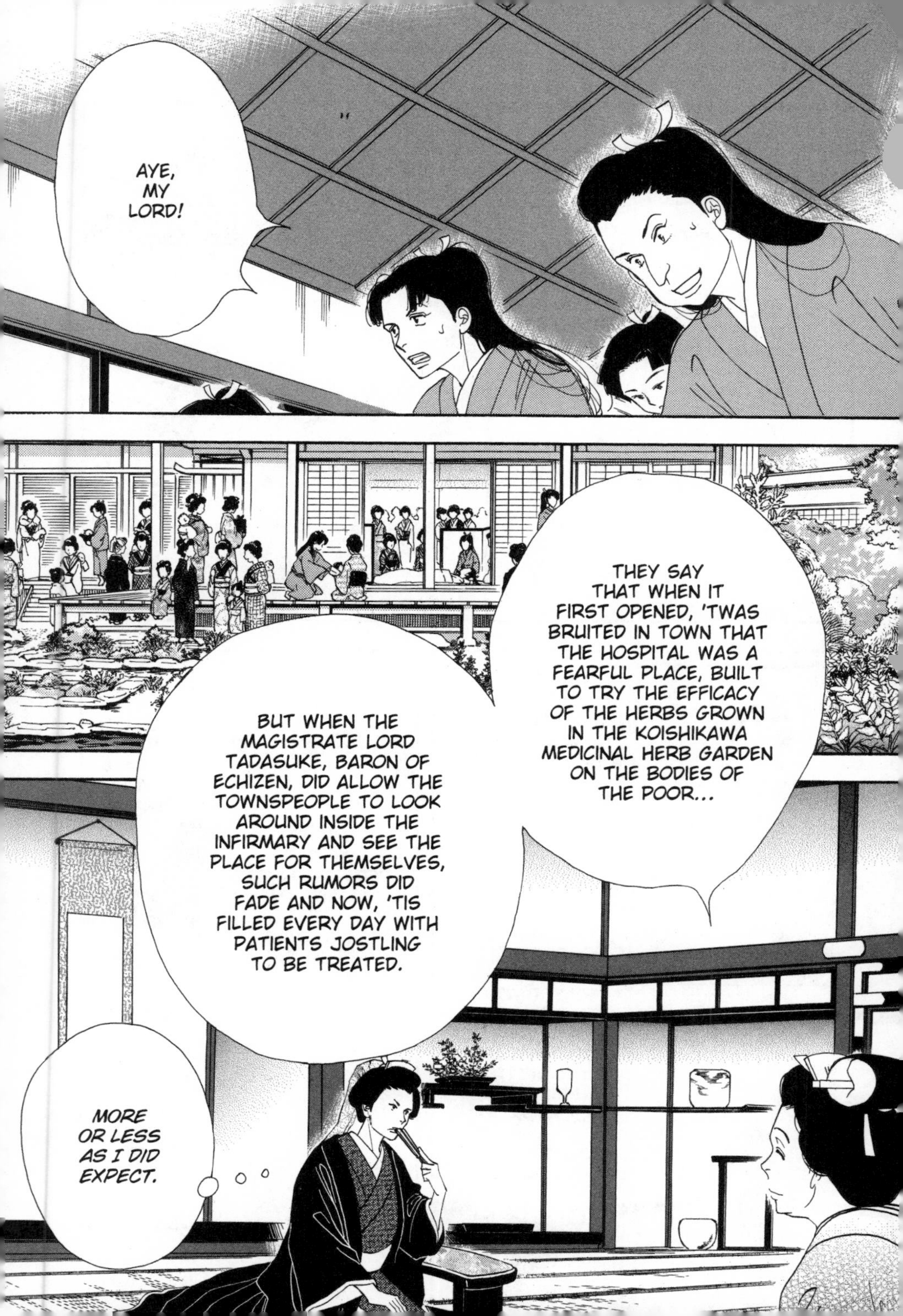
AYE, MY LORD!
THEY SAY THAT WHEN IT FIRST OPENED, 'TWAS BRUITED IN TOWN THAT THE HOSPITAL WAS A FEARFUL PLACE, BUILT TO TRY THE EFFICACY OF THE HERBS GROWN IN THE KOISHIKAWA MEDICINAL HERB GARDEN ON THE BODIES OF THE POOR...
BUT WHEN THE MAGISTRATE LORD TADASUKE, BARON OF ECHIZEN, DID ALLOW THE TOWNSPEOPLE TO LOOK AROUND INSIDE THE INFIRMARY AND SEE THE PLACE FOR THEMSELVES, SUCH RUMORS DID FADE AND NOW, 'TIS FILLED EVERY DAY WITH PATIENTS JOSTLING TO BE TREATED.
MORE OR LESS AS I DID EXPECT.

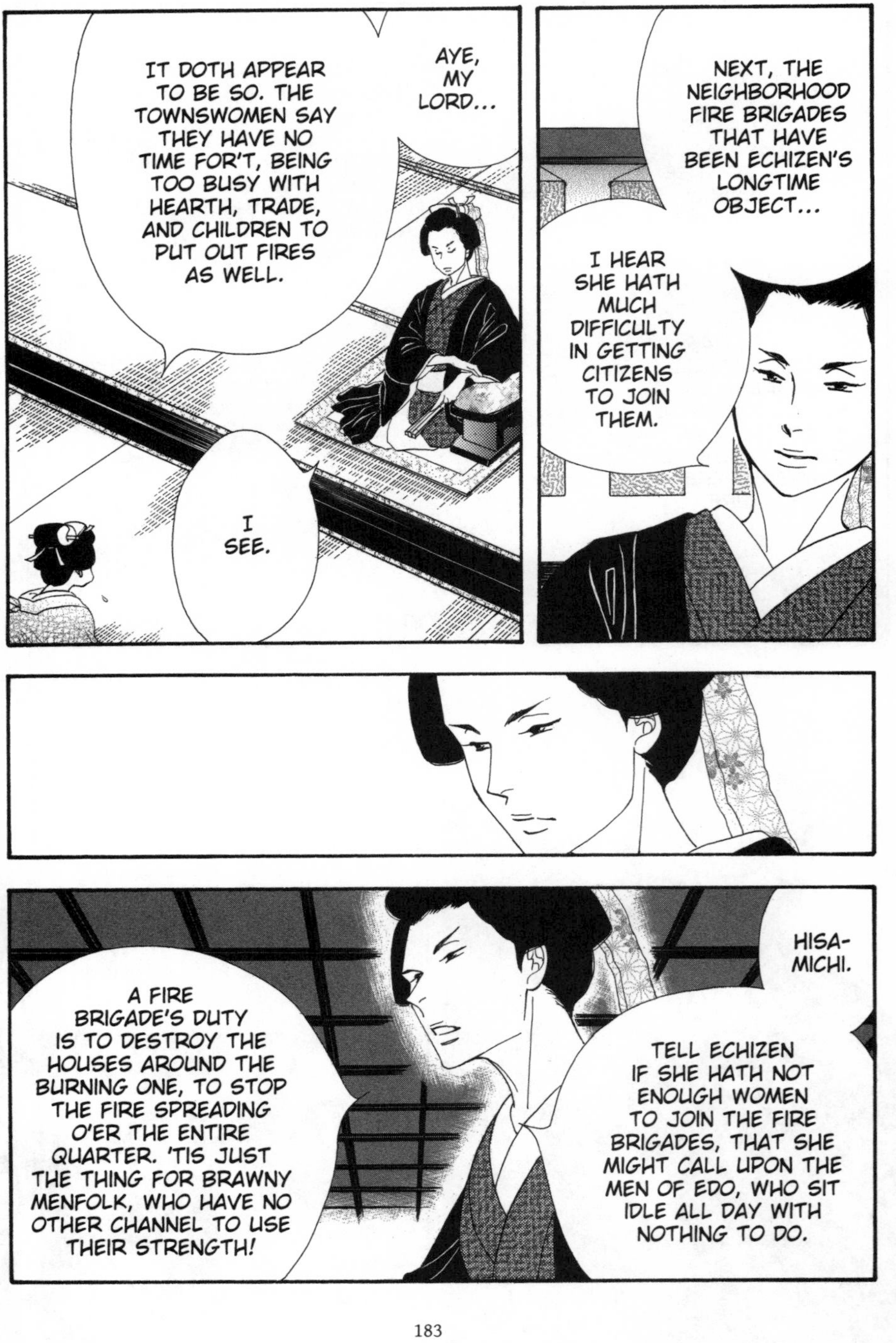
NEXT, THE NEIGHBORHOOD FIRE BRIGADES THAT HAVE BEEN ECHIZEN'S LONGTIME OBJECT...
I HEAR SHE HATH MUCH DIFFICULTY IN GETTING CITIZENS TO JOIN THEM.
AYE, MY LORD...
IT DOTH APPEAR TO BE SO. THE TOWNSWOMEN SAY THEY HAVE NO TIME FOR'T, BEING TOO BUSY WITH HEARTH, TRADE, AND CHILDREN TO PUT OUT FIRES AS WELL.
I SEE.
HISA-MICHI.
TELL ECHIZEN IF SHE HATH NOT ENOUGH WOMEN TO JOIN THE FIRE BRIGADES, THAT SHE MIGHT CALL UPON THE MEN OF EDO, WHO SIT IDLE ALL DAY WITH NOTHING TO DO.
A FIRE BRIGADE'S DUTY IS TO DESTROY THE HOUSES AROUND THE BURNING ONE, TO STOP THE FIRE SPREADING O'ER THE ENTIRE QUARTER. 'TIS JUST THE THING FOR BRAWNY MENFOLK, WHO HAVE NO OTHER CHANNEL TO USE THEIR STRENGTH!

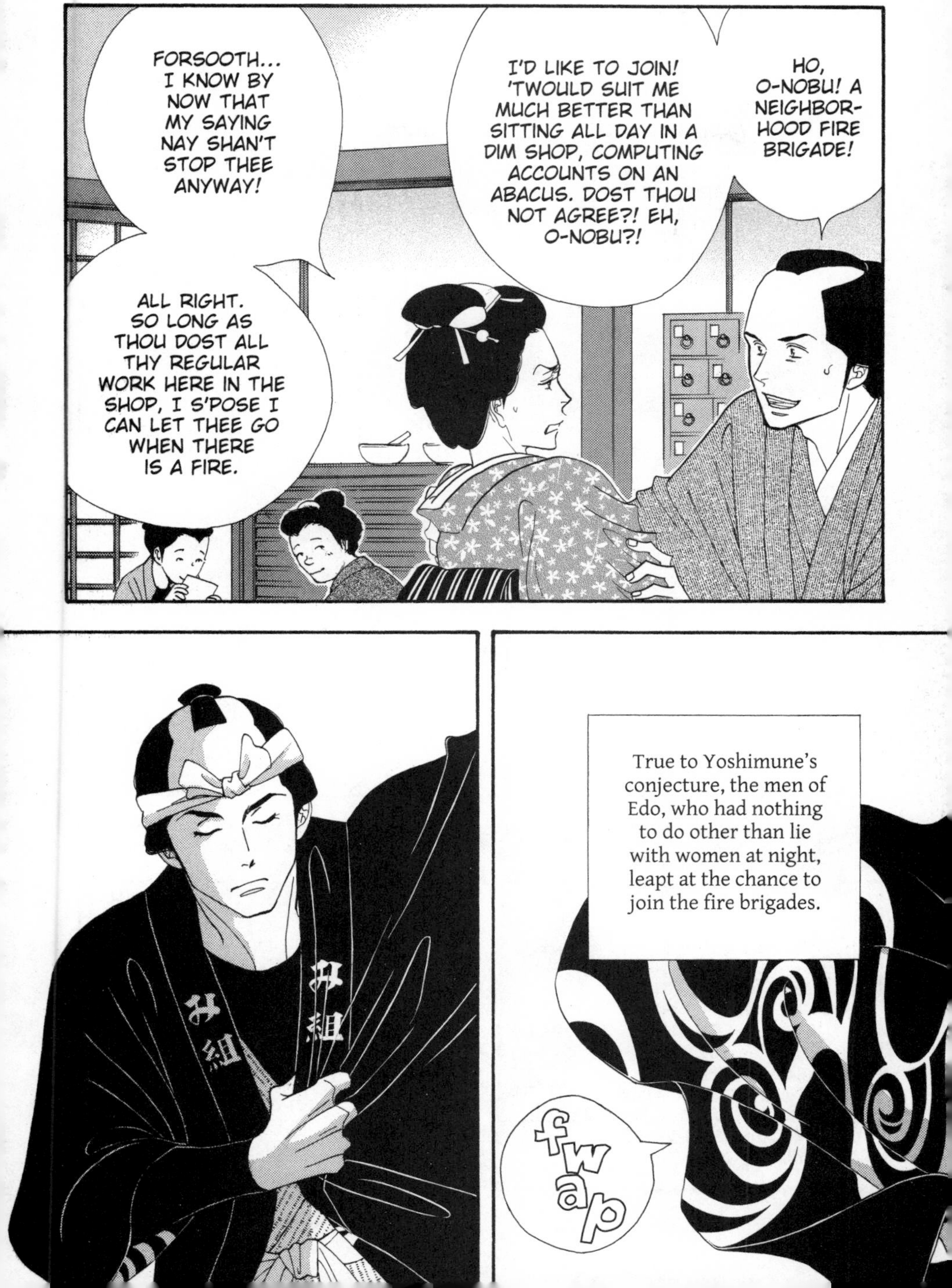
HO, O-NOBU! A NEIGHBORHOOD FIRE BRIGADE!
I'D LIKE TO JOIN! 'TWOULD SUIT ME MUCH BETTER THAN SITTING ALL DAY IN A DIM SHOP, COMPUTING ACCOUNTS ON AN ABACUS. DOST THOU NOT AGREE?! EH, O-NOBU?!
FORSOOTH... I KNOW BY NOW THAT MY SAYING NAY SHAN'T STOP THEE ANYWAY!
ALL RIGHT. SO LONG AS THOU DOST ALL THY REGULAR WORK HERE IN THE SHOP, I S'POSE I CAN LET THEE GO WHEN THERE IS A FIRE.
True to Yoshimune's conjecture, the men of Edo, who had nothing to do other than lie with women at night, leapt at the chance to join the fire brigades.
fwap

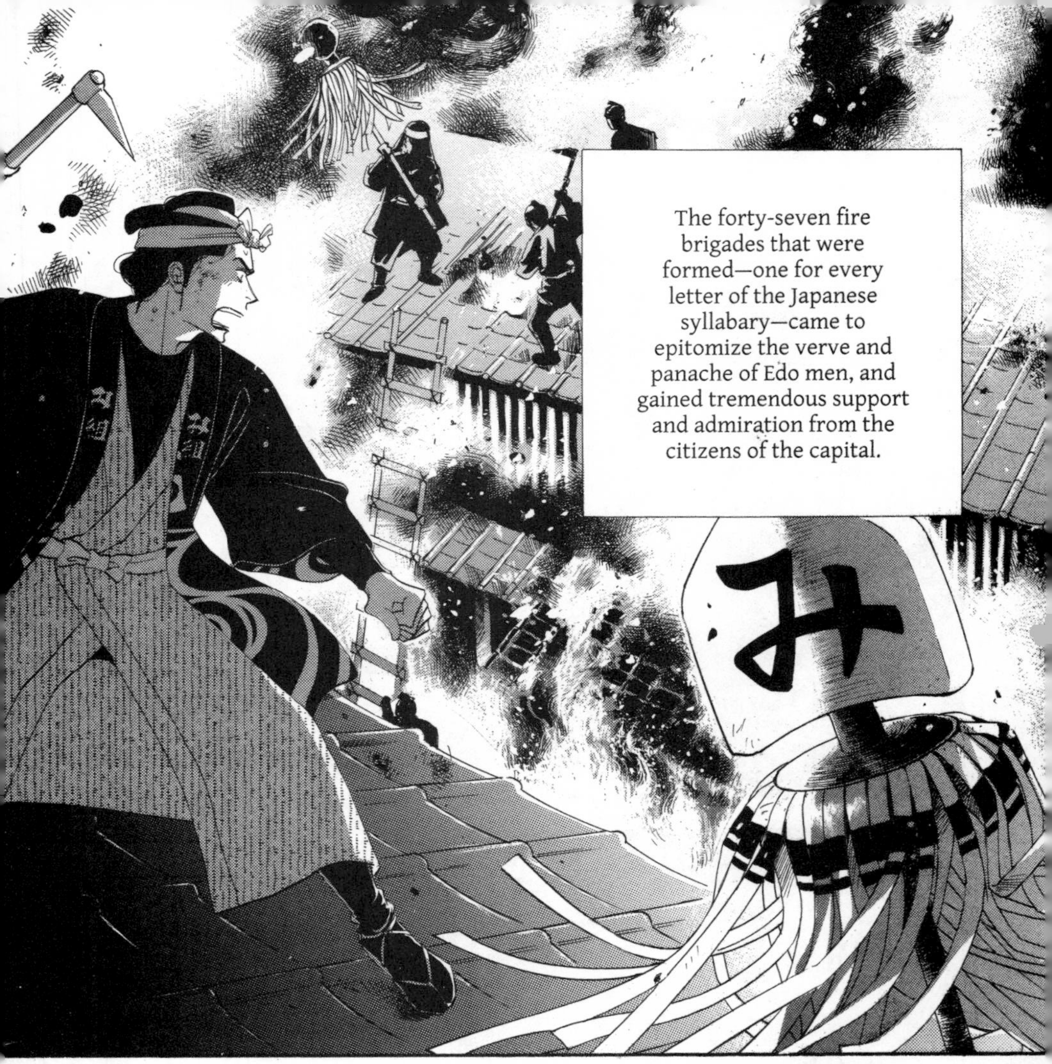
The forty-seven fire brigades that were formed—one for every letter of the Japanese syllabary—came to epitomize the verve and panache of Edo men, and gained tremendous support and admiration from the citizens of the capital.
み
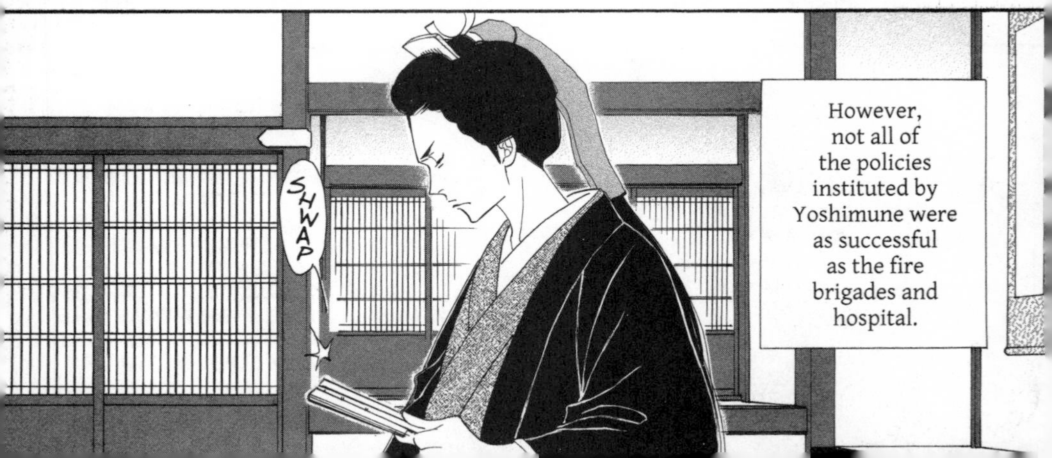
However, not all of the policies instituted by Yoshimune were as successful as the fire brigades and hospital.
SHWAP

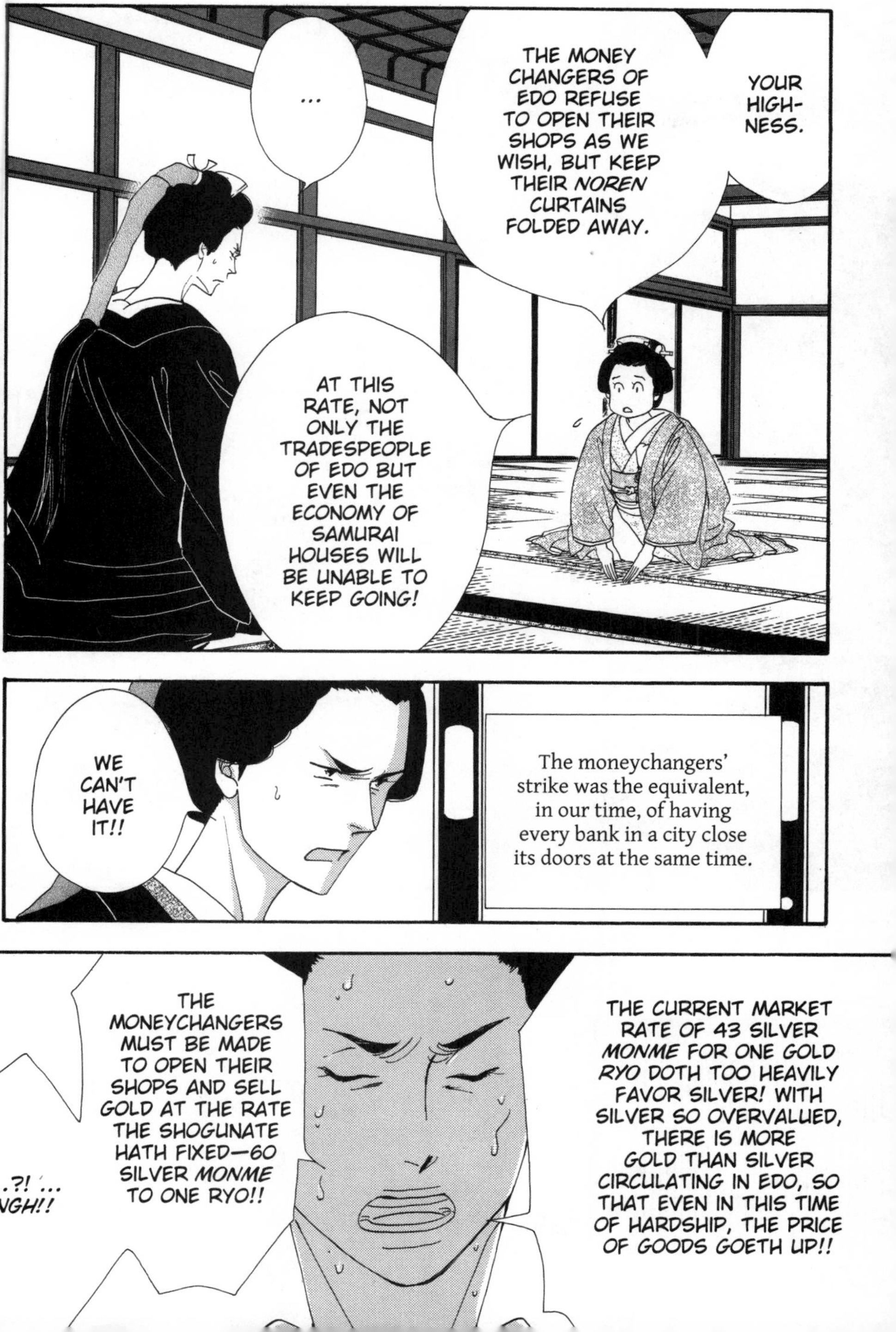
YOUR HIGHNESS.
THE MONEY CHANGERS OF EDO REFUSE TO OPEN THEIR SHOPS AS WE WISH, BUT KEEP THEIR *NOREN* CURTAINS FOLDED AWAY.
...
AT THIS RATE, NOT ONLY THE TRADESPEOPLE OF EDO BUT EVEN THE ECONOMY OF SAMURAI HOUSES WILL BE UNABLE TO KEEP GOING!
The moneychangers' strike was the equivalent, in our time, of having every bank in a city close its doors at the same time.
WE CAN'T HAVE IT!!
THE CURRENT MARKET RATE OF 43 SILVER *MONME* FOR ONE GOLD *RYO* DOTH TOO HEAVILY FAVOR SILVER! WITH SILVER SO OVERVALUED, THERE IS MORE GOLD THAN SILVER CIRCULATING IN EDO, SO THAT EVEN IN THIS TIME OF HARDSHIP, THE PRICE OF GOODS GOETH UP!!
THE MONEYCHANGERS MUST BE MADE TO OPEN THEIR SHOPS AND SELL GOLD AT THE RATE THE SHOGUNATE HATH FIXED—60 SILVER *MONME* TO ONE RYO!!
...?! ... NGH!!

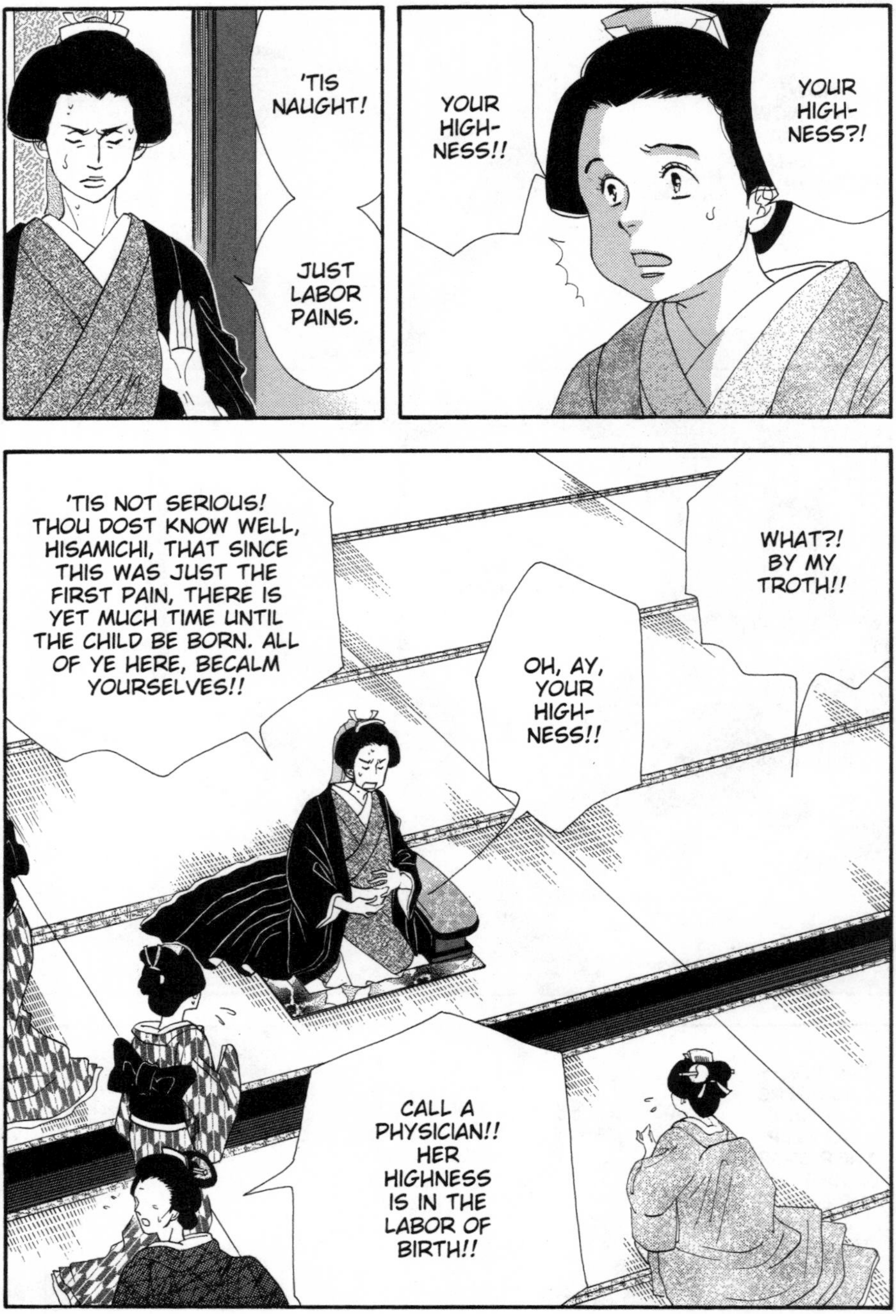
YOUR HIGH-NESS?!
YOUR HIGH-NESS!!
'TIS NAUGHT!
JUST LABOR PAINS.
WHAT?! BY MY TROTH!!
OH, AY, YOUR HIGH-NESS!!
'TIS NOT SERIOUS! THOU DOST KNOW WELL, HISAMICHI, THAT SINCE THIS WAS JUST THE FIRST PAIN, THERE IS YET MUCH TIME UNTIL THE CHILD BE BORN. ALL OF YE HERE, BECALM YOURSELVES!!
CALL A PHYSICIAN!! HER HIGHNESS IS IN THE LABOR OF BIRTH!!

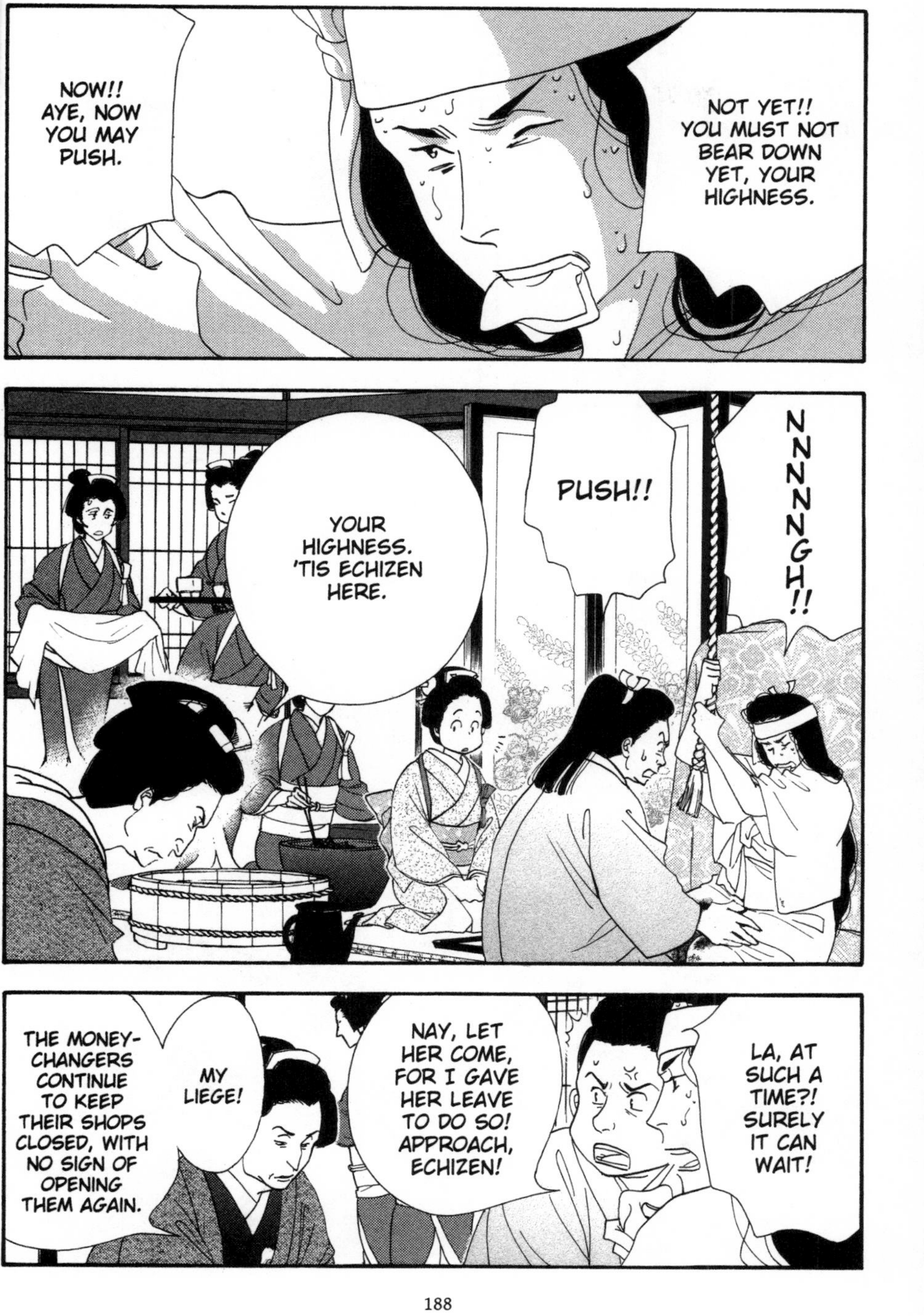
NOT YET!! YOU MUST NOT BEAR DOWN YET, YOUR HIGHNESS.
NOW!! AYE, NOW YOU MAY PUSH.
NNNNNGH!!
PUSH!!
YOUR HIGHNESS. 'TIS ECHIZEN HERE.
LA, AT SUCH A TIME?! SURELY IT CAN WAIT!
NAY, LET HER COME, FOR I GAVE HER LEAVE TO DO SO! APPROACH, ECHIZEN!
MY LIEGE!
THE MONEY-CHANGERS CONTINUE TO KEEP THEIR SHOPS CLOSED, WITH NO SIGN OF OPENING THEM AGAIN.

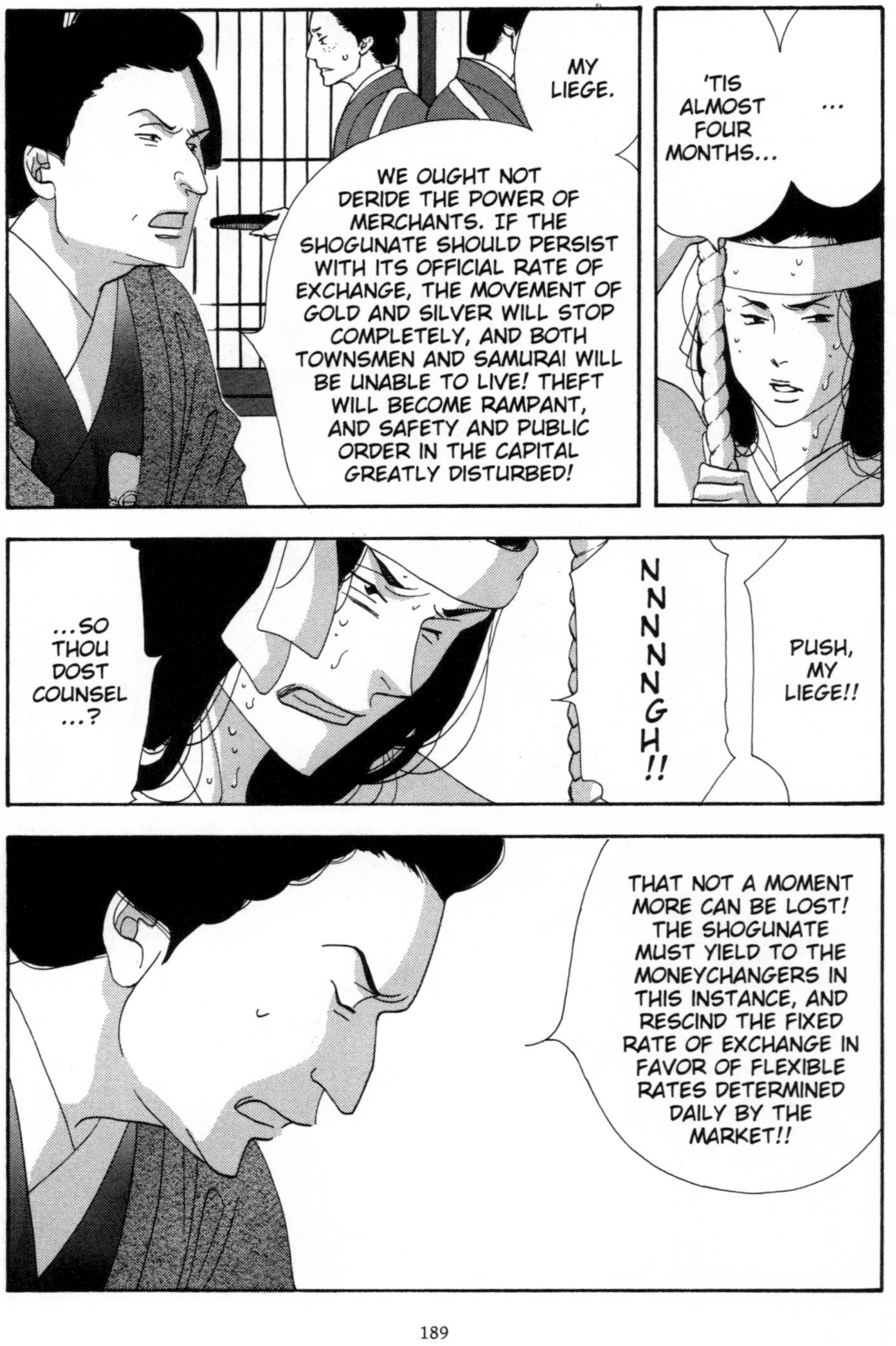
...
'TIS ALMOST FOUR MONTHS...
MY LIEGE.
WE OUGHT NOT DERIDE THE POWER OF MERCHANTS. IF THE SHOGUNATE SHOULD PERSIST WITH ITS OFFICIAL RATE OF EXCHANGE, THE MOVEMENT OF GOLD AND SILVER WILL STOP COMPLETELY, AND BOTH TOWNSMEN AND SAMURAI WILL BE UNABLE TO LIVE! THEFT WILL BECOME RAMPANT, AND SAFETY AND PUBLIC ORDER IN THE CAPITAL GREATLY DISTURBED!
PUSH, MY LIEGE!!
NNNNNGH!!
...SO THOU DOST COUNSEL ...?
THAT NOT A MOMENT MORE CAN BE LOST! THE SHOGUNATE MUST YIELD TO THE MONEYCHANGERS IN THIS INSTANCE, AND RESCIND THE FIXED RATE OF EXCHANGE IN FAVOR OF FLEXIBLE RATES DETERMINED DAILY BY THE MARKET!!

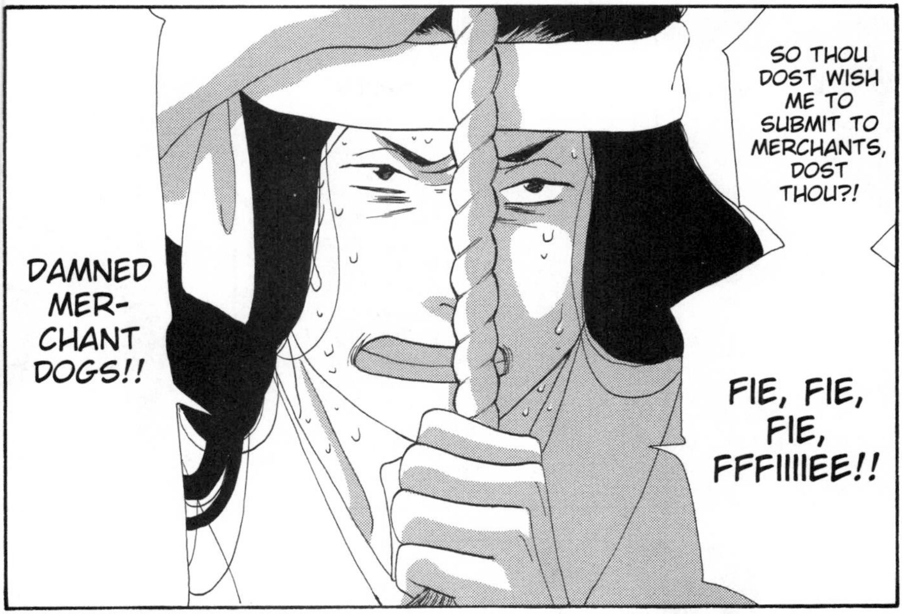
SO THOU DOST WISH ME TO SUBMIT TO MERCHANTS, DOST THOU?!
FIE, FIE, FIE, FFFIIIIIEE!!
DAMNED MER-CHANT DOGS!!

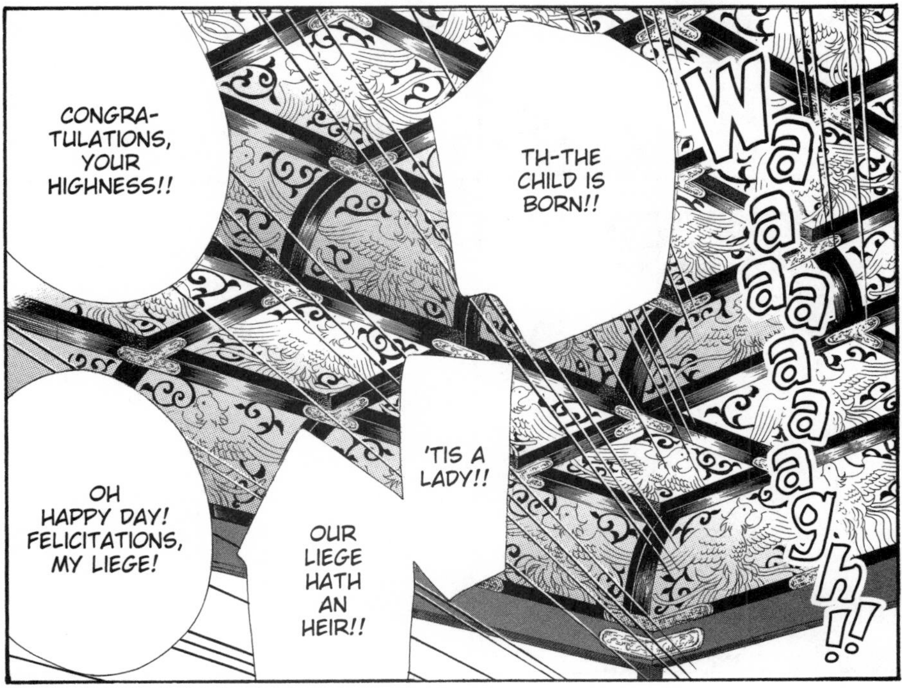
Waaaaaagh!!
TH-THE CHILD IS BORN!!
CONGRA-TULATIONS, YOUR HIGHNESS!!
'TIS A LADY!!
OUR LIEGE HATH AN HEIR!!
OH HAPPY DAY! FELICITATIONS, MY LIEGE!

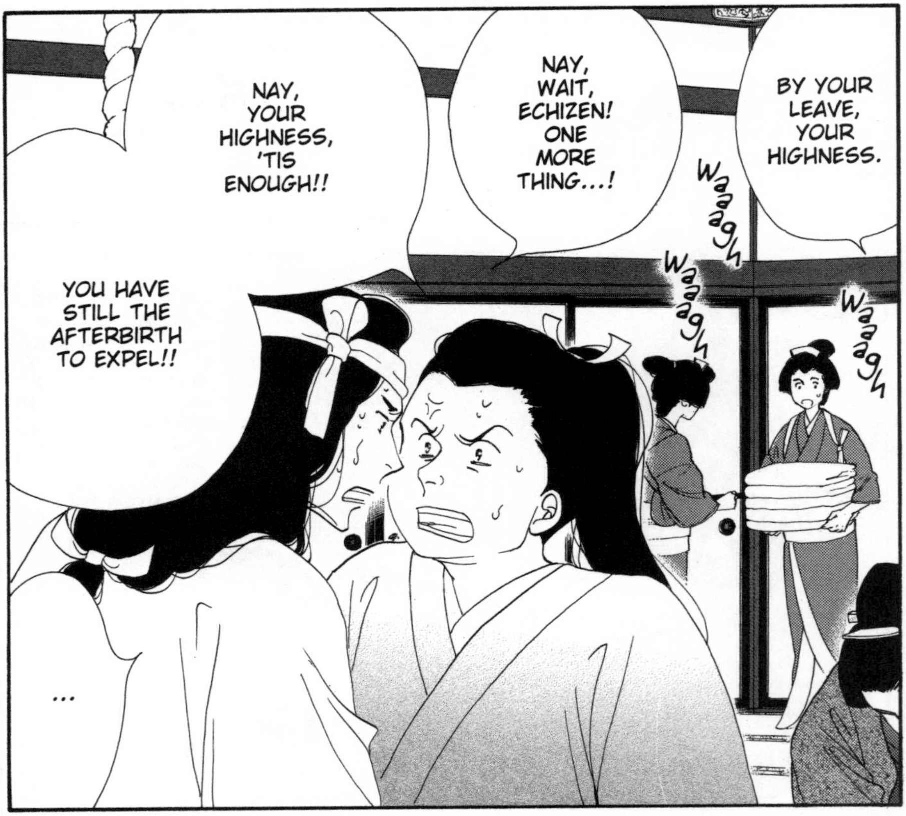
BY YOUR LEAVE, YOUR HIGHNESS.
Waaagh
Waaagh
Waaagh
NAY, WAIT, ECHIZEN! ONE MORE THING...!
NAY, YOUR HIGHNESS, 'TIS ENOUGH!!
YOU HAVE STILL THE AFTERBIRTH TO EXPEL!!
...

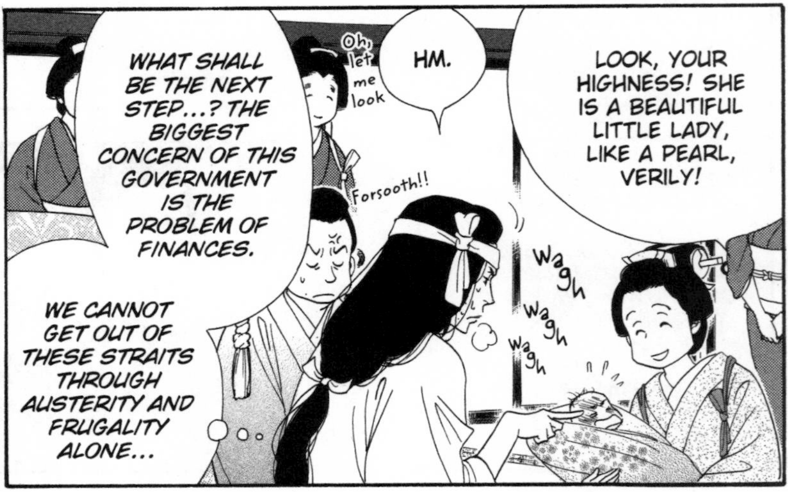
LOOK, YOUR HIGHNESS! SHE IS A BEAUTIFUL LITTLE LADY, LIKE A PEARL, VERILY!
HM.
Oh, let me look
Forsooth!!
WHAT SHALL BE THE NEXT STEP...? THE BIGGEST CONCERN OF THIS GOVERNMENT IS THE PROBLEM OF FINANCES.
Wagh
Wagh
Wagh
WE CANNOT GET OUT OF THESE STRAITS THROUGH AUSTERITY AND FRUGALITY ALONE...

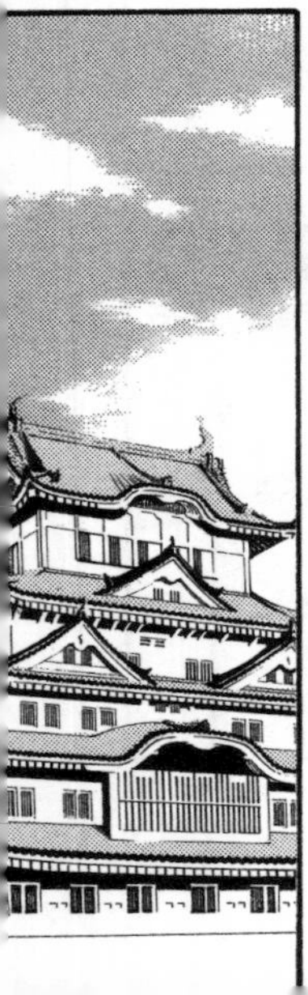

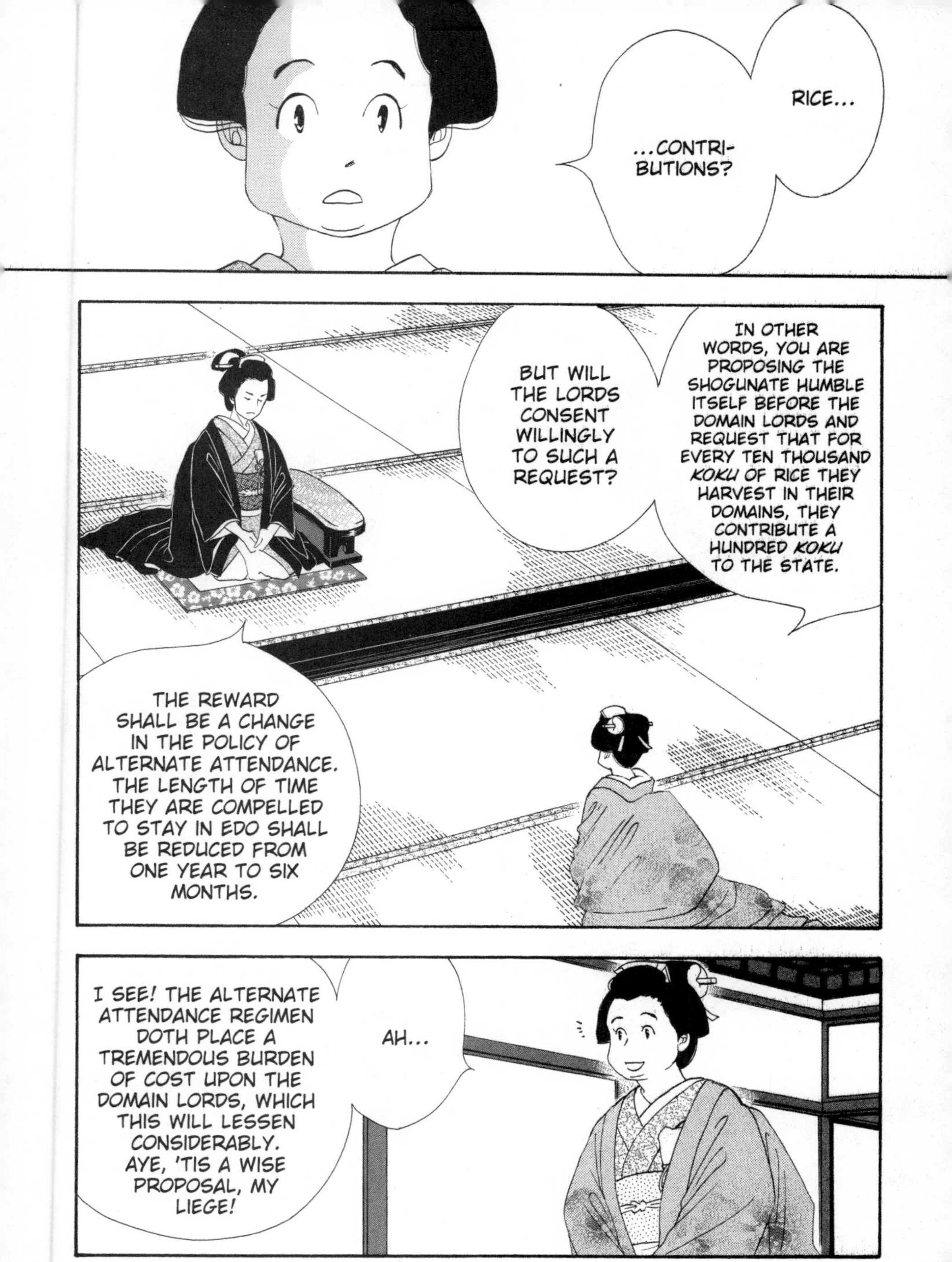
RICE...
...CONTRI-BUTIONS?
IN OTHER WORDS, YOU ARE PROPOSING THE SHOGUNATE HUMBLE ITSELF BEFORE THE DOMAIN LORDS AND REQUEST THAT FOR EVERY TEN THOUSAND *KOKU* OF RICE THEY HARVEST IN THEIR DOMAINS, THEY CONTRIBUTE A HUNDRED *KOKU* TO THE STATE.
BUT WILL THE LORDS CONSENT WILLINGLY TO SUCH A REQUEST?
THE REWARD SHALL BE A CHANGE IN THE POLICY OF ALTERNATE ATTENDANCE. THE LENGTH OF TIME THEY ARE COMPELLED TO STAY IN EDO SHALL BE REDUCED FROM ONE YEAR TO SIX MONTHS.
AH...
I SEE! THE ALTERNATE ATTENDANCE REGIMEN DOTH PLACE A TREMENDOUS BURDEN OF COST UPON THE DOMAIN LORDS, WHICH THIS WILL LESSEN CONSIDERABLY. AYE, 'TIS A WISE PROPOSAL, MY LIEGE!

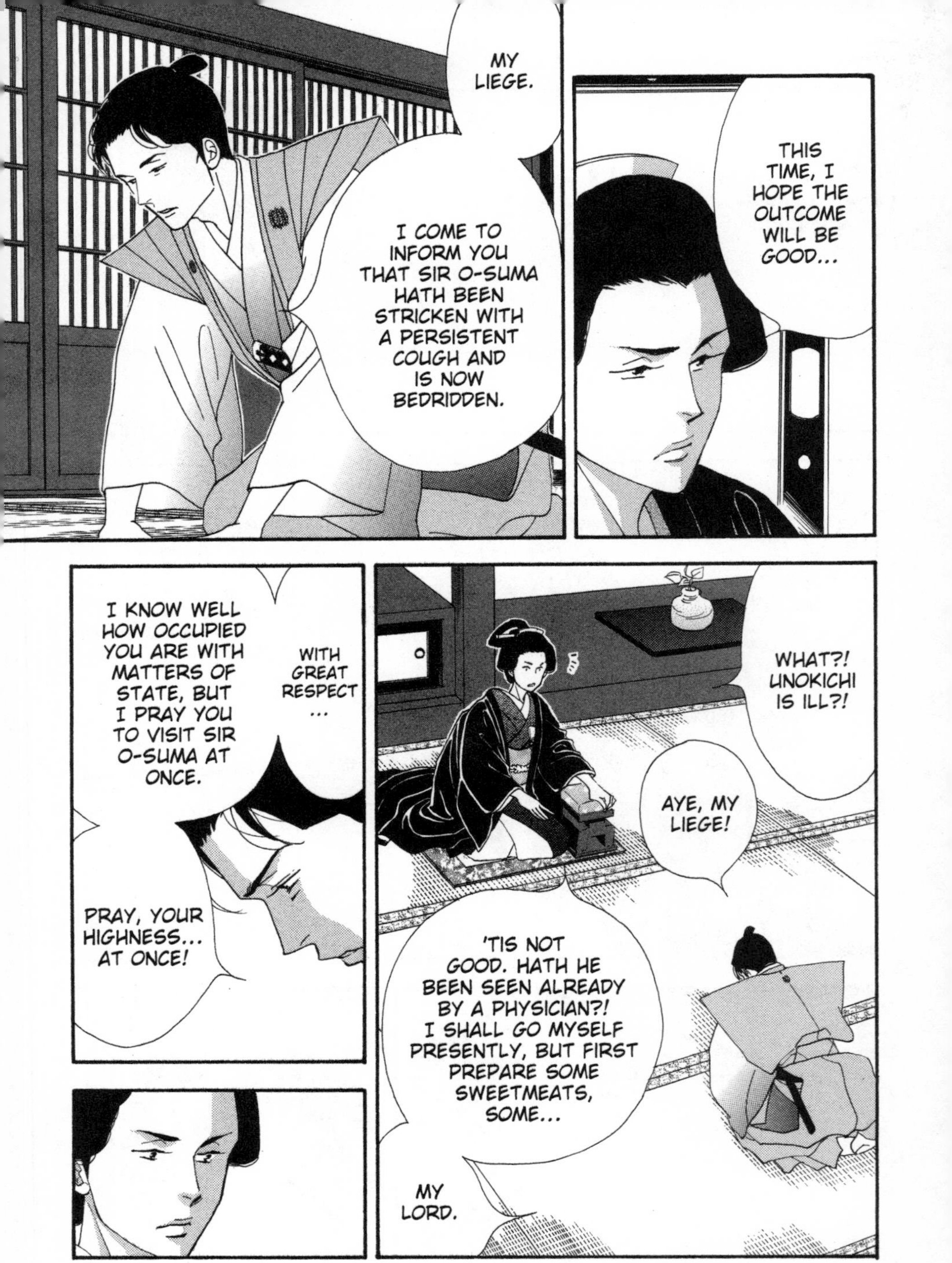
THIS TIME, I HOPE THE OUTCOME WILL BE GOOD...
MY LIEGE.
I COME TO INFORM YOU THAT SIR O-SUMA HATH BEEN STRICKEN WITH A PERSISTENT COUGH AND IS NOW BEDRIDDEN.
WHAT?! UNOKICHI IS ILL?!
AYE, MY LIEGE!
'TIS NOT GOOD. HATH HE BEEN SEEN ALREADY BY A PHYSICIAN?! I SHALL GO MYSELF PRESENTLY, BUT FIRST PREPARE SOME SWEETMEATS, SOME...
MY LORD.
WITH GREAT RESPECT...
I KNOW WELL HOW OCCUPIED YOU ARE WITH MATTERS OF STATE, BUT I PRAY YOU TO VISIT SIR O-SUMA AT ONCE.
PRAY, YOUR HIGHNESS... AT ONCE!

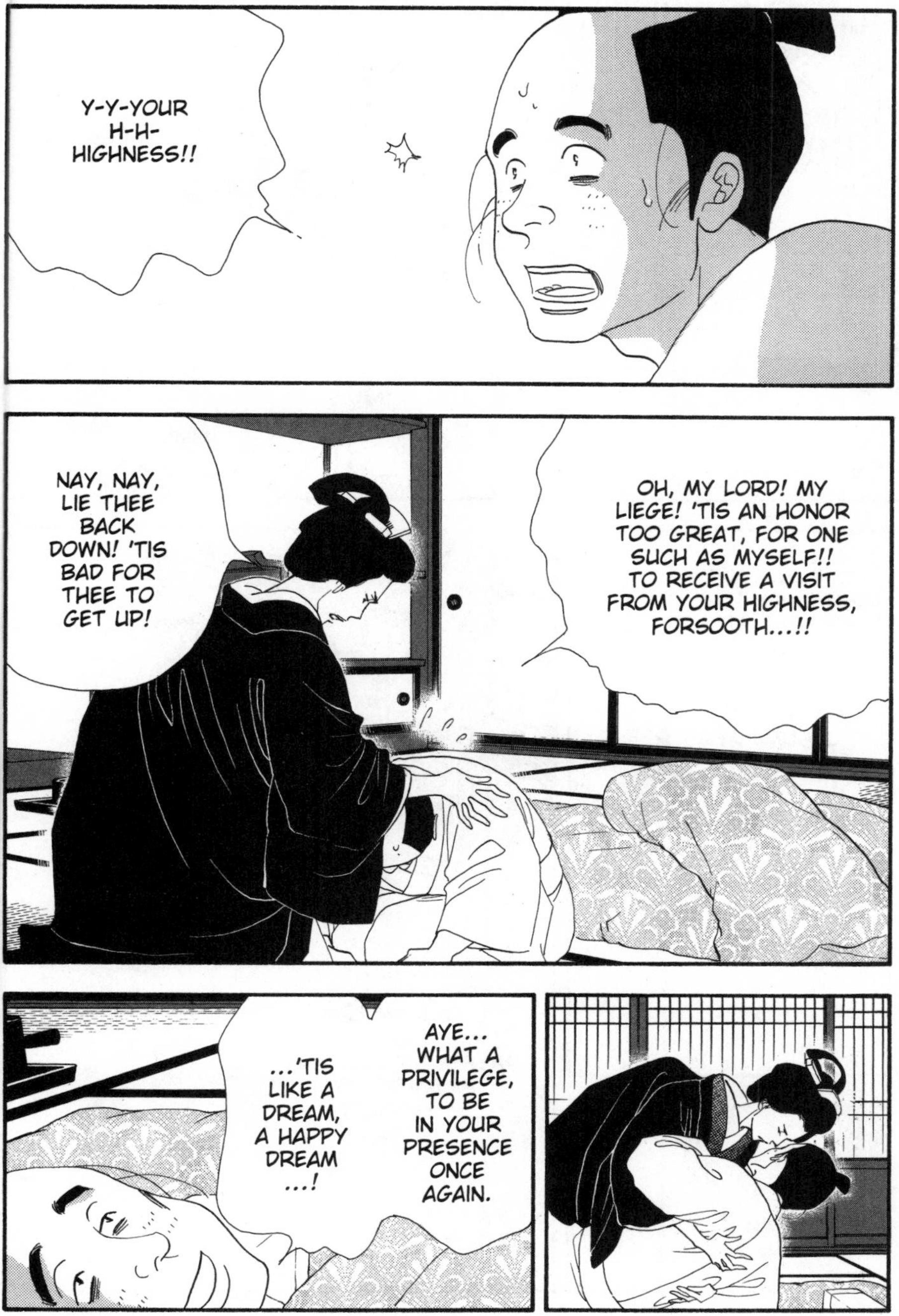
Y-Y-YOUR H-H-HIGHNESS!!
OH, MY LORD! MY LIEGE! 'TIS AN HONOR TOO GREAT, FOR ONE SUCH AS MYSELF!! TO RECEIVE A VISIT FROM YOUR HIGHNESS, FORSOOTH...!!
NAY, NAY, LIE THEE BACK DOWN! 'TIS BAD FOR THEE TO GET UP!
AYE... WHAT A PRIVILEGE, TO BE IN YOUR PRESENCE ONCE AGAIN.
...'TIS LIKE A DREAM, A HAPPY DREAM...!

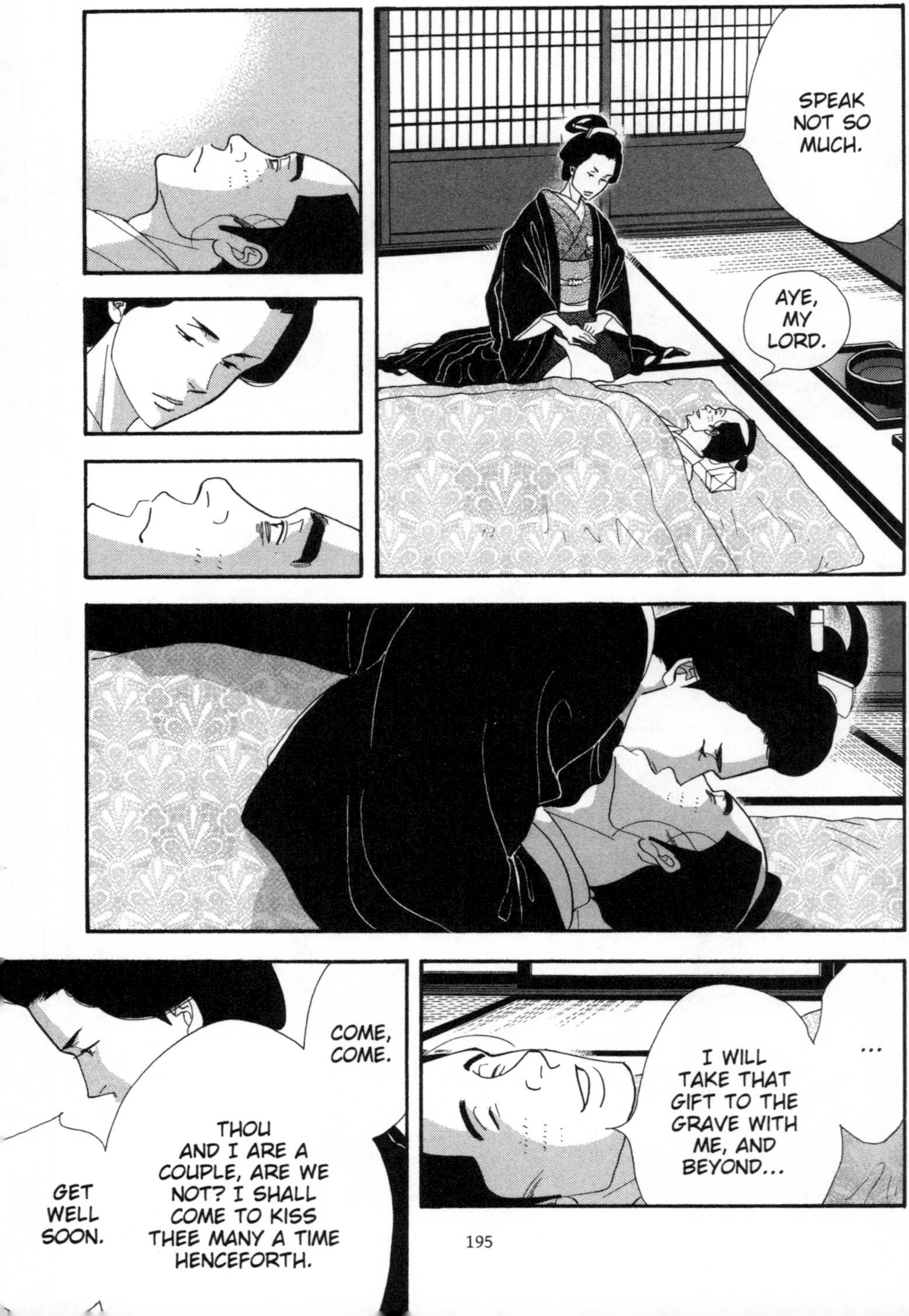
SPEAK NOT SO MUCH.
AYE, MY LORD.
...
I WILL TAKE THAT GIFT TO THE GRAVE WITH ME, AND BEYOND...
COME, COME.
THOU AND I ARE A COUPLE, ARE WE NOT? I SHALL COME TO KISS THEE MANY A TIME HENCEFORTH.
GET WELL SOON.

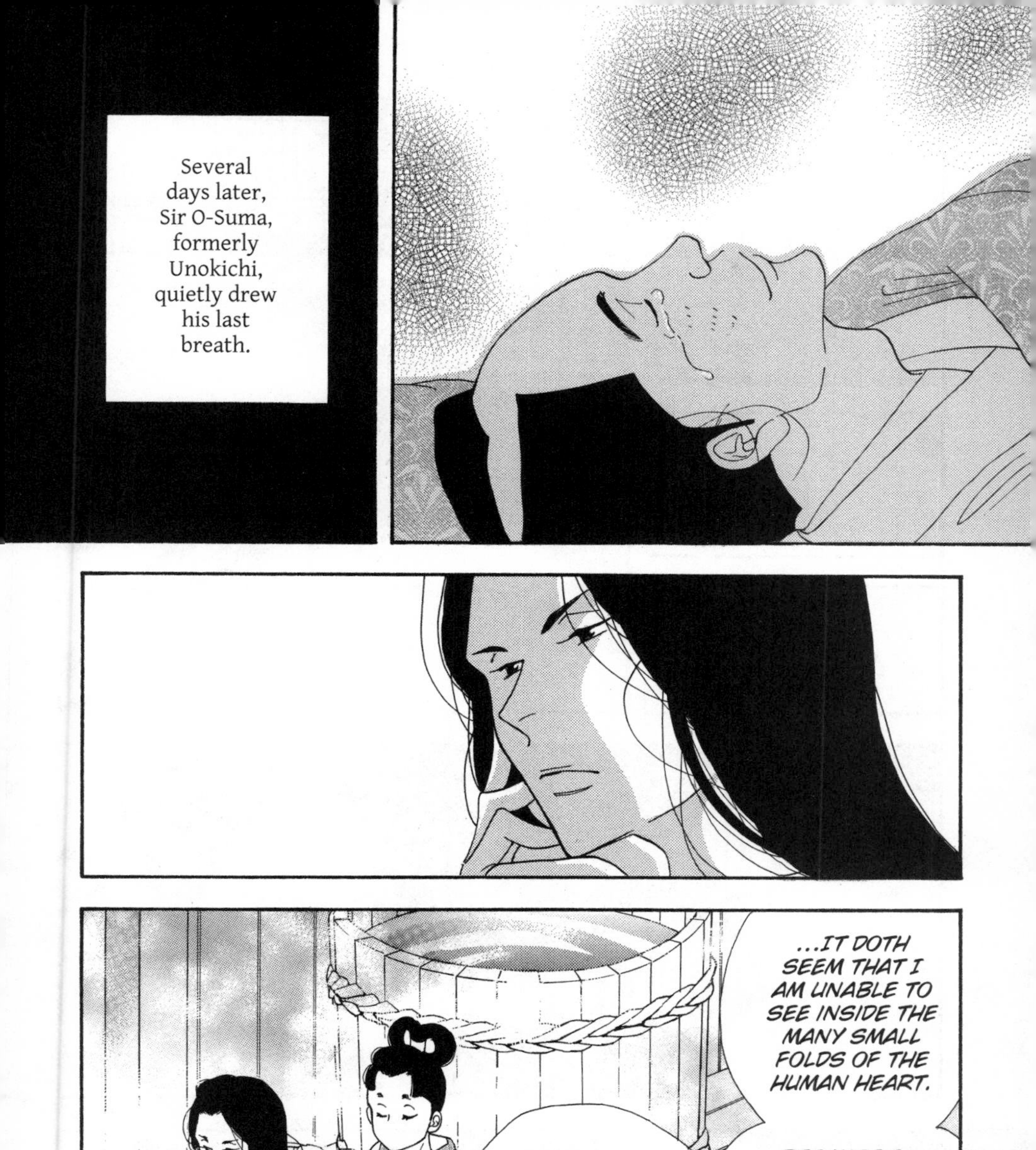
Several days later, Sir O-Suma, formerly Unokichi, quietly drew his last breath.
...IT DOTH SEEM THAT I AM UNABLE TO SEE INSIDE THE MANY SMALL FOLDS OF THE HUMAN HEART.
BECAUSE I COULD NOT LOOK INTO THE MINDS OF THOSE WHO BUY AND SELL FOR A LIVING, THE MERCHANTS DID TURN THEIR BACKS ON ME.
AND POOR UNOKICHI... I THOUGHT 'TWAS ENOUGH TO LET HIM SEE HIS LITTLE DAUGHTER, LADY FUKU. I SHOULD HAVE GONE TO VISIT HIM SOONER...

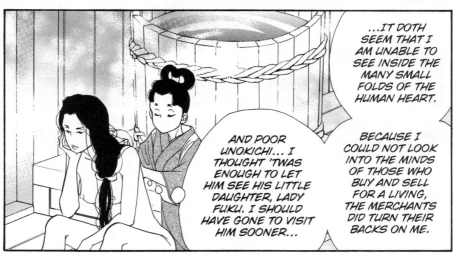

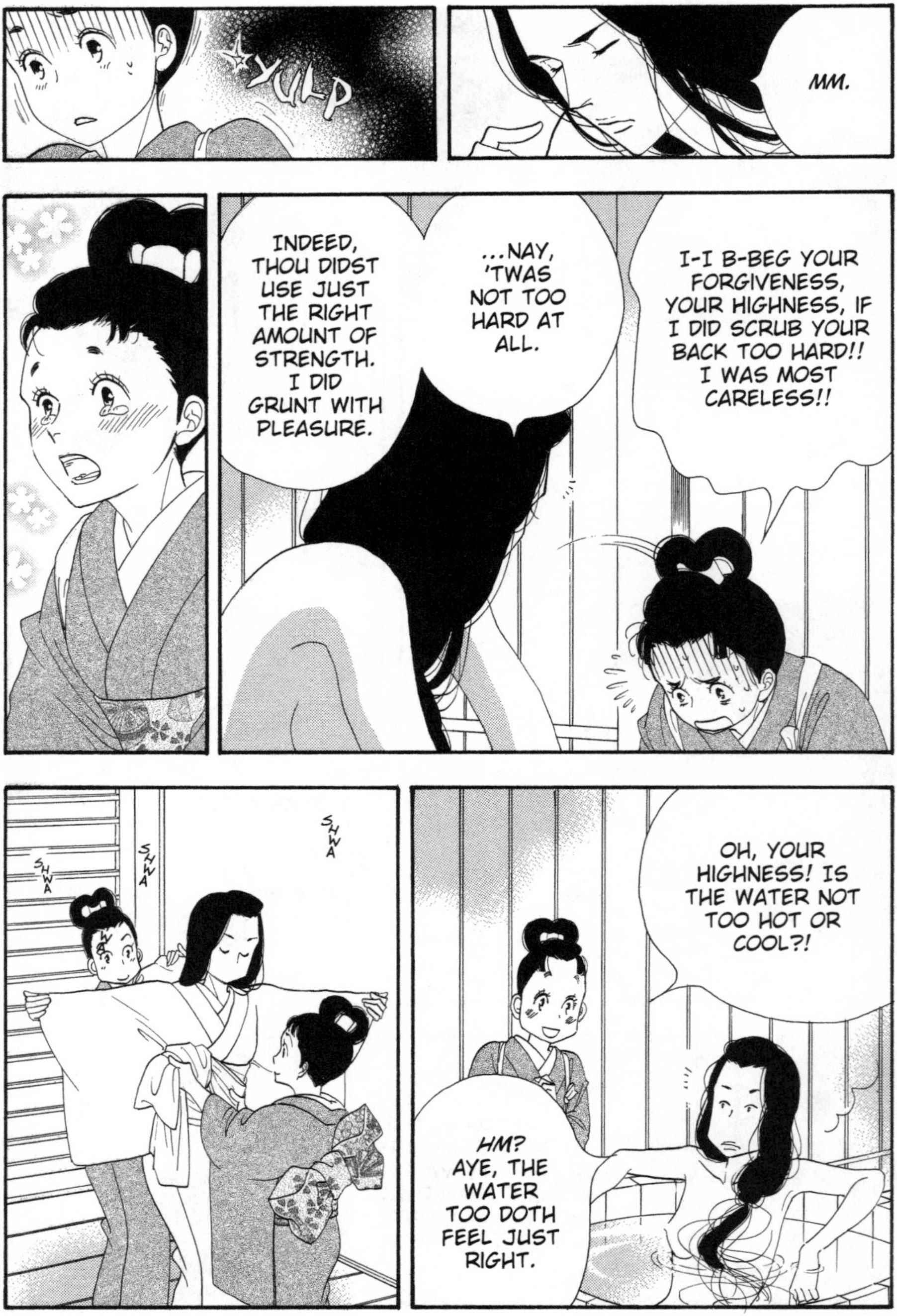
MM.
YULP
I-I B-BEG YOUR FORGIVENESS, YOUR HIGHNESS, IF I DID SCRUB YOUR BACK TOO HARD!! I WAS MOST CARELESS!!
...NAY, 'TWAS NOT TOO HARD AT ALL.
INDEED, THOU DIDST USE JUST THE RIGHT AMOUNT OF STRENGTH. I DID GRUNT WITH PLEASURE.
OH, YOUR HIGHNESS! IS THE WATER NOT TOO HOT OR COOL?!
HM? AYE, THE WATER TOO DOTH FEEL JUST RIGHT.
SHWA
SHWA
SHWA

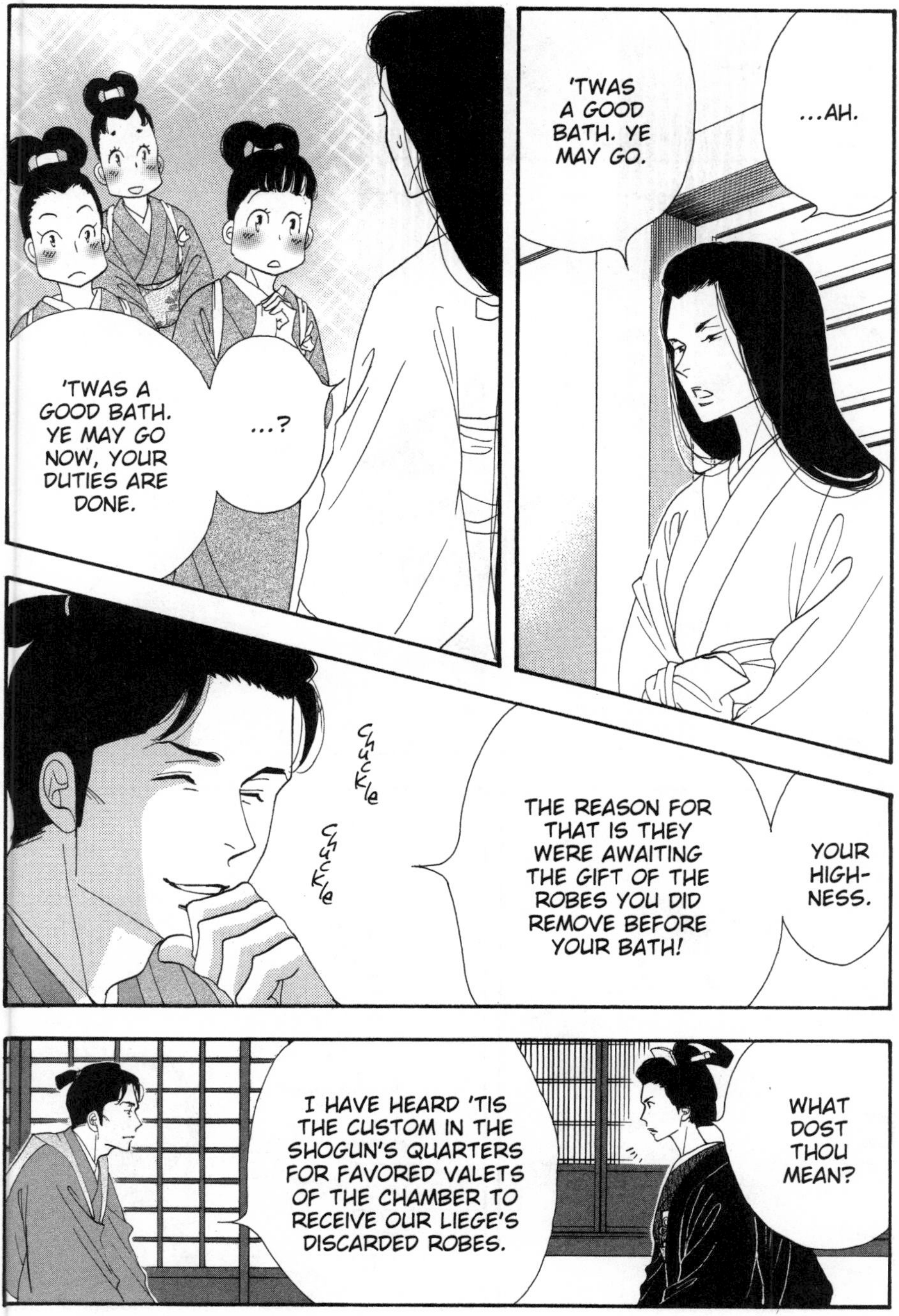
...AH.
'TWAS A GOOD BATH. YE MAY GO.
...?
'TWAS A GOOD BATH. YE MAY GO NOW, YOUR DUTIES ARE DONE.
YOUR HIGHNESS.
THE REASON FOR THAT IS THEY WERE AWAITING THE GIFT OF THE ROBES YOU DID REMOVE BEFORE YOUR BATH!
Chuckle
Chuckle
WHAT DOST THOU MEAN?
I HAVE HEARD 'TIS THE CUSTOM IN THE SHOGUN'S QUARTERS FOR FAVORED VALETS OF THE CHAMBER TO RECEIVE OUR LIEGE'S DISCARDED ROBES.

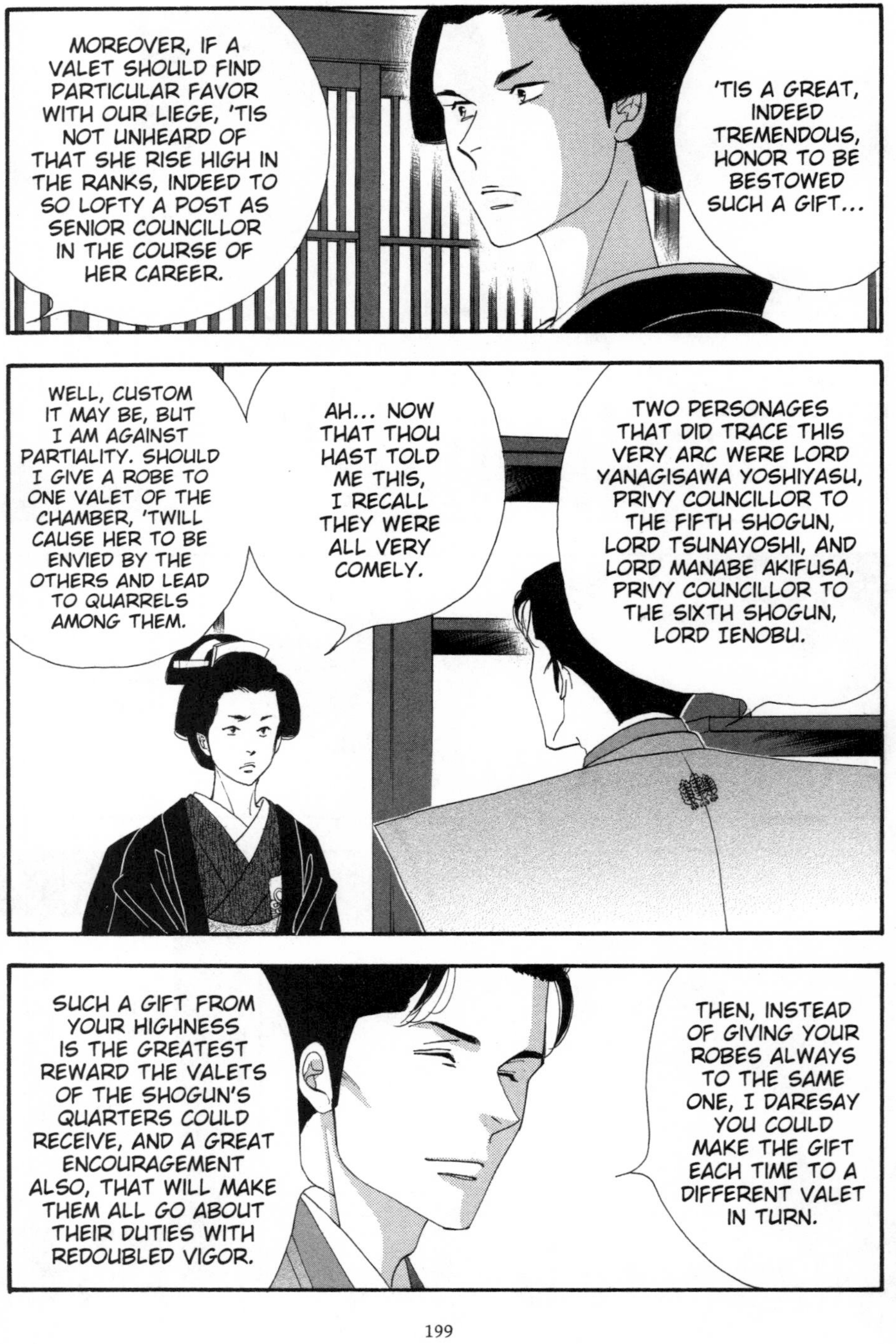
'TIS A GREAT, INDEED TREMENDOUS, HONOR TO BE BESTOWED SUCH A GIFT...
MOREOVER, IF A VALET SHOULD FIND PARTICULAR FAVOR WITH OUR LIEGE, 'TIS NOT UNHEARD OF THAT SHE RISE HIGH IN THE RANKS, INDEED TO SO LOFTY A POST AS SENIOR COUNCILLOR IN THE COURSE OF HER CAREER.
TWO PERSONAGES THAT DID TRACE THIS VERY ARC WERE LORD YANAGISAWA YOSHIYASU, PRIVY COUNCILLOR TO THE FIFTH SHOGUN, LORD TSUNAYOSHI, AND LORD MANABE AKIFUSA, PRIVY COUNCILLOR TO THE SIXTH SHOGUN, LORD IENOBU.
AH... NOW THAT THOU HAST TOLD ME THIS, I RECALL THEY WERE ALL VERY COMELY.
WELL, CUSTOM IT MAY BE, BUT I AM AGAINST PARTIALITY. SHOULD I GIVE A ROBE TO ONE VALET OF THE CHAMBER, 'TWILL CAUSE HER TO BE ENVIED BY THE OTHERS AND LEAD TO QUARRELS AMONG THEM.
THEN, INSTEAD OF GIVING YOUR ROBES ALWAYS TO THE SAME ONE, I DARESAY YOU COULD MAKE THE GIFT EACH TIME TO A DIFFERENT VALET IN TURN.
SUCH A GIFT FROM YOUR HIGHNESS IS THE GREATEST REWARD THE VALETS OF THE SHOGUN'S QUARTERS COULD RECEIVE, AND A GREAT ENCOURAGEMENT ALSO, THAT WILL MAKE THEM ALL GO ABOUT THEIR DUTIES WITH REDOUBLED VIGOR.

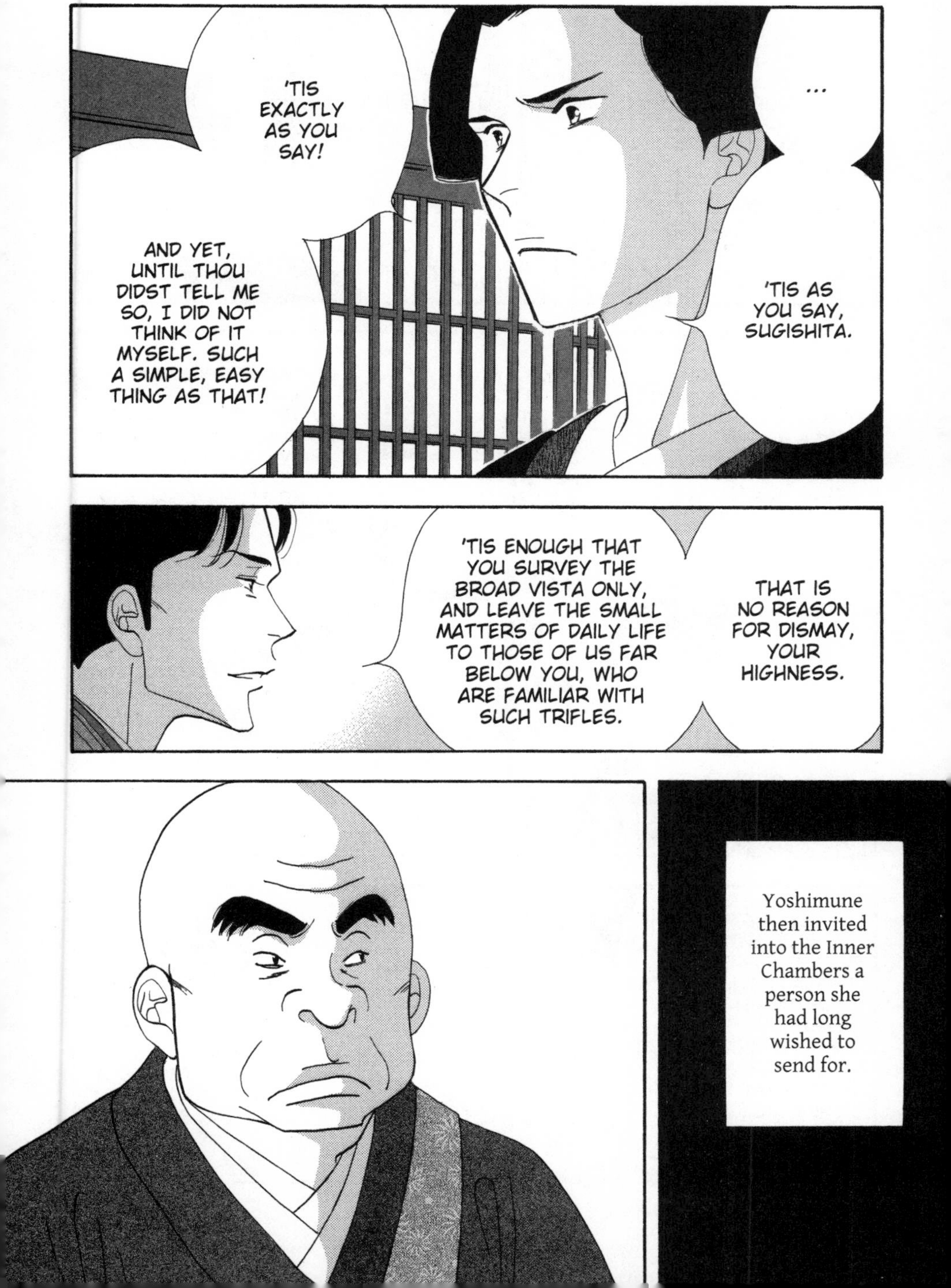
...
'TIS AS YOU SAY, SUGISHITA.
'TIS EXACTLY AS YOU SAY!
AND YET, UNTIL THOU DIDST TELL ME SO, I DID NOT THINK OF IT MYSELF. SUCH A SIMPLE, EASY THING AS THAT!
THAT IS NO REASON FOR DISMAY, YOUR HIGHNESS.
'TIS ENOUGH THAT YOU SURVEY THE BROAD VISTA ONLY, AND LEAVE THE SMALL MATTERS OF DAILY LIFE TO THOSE OF US FAR BELOW YOU, WHO ARE FAMILIAR WITH SUCH TRIFLES.
Yoshimune then invited into the Inner Chambers a person she had long wished to send for.

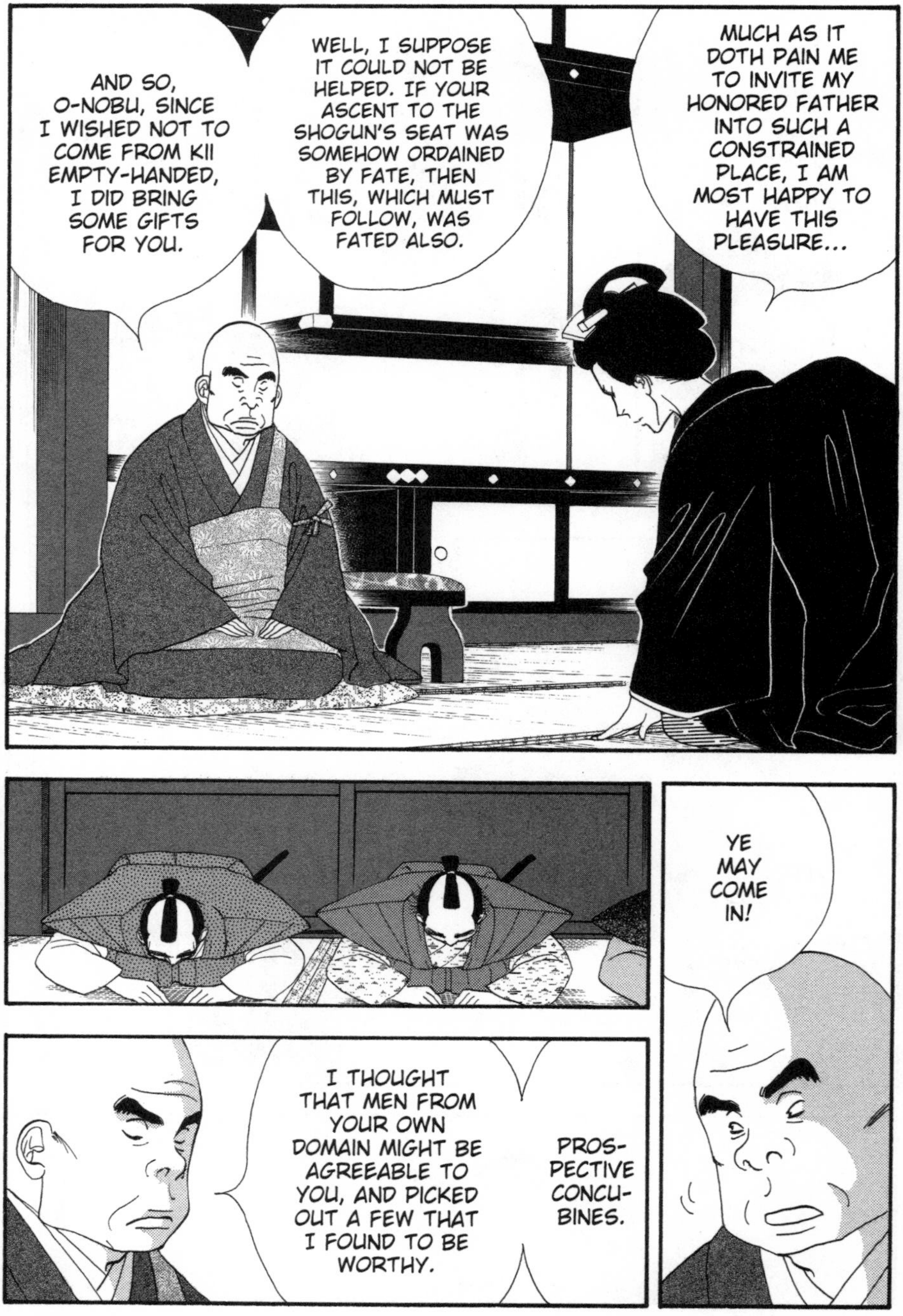
MUCH AS IT DOTH PAIN ME TO INVITE MY HONORED FATHER INTO SUCH A CONSTRAINED PLACE, I AM MOST HAPPY TO HAVE THIS PLEASURE...
WELL, I SUPPOSE IT COULD NOT BE HELPED. IF YOUR ASCENT TO THE SHOGUN'S SEAT WAS SOMEHOW ORDAINED BY FATE, THEN THIS, WHICH MUST FOLLOW, WAS FATED ALSO.
AND SO, O-NOBU, SINCE I WISHED NOT TO COME FROM KII EMPTY-HANDED, I DID BRING SOME GIFTS FOR YOU.
YE MAY COME IN!
PROS-PECTIVE CONCU-BINES.
I THOUGHT THAT MEN FROM YOUR OWN DOMAIN MIGHT BE AGREEABLE TO YOU, AND PICKED OUT A FEW THAT I FOUND TO BE WORTHY.

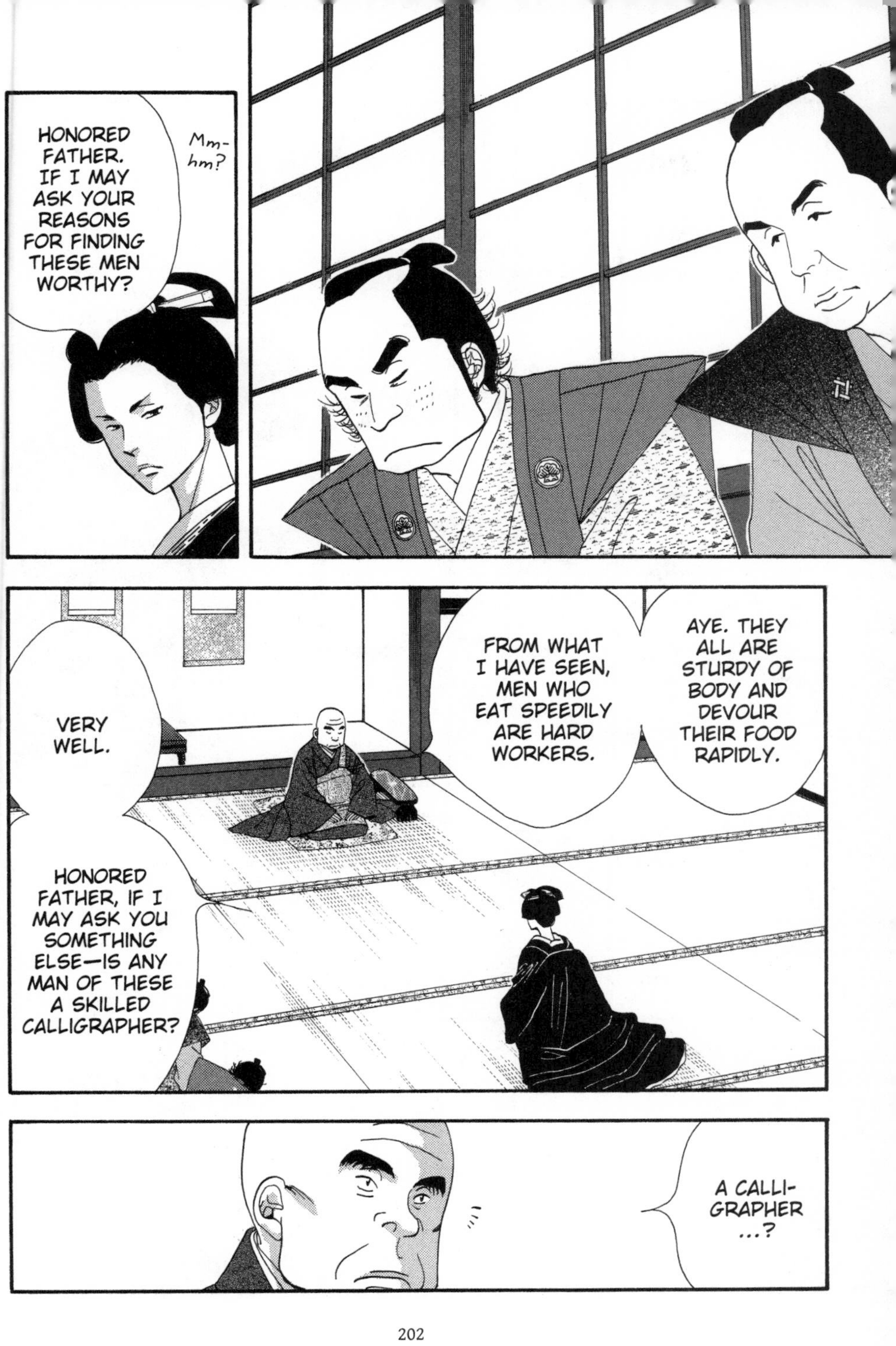
HONORED FATHER. IF I MAY ASK YOUR REASONS FOR FINDING THESE MEN WORTHY?
Mm-hm?
AYE. THEY ALL ARE STURDY OF BODY AND DEVOUR THEIR FOOD RAPIDLY.
FROM WHAT I HAVE SEEN, MEN WHO EAT SPEEDILY ARE HARD WORKERS.
VERY WELL.
HONORED FATHER, IF I MAY ASK YOU SOMETHING ELSE—IS ANY MAN OF THESE A SKILLED CALLIGRAPHER?
A CALLI-GRAPHER ...?

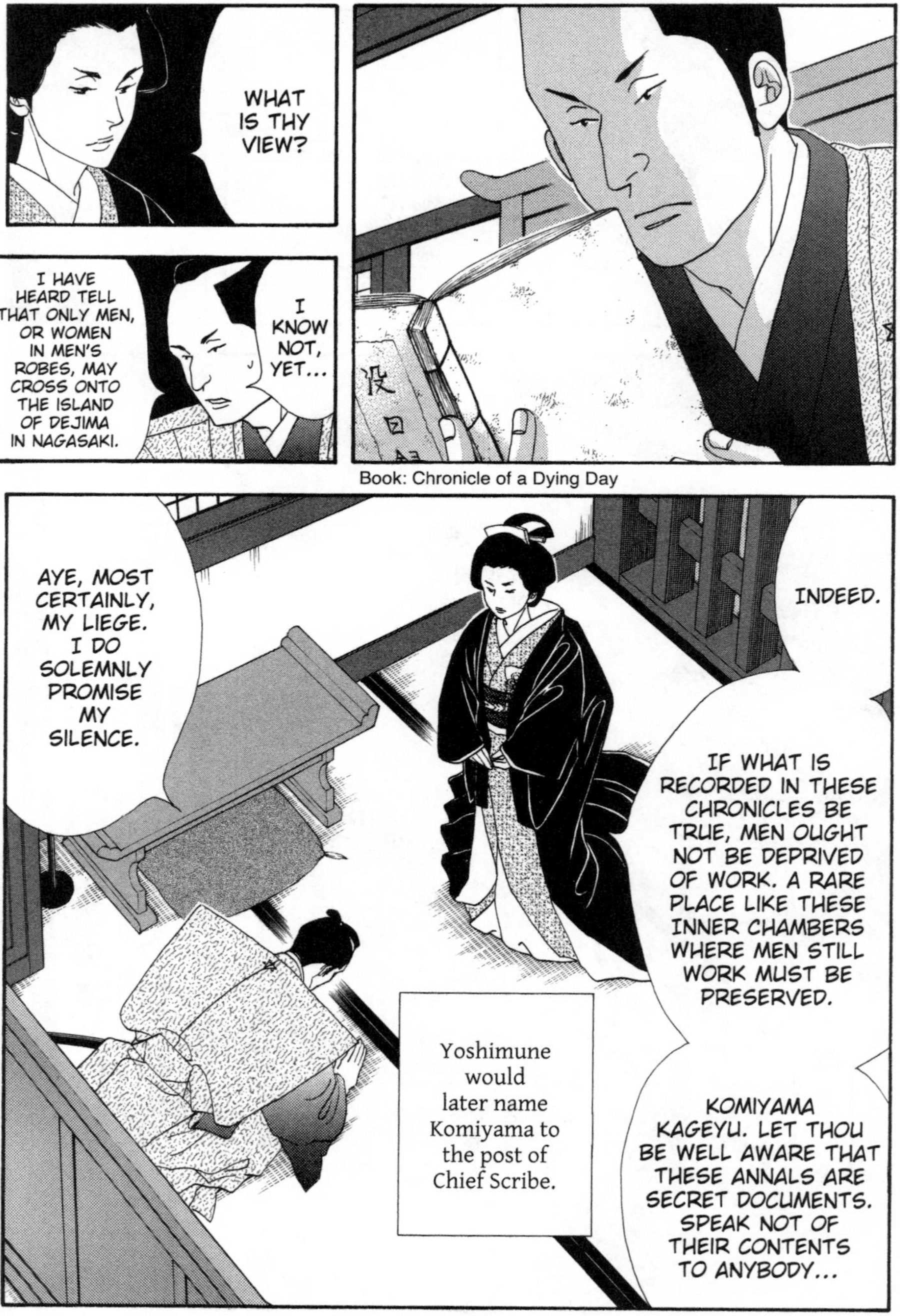

Book: Chronicle of a Dying Day
WHAT IS THY VIEW?
I KNOW NOT, YET...
I HAVE HEARD TELL THAT ONLY MEN, OR WOMEN IN MEN'S ROBES, MAY CROSS ONTO THE ISLAND OF DEJIMA IN NAGASAKI.
INDEED.
IF WHAT IS RECORDED IN THESE CHRONICLES BE TRUE, MEN OUGHT NOT BE DEPRIVED OF WORK. A RARE PLACE LIKE THESE INNER CHAMBERS WHERE MEN STILL WORK MUST BE PRESERVED.
KOMIYAMA KAGEYU. LET THOU BE WELL AWARE THAT THESE ANNALS ARE SECRET DOCUMENTS. SPEAK NOT OF THEIR CONTENTS TO ANYBODY...
AYE, MOST CERTAINLY, MY LIEGE. I DO SOLEMNLY PROMISE MY SILENCE.
Yoshimune would later name Komiyama to the post of Chief Scribe.

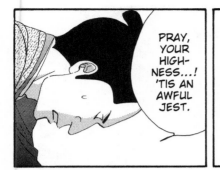

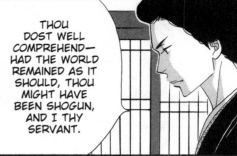

THOU DOST WELL COMPREHEND—HAD THE WORLD REMAINED AS IT SHOULD, THOU MIGHT HAVE BEEN SHOGUN, AND I THY SERVANT.
PRAY, YOUR HIGH-NESS...! 'TIS AN AWFUL JEST.
BOW YE DOWN FOR THE ENTRANCE OF OUR LIEGE!!

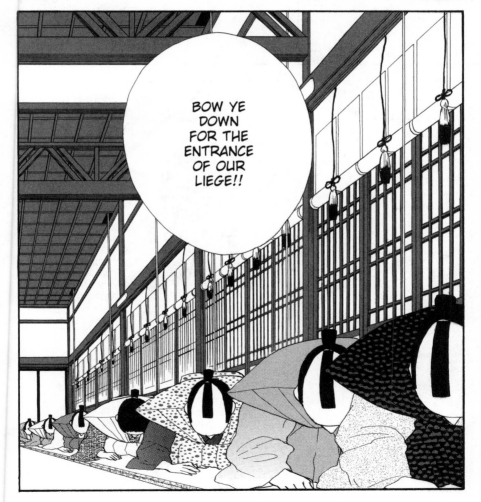

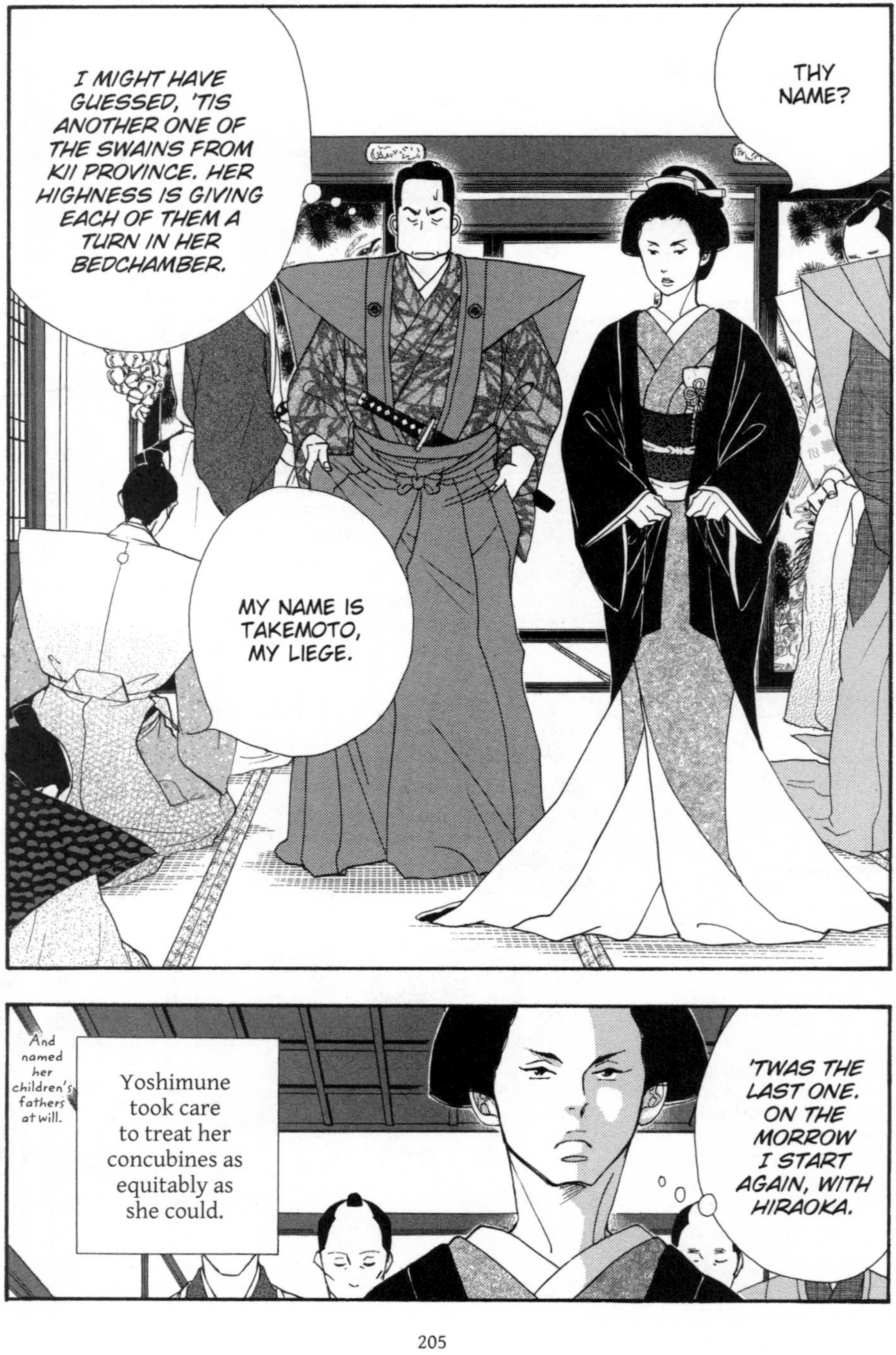
THY NAME?
I MIGHT HAVE GUESSED, 'TIS ANOTHER ONE OF THE SWAINS FROM KII PROVINCE. HER HIGHNESS IS GIVING EACH OF THEM A TURN IN HER BEDCHAMBER.
MY NAME IS TAKEMOTO, MY LIEGE.
'TWAS THE LAST ONE. ON THE MORROW I START AGAIN, WITH HIRAOKA.
Yoshimune took care to treat her concubines as equitably as she could.
And named her children's fathers at will.

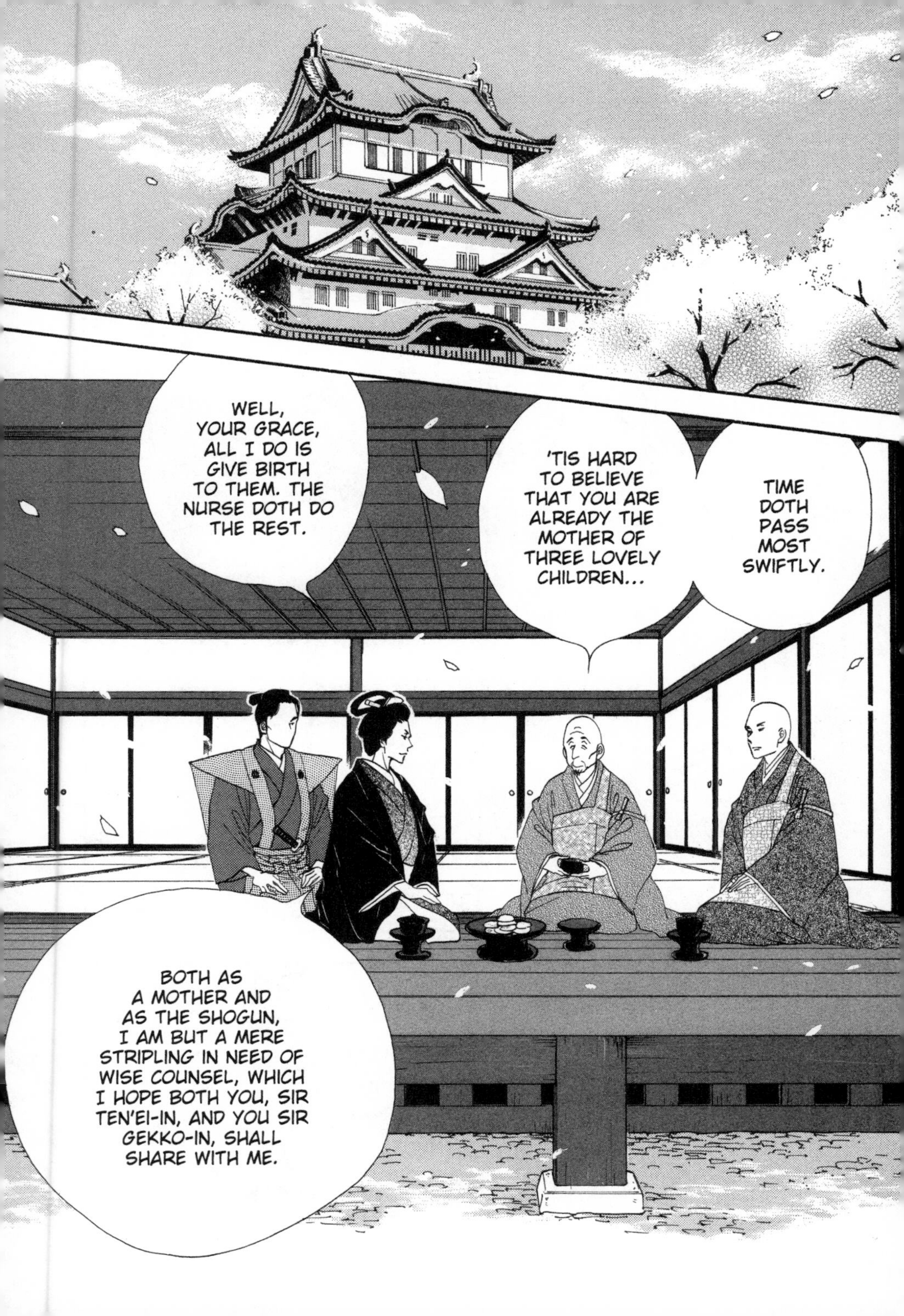
TIME DOTH PASS MOST SWIFTLY.
'TIS HARD TO BELIEVE THAT YOU ARE ALREADY THE MOTHER OF THREE LOVELY CHILDREN...
WELL, YOUR GRACE, ALL I DO IS GIVE BIRTH TO THEM. THE NURSE DOTH DO THE REST.
BOTH AS A MOTHER AND AS THE SHOGUN, I AM BUT A MERE STRIPLING IN NEED OF WISE COUNSEL, WHICH I HOPE BOTH YOU, SIR TEN'EI-IN, AND YOU SIR GEKKO-IN, SHALL SHARE WITH ME.

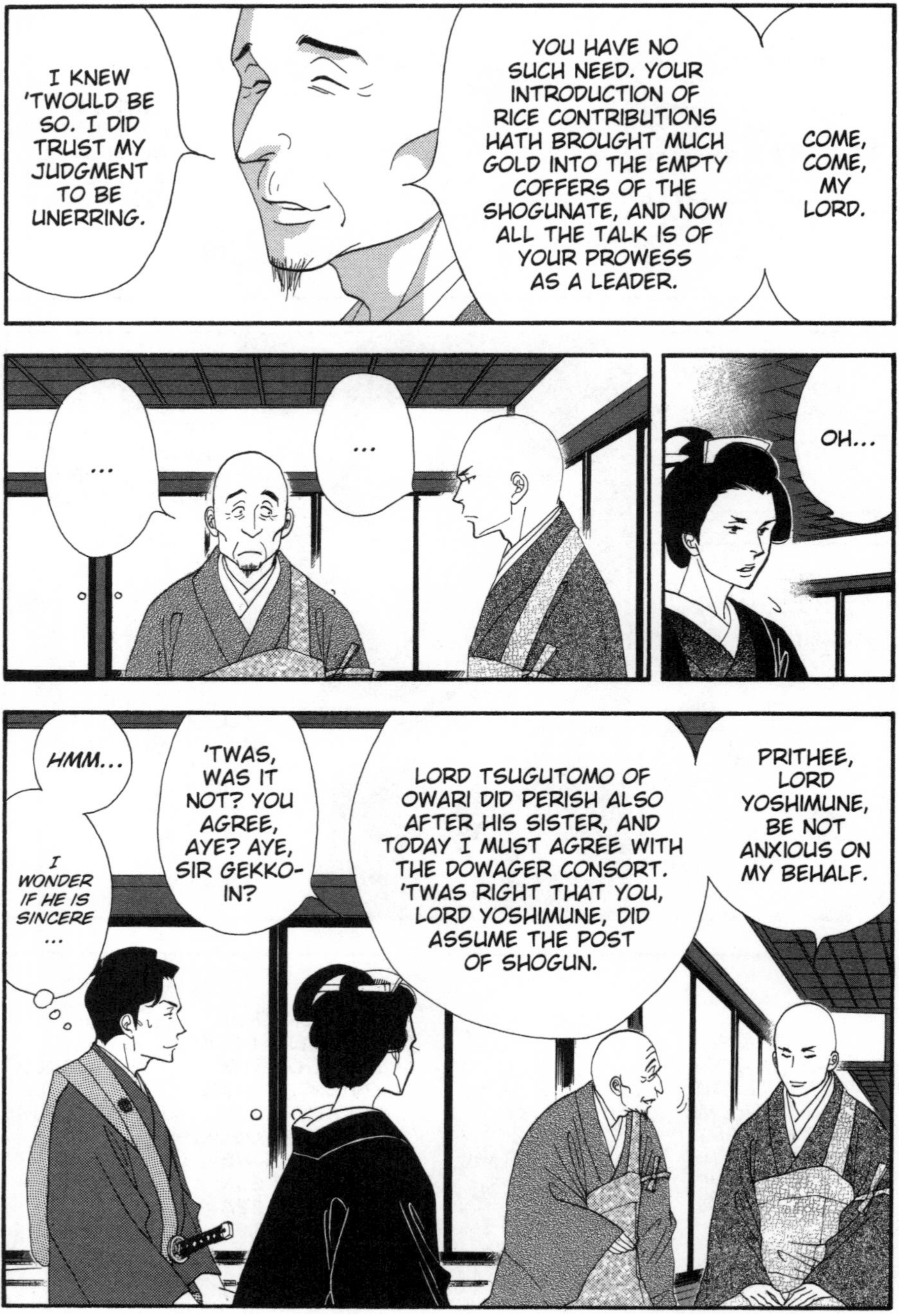
COME, COME, MY LORD.
YOU HAVE NO SUCH NEED. YOUR INTRODUCTION OF RICE CONTRIBUTIONS HATH BROUGHT MUCH GOLD INTO THE EMPTY COFFERS OF THE SHOGUNATE, AND NOW ALL THE TALK IS OF YOUR PROWESS AS A LEADER.
I KNEW 'TWOULD BE SO. I DID TRUST MY JUDGMENT TO BE UNERRING.
OH...
...
...
PRITHEE, LORD YOSHIMUNE, BE NOT ANXIOUS ON MY BEHALF.
LORD TSUGUTOMO OF OWARI DID PERISH ALSO AFTER HIS SISTER, AND TODAY I MUST AGREE WITH THE DOWAGER CONSORT. 'TWAS RIGHT THAT YOU, LORD YOSHIMUNE, DID ASSUME THE POST OF SHOGUN.
'TWAS, WAS IT NOT? YOU AGREE, AYE? AYE, SIR GEKKO-IN?
HMM...
I WONDER IF HE IS SINCERE ...

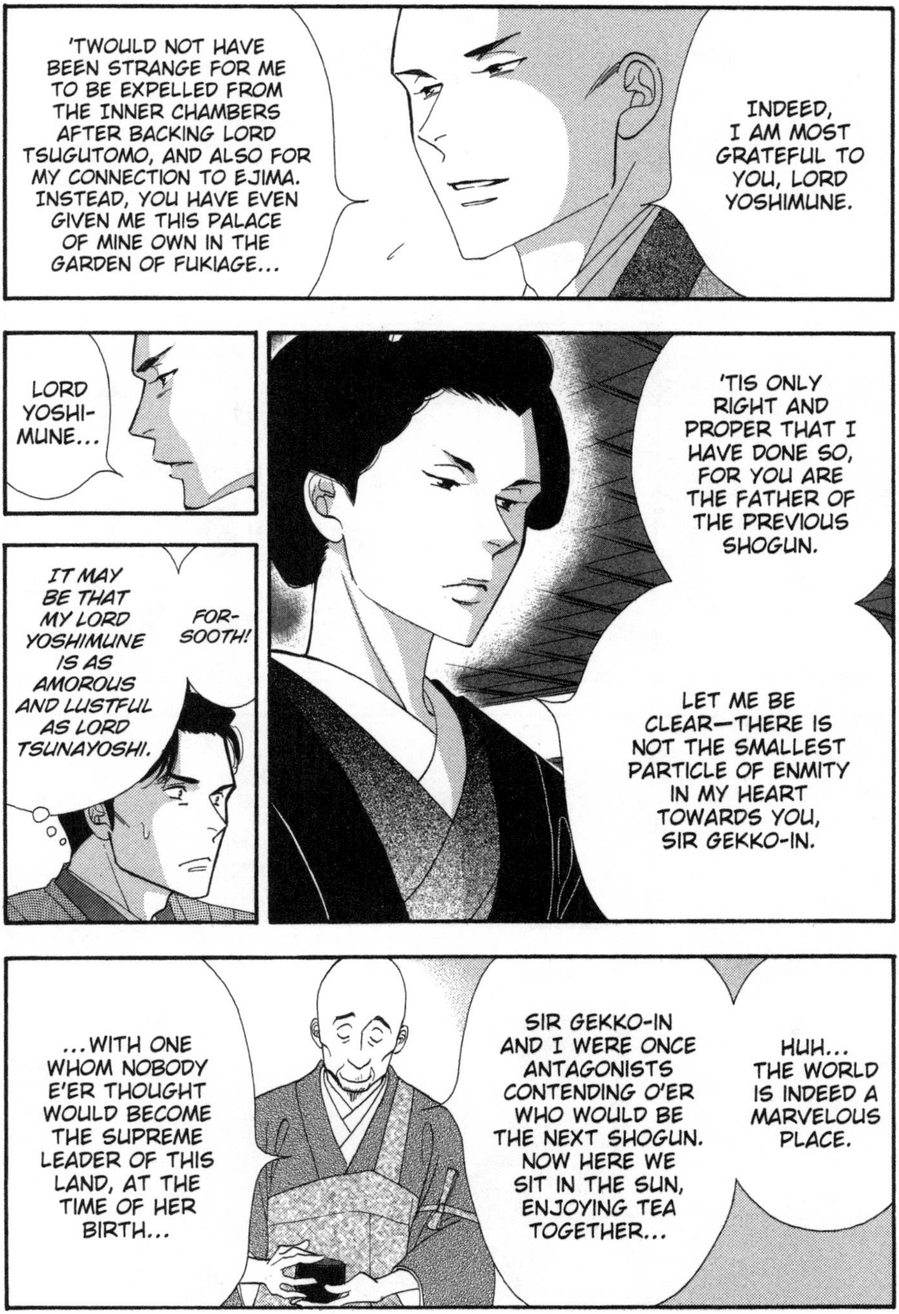
INDEED, I AM MOST GRATEFUL TO YOU, LORD YOSHIMUNE.
'TWOULD NOT HAVE BEEN STRANGE FOR ME TO BE EXPELLED FROM THE INNER CHAMBERS AFTER BACKING LORD TSUGUTOMO, AND ALSO FOR MY CONNECTION TO EJIMA. INSTEAD, YOU HAVE EVEN GIVEN ME THIS PALACE OF MINE OWN IN THE GARDEN OF FUKIAGE...
'TIS ONLY RIGHT AND PROPER THAT I HAVE DONE SO, FOR YOU ARE THE FATHER OF THE PREVIOUS SHOGUN.
LET ME BE CLEAR—THERE IS NOT THE SMALLEST PARTICLE OF ENMITY IN MY HEART TOWARDS YOU, SIR GEKKO-IN.
LORD YOSHI-MUNE...
FOR-SOOTH!
IT MAY BE THAT MY LORD YOSHIMUNE IS AS AMOROUS AND LUSTFUL AS LORD TSUNAYOSHI.
HUH... THE WORLD IS INDEED A MARVELOUS PLACE.
SIR GEKKO-IN AND I WERE ONCE ANTAGONISTS CONTENDING O'ER WHO WOULD BE THE NEXT SHOGUN. NOW HERE WE SIT IN THE SUN, ENJOYING TEA TOGETHER...
...WITH ONE WHOM NOBODY E'ER THOUGHT WOULD BECOME THE SUPREME LEADER OF THIS LAND, AT THE TIME OF HER BIRTH...

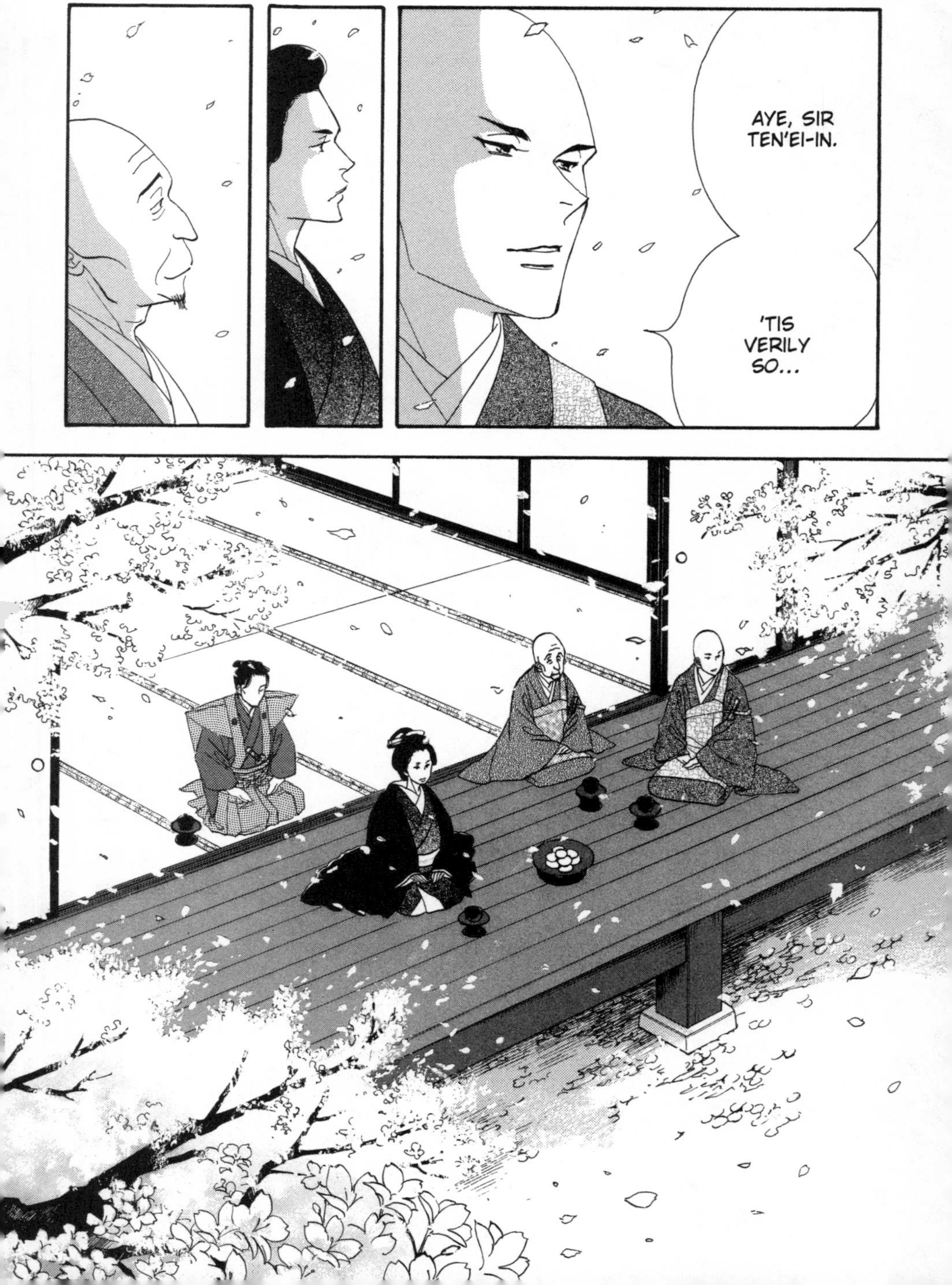
AYE, SIR TEN'EI-IN.
'TIS VERILY SO...

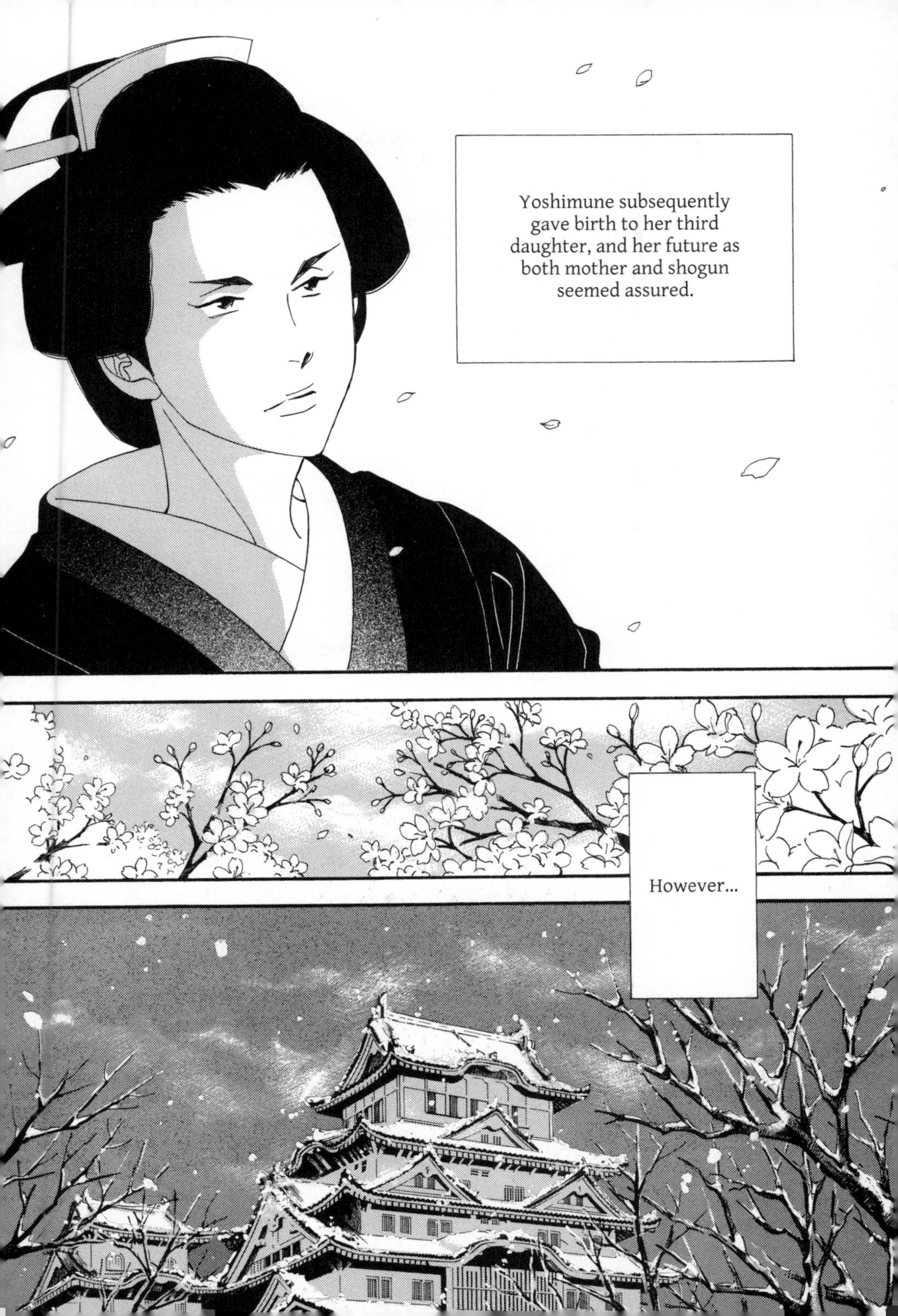
Yoshimune subsequently gave birth to her third daughter, and her future as both mother and shogun seemed assured.
However...

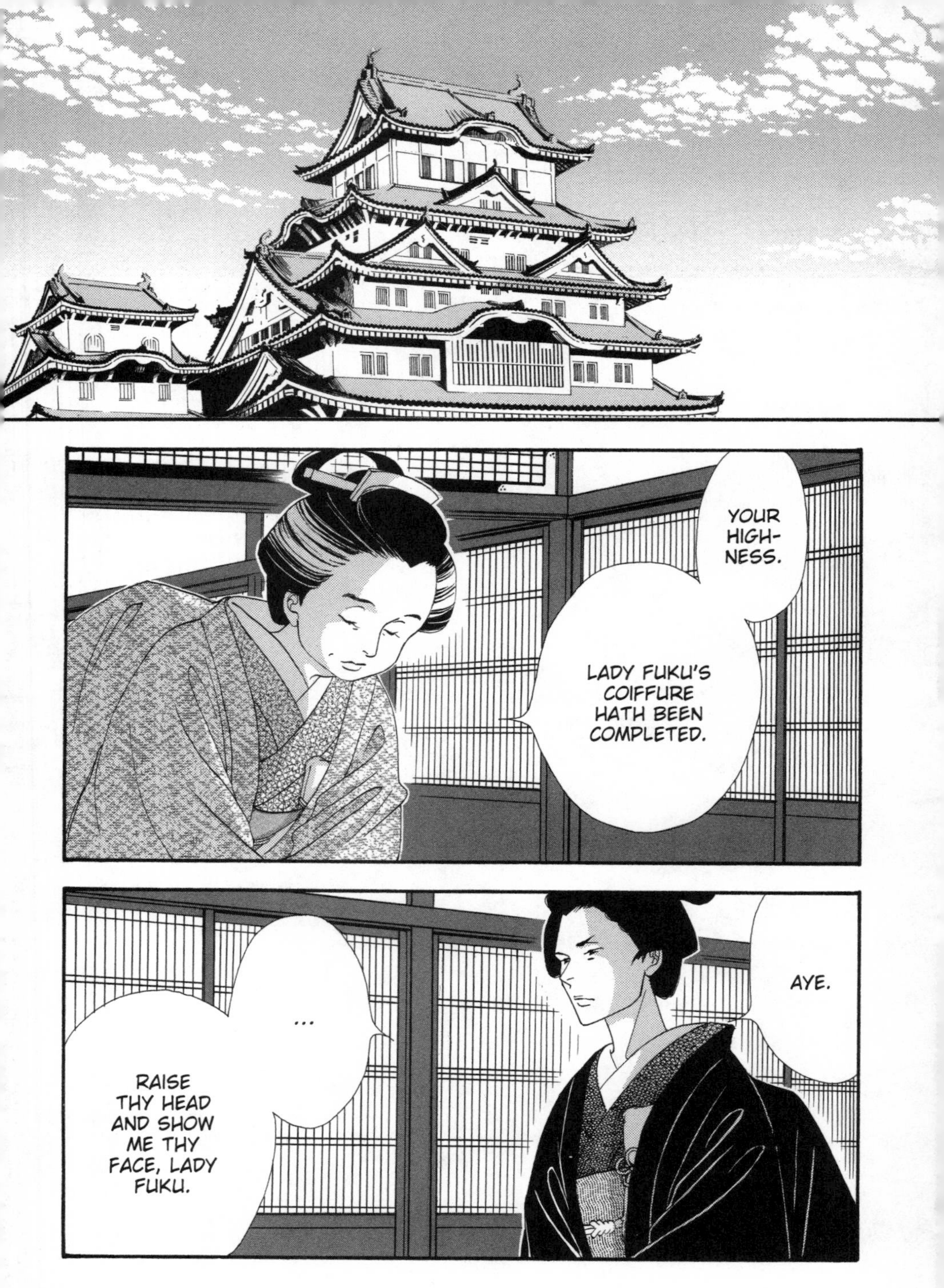
YOUR HIGHNESS.
LADY FUKU'S COIFFURE HATH BEEN COMPLETED.
AYE.
...
RAISE THY HEAD AND SHOW ME THY FACE, LADY FUKU.

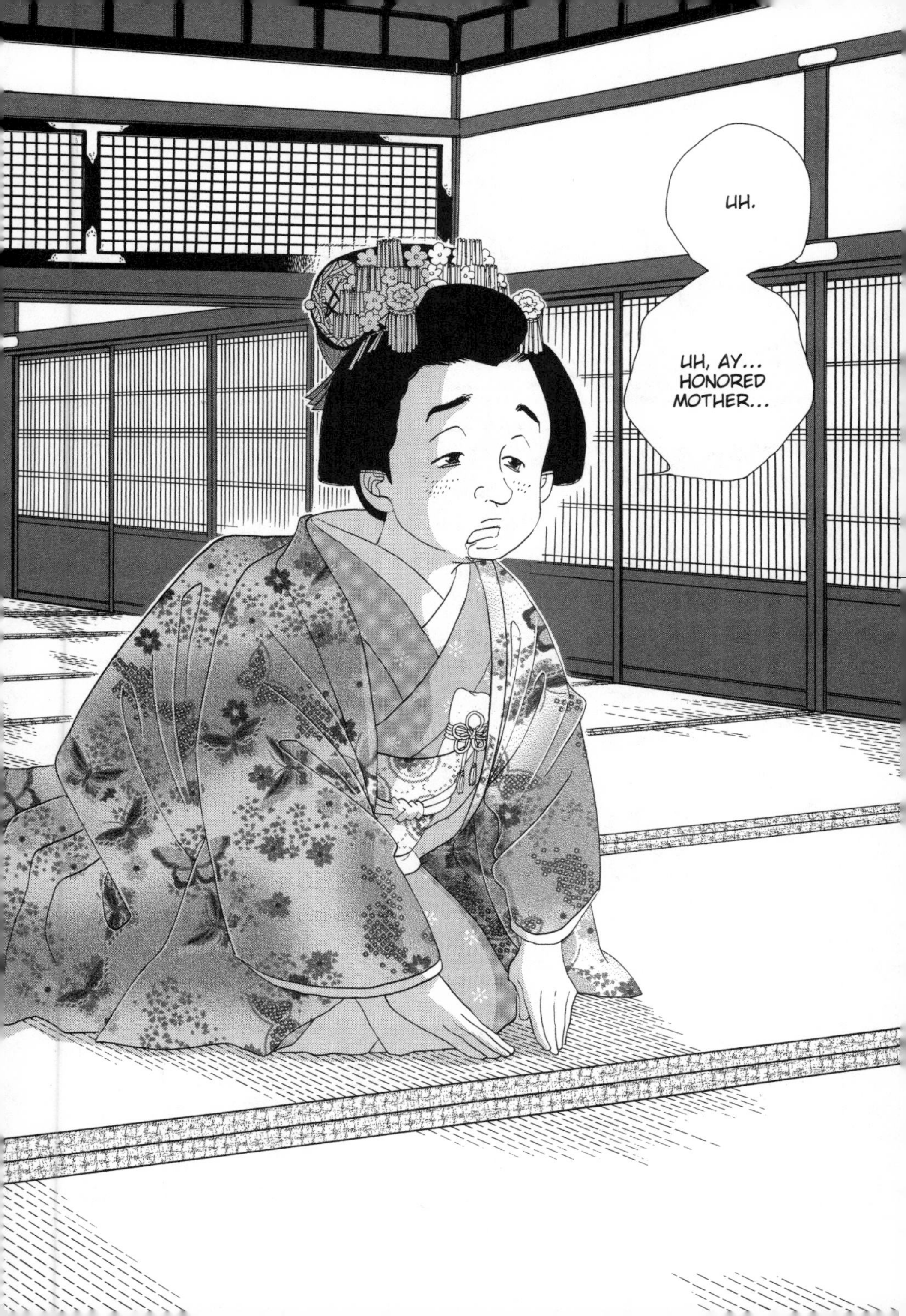
UH.
UH, AY... HONORED MOTHER...

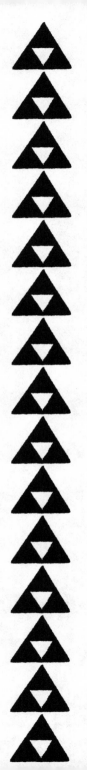

Ōoku

✿ THE INNER CHAMBERS

Ōoku: The Inner Chambers

VOLUME 7 · END NOTES

by Akemi Wegmüller

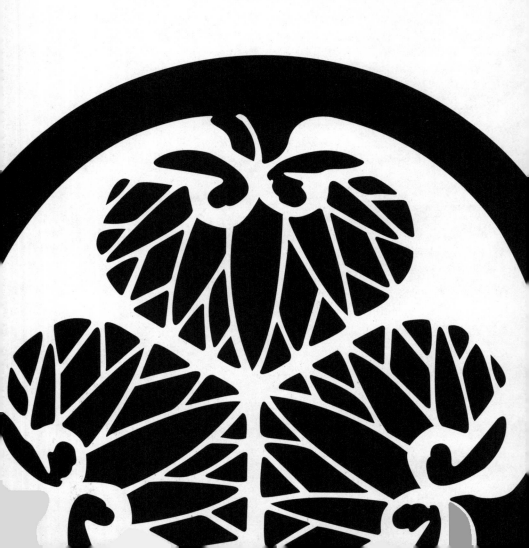

Page 36, panel 2 · YAMAMURA-ZA

Za means "guild," and when attached as a suffix to a name, means "theater" and refers to both the name of the playhouse and the name of the acting troupe or company.

Page 37, panel 2 · FROM MT. FUJI TO TSUKUBA

A line from the opening of the play *Sukeroku*, traditionally sung by storyteller-singers.

Page 37, panel 3 · DANJURO, NARITA-YA

The Kabuki actor here is based on the historic Ichikawa Danjuro I, whose stage nickname (*yago*) was Narita-ya. In Kabuki tradition, the audience calls out the actors name or yago during favorite scenes.

Page 38, panel 3 · ARAGOTO, KAMIGATA

Aragoto is a part of *aramushagoto*, a kabuki style that uses exaggerated, bold movements and costumes. Ichikawa Danjuro I unified aramushagoto and created the act in which the hero defeats the villain, or aragoto. *Wagoto*, in contrast to aragoto, is the act in which a love affair occurs. During the Edo period, Kamigata was the region where the big cities were located.

Page 41, panel 1 · ZOJO-JI AND KAN'EI-JI

These are the two Tokugawa *bodaiji* (family temple and burial grounds.)

Page 61, panel 1 · HOUR OF THE SHEEP

Yatsudoki in Japanese. Around two a.m. and two p.m. Also called Eighth Hour of the Afternoon.

Page 99, panel 5 · UKIYO-E

Literally means "pictures of the floating world." A genre of woodblock prints.

Page 138, panel 2 · OFFICIAL CENSOR

Metsuke were inspectors tasked with investigating corruption and fraud in those below daimyo (lord) status. They served a function somewhat similar to modern FBI agents.

Page 211, panel 2 · COIFFURE

This indicates she has come of age and is ready for her hair to be put up in a woman's style. The coiffure ceremony was called *O-gushi-age*.

CREATOR BIOGRAPHY

FUMI YOSHINAGA

Fumi Yoshinaga is a Tokyo-born manga creator who debuted in 1994 with *Tsuki to Sandaru* (*The Moon and the Sandals*). Yoshinaga has won numerous awards, including the 2009 Osamu Tezuka Cultural Prize for *Ōoku*, the 2002 Kodansha Manga Award for her series *Antique Bakery* and the 2006 Japan Media Arts Festival Excellence Award for *Ōoku*. She was also nominated for the 2008 Eisner Award for Best Writer/Artist.

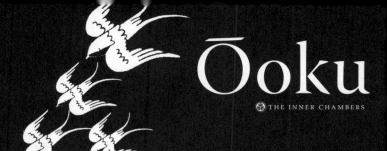

Ōoku: The Inner Chambers
Vol. 7

VIZ Signature Edition

Story and Art by Fumi Yoshinaga

Translation & Adaptation/Akemi Wegmüller
Touch-up Art & Lettering/Monalisa De Asis
Design/Fawn Lau
Editor/Pancha Diaz

Ōoku by Fumi Yoshinaga © Fumi Yoshinaga 2011
All rights reserved. First published in Japan in 2011 by
HAKUSENSHA, Inc., Tokyo. English language translation
rights arranged with HAKUSENSHA, Inc., Tokyo.

Printed in the U.S.A.

Published by VIZ Media, LLC
P.O. Box 77010
San Francisco, CA 94107

10 9 8 7 6 5 4 3 2 1
First printing, July 2012

www.viz.com

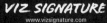
www.vizsignature.com

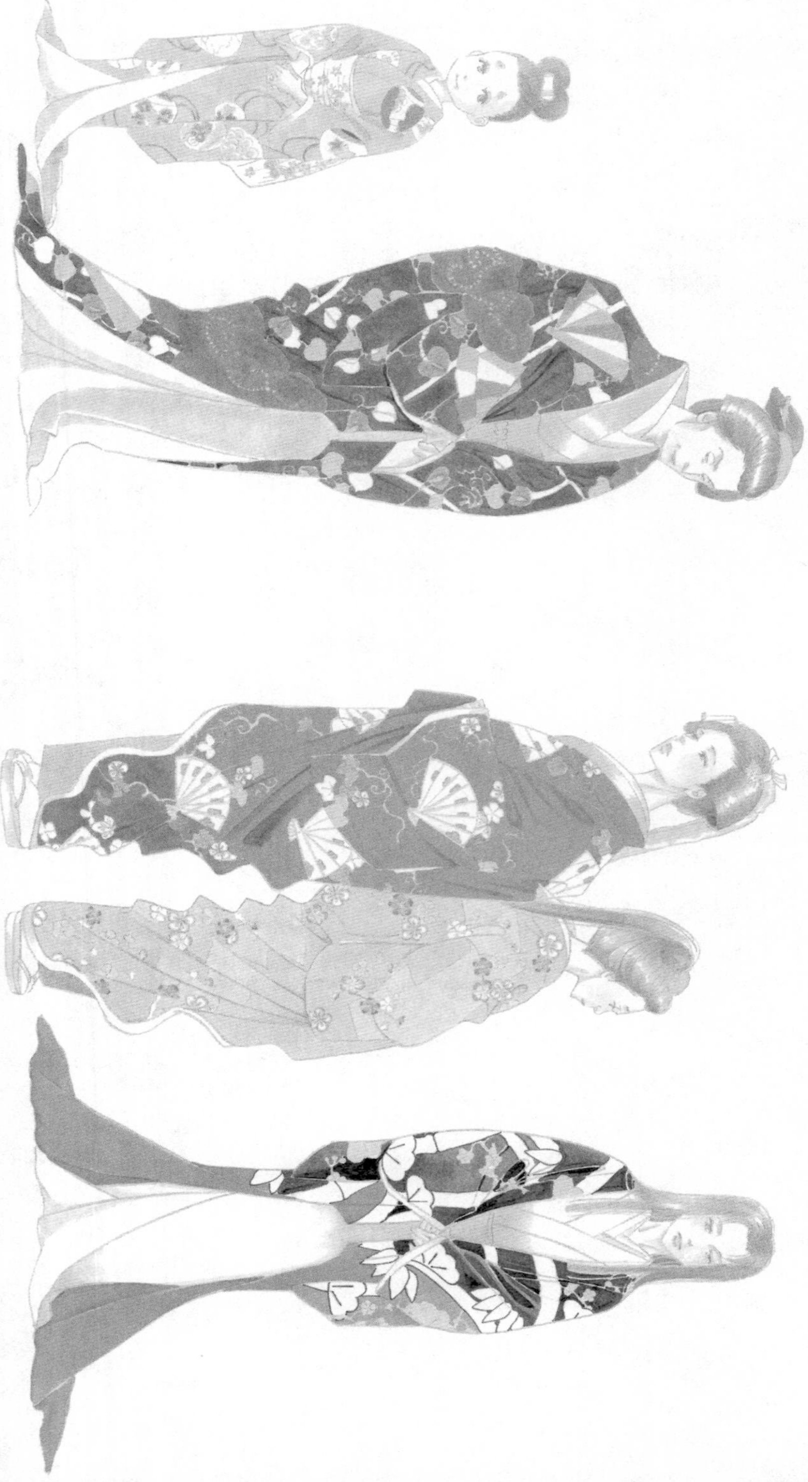

THIS IS THE LAST PAGE.

Ōoku: The Inner Chambers has been printed in the original Japanese format in order to preserve the orientation of the original artwork.

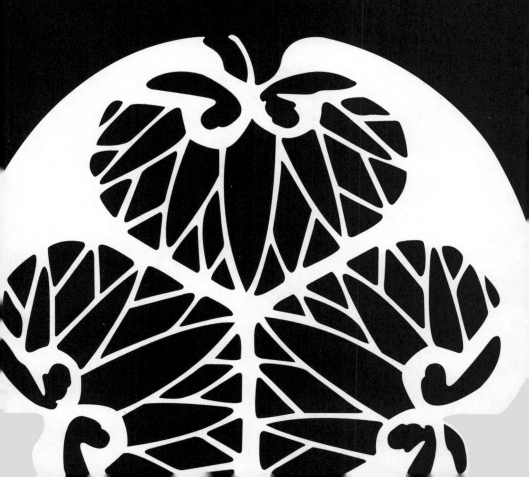